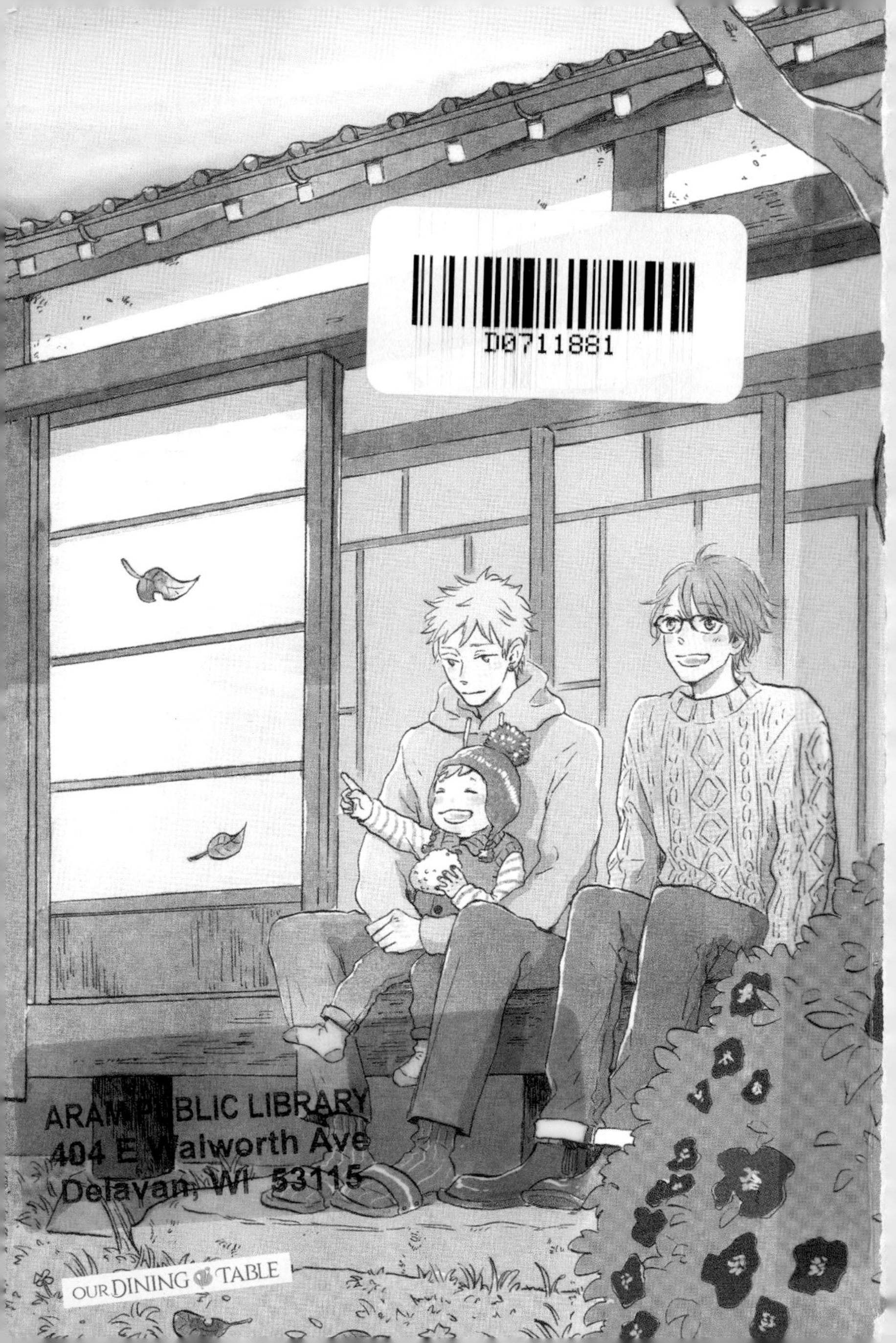
OUR DINING TABLE

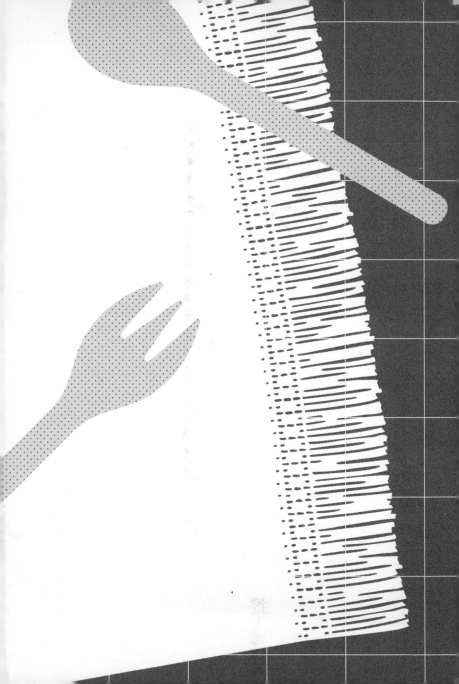

OUR DINING TABLE

story & art by
Mita Ori

contents

Chapter 0

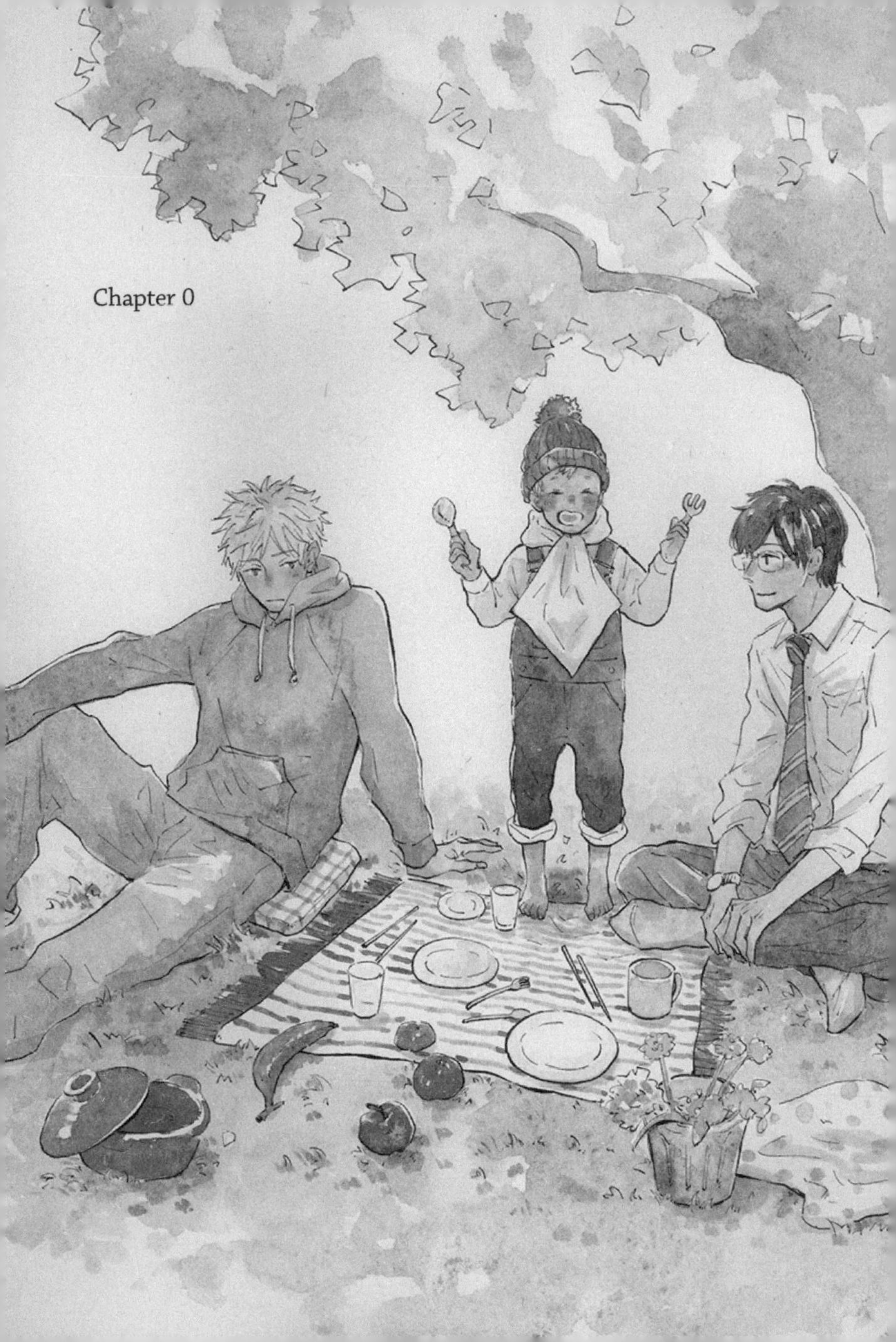

OUR DINING TABLE

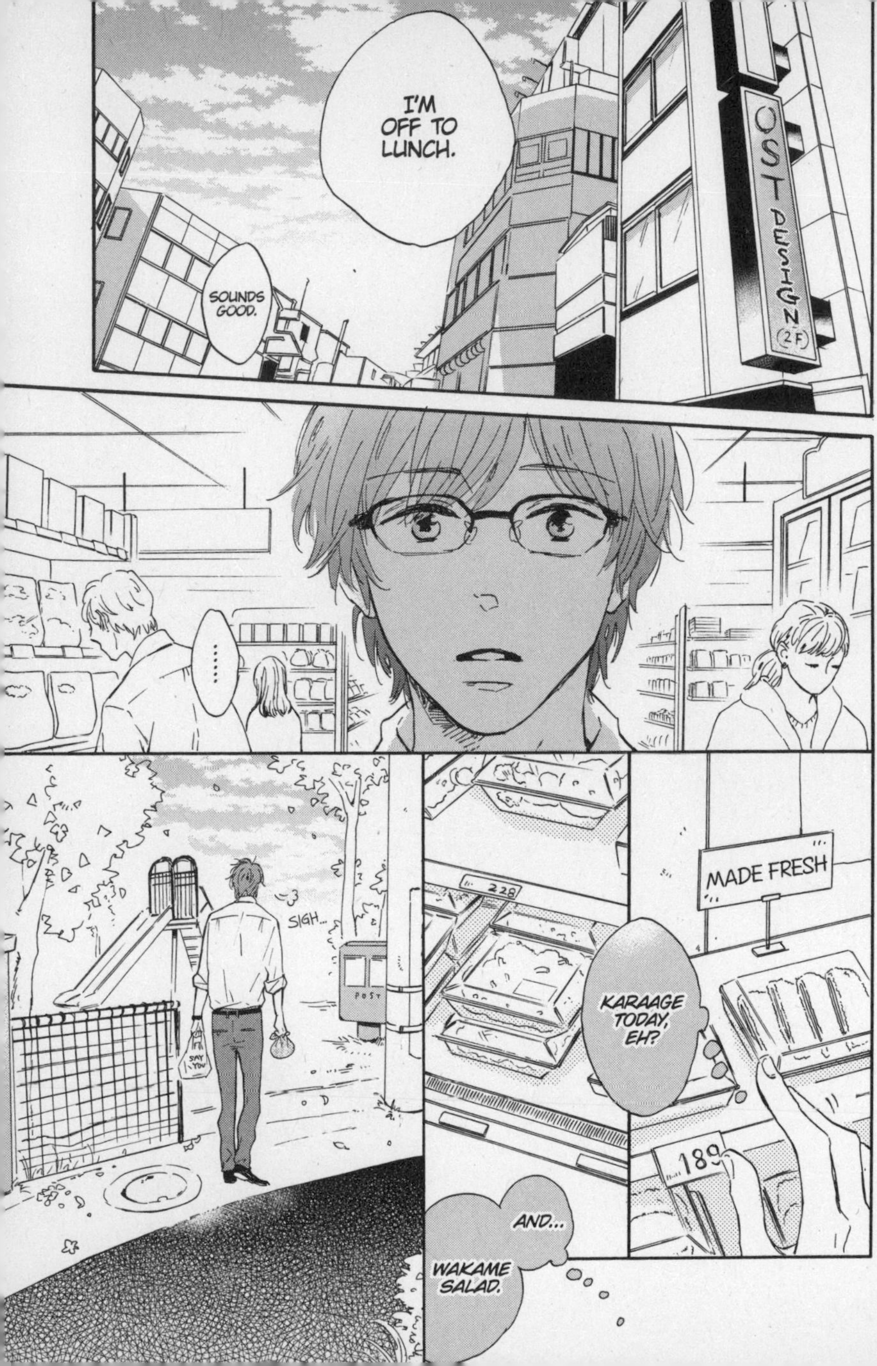
OST DESIGN 2F
I'M OFF TO LUNCH.
SOUNDS GOOD.
......
MADE FRESH
228
KARAAGE TODAY, EH?
189
AND...
WAKAME SALAD.
SIGH...
POST
SAY YOU

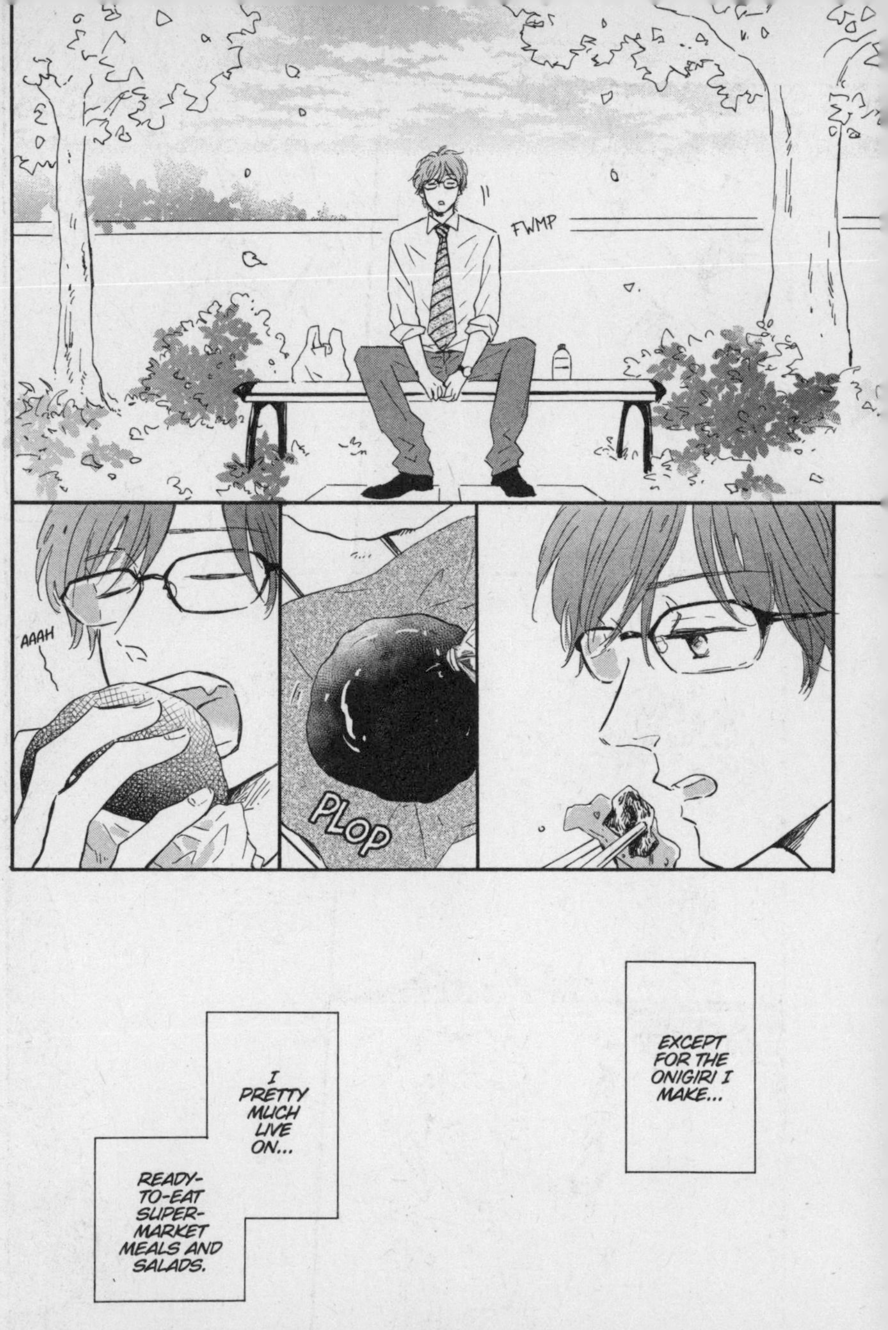
FWMP
PLOP
AAAH
EXCEPT FOR THE ONIGIRI I MAKE...
I PRETTY MUCH LIVE ON...
READY-TO-EAT SUPER-MARKET MEALS AND SALADS.

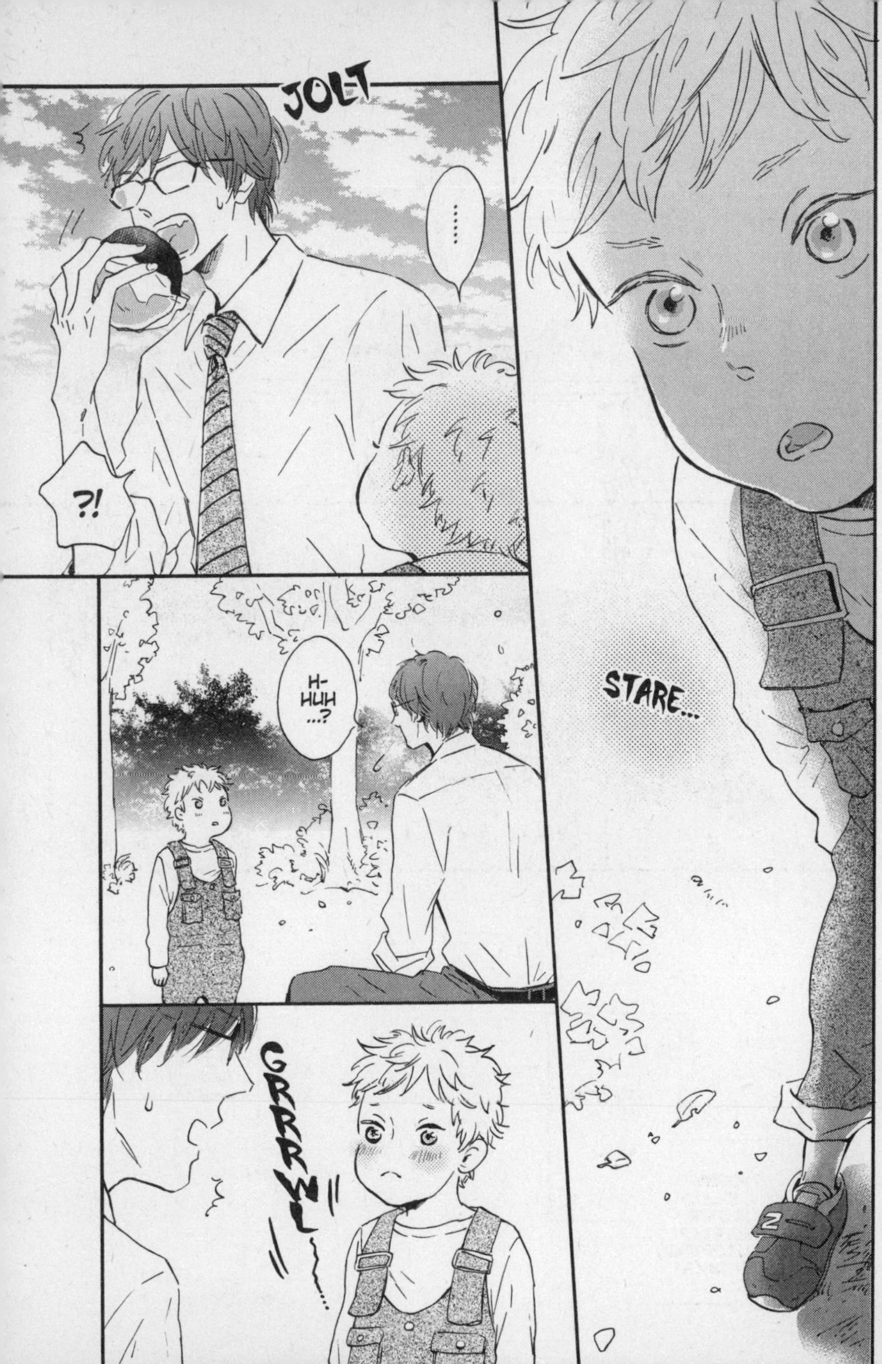
STARE...
JOLT
......
?!
H-HUH...?
GRRRWL...

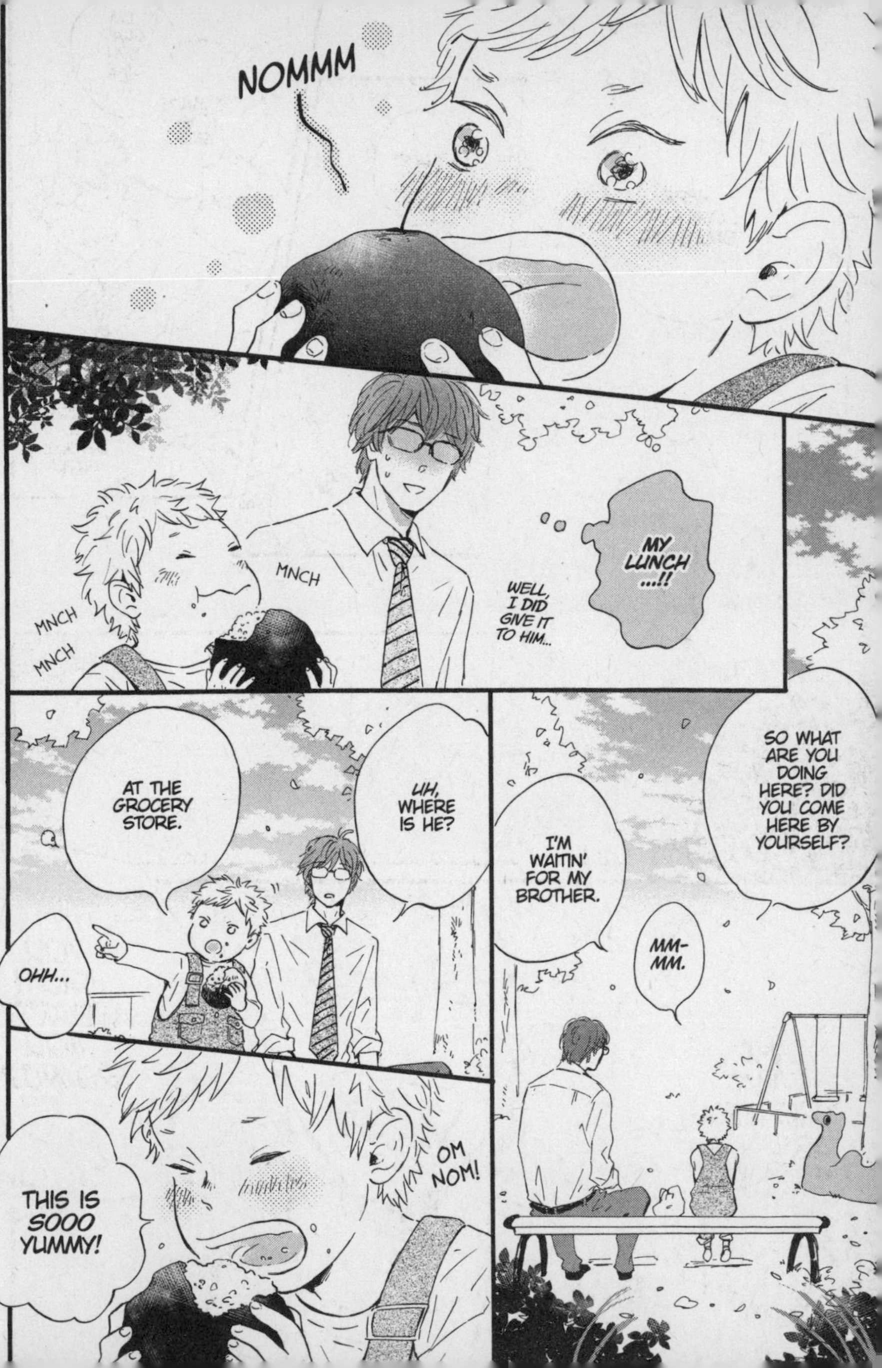
NOMMM
MY LUNCH ...!!
WELL, I DID GIVE IT TO HIM...
MNCH
MNCH
MNCH
SO WHAT ARE YOU DOING HERE? DID YOU COME HERE BY YOURSELF?
I'M WAITIN' FOR MY BROTHER.
MM-MM.
UH, WHERE IS HE?
AT THE GROCERY STORE.
OHH...
OM NOM!
THIS IS SOOO YUMMY!

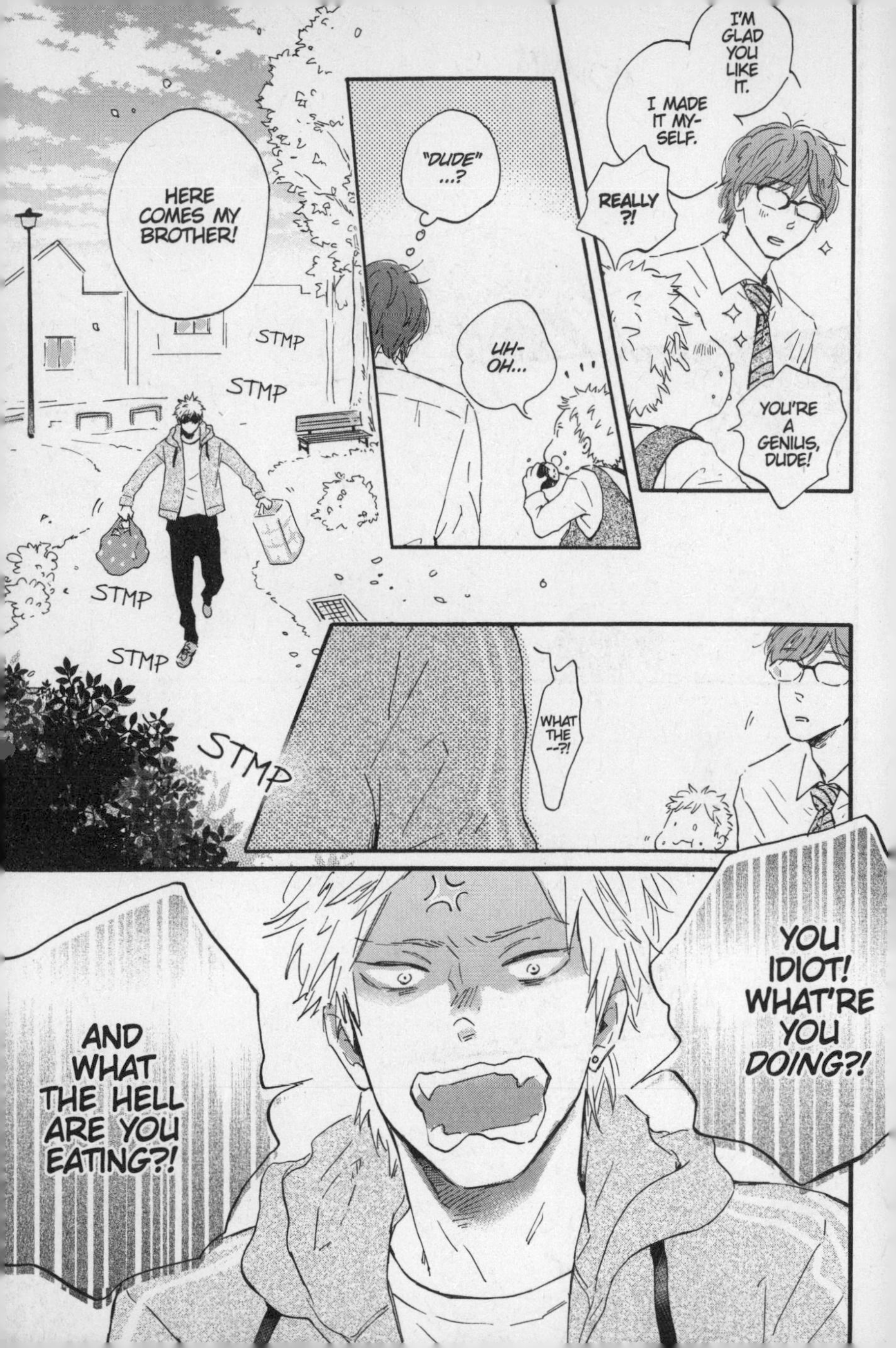
REALLY?!
YOU'RE A GENIUS, DUDE!
I'M GLAD YOU LIKE IT.
I MADE IT MY-SELF.
"DUDE"...?
UH-OH...
WHAT THE--?!
HERE COMES MY BROTHER!
STMP
STMP
STMP
STMP
STMP
YOU IDIOT! WHAT'RE YOU DOING?!
AND WHAT THE HELL ARE YOU EATING?!

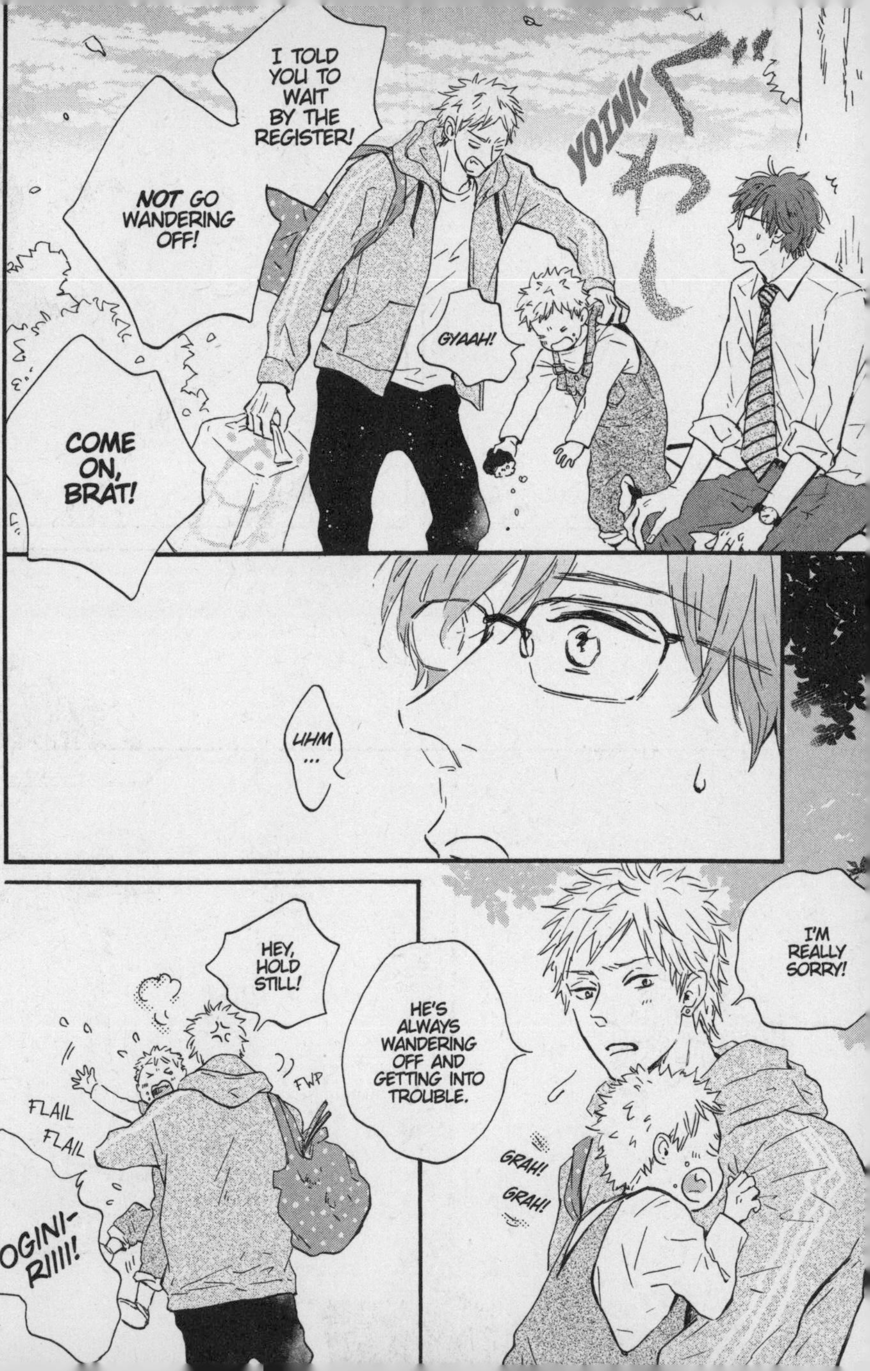
YOINK
I TOLD YOU TO WAIT BY THE REGISTER!
NOT GO WANDERING OFF!
GYAAH!
COME ON, BRAT!
UHM...
I'M REALLY SORRY!
HE'S ALWAYS WANDERING OFF AND GETTING INTO TROUBLE.
GRAH!
GRAH!
HEY, HOLD STILL!
FWP
FLAIL
FLAIL
OGINI-RIIII!

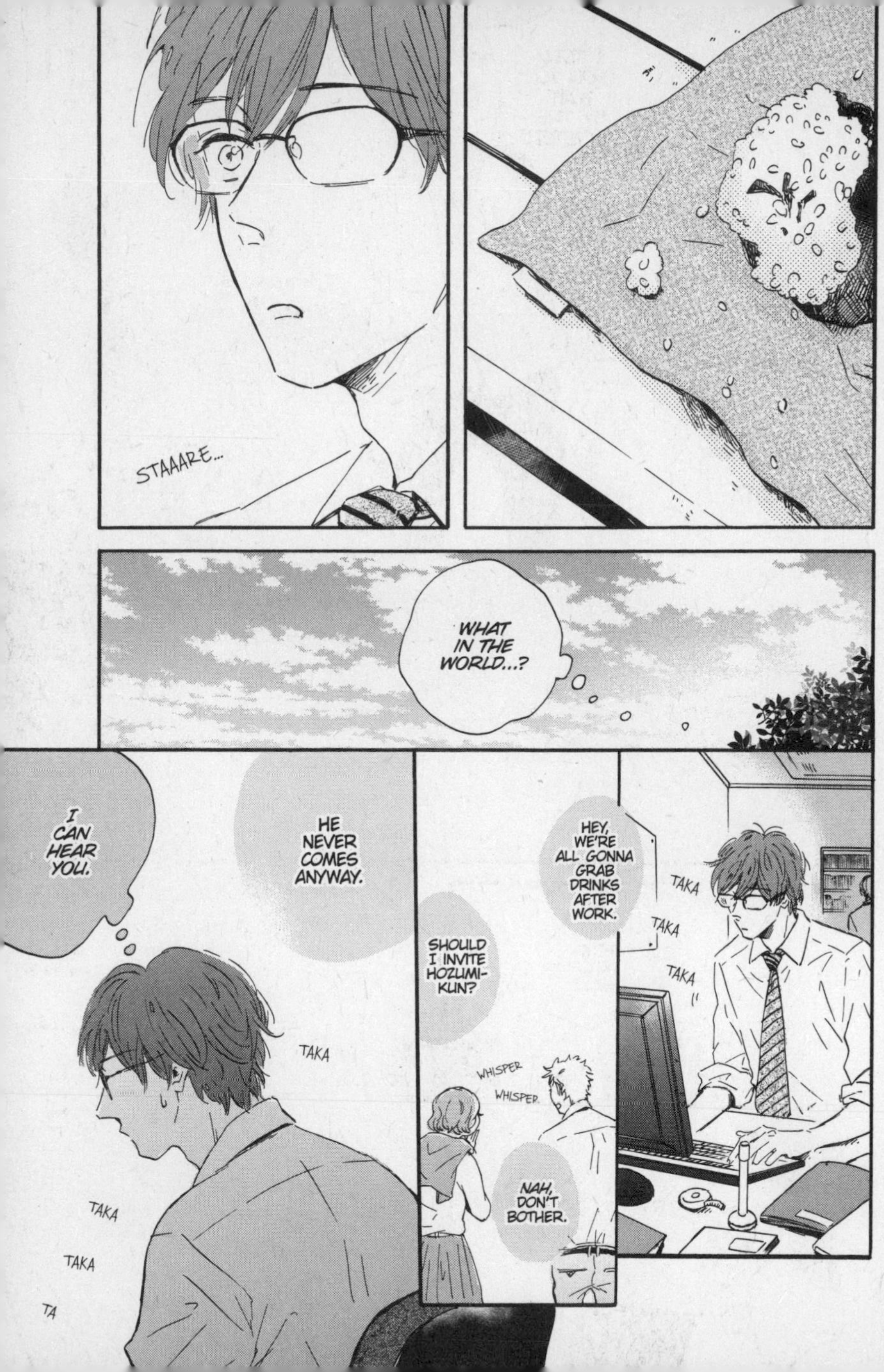
STAAARE...
WHAT IN THE WORLD...?
TAKA
TAKA
TAKA
HEY, WE'RE ALL GONNA GRAB DRINKS AFTER WORK.
SHOULD I INVITE HOZUMI-KUN?
WHISPER
WHISPER
NAH, DON'T BOTHER.
HE NEVER COMES ANYWAY.
I CAN HEAR YOU.
TAKA
TAKA
TAKA
TA

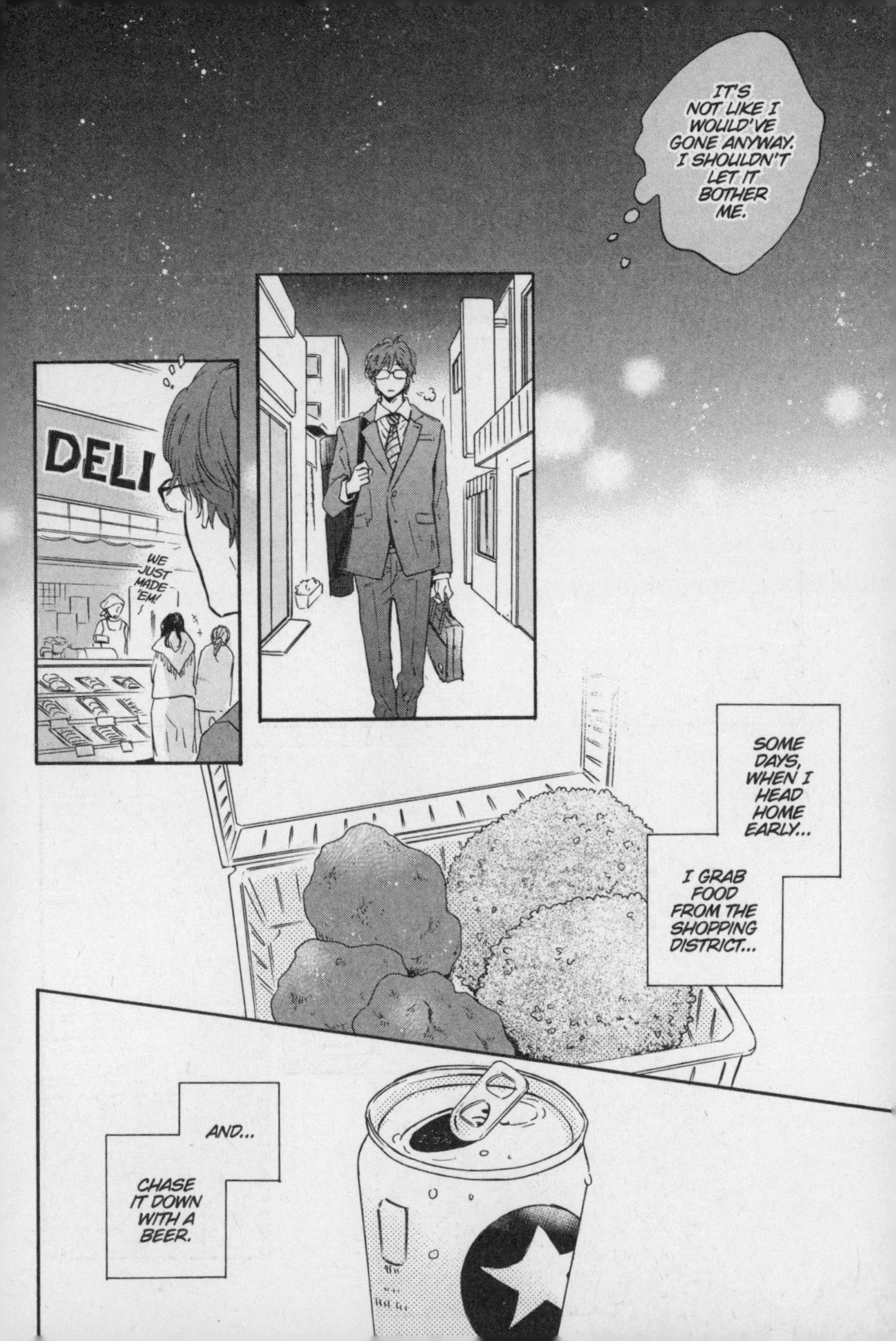
IT'S NOT LIKE I WOULD'VE GONE ANYWAY. I SHOULDN'T LET IT BOTHER ME.
DELI
WE JUST MADE 'EM!
SOME DAYS, WHEN I HEAD HOME EARLY...
I GRAB FOOD FROM THE SHOPPING DISTRICT...
AND...
CHASE IT DOWN WITH A BEER.

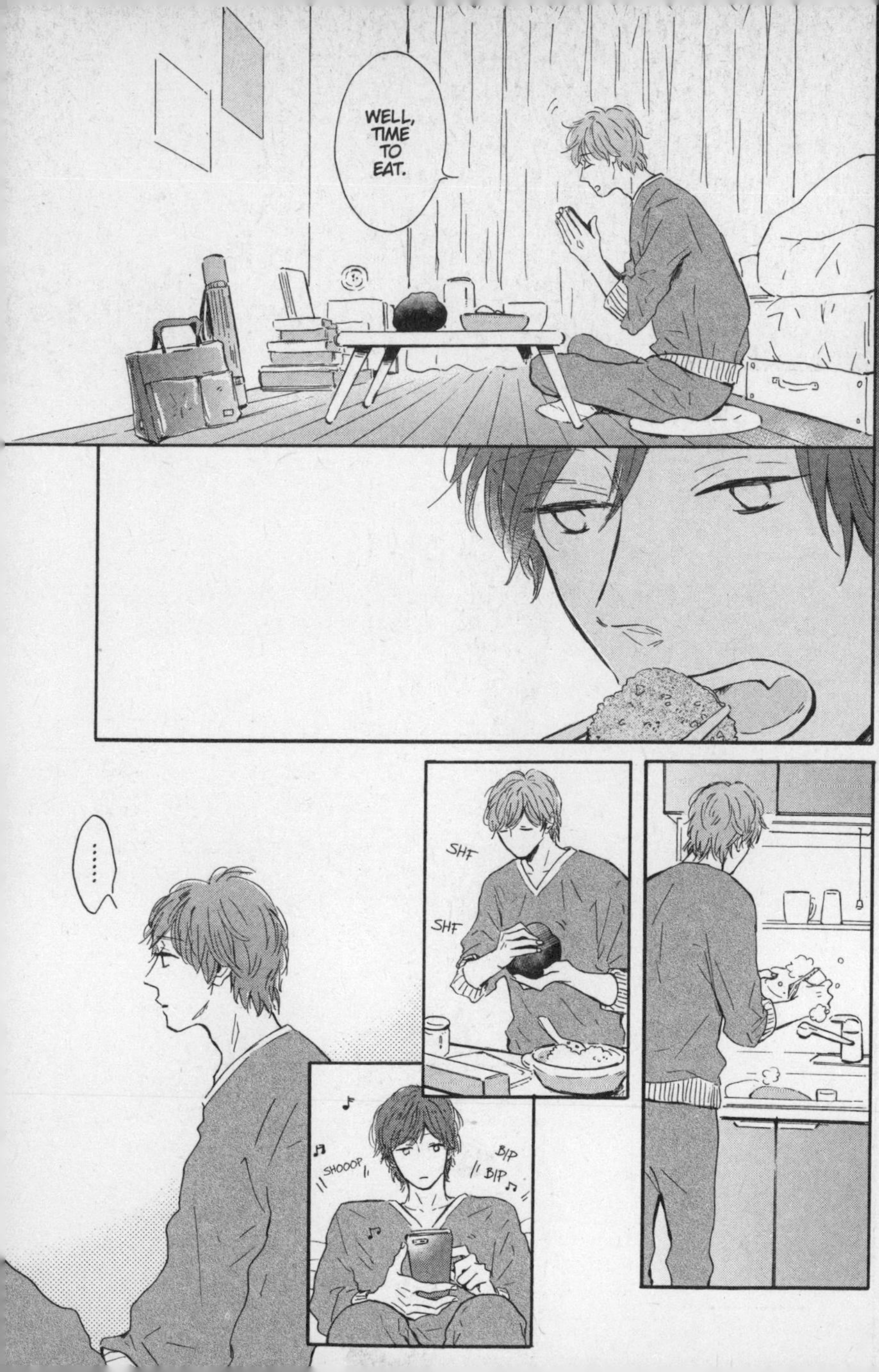
WELL, TIME TO EAT.
SHF
SHF
SHOOOP
BIP BIP
......

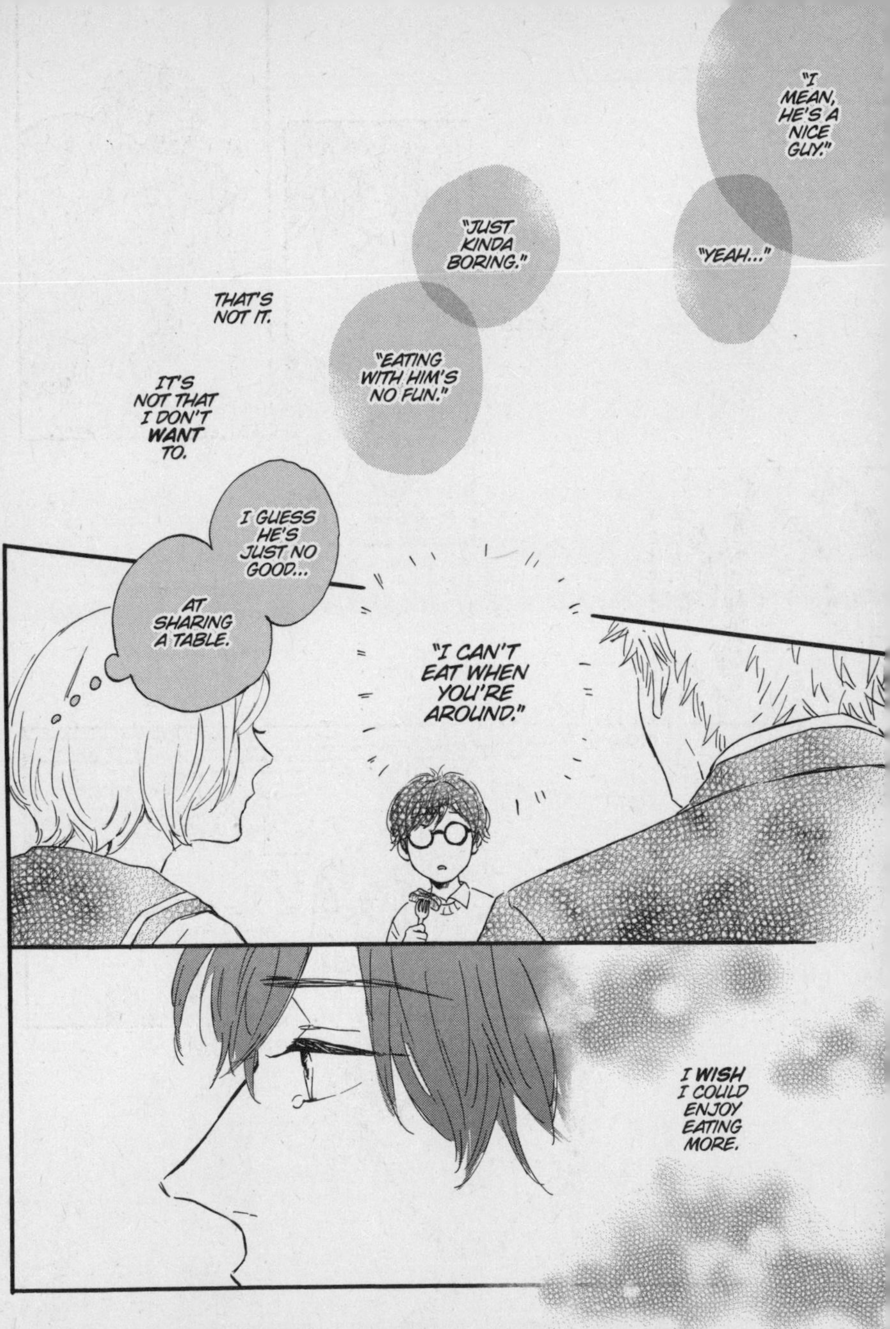
"I MEAN, HE'S A NICE GUY."
"YEAH..."
"JUST KINDA BORING."
"EATING WITH HIM'S NO FUN."
THAT'S NOT IT.
IT'S NOT THAT I DON'T WANT TO.
"I CAN'T EAT WHEN YOU'RE AROUND."
I GUESS HE'S JUST NO GOOD...
AT SHARING A TABLE.
I WISH I COULD ENJOY EATING MORE.

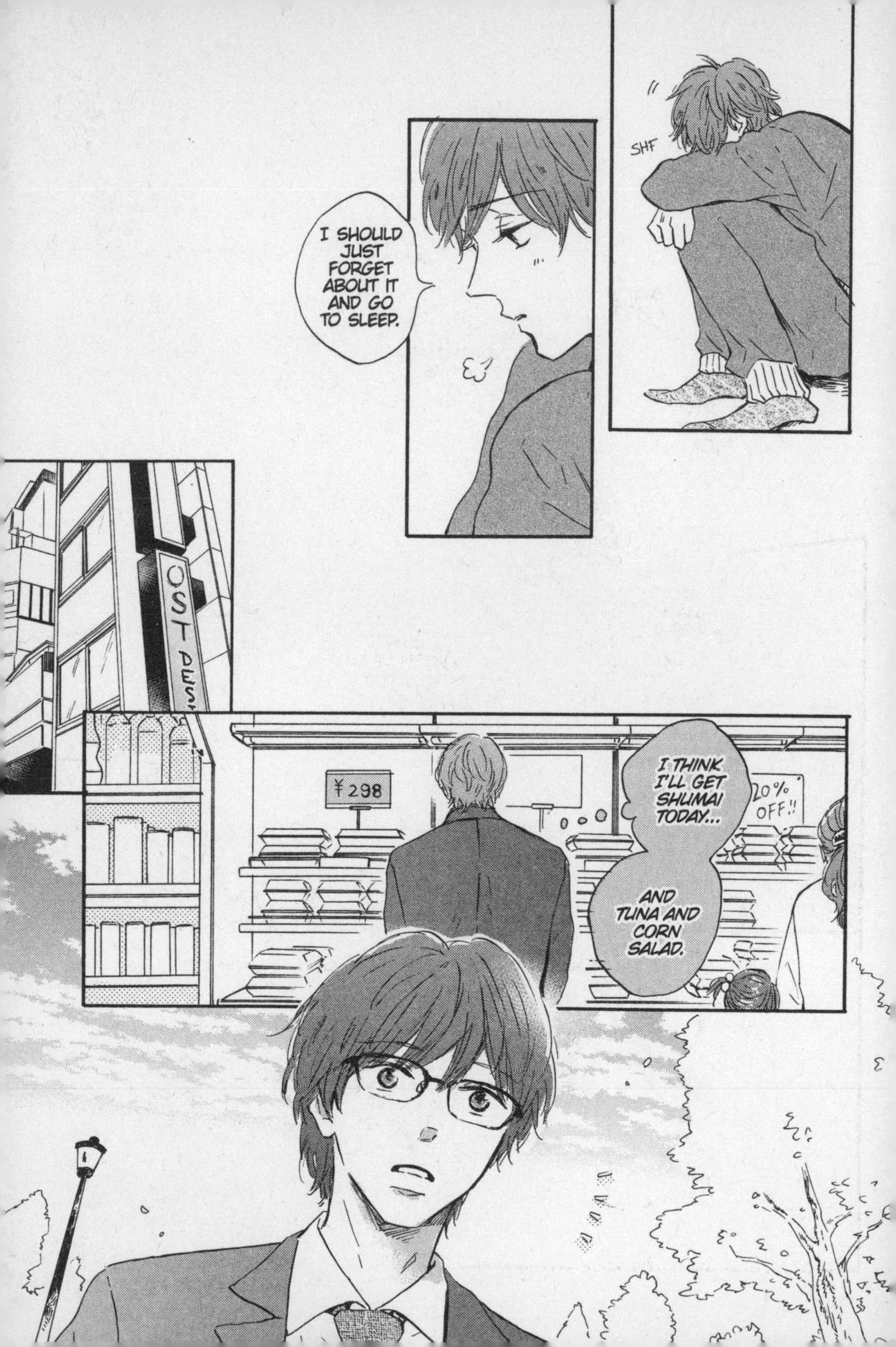
SHF
I SHOULD JUST FORGET ABOUT IT AND GO TO SLEEP.
¥298
I THINK I'LL GET SHUMAI TODAY...
AND TUNA AND CORN SALAD.
20% OFF!!

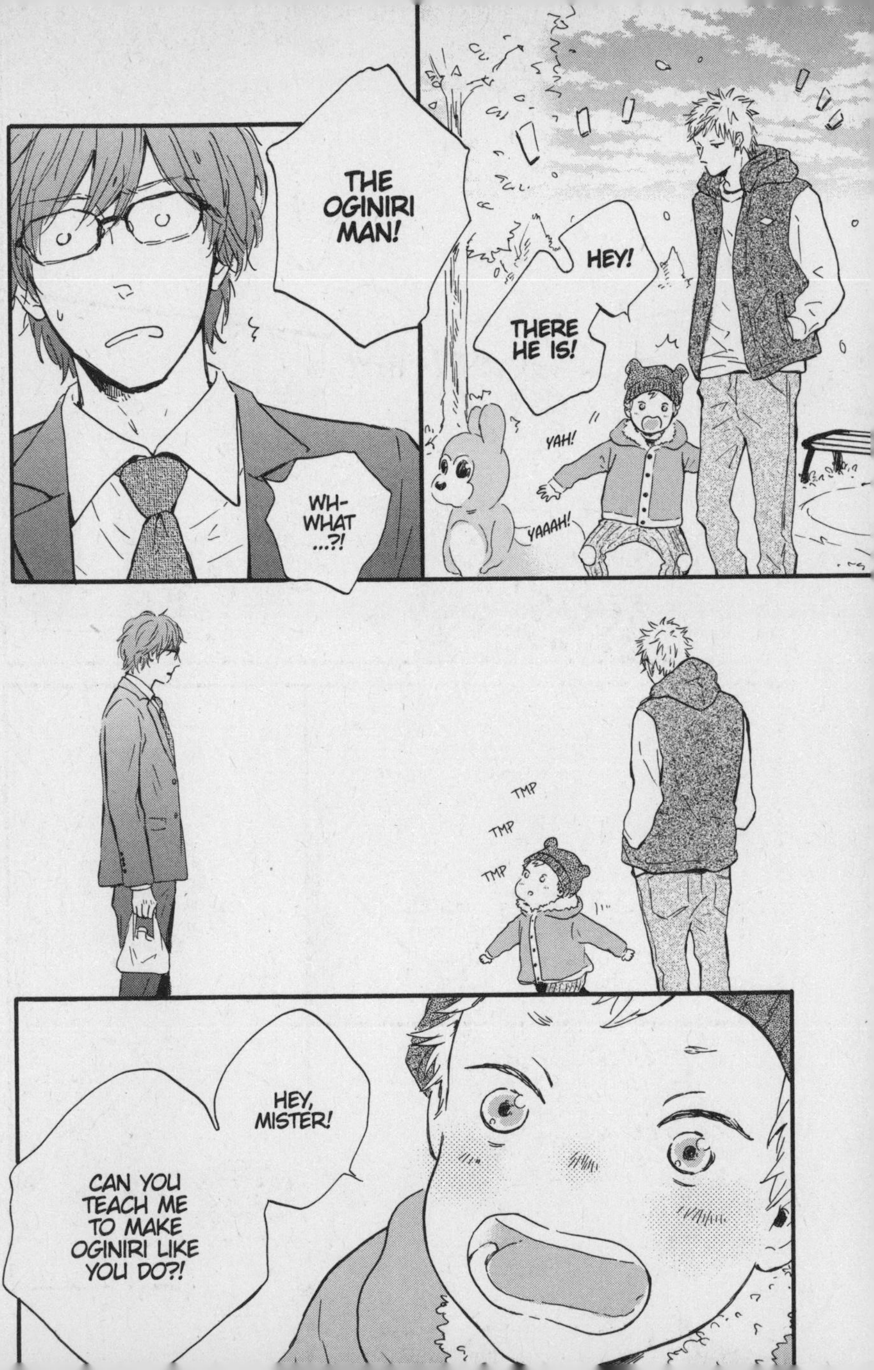
HEY!
THERE HE IS!
YAH!
YAAAH!
THE OGINIRI MAN!
WH-WHAT ...?!
TMP
TMP
TMP
HEY, MISTER!
CAN YOU TEACH ME TO MAKE OGINIRI LIKE YOU DO?!

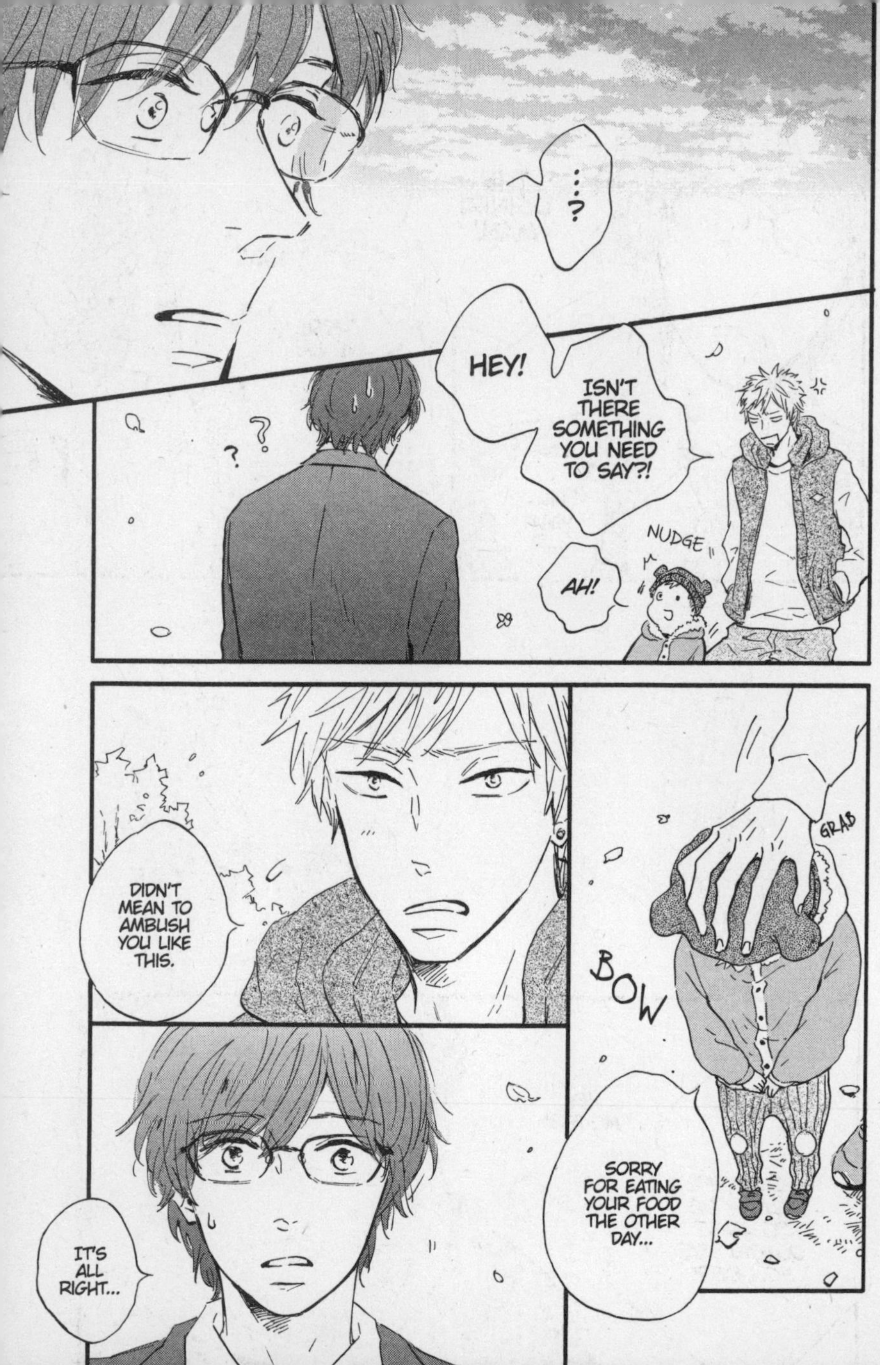
...?
HEY!
ISN'T THERE SOMETHING YOU NEED TO SAY?!
NUDGE
AH!
GRAB
BOW
SORRY FOR EATING YOUR FOOD THE OTHER DAY...
DIDN'T MEAN TO AMBUSH YOU LIKE THIS.
IT'S ALL RIGHT...

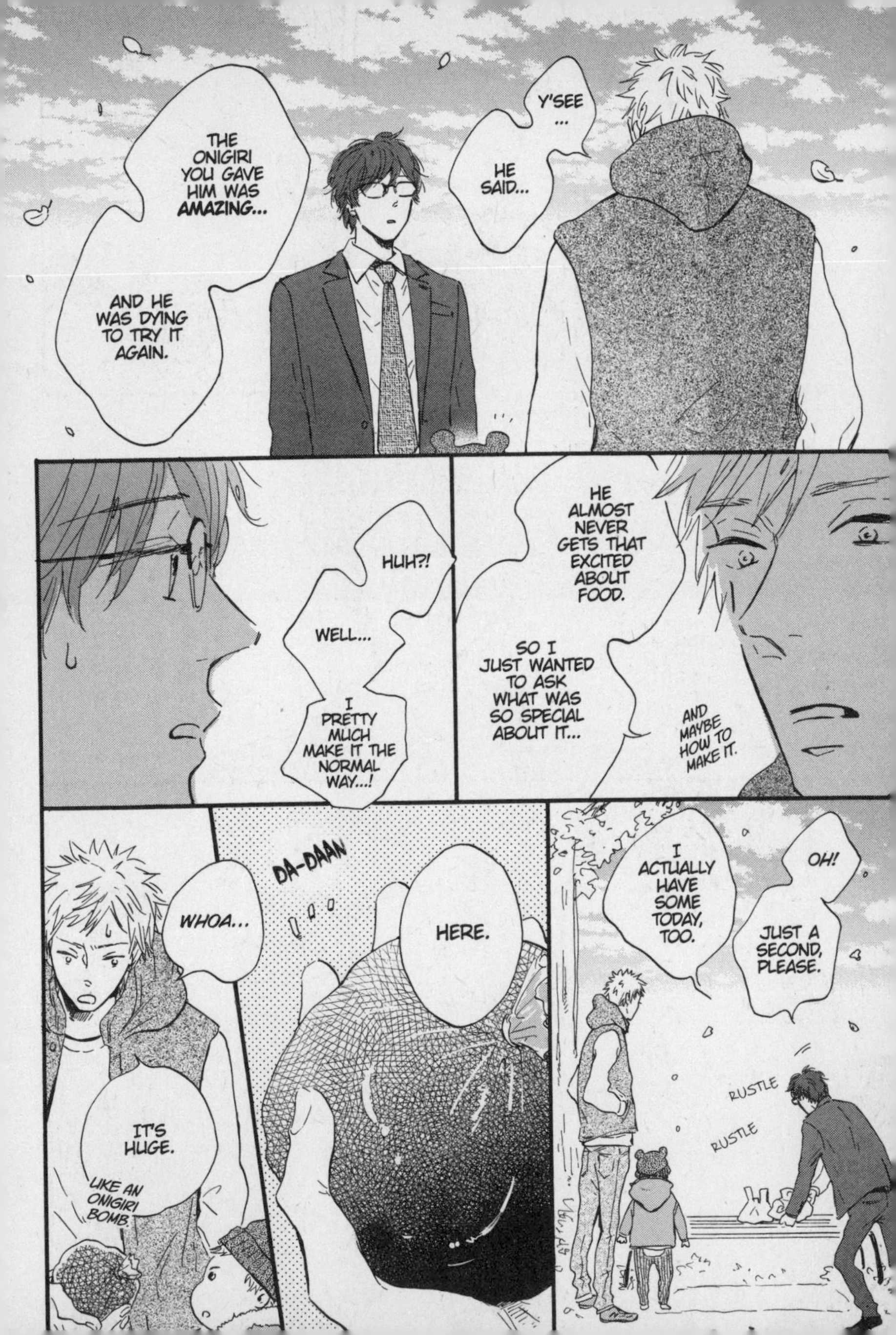
Y'SEE ...
HE SAID...
THE ONIGIRI YOU GAVE HIM WAS AMAZING...
AND HE WAS DYING TO TRY IT AGAIN.
HE ALMOST NEVER GETS THAT EXCITED ABOUT FOOD.
SO I JUST WANTED TO ASK WHAT WAS SO SPECIAL ABOUT IT...
AND MAYBE HOW TO MAKE IT.
HUH?!
WELL...
I PRETTY MUCH MAKE IT THE NORMAL WAY...!
OH!
I ACTUALLY HAVE SOME TODAY, TOO.
JUST A SECOND, PLEASE.
RUSTLE
RUSTLE
DA-DAAN
HERE.
WHOA...
IT'S HUGE.
LIKE AN ONIGIRI BOMB.

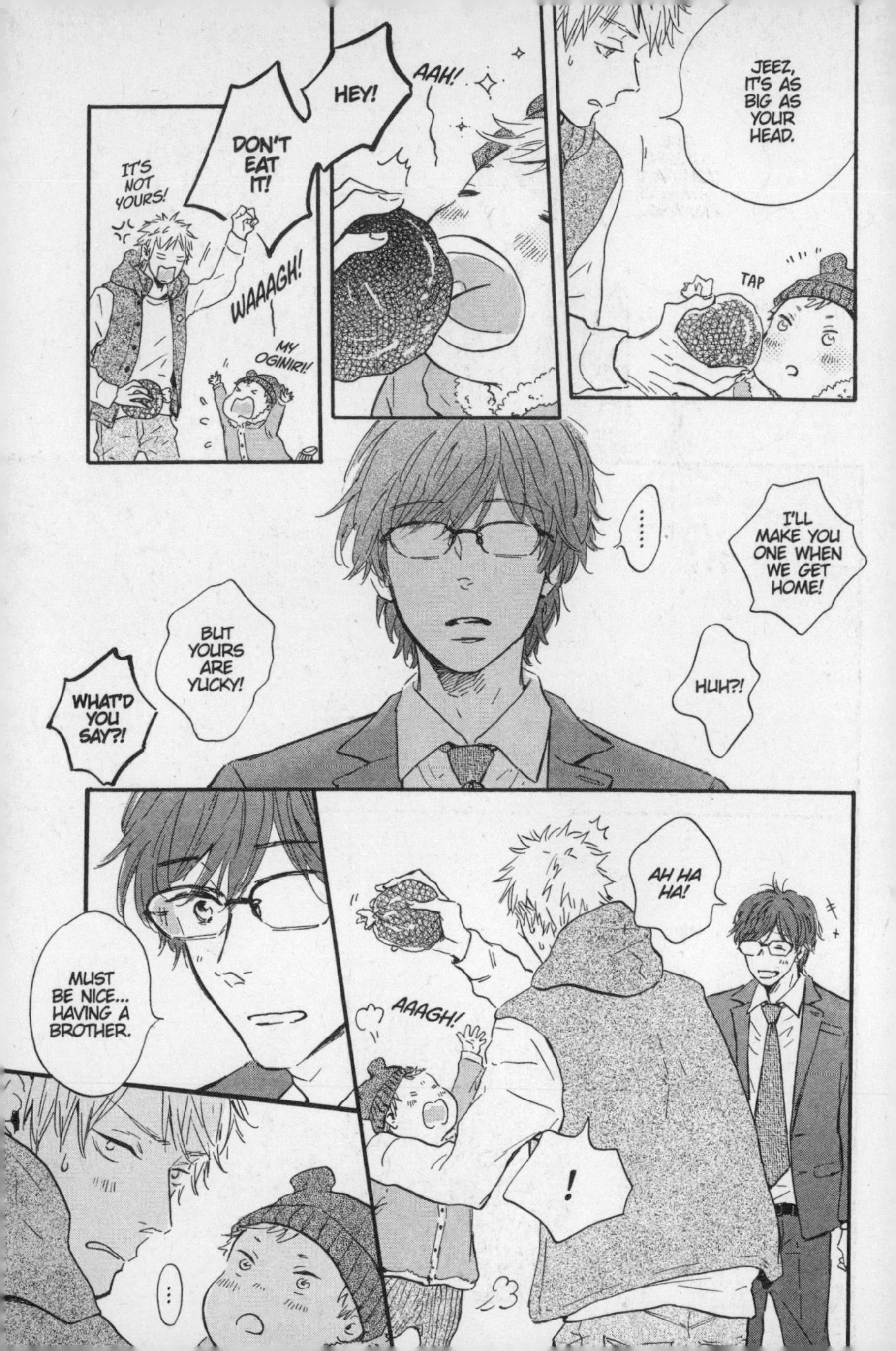
JEEZ, IT'S AS BIG AS YOUR HEAD.
TAP
AAH!
HEY!
DON'T EAT IT!
IT'S NOT YOURS!
WAAAGH!
MY OGINIRI!
......
I'LL MAKE YOU ONE WHEN WE GET HOME!
HUH?!
BUT YOURS ARE YUCKY!
WHAT'D YOU SAY?!
AH HA HA!
AAAGH!
!
MUST BE NICE... HAVING A BROTHER.
...

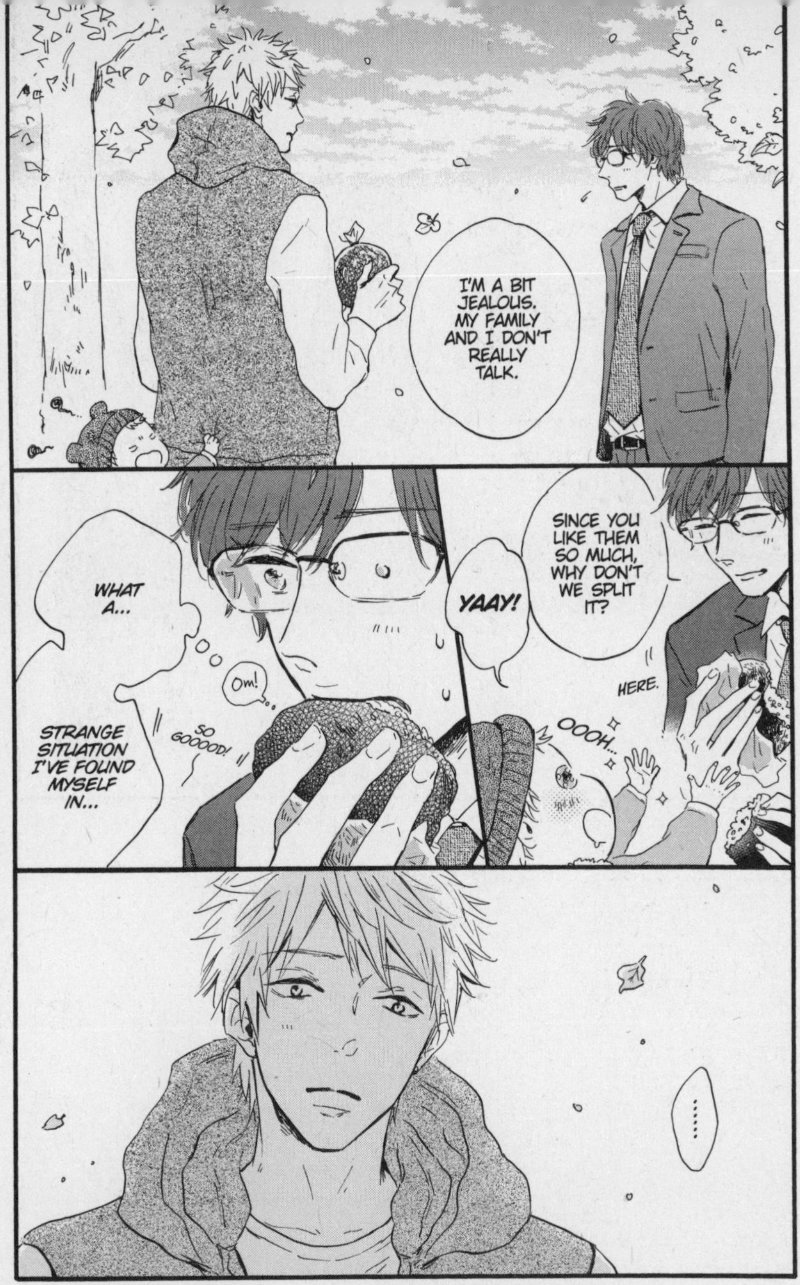

I'M A BIT JEALOUS. MY FAMILY AND I DON'T REALLY TALK.
SINCE YOU LIKE THEM SO MUCH, WHY DON'T WE SPLIT IT?
HERE.
OOOH...
YAAY!
WHAT A...
Om!
SO GOOOOD!
STRANGE SITUATION I'VE FOUND MYSELF IN...
......

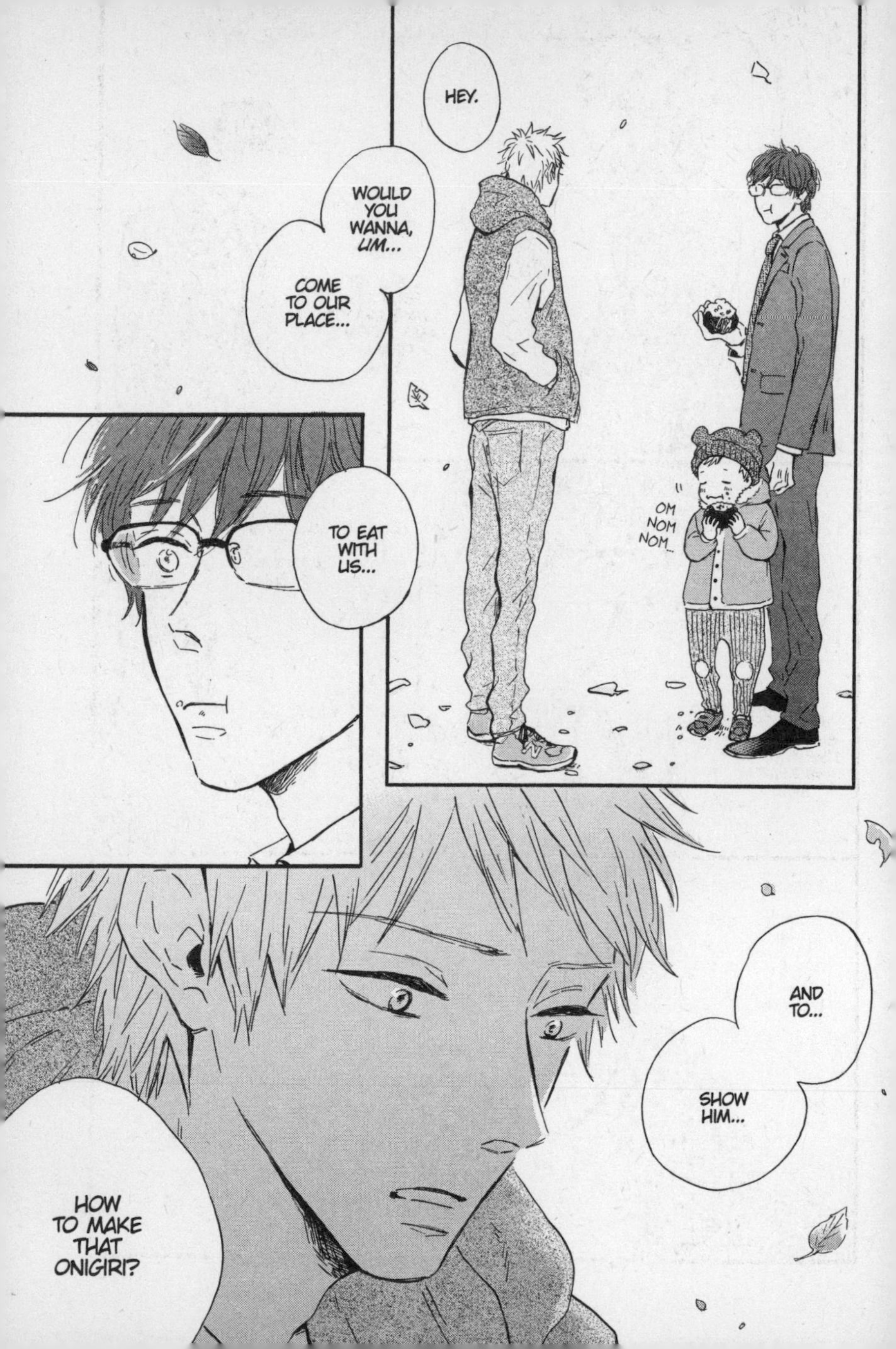
HEY.
OM NOM NOM...
WOULD YOU WANNA, UM...
COME TO OUR PLACE...
TO EAT WITH US...
AND TO...
SHOW HIM...
HOW TO MAKE THAT ONIGIRI?

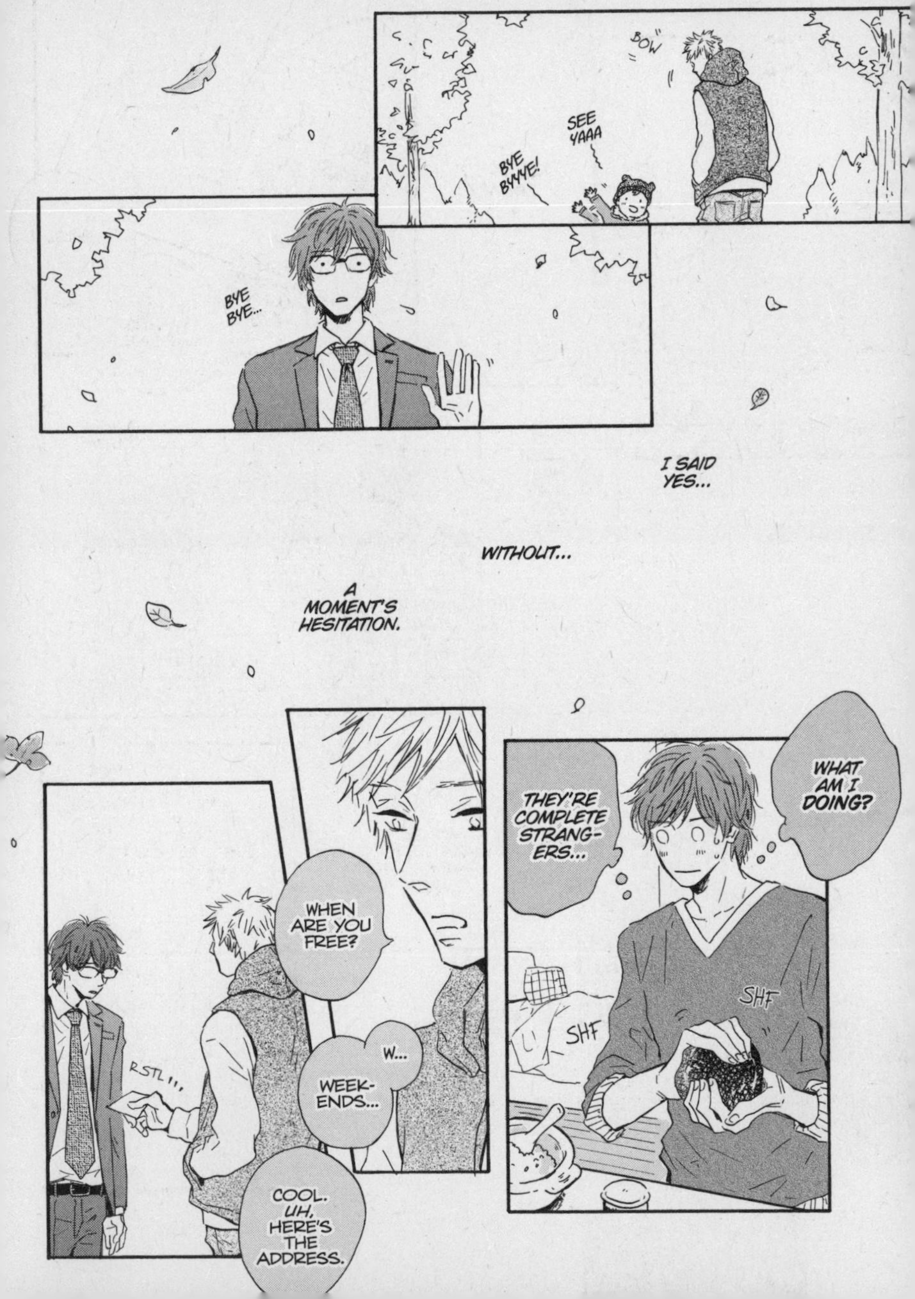
BOW
SEE YAAA
BYE BYYYE!
BYE BYE...
I SAID YES...
WITHOUT...
A MOMENT'S HESITATION.
WHAT AM I DOING?
THEY'RE COMPLETE STRANG- ERS...
SHF
SHF
WHEN ARE YOU FREE?
W...
WEEK- ENDS...
RSTL
COOL. UH, HERE'S THE ADDRESS.

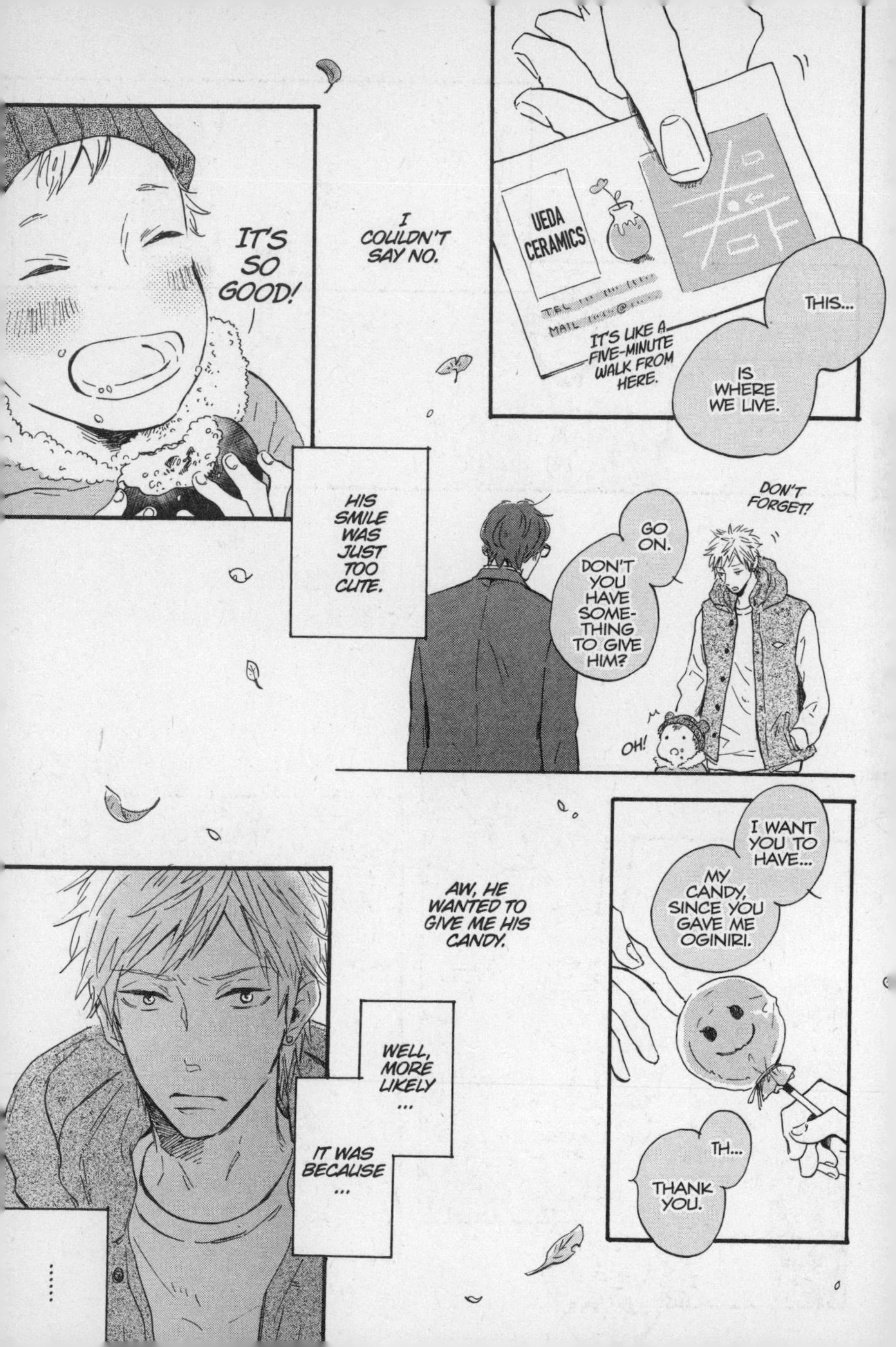
UEDA CERAMICS
THIS...
IS WHERE WE LIVE.
IT'S LIKE A FIVE-MINUTE WALK FROM HERE.
I COULDN'T SAY NO.
IT'S SO GOOD!
HIS SMILE WAS JUST TOO CUTE.
DON'T FORGET!
GO ON.
DON'T YOU HAVE SOMETHING TO GIVE HIM?
OH!
I WANT YOU TO HAVE...
MY CANDY, SINCE YOU GAVE ME OGINIRI.
TH...
THANK YOU.
AW, HE WANTED TO GIVE ME HIS CANDY.
WELL, MORE LIKELY...
IT WAS BECAUSE...
......

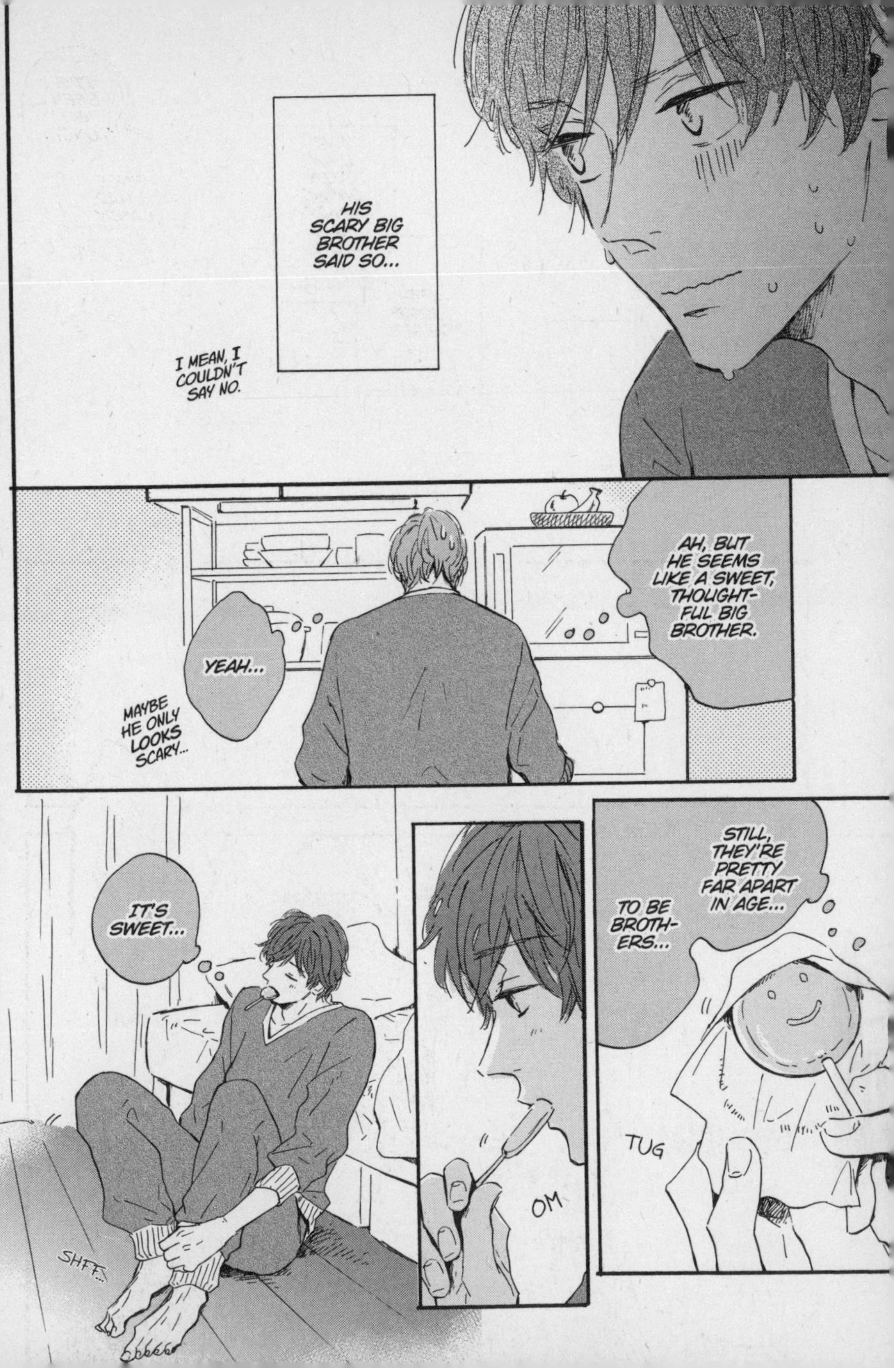
HIS SCARY BIG BROTHER SAID SO...
I MEAN, I COULDN'T SAY NO.
AH, BUT HE SEEMS LIKE A SWEET, THOUGHT-FUL BIG BROTHER.
YEAH...
MAYBE HE ONLY LOOKS SCARY...
STILL, THEY'RE PRETTY FAR APART IN AGE...
TO BE BROTH-ERS...
TUG
OM
IT'S SWEET...
SHFF...

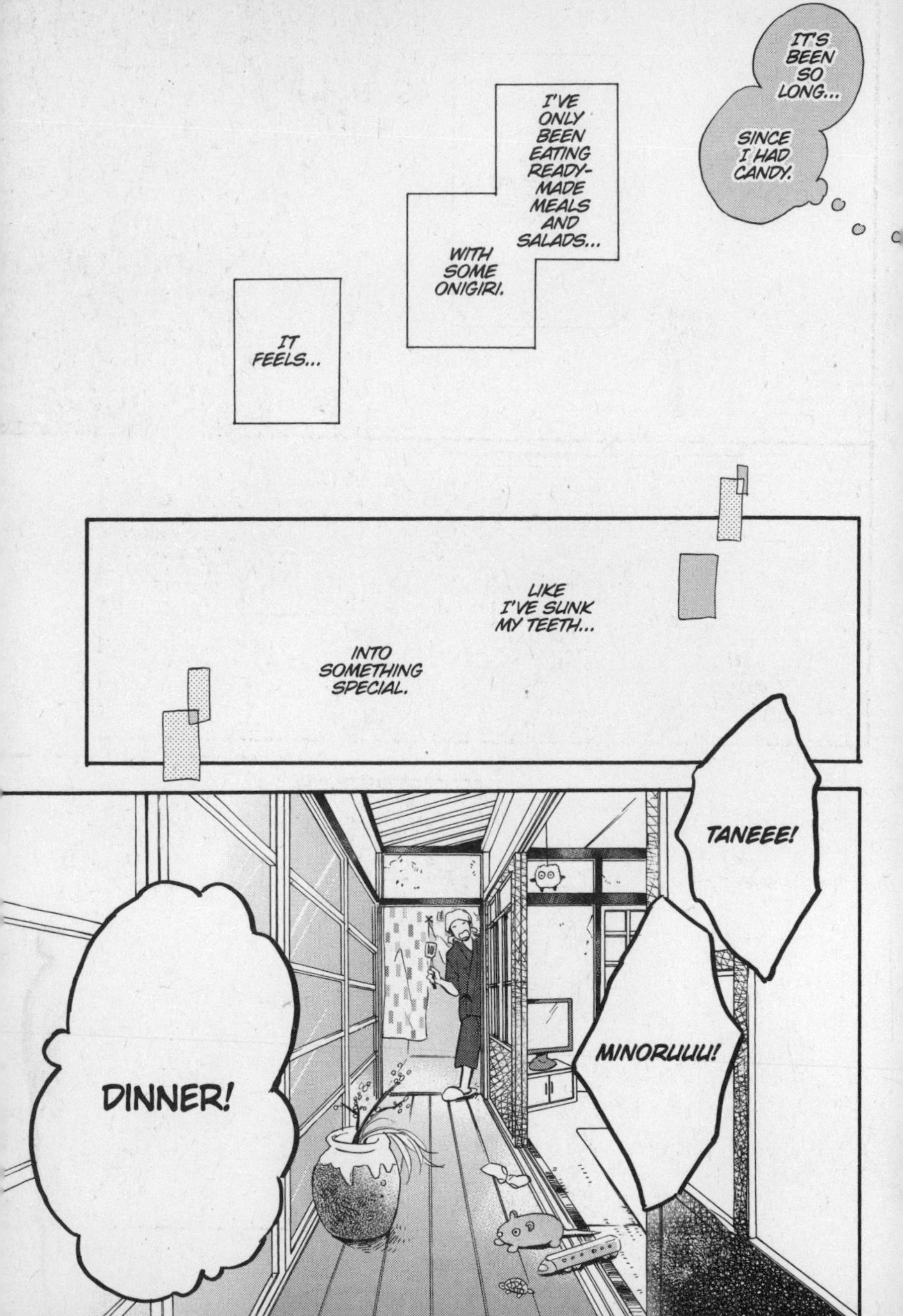
IT'S BEEN SO LONG...
SINCE I HAD CANDY.
I'VE ONLY BEEN EATING READY-MADE MEALS AND SALADS...
WITH SOME ONIGIRI.
IT FEELS...
LIKE I'VE SUNK MY TEETH...
INTO SOMETHING SPECIAL.
TANEEE!
MINORUUU!
DINNER!

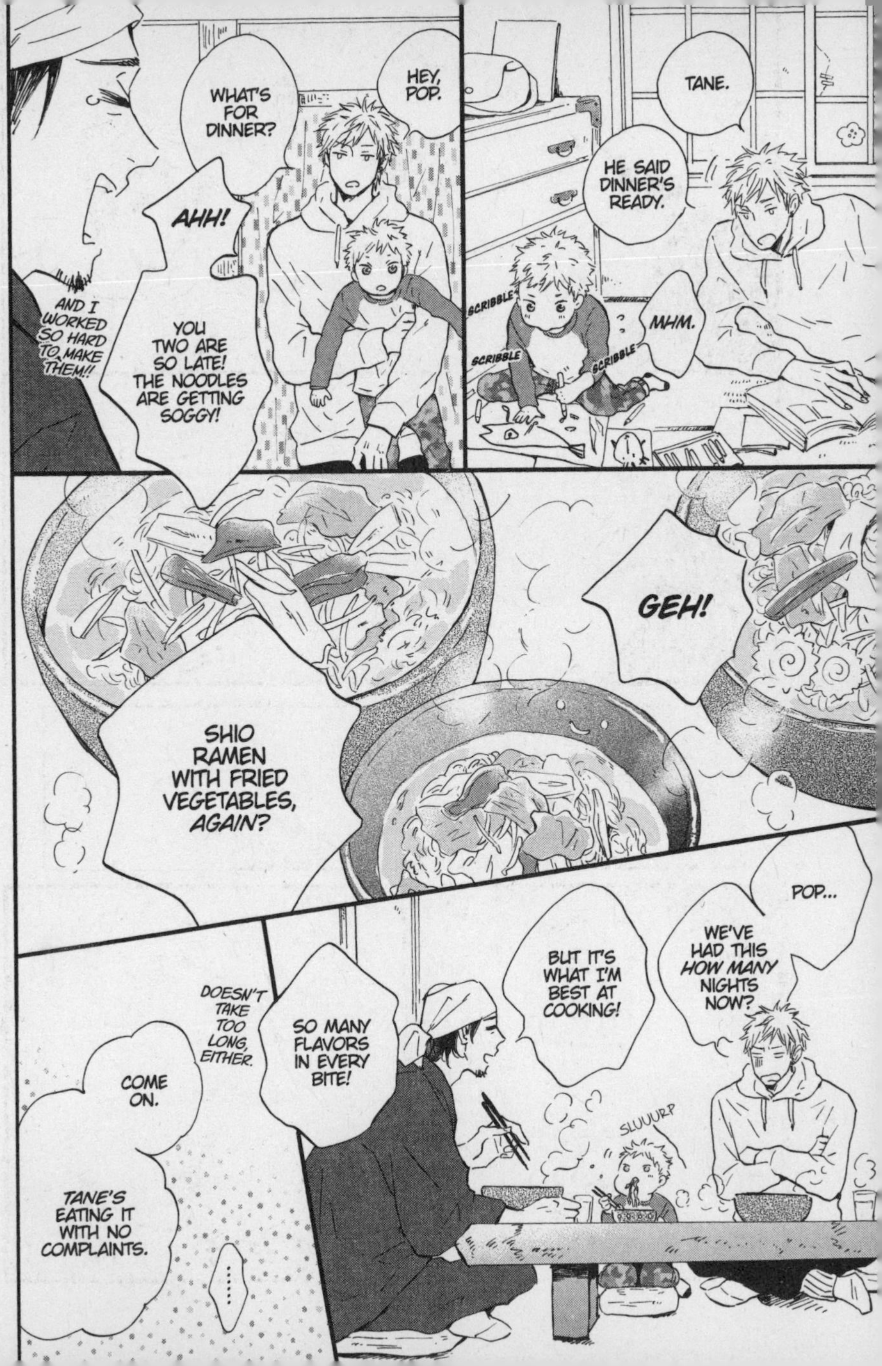

TANE.
HE SAID DINNER'S READY.
SCRIBBLE
SCRIBBLE
SCRIBBLE
MHM.
HEY, POP.
WHAT'S FOR DINNER?
AHH!
YOU TWO ARE SO LATE! THE NOODLES ARE GETTING SOGGY!
AND I WORKED SO HARD TO MAKE THEM!!
GEH!
SHIO RAMEN WITH FRIED VEGETABLES, *AGAIN?*
POP...
WE'VE HAD THIS *HOW MANY* NIGHTS NOW?
BUT IT'S WHAT I'M BEST AT COOKING!
SLUUURP
SO MANY FLAVORS IN EVERY BITE!
DOESN'T TAKE TOO LONG, EITHER.
COME ON.
TANE'S EATING IT WITH NO COMPLAINTS.
......

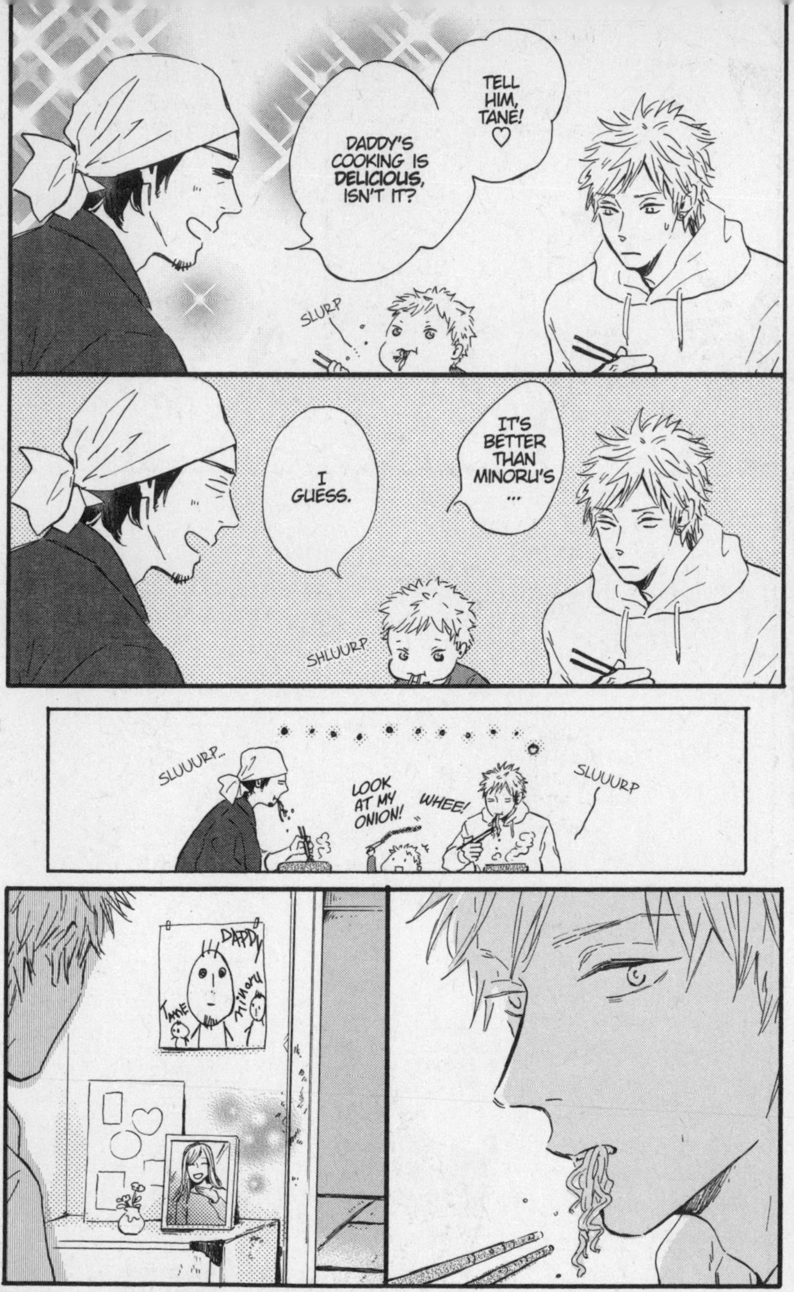

TELL HIM, TANE! ♡
DADDY'S COOKING IS DELICIOUS, ISN'T IT?
SLURP
IT'S BETTER THAN MINORU'S ...
I GUESS.
SHLUURP
SLUUURP
WHEE!
LOOK AT MY ONION!
SLUUURP...
DADDY
minoru
TANE

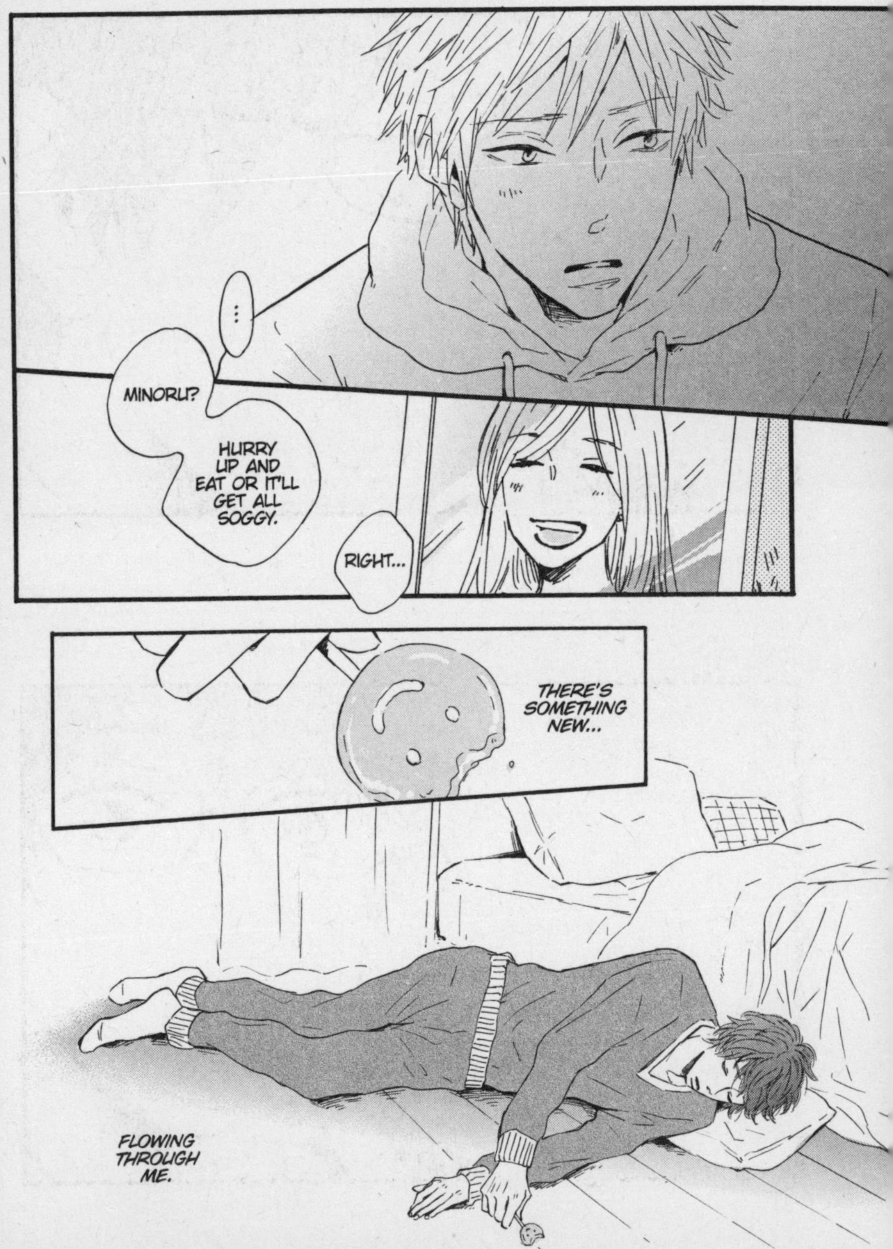
...
MINORU?
HURRY UP AND EAT OR IT'LL GET ALL SOGGY.
RIGHT...
THERE'S SOMETHING NEW...
FLOWING THROUGH ME.

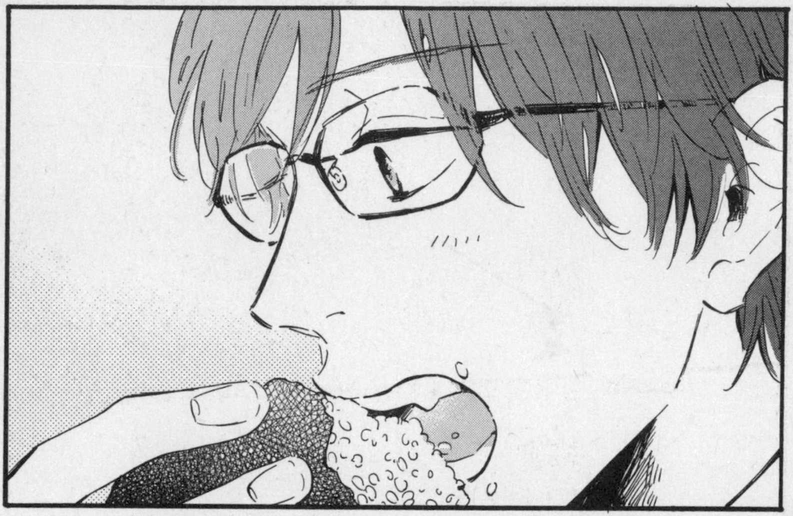

Chapter 1

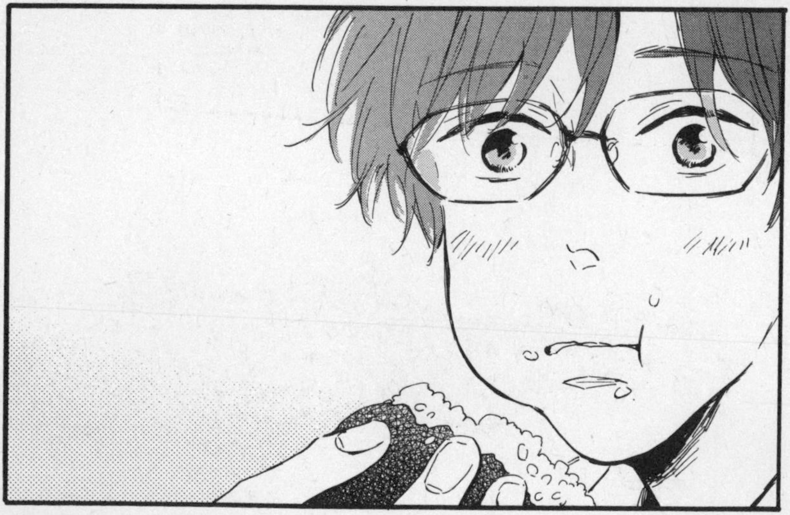

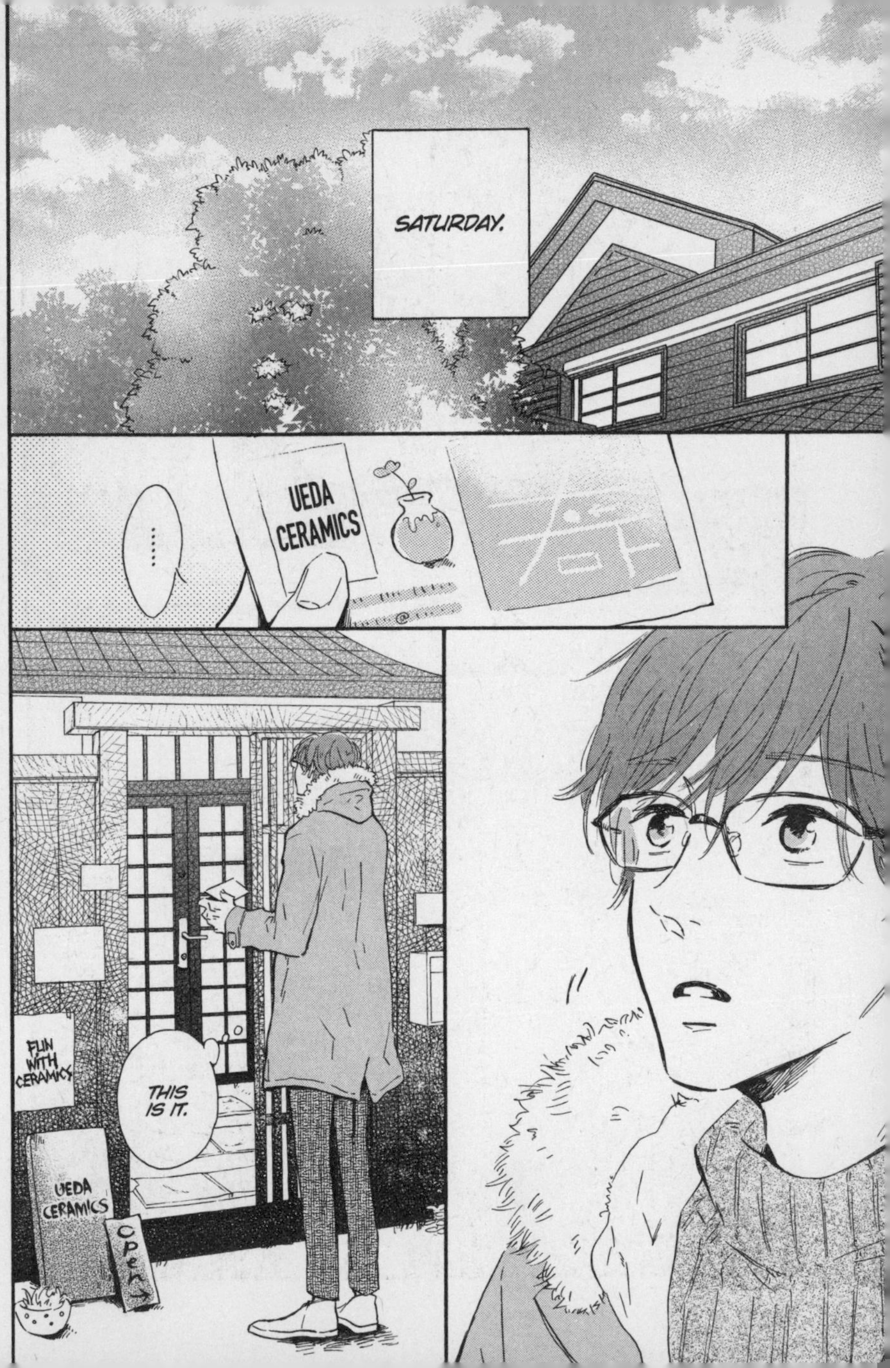
SATURDAY.
UEDA CERAMICS
......
THIS IS IT.
FUN WITH CERAMICS
UEDA CERAMICS
Open →

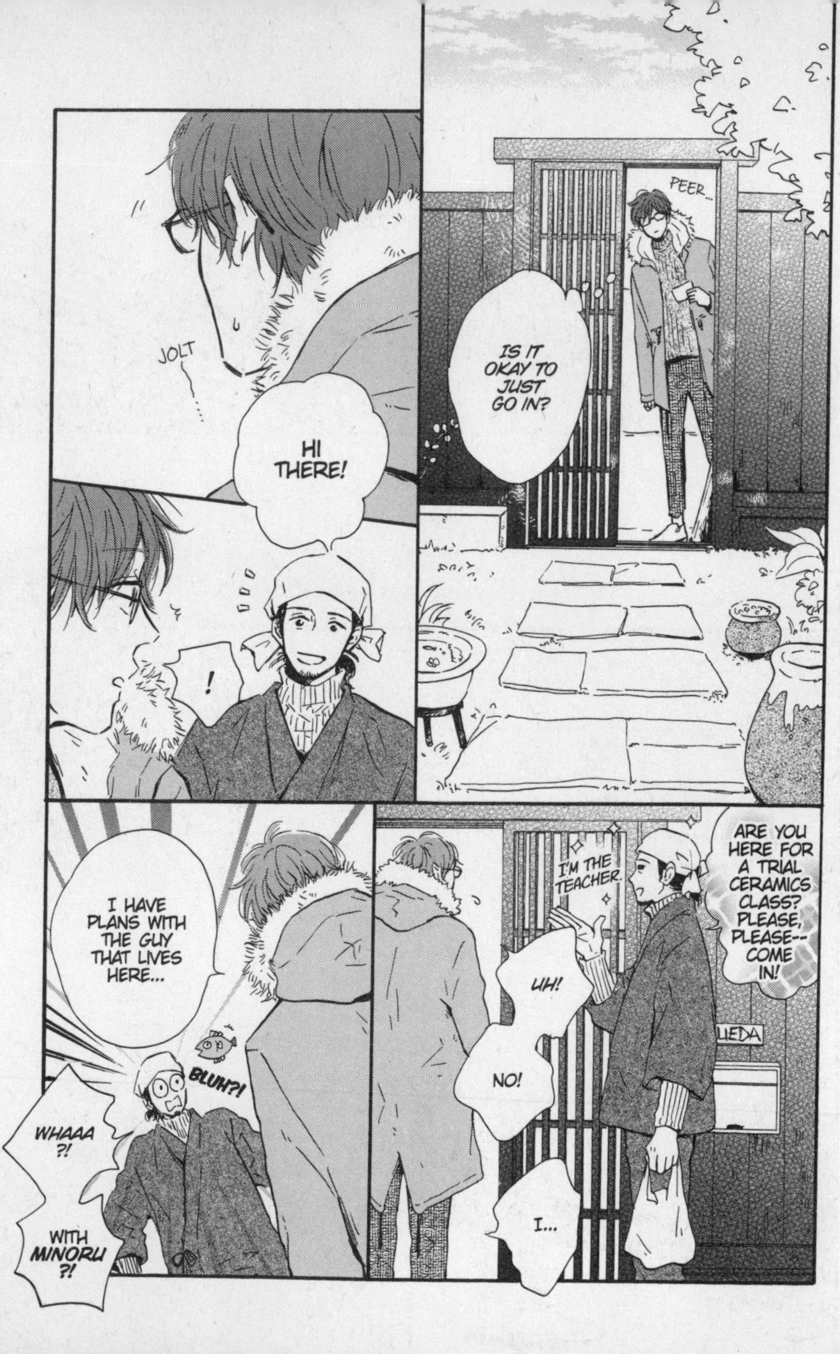
PEER...
IS IT OKAY TO JUST GO IN?
JOLT
HI THERE!
!
ARE YOU HERE FOR A TRIAL CERAMICS CLASS? PLEASE, PLEASE--COME IN!
I'M THE TEACHER.
UEDA
UH!
NO!
I...
I HAVE PLANS WITH THE GUY THAT LIVES HERE...
BLUH?!
WHAAA?!
WITH MINORU?!

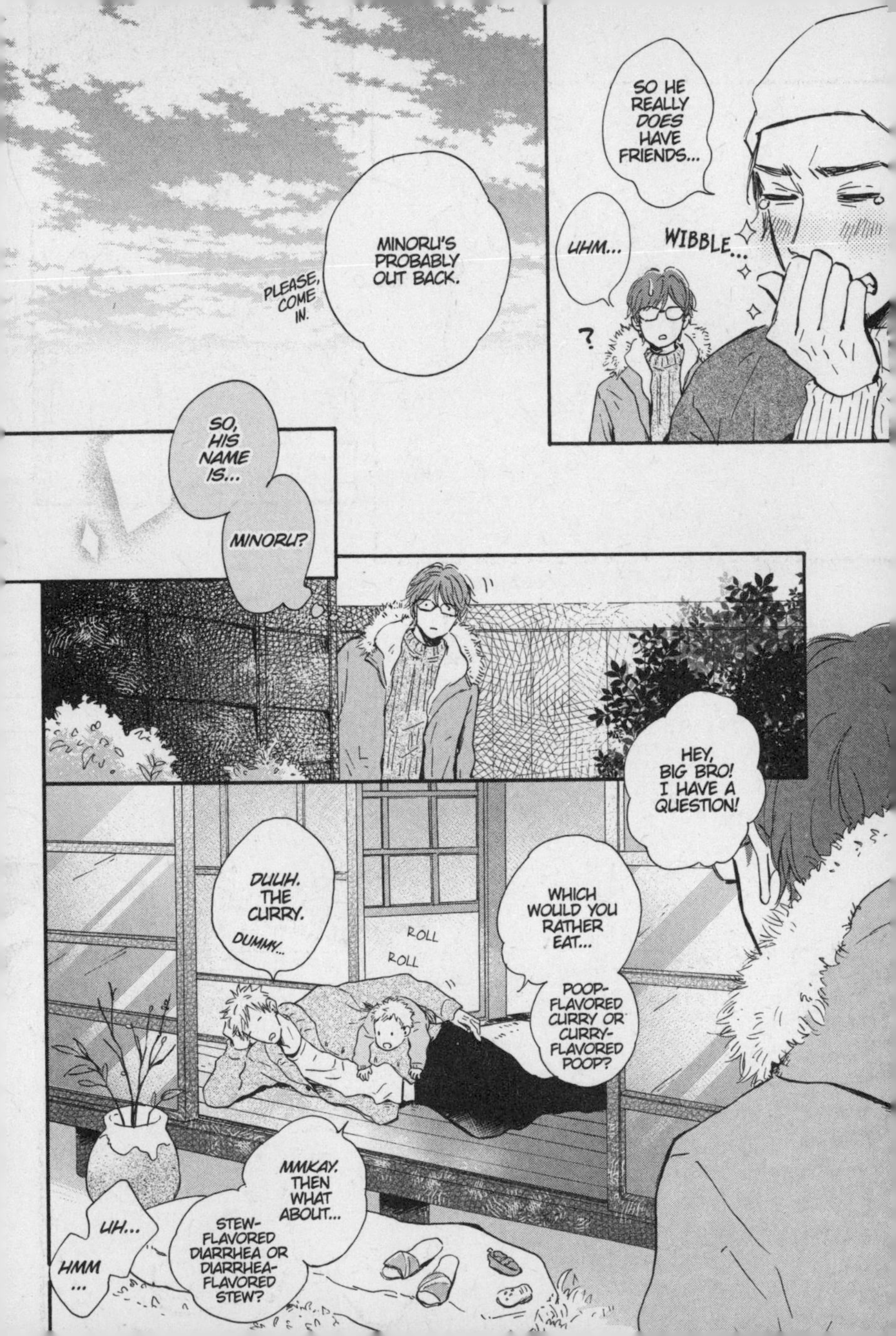
SO HE REALLY DOES HAVE FRIENDS...
WIBBLE...
UHM...
?
MINORU'S PROBABLY OUT BACK.
PLEASE, COME IN.
SO, HIS NAME IS...
MINORU?
HEY, BIG BRO! I HAVE A QUESTION!
WHICH WOULD YOU RATHER EAT...
POOP-FLAVORED CURRY OR CURRY-FLAVORED POOP?
ROLL
ROLL
DUUH. THE CURRY.
DUMMY...
MMKAY. THEN WHAT ABOUT...
STEW-FLAVORED DIARRHEA OR DIARRHEA-FLAVORED STEW?
UH...
HMM ...

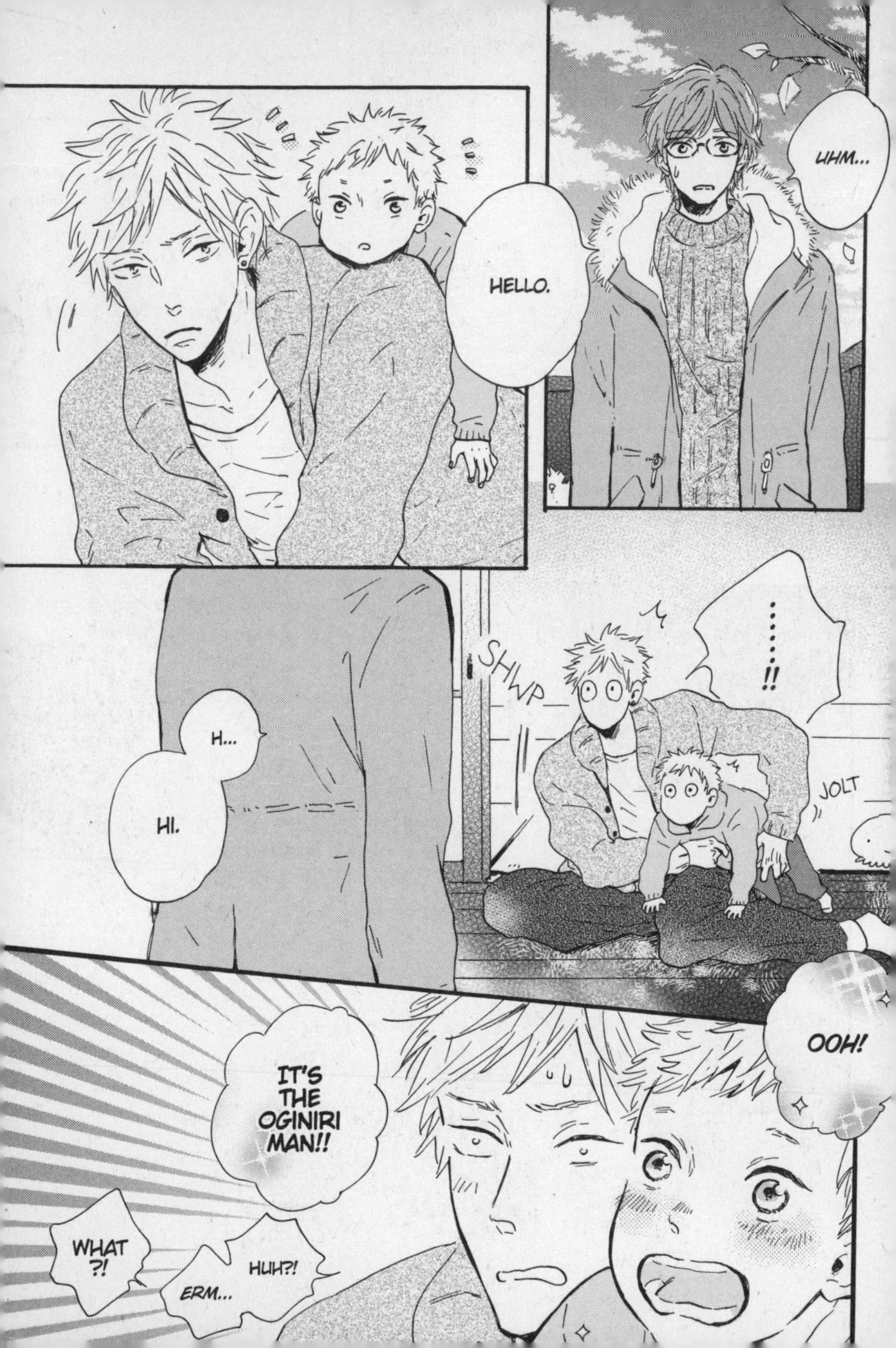
UHM...
HELLO.
......!!
SHWP
JOLT
H...
HI.
OOH!
IT'S THE OGINIRI MAN!!
HUH?!
WHAT?!
ERM...

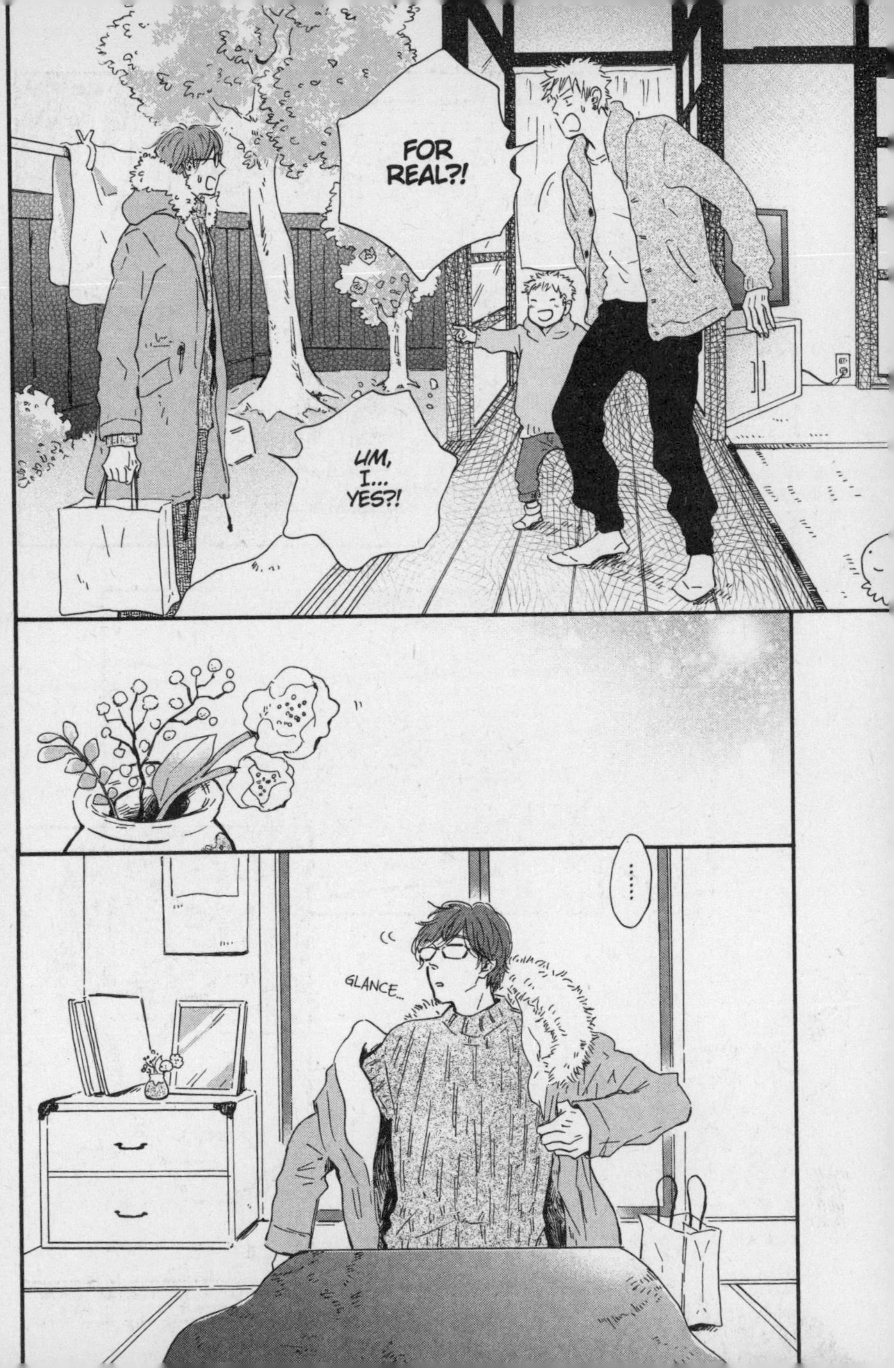
FOR REAL?!
UM, I... YES?!
......
GLANCE...

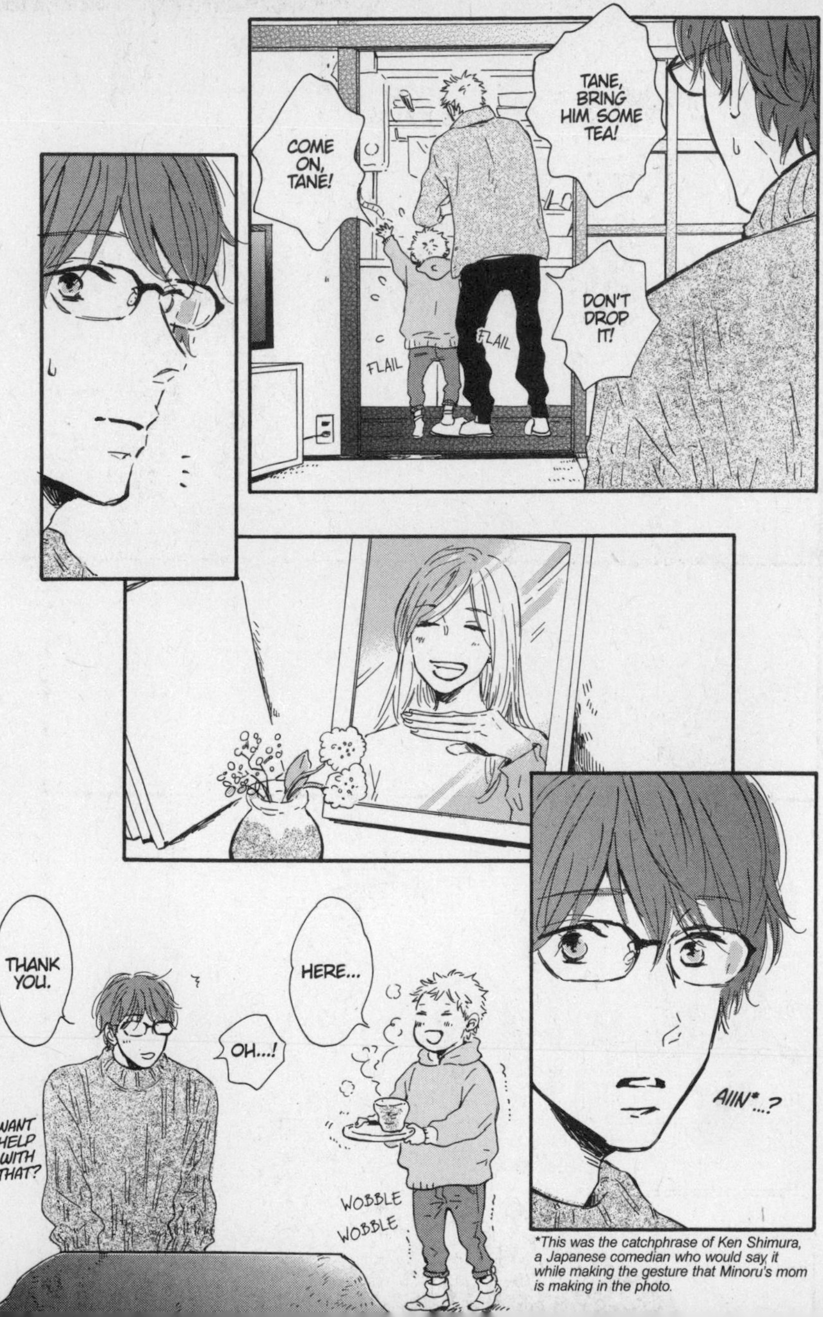
TANE, BRING HIM SOME TEA!
COME ON, TANE!
DON'T DROP IT!
FLAIL
FLAIL
AIIN*...?
HERE...
OH...!
THANK YOU.
WANT HELP WITH THAT?
WOBBLE WOBBLE

*This was the catchphrase of Ken Shimura, a Japanese comedian who would say it while making the gesture that Minoru's mom is making in the photo.

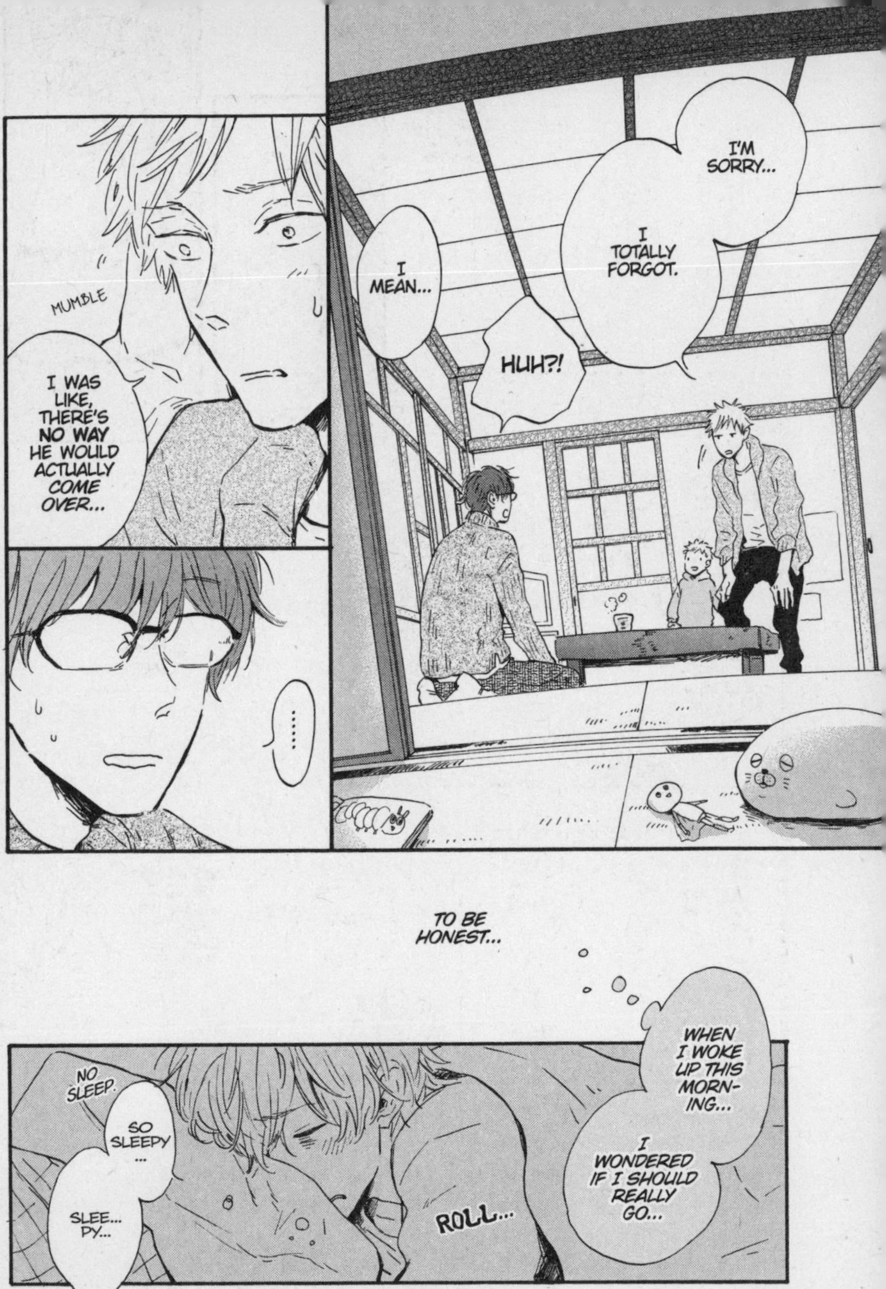
I'M SORRY...
I TOTALLY FORGOT.
I MEAN...
HUH?!
MUMBLE
I WAS LIKE, THERE'S NO WAY HE WOULD ACTUALLY COME OVER...
......
TO BE HONEST...
WHEN I WOKE UP THIS MORN-ING...
I WONDERED IF I SHOULD REALLY GO...
ROLL...
NO SLEEP.
SO SLEEPY ...
SLEE... PY...

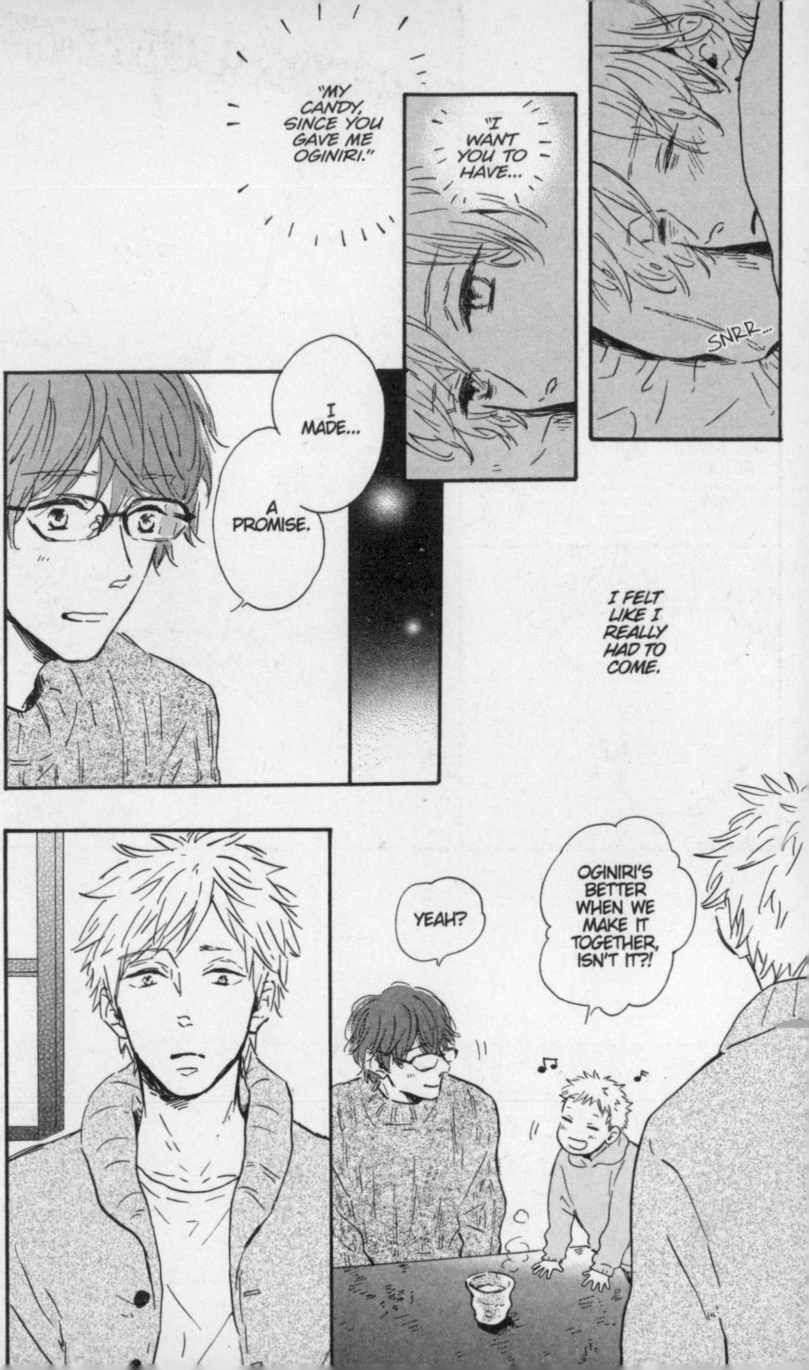
SNRR...
"I WANT YOU TO HAVE...
"MY CANDY, SINCE YOU GAVE ME OGINIRI."
I FELT LIKE I REALLY HAD TO COME.
I MADE...
A PROMISE.
OGINIRI'S BETTER WHEN WE MAKE IT TOGETHER, ISN'T IT?!
YEAH?

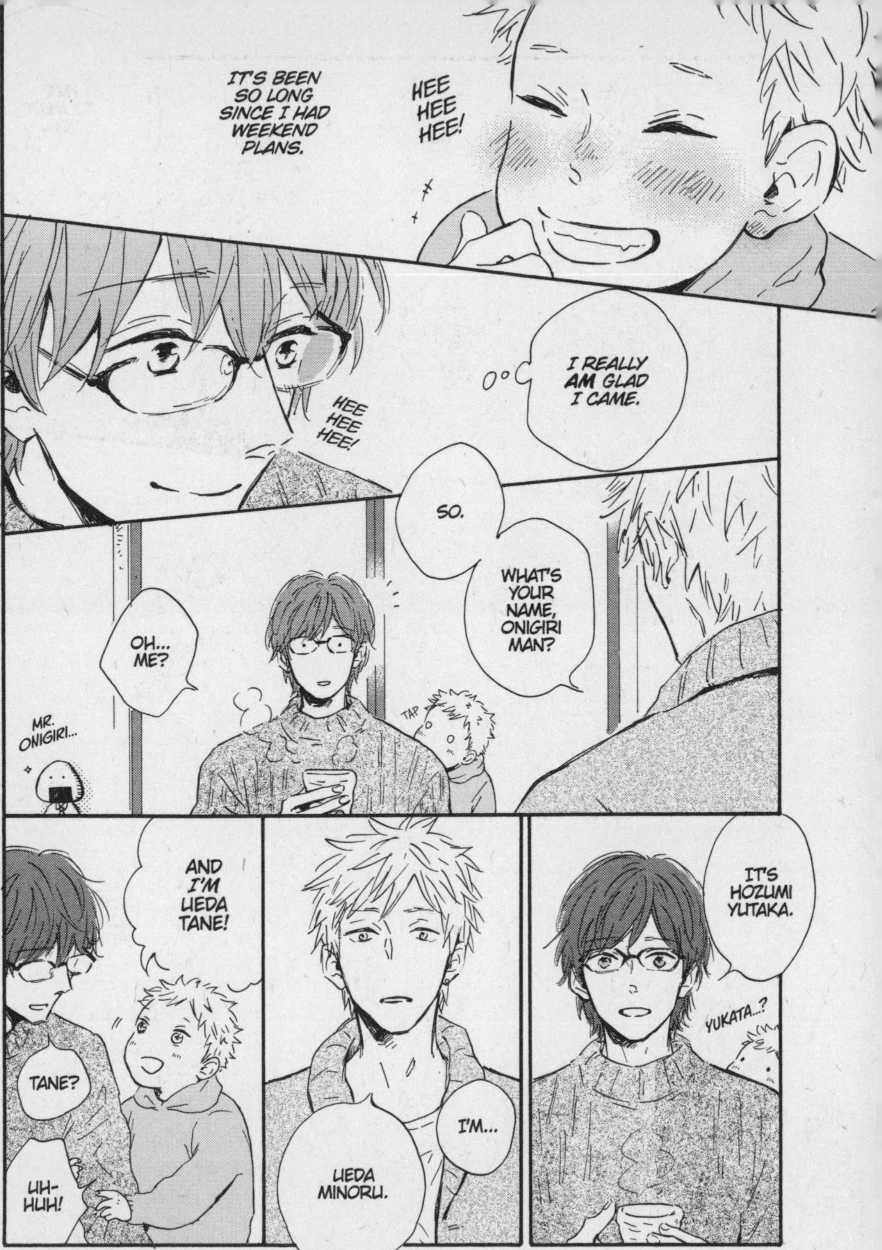

IT'S BEEN SO LONG SINCE I HAD WEEKEND PLANS.
HEE HEE HEE!
I REALLY AM GLAD I CAME.
HEE HEE HEE!
SO.
WHAT'S YOUR NAME, ONIGIRI MAN?
OH... ME?
TAP
MR. ONIGIRI...
IT'S HOZUMI YUTAKA.
YUKATA...?
I'M...
UEDA MINORU.
AND I'M UEDA TANE!
TANE?
UH-HUH!

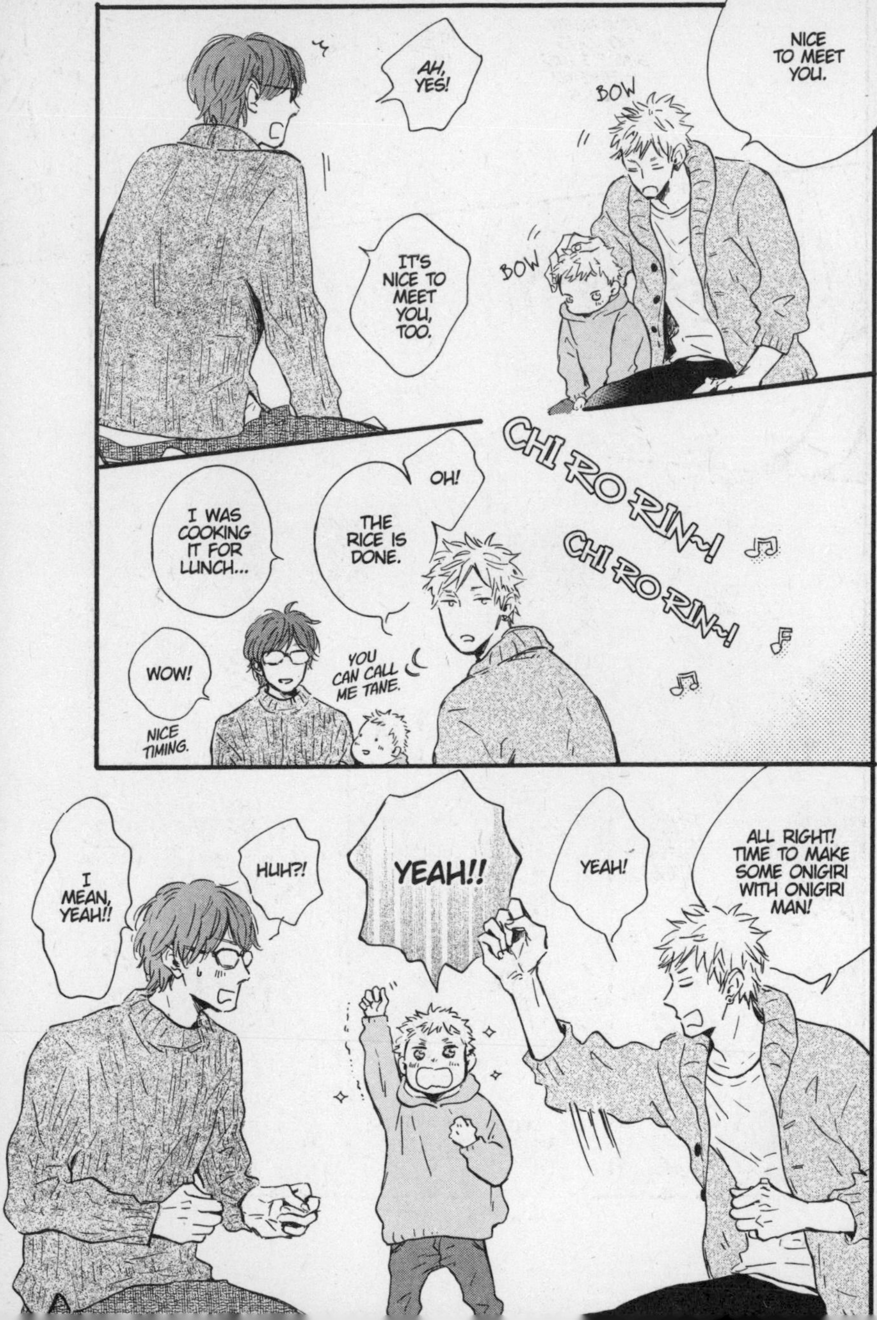
NICE TO MEET YOU.
BOW
BOW
AH, YES!
IT'S NICE TO MEET YOU, TOO.
CHI RO RIN~!
CHI RO RIN~!
OH!
THE RICE IS DONE.
YOU CAN CALL ME TANE.
I WAS COOKING IT FOR LUNCH...
WOW!
NICE TIMING.
ALL RIGHT! TIME TO MAKE SOME ONIGIRI WITH ONIGIRI MAN!
YEAH!
YEAH!!
HUH?!
I MEAN, YEAH!!

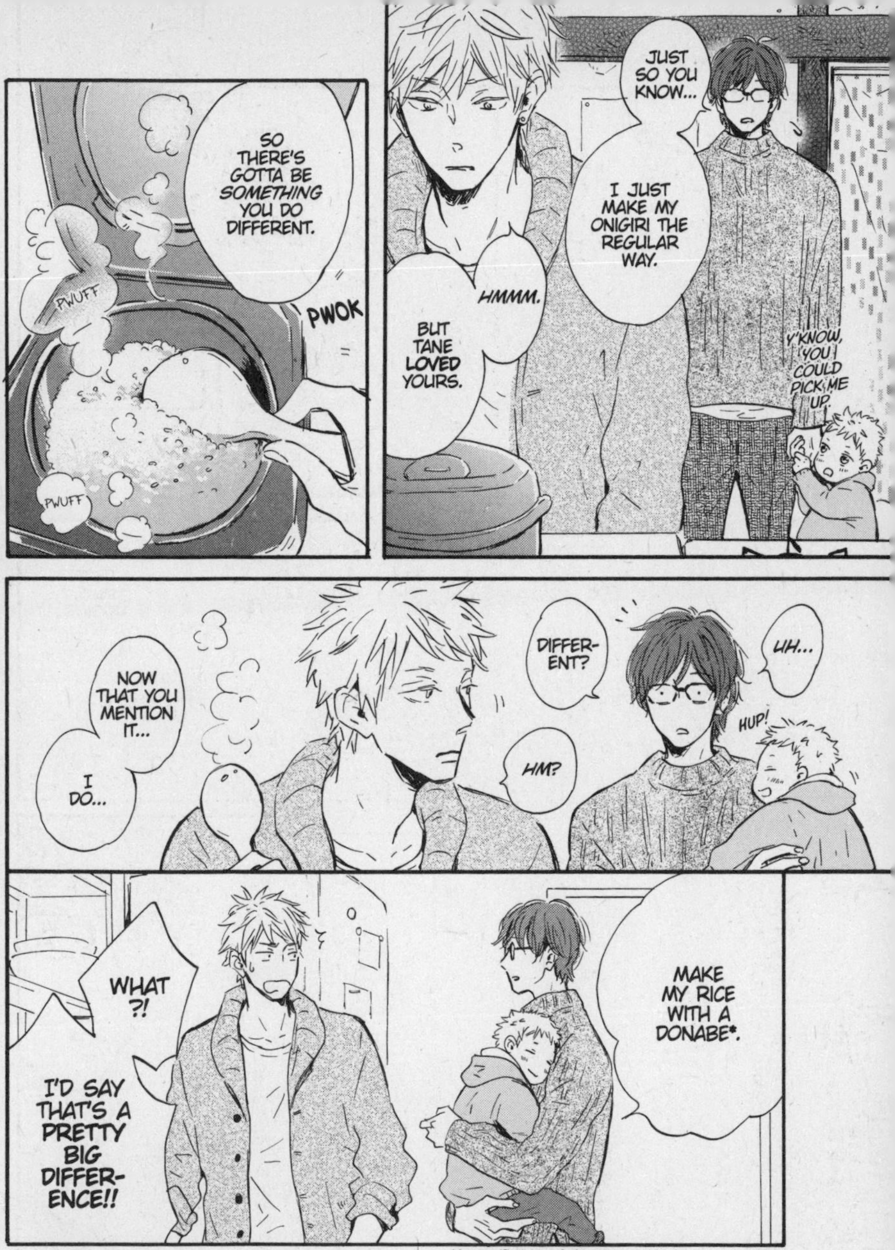
JUST SO YOU KNOW...
I JUST MAKE MY ONIGIRI THE REGULAR WAY.
Y'KNOW, YOU COULD PICK ME UP.
HMMM.
BUT TANE LOVED YOURS.
SO THERE'S GOTTA BE SOMETHING YOU DO DIFFERENT.
PWOK
PWUFF
PWUFF
UH...
DIFFER-ENT?
HUP!
HM?
NOW THAT YOU MENTION IT...
I DO...
MAKE MY RICE WITH A DONABE*.
WHAT ?!
I'D SAY THAT'S A PRETTY BIG DIFFER-ENCE!!

*A specific type of clay pot used in Japanese cooking.

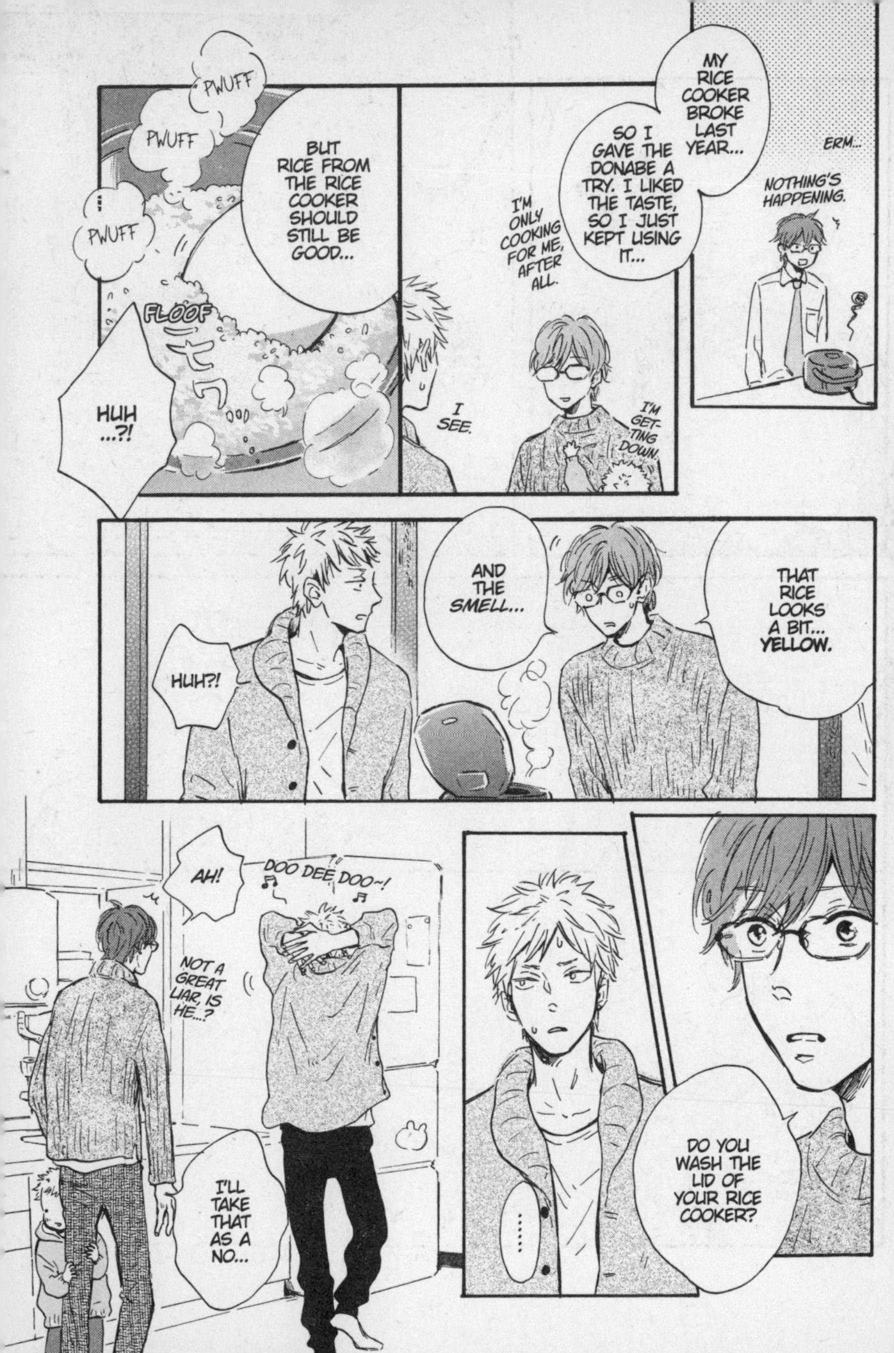

MY RICE COOKER BROKE LAST YEAR...
ERM...
NOTHING'S HAPPENING.
SO I GAVE THE DONABE A TRY. I LIKED THE TASTE, SO I JUST KEPT USING IT...
I'M ONLY COOKING FOR ME, AFTER ALL.
I SEE.
I'M GETTING DOWN.
BUT RICE FROM THE RICE COOKER SHOULD STILL BE GOOD...
PWUFF
PWUFF
PWUFF
FLOOF
HUH ...?!
THAT RICE LOOKS A BIT... YELLOW.
AND THE SMELL...
HUH?!
DO YOU WASH THE LID OF YOUR RICE COOKER?
......
AH!
DOO DEE DOO~!
NOT A GREAT LIAR, IS HE...?
I'LL TAKE THAT AS A NO...

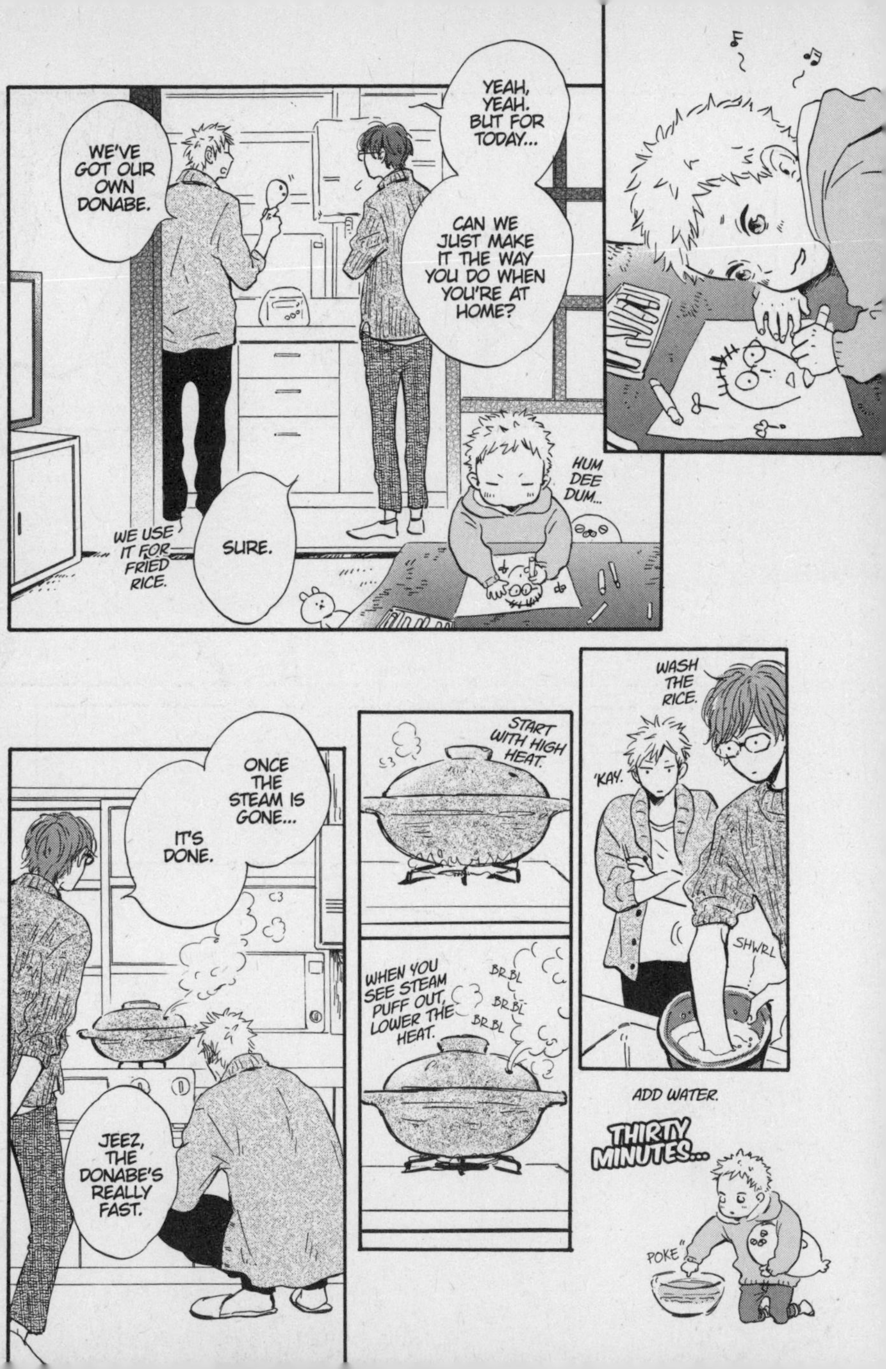

YEAH, YEAH. BUT FOR TODAY...
CAN WE JUST MAKE IT THE WAY YOU DO WHEN YOU'RE AT HOME?
WE'VE GOT OUR OWN DONABE.
HUM DEE DUM...
SURE.
WE USE IT FOR FRIED RICE.
WASH THE RICE.
'KAY.
SHWRL
ADD WATER.
THIRTY MINUTES...
POKE
START WITH HIGH HEAT.
BR BL
BR BL
BR BL
WHEN YOU SEE STEAM PUFF OUT, LOWER THE HEAT.
ONCE THE STEAM IS GONE...
IT'S DONE.
JEEZ, THE DONABE'S REALLY FAST.

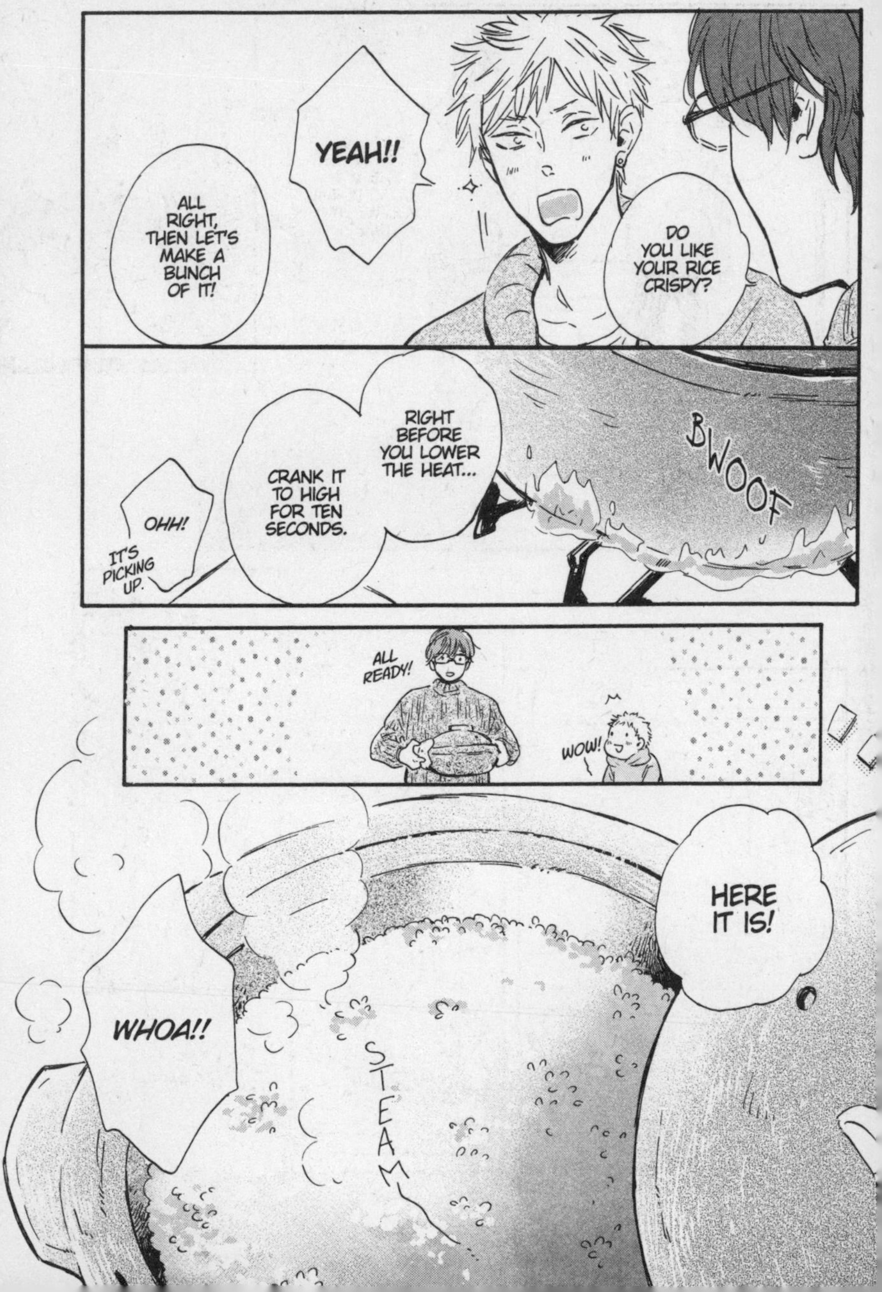
DO YOU LIKE YOUR RICE CRISPY?
YEAH!!
ALL RIGHT, THEN LET'S MAKE A BUNCH OF IT!
BWOOF
RIGHT BEFORE YOU LOWER THE HEAT...
CRANK IT TO HIGH FOR TEN SECONDS.
OHH!
IT'S PICKING UP.
ALL READY!
WOW!
HERE IT IS!
WHOA!!
STEAM

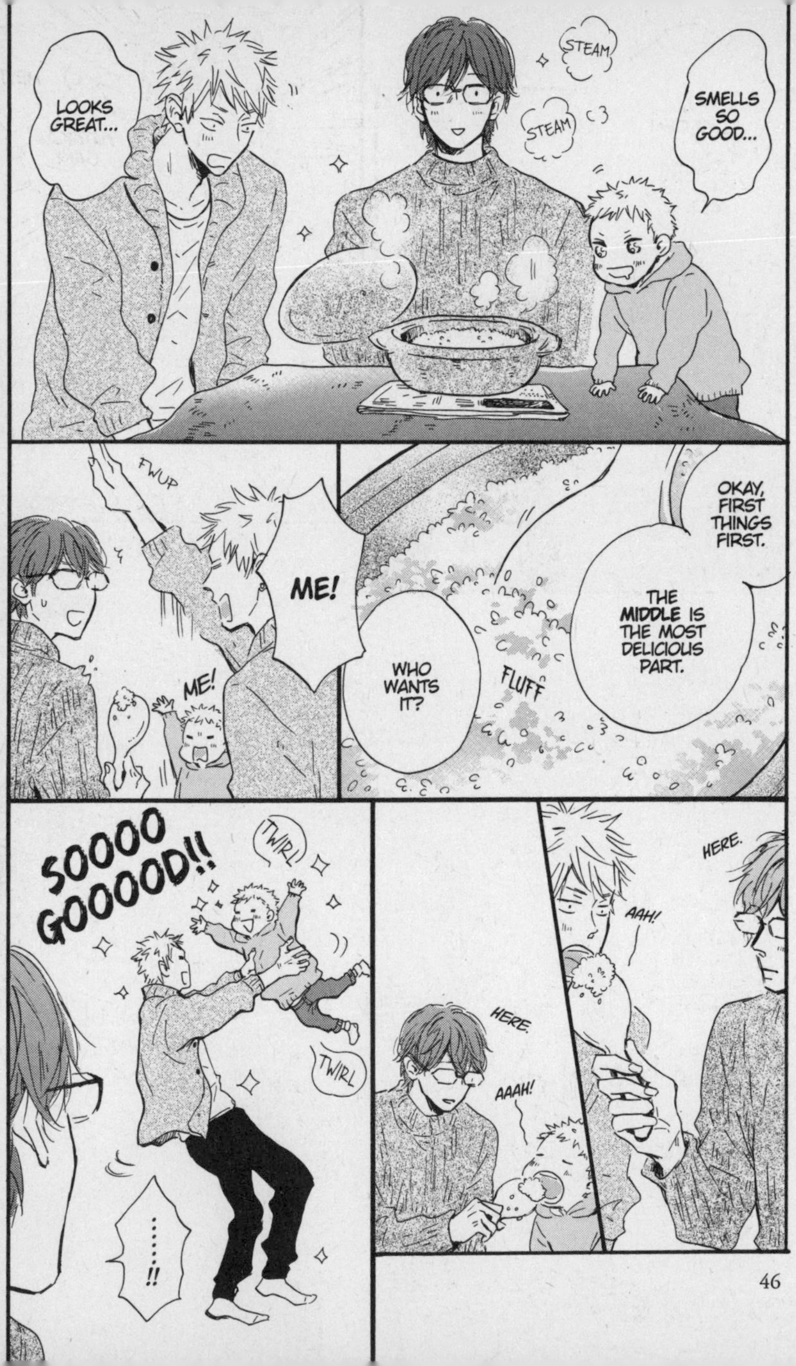
SMELLS SO GOOD...
STEAM
STEAM
LOOKS GREAT...
OKAY, FIRST THINGS FIRST.
THE MIDDLE IS THE MOST DELICIOUS PART.
FLUFF
WHO WANTS IT?
ME!
FWUP
ME!
HERE.
AAH!
HERE.
AAAH!
SOOOO GOOOOD!!
TWIRL
TWIRL
......!!

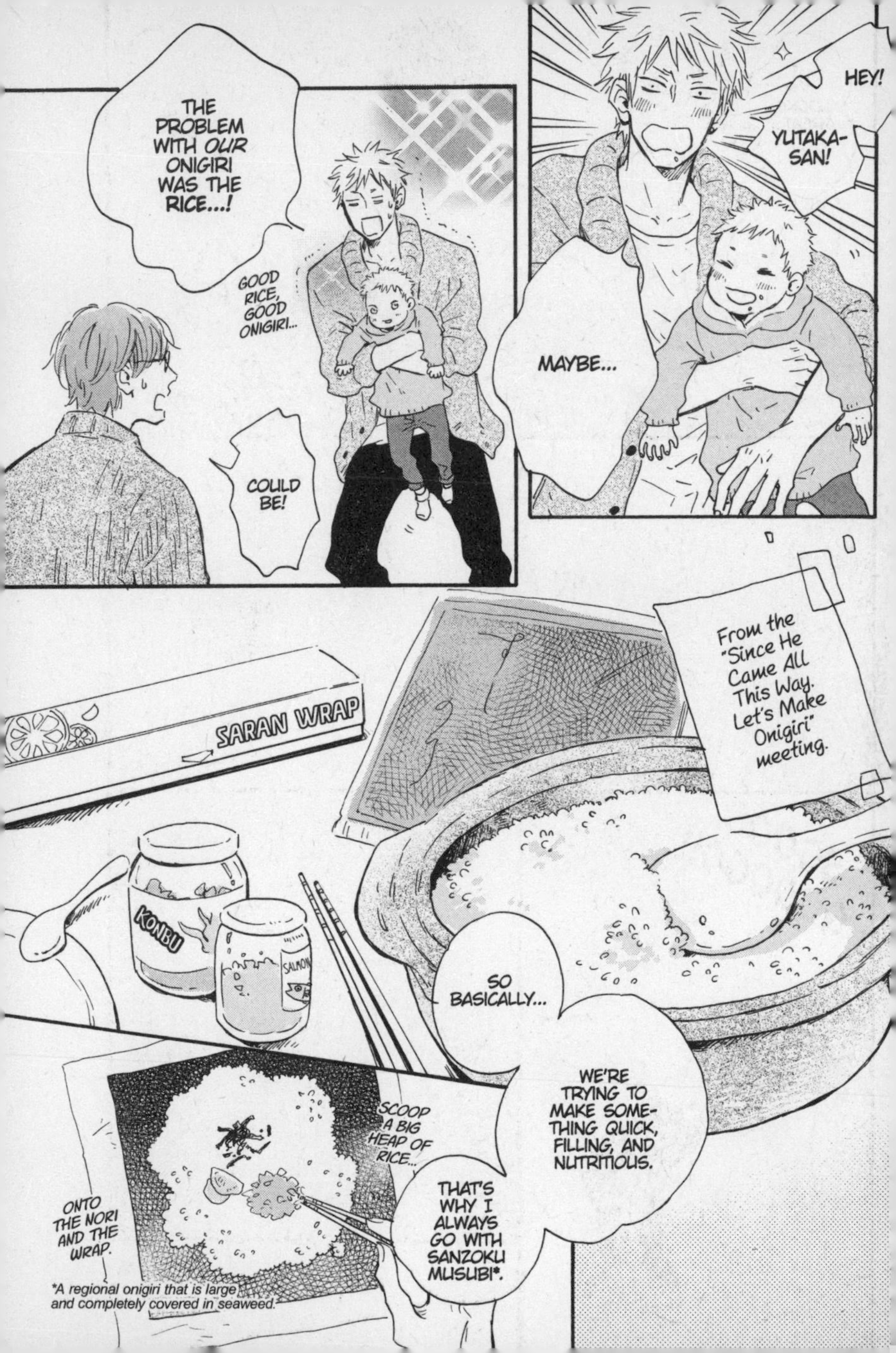
HEY!
YUTAKA-SAN!
MAYBE...
THE PROBLEM WITH OUR ONIGIRI WAS THE RICE...!
GOOD RICE, GOOD ONIGIRI...
COULD BE!
From the "Since He Came All This Way. Let's Make Onigiri" meeting.
SARAN WRAP
KONBU
SALMON
SO BASICALLY...
WE'RE TRYING TO MAKE SOME-THING QUICK, FILLING, AND NUTRITIOUS.
SCOOP A BIG HEAP OF RICE...
THAT'S WHY I ALWAYS GO WITH SANZOKU MUSUBI*.
ONTO THE NORI AND THE WRAP.

*A regional onigiri that is large and completely covered in seaweed.

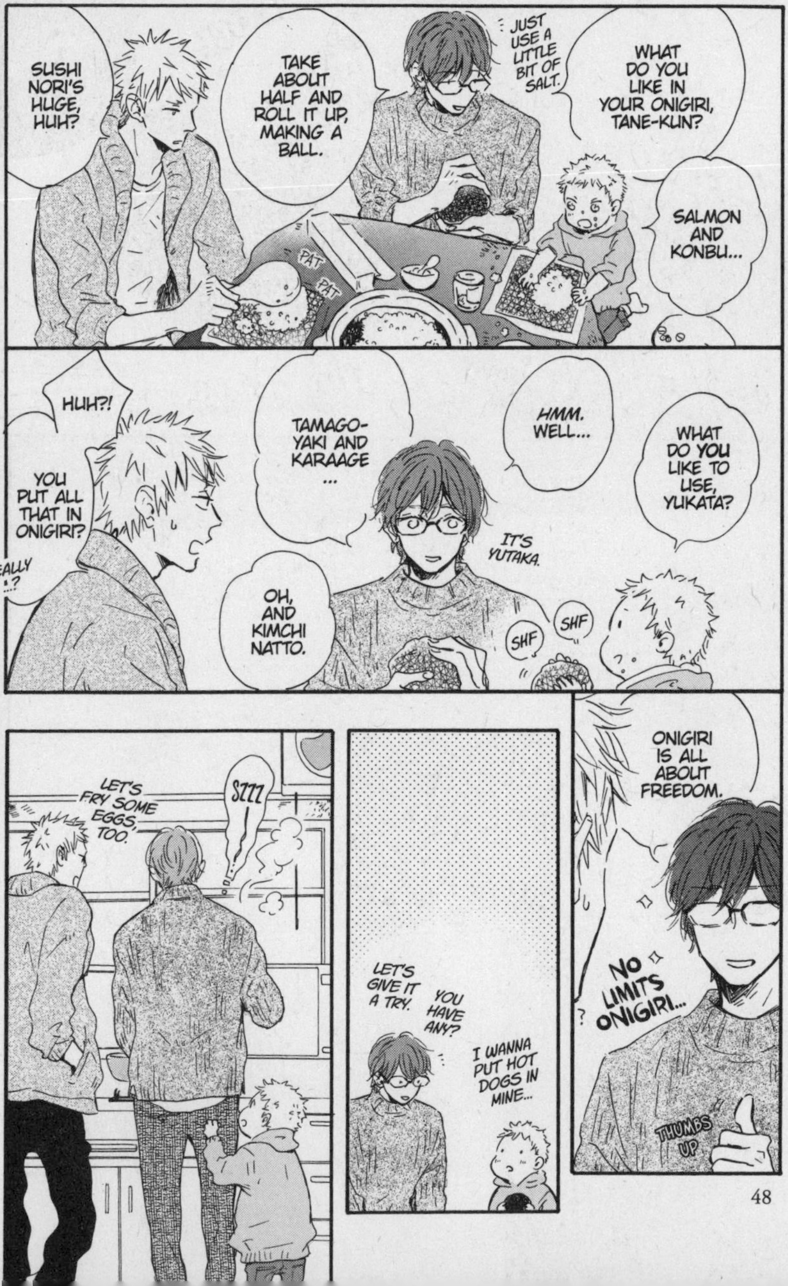

WHAT DO YOU LIKE IN YOUR ONIGIRI, TANE-KUN?
JUST USE A LITTLE BIT OF SALT.
SALMON AND KONBU...
TAKE ABOUT HALF AND ROLL IT UP, MAKING A BALL.
PAT PAT
SUSHI NORI'S HUGE, HUH?
WHAT DO YOU LIKE TO USE, YUKATA?
HMM. WELL...
IT'S YUTAKA.
TAMAGO-YAKI AND KARAAGE ...
HUH?!
OH, AND KIMCHI NATTO.
SHF
SHF
YOU PUT ALL THAT IN ONIGIRI?
REALLY ...?
ONIGIRI IS ALL ABOUT FREEDOM.
NO LIMITS ONIGIRI...
THUMBS UP
I WANNA PUT HOT DOGS IN MINE...
YOU HAVE ANY?
LET'S GIVE IT A TRY.
SZZZ
LET'S FRY SOME EGGS, TOO.

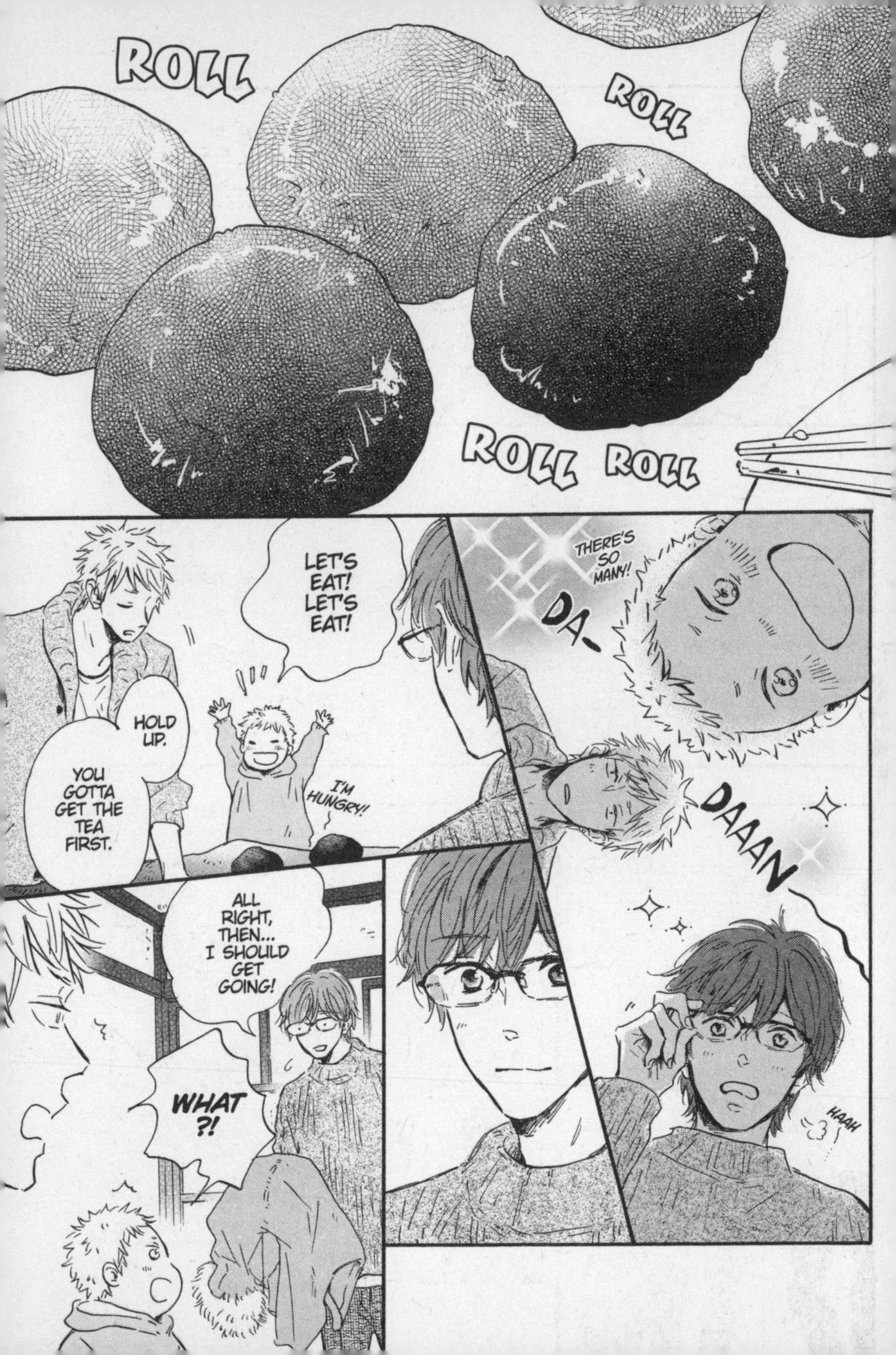
ROLL
ROLL
ROLL ROLL
THERE'S SO MANY!
DA-
DAAAN
LET'S EAT! LET'S EAT!
I'M HUNGRY!
HOLD UP.
YOU GOTTA GET THE TEA FIRST.
HAAH
ALL RIGHT, THEN... I SHOULD GET GOING!
WHAT?!

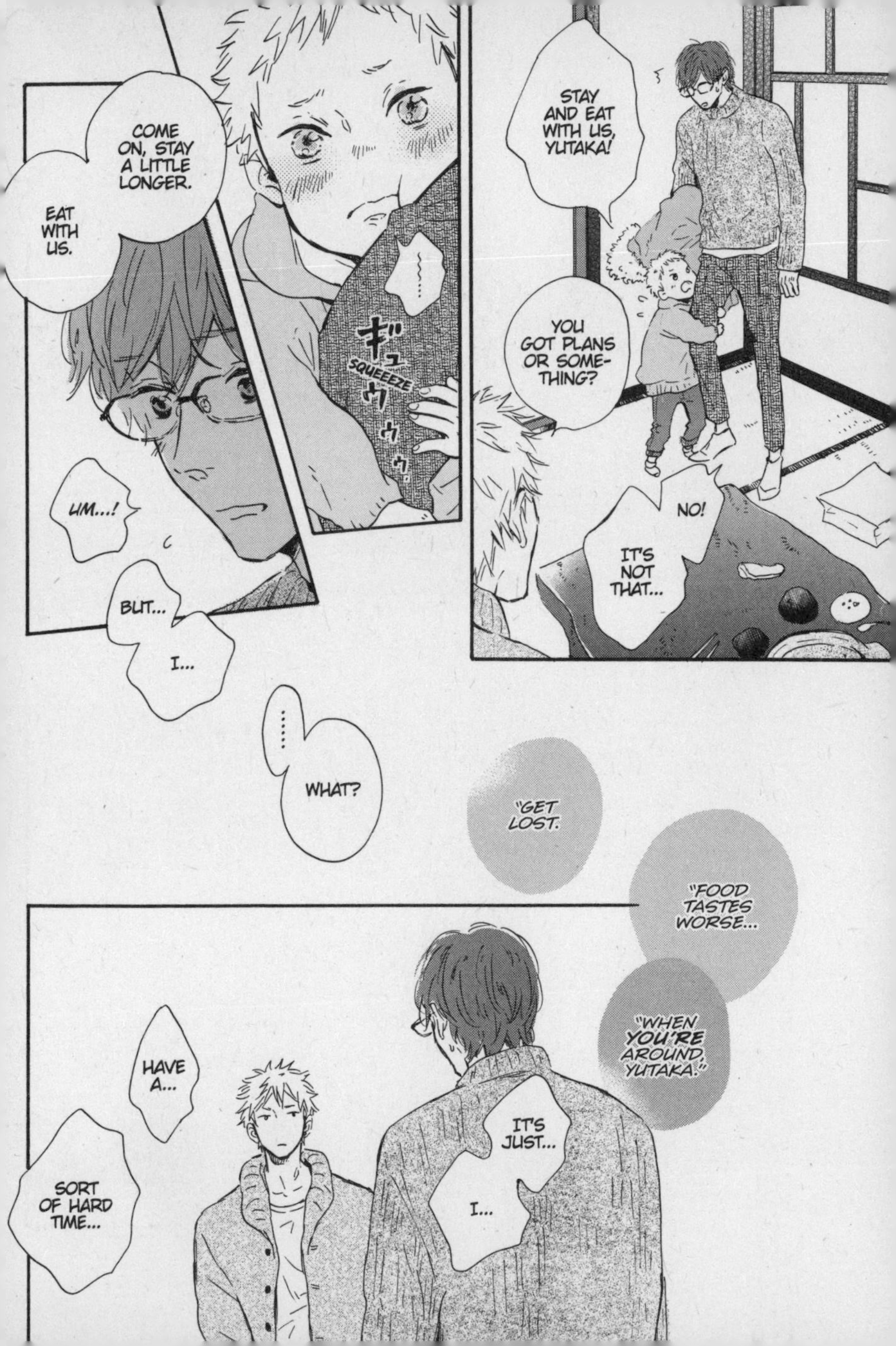
STAY AND EAT WITH US, YUTAKA!
YOU GOT PLANS OR SOME-THING?
NO!
IT'S NOT THAT...
COME ON, STAY A LITTLE LONGER.
EAT WITH US.
......
ギュウウウ
SQUEEEZE
UM...!
BUT...
I...
......
WHAT?
"GET LOST.
"FOOD TASTES WORSE...
"WHEN YOU'RE AROUND, YUTAKA."
IT'S JUST...
I...
HAVE A...
SORT OF HARD TIME...

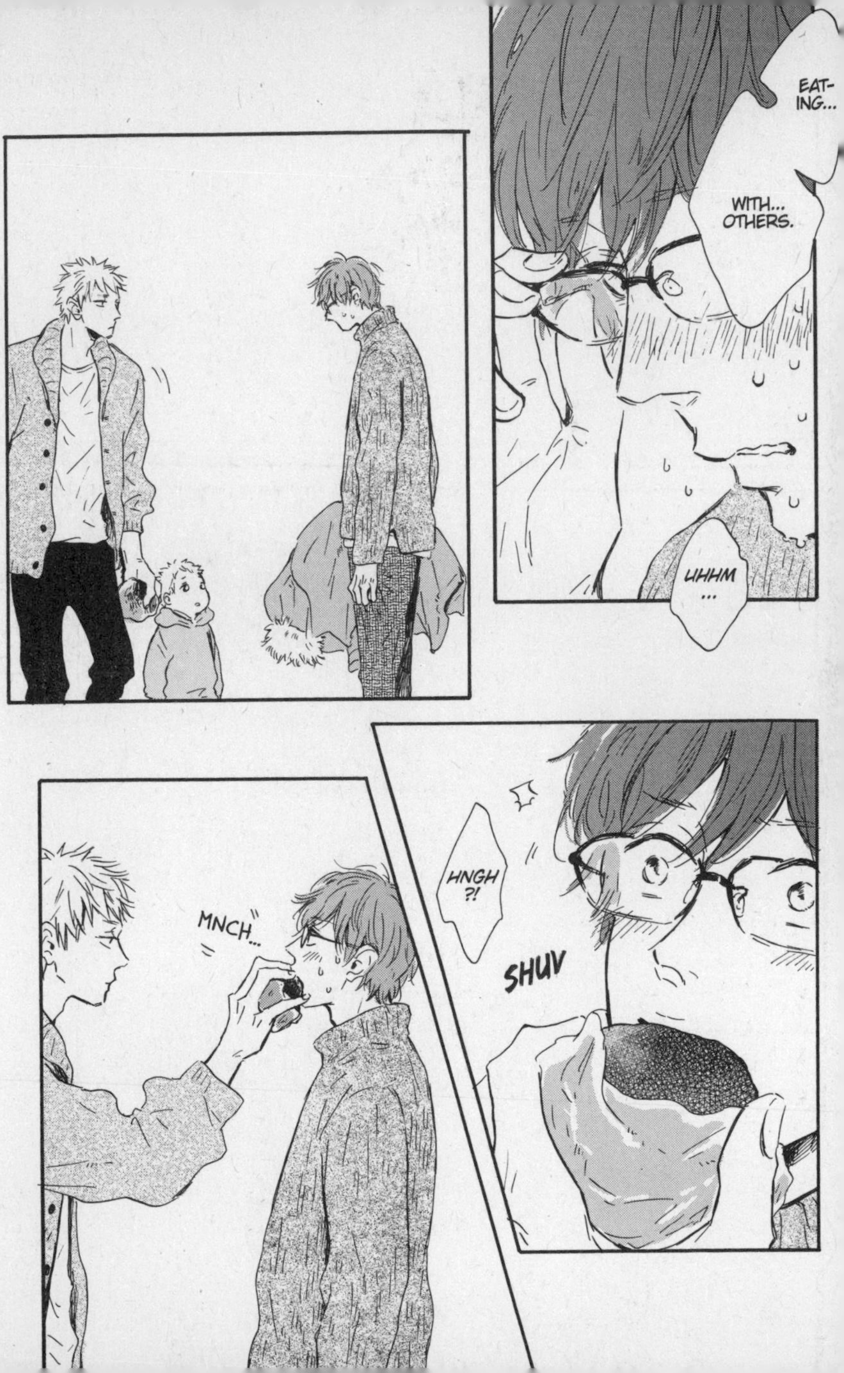
EAT-ING...
WITH... OTHERS.
UHHM ...
HNGH ?!
SHUV
MNCH...

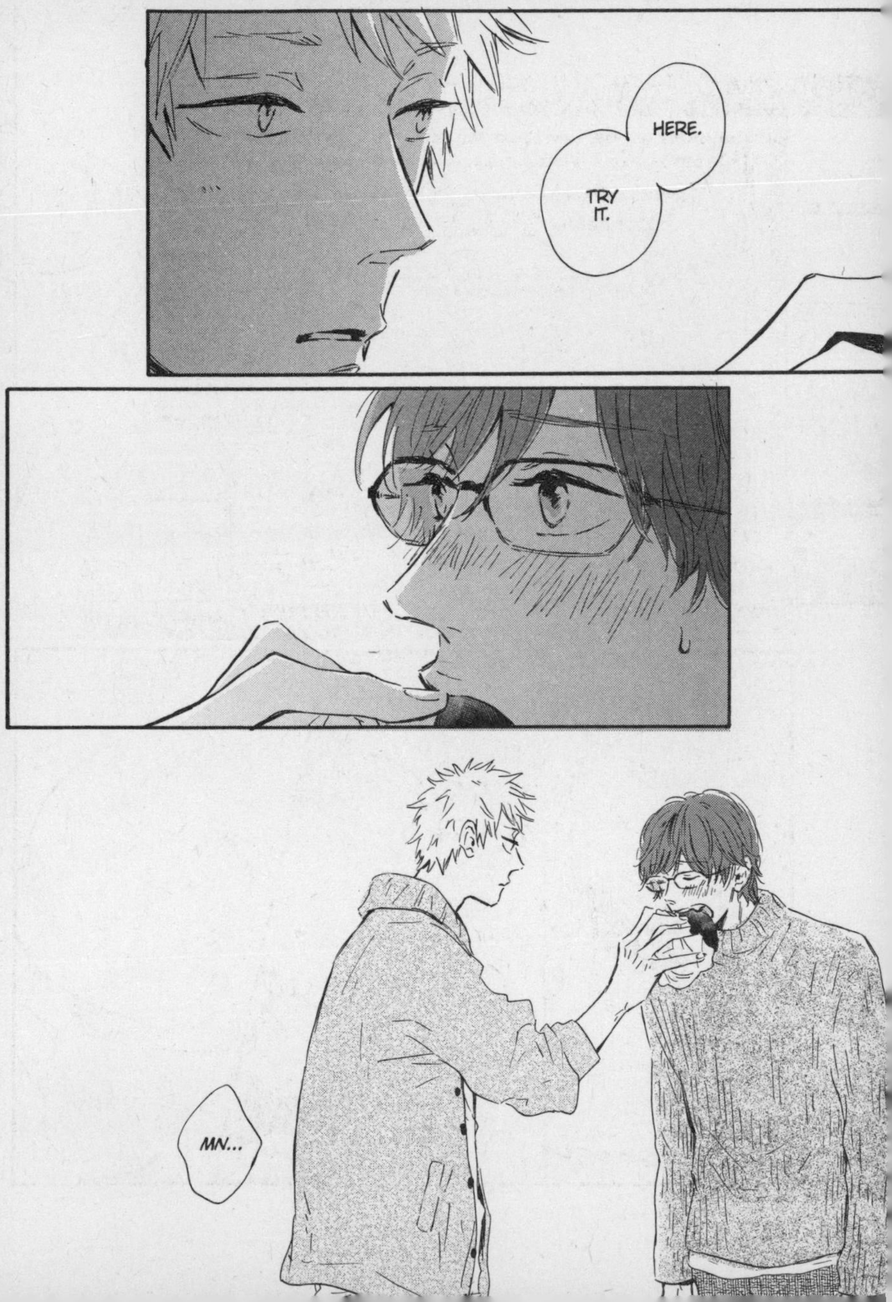
HERE.
TRY IT.
MN...

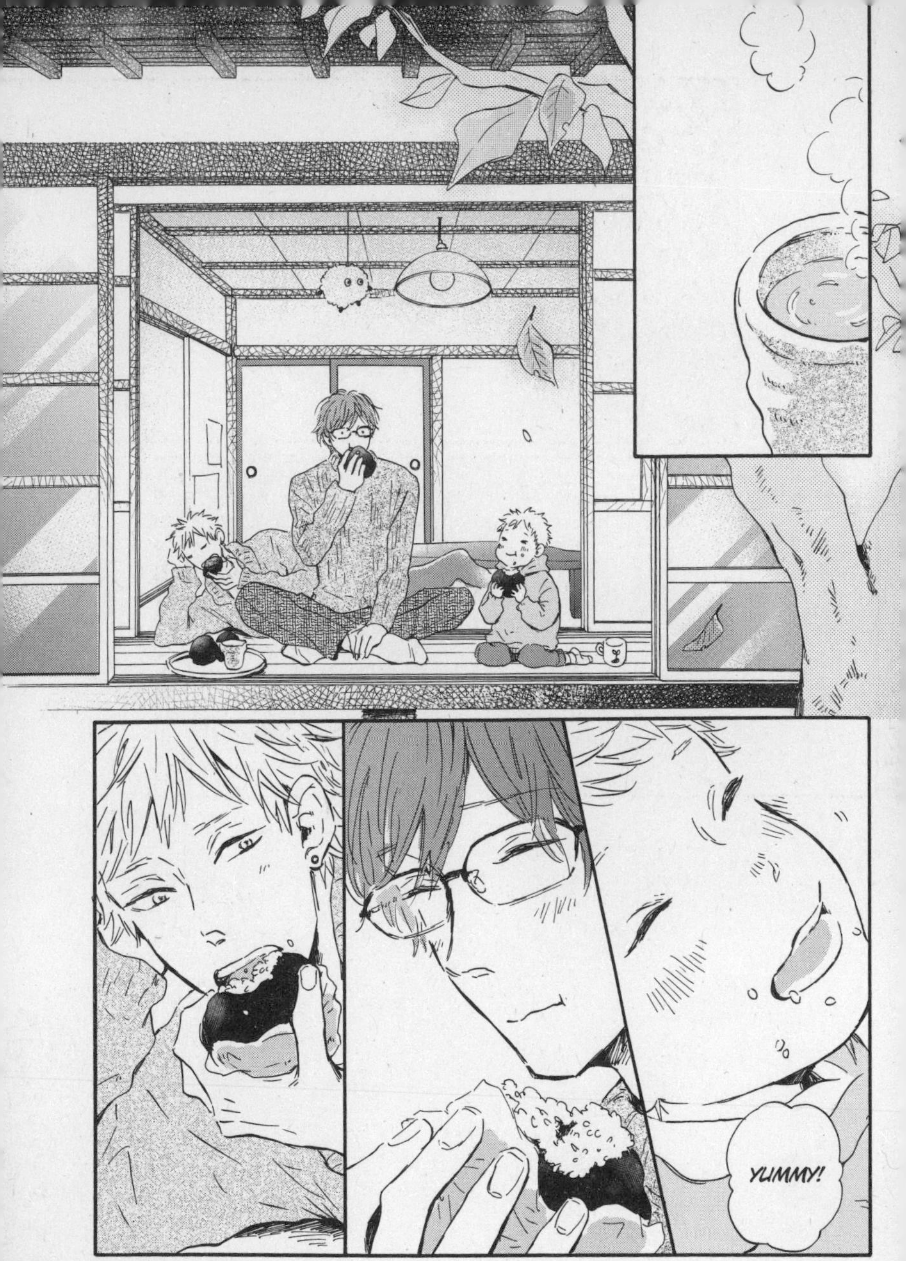
YUMMY!

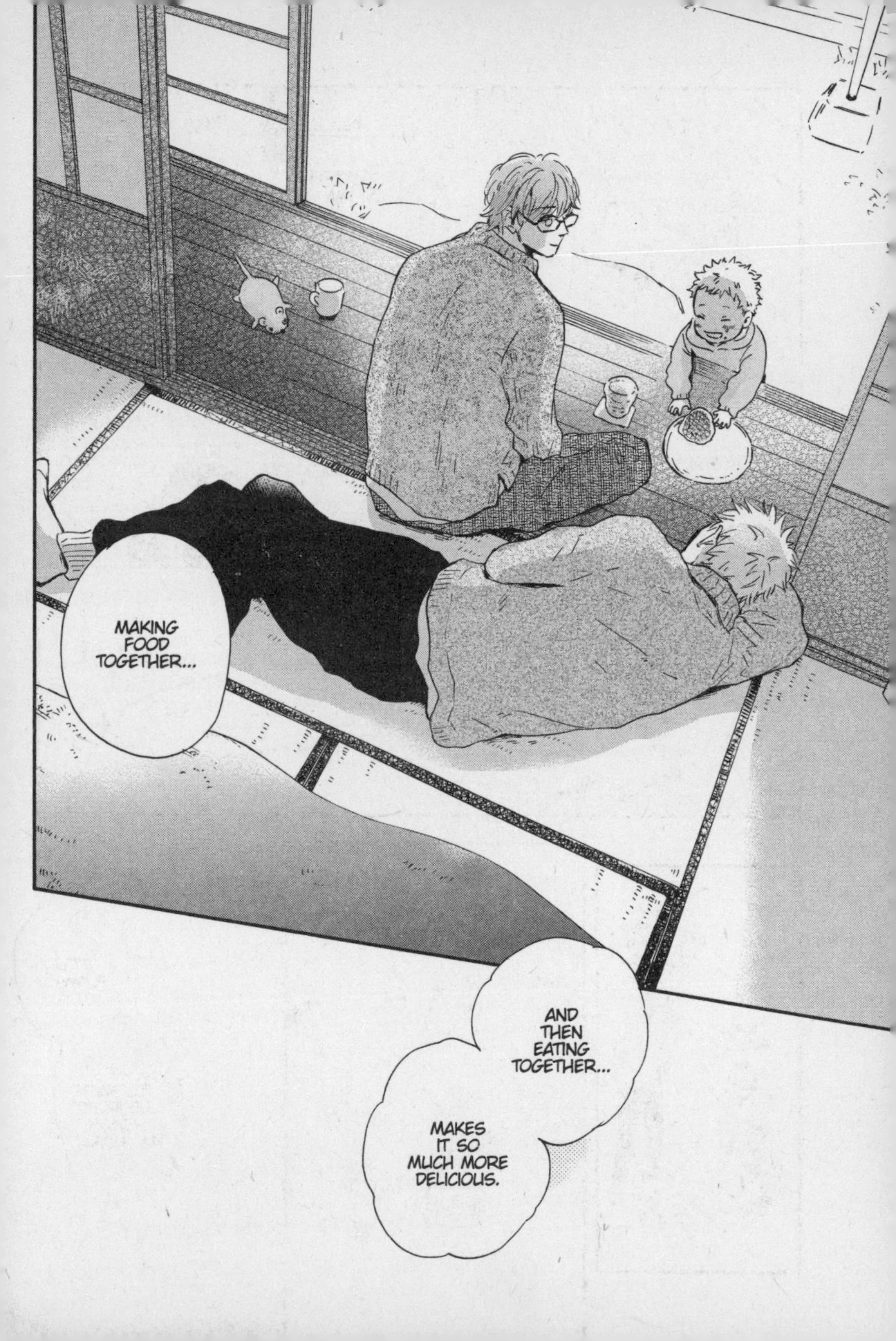
MAKING FOOD TOGETHER...
AND THEN EATING TOGETHER...
MAKES IT SO MUCH MORE DELICIOUS.

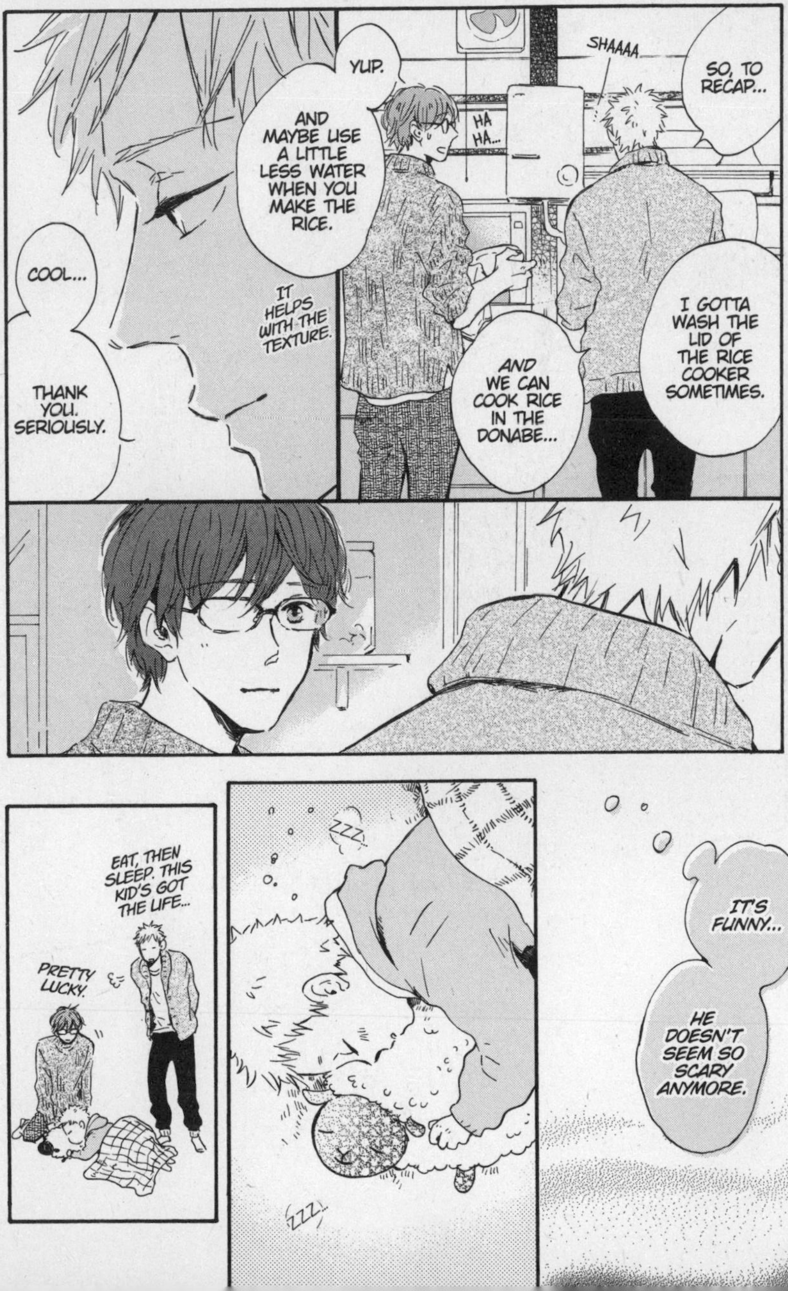
SO, TO RECAP...
SHAAAA
I GOTTA WASH THE LID OF THE RICE COOKER SOMETIMES.
HA HA...
AND WE CAN COOK RICE IN THE DONABE...
YUP.
AND MAYBE USE A LITTLE LESS WATER WHEN YOU MAKE THE RICE.
IT HELPS WITH THE TEXTURE.
COOL...
THANK YOU. SERIOUSLY.
IT'S FUNNY...
HE DOESN'T SEEM SO SCARY ANYMORE.
ZZZ
ZZZ
EAT, THEN SLEEP. THIS KID'S GOT THE LIFE...
PRETTY LUCKY.

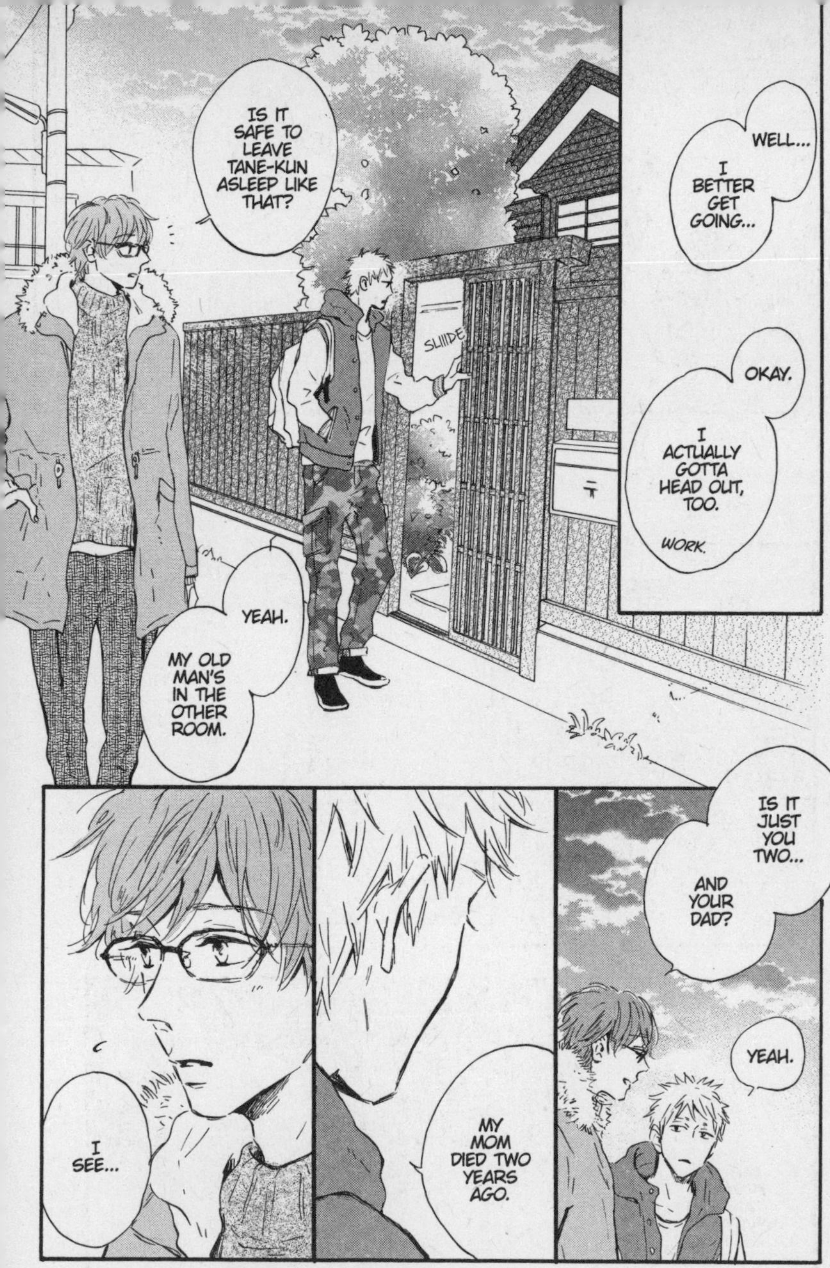
WELL... I BETTER GET GOING...
OKAY. I ACTUALLY GOTTA HEAD OUT, TOO.
WORK.
IS IT SAFE TO LEAVE TANE-KUN ASLEEP LIKE THAT?
SLIIIDE
YEAH. MY OLD MAN'S IN THE OTHER ROOM.
IS IT JUST YOU TWO... AND YOUR DAD?
YEAH.
MY MOM DIED TWO YEARS AGO.
I SEE...

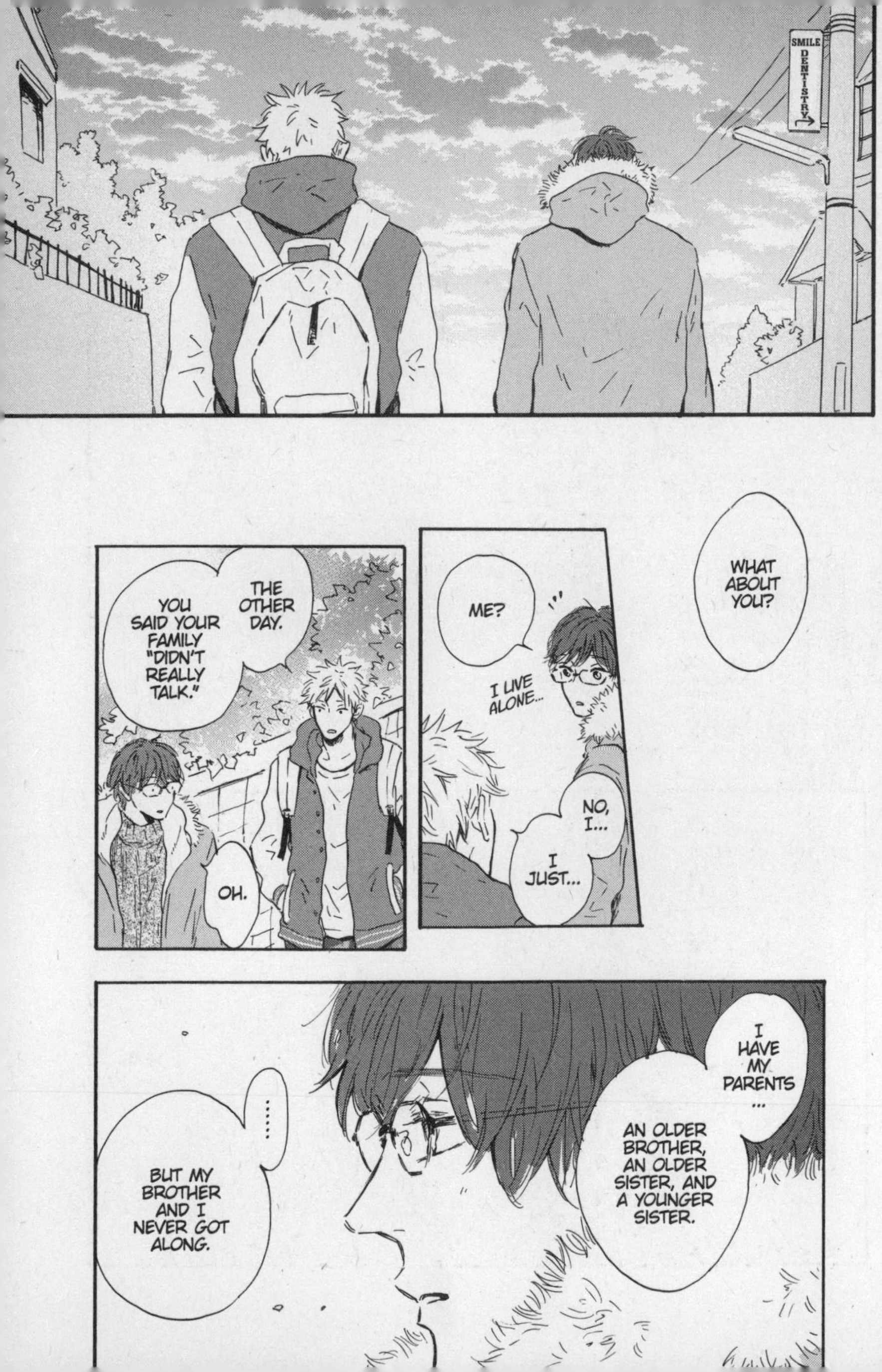
SMILE DENTISTRY
WHAT ABOUT YOU?
ME?
I LIVE ALONE...
NO, I...
I JUST...
THE OTHER DAY.
YOU SAID YOUR FAMILY "DIDN'T REALLY TALK."
OH.
I HAVE MY PARENTS...
AN OLDER BROTHER, AN OLDER SISTER, AND A YOUNGER SISTER.
......
BUT MY BROTHER AND I NEVER GOT ALONG.

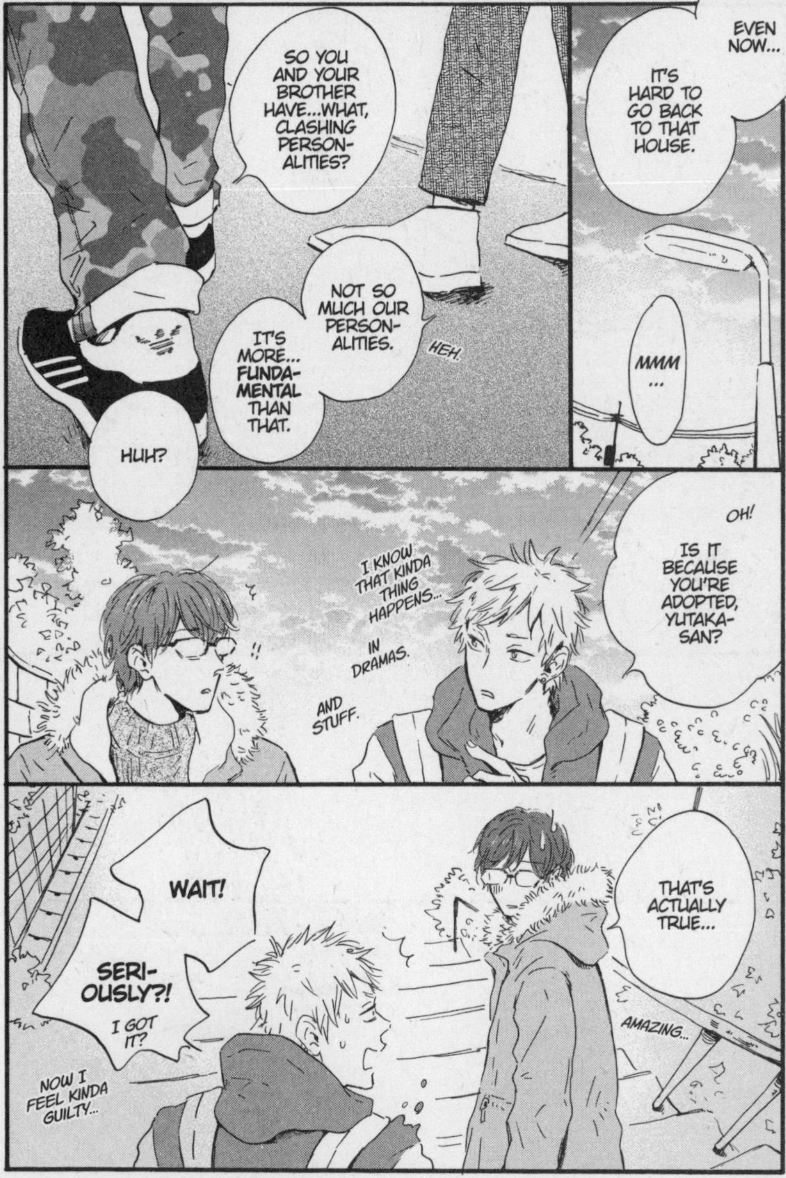
EVEN NOW...
IT'S HARD TO GO BACK TO THAT HOUSE.
MMM...
SO YOU AND YOUR BROTHER HAVE...WHAT, CLASHING PERSON-ALITIES?
NOT SO MUCH OUR PERSON-ALITIES.
HEH.
IT'S MORE... FUNDA-MENTAL THAN THAT.
HUH?
OH!
IS IT BECAUSE YOU'RE ADOPTED, YUTAKA-SAN?
I KNOW THAT KINDA THING HAPPENS...
IN DRAMAS.
AND STUFF.
THAT'S ACTUALLY TRUE...
AMAZING...
WAIT!
SERI-OUSLY?!
I GOT IT?
NOW I FEEL KINDA GUILTY...

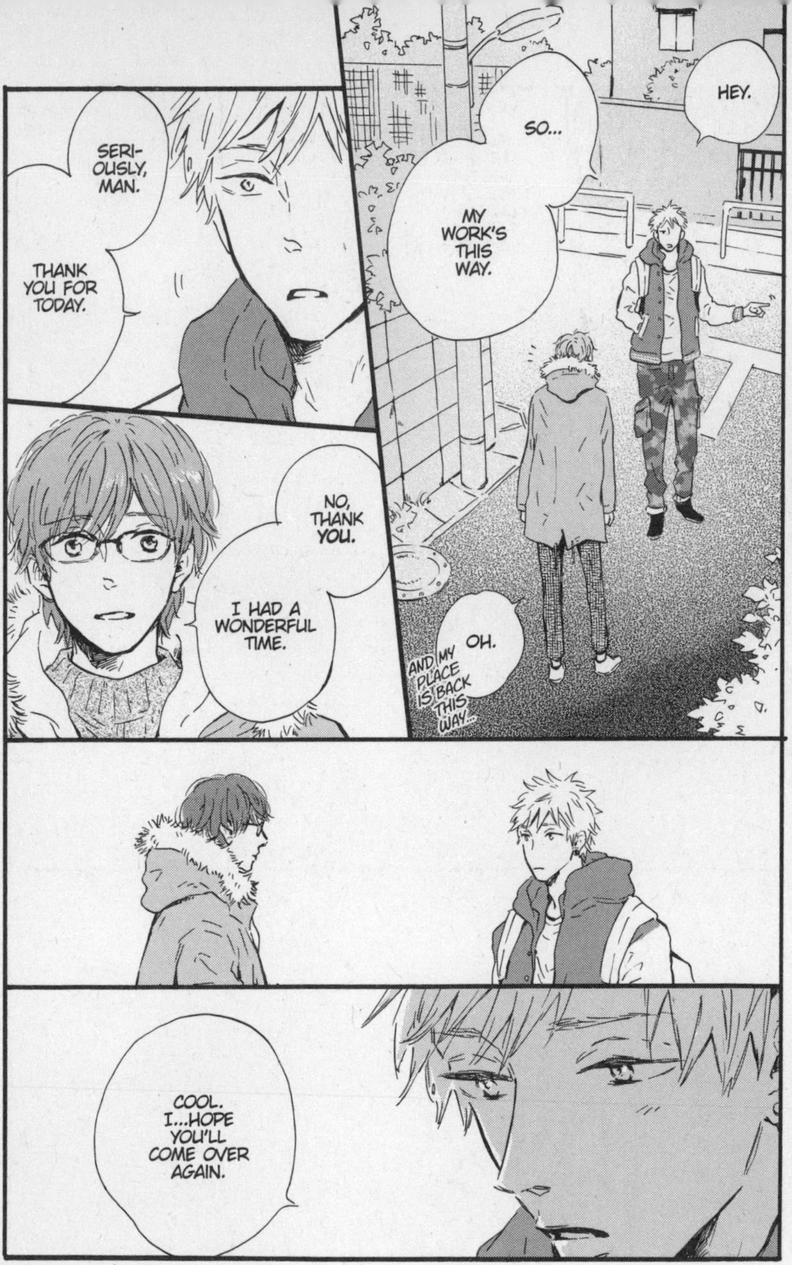
HEY.
SO...
MY WORK'S THIS WAY.
OH.
AND MY PLACE IS BACK THIS WAY...
SERI-OUSLY, MAN.
THANK YOU FOR TODAY.
NO, THANK YOU.
I HAD A WONDERFUL TIME.
COOL. I...HOPE YOU'LL COME OVER AGAIN.

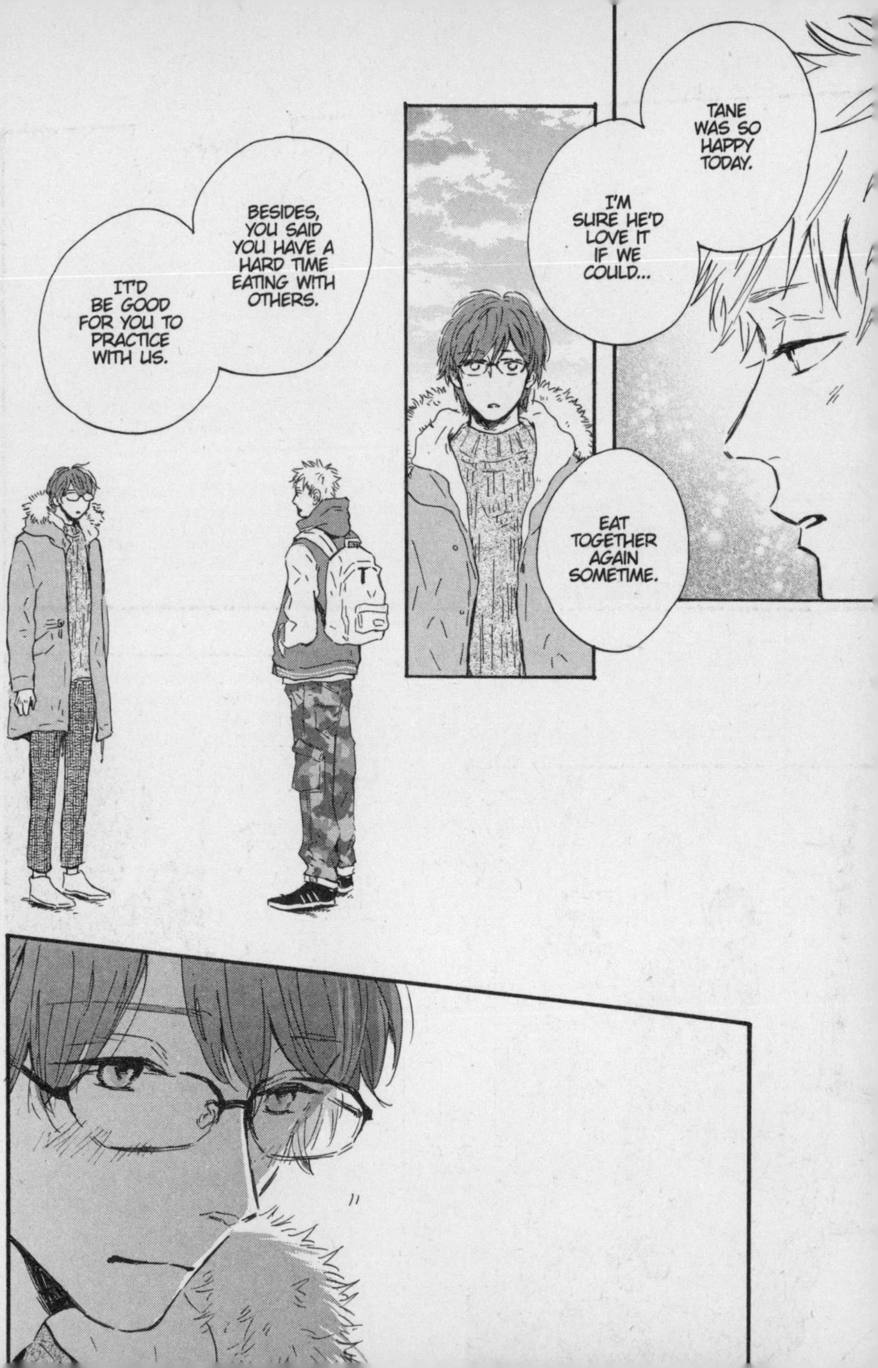
TANE WAS SO HAPPY TODAY.
I'M SURE HE'D LOVE IT IF WE COULD...
EAT TOGETHER AGAIN SOMETIME.
BESIDES, YOU SAID YOU HAVE A HARD TIME EATING WITH OTHERS.
IT'D BE GOOD FOR YOU TO PRACTICE WITH US.

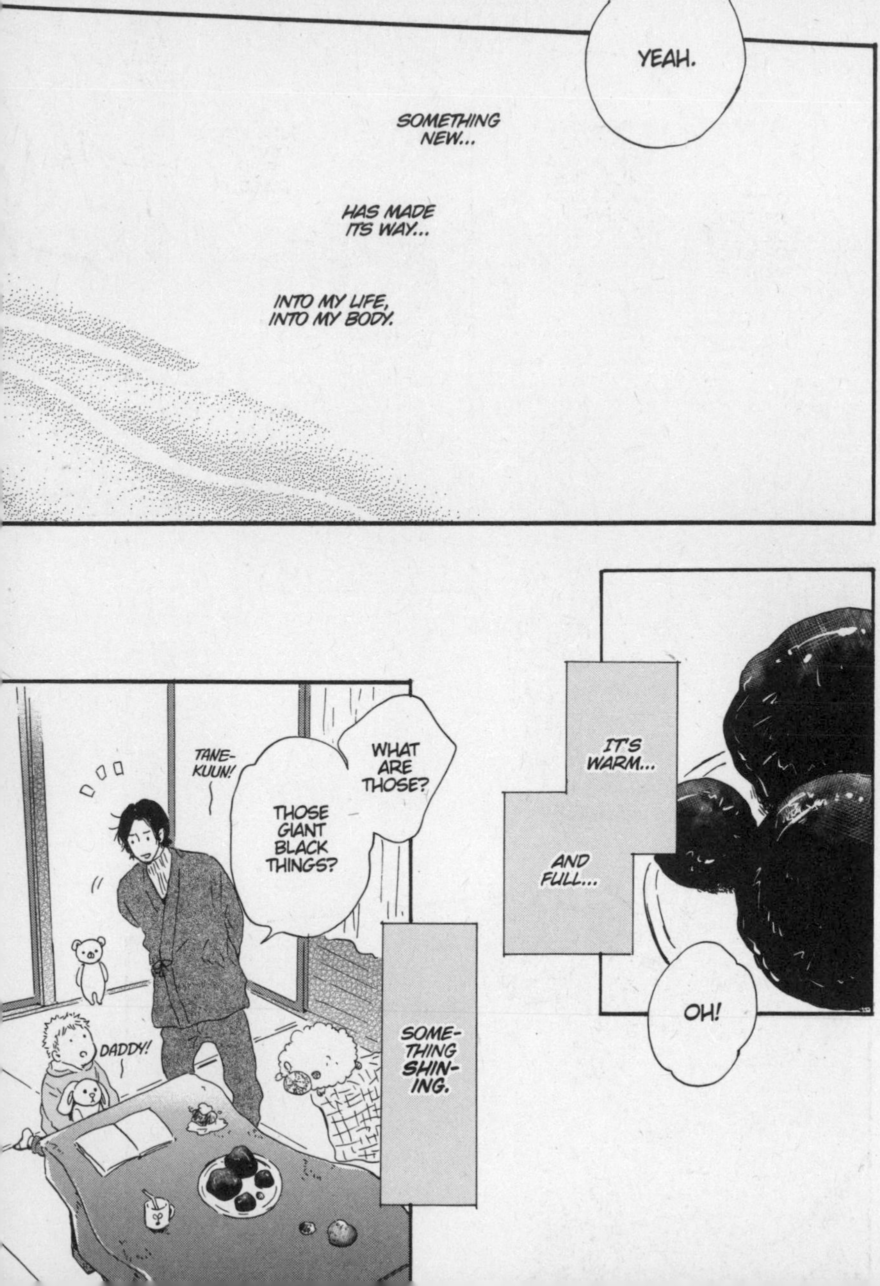
YEAH.
SOMETHING NEW...
HAS MADE ITS WAY...
INTO MY LIFE, INTO MY BODY.
IT'S WARM...
AND FULL...
OH!
SOME-THING SHIN-ING.
WHAT ARE THOSE?
THOSE GIANT BLACK THINGS?
TANE-KUUN!
DADDY!

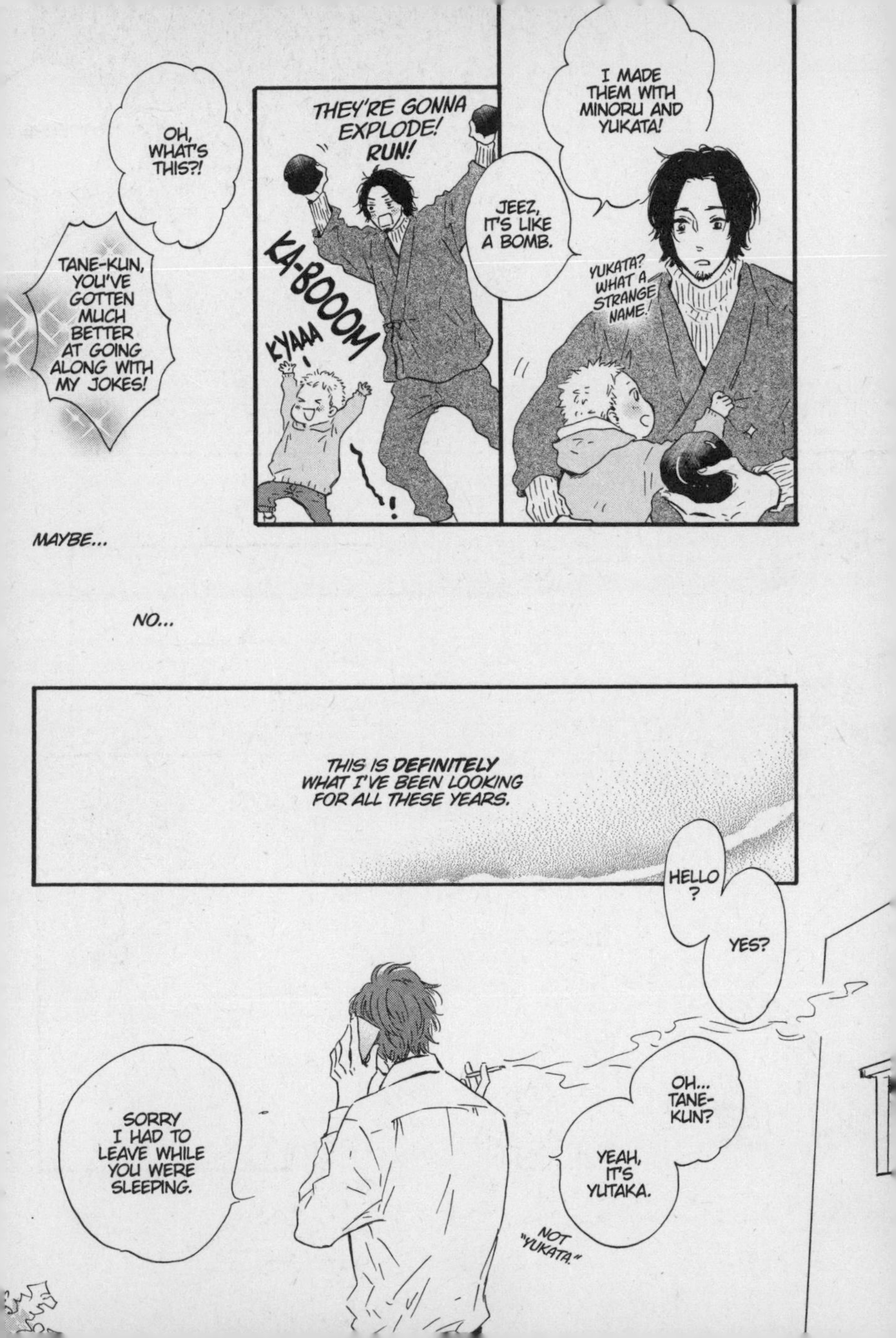
I MADE THEM WITH MINORU AND YUKATA!
YUKATA? WHAT A STRANGE NAME!
JEEZ, IT'S LIKE A BOMB.
THEY'RE GONNA EXPLODE! RUN!
KA-BOOOM
KYAAA
!
OH, WHAT'S THIS?!
TANE-KUN, YOU'VE GOTTEN MUCH BETTER AT GOING ALONG WITH MY JOKES!
MAYBE...
NO...
THIS IS DEFINITELY WHAT I'VE BEEN LOOKING FOR ALL THESE YEARS.
HELLO?
YES?
OH... TANE-KUN?
YEAH, IT'S YUTAKA.
NOT "YUKATA."
SORRY I HAD TO LEAVE WHILE YOU WERE SLEEPING.

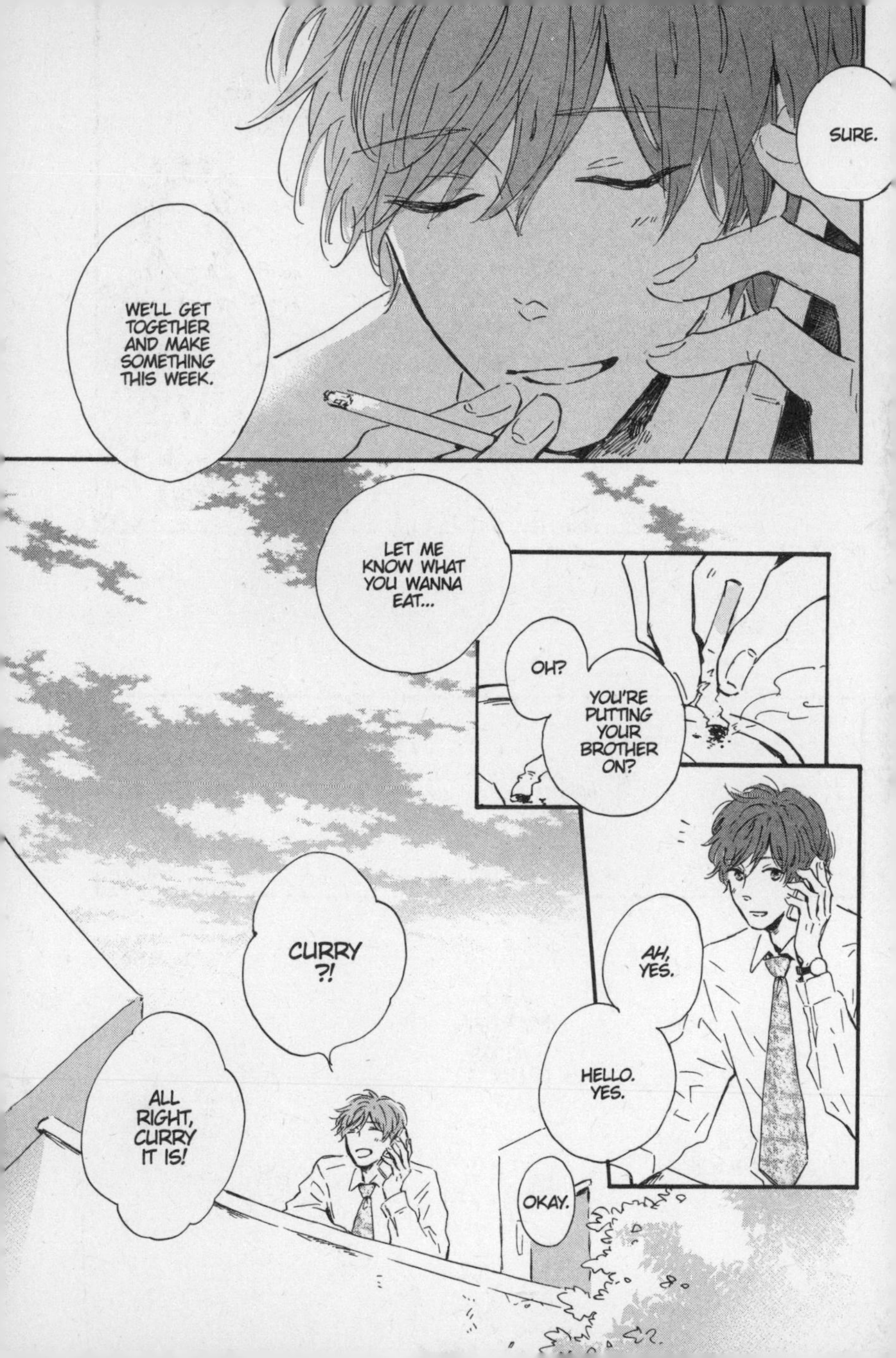
SURE.
WE'LL GET TOGETHER AND MAKE SOMETHING THIS WEEK.
LET ME KNOW WHAT YOU WANNA EAT...
OH?
YOU'RE PUTTING YOUR BROTHER ON?
AH, YES.
HELLO. YES.
CURRY?!
ALL RIGHT, CURRY IT IS!
OKAY.

OUR DINING TABLE

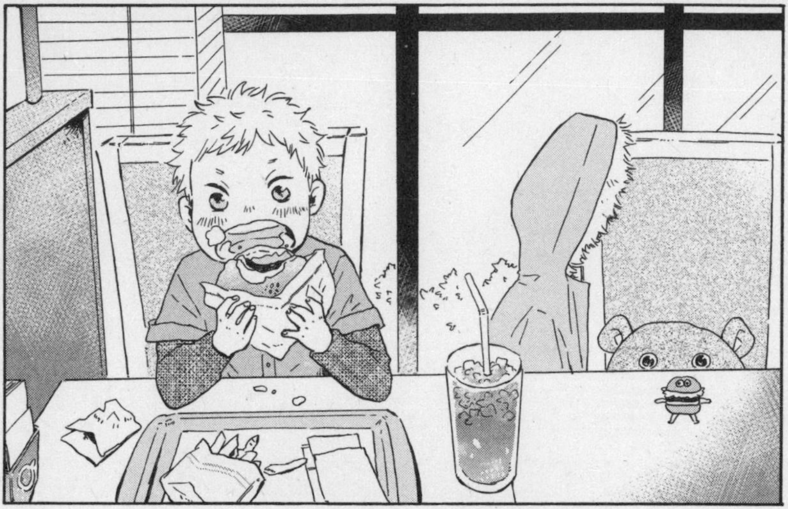

Chapter 2

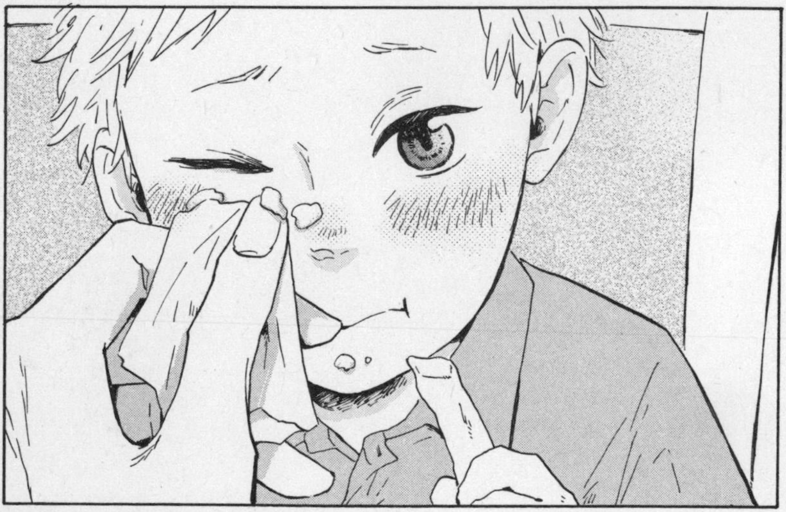

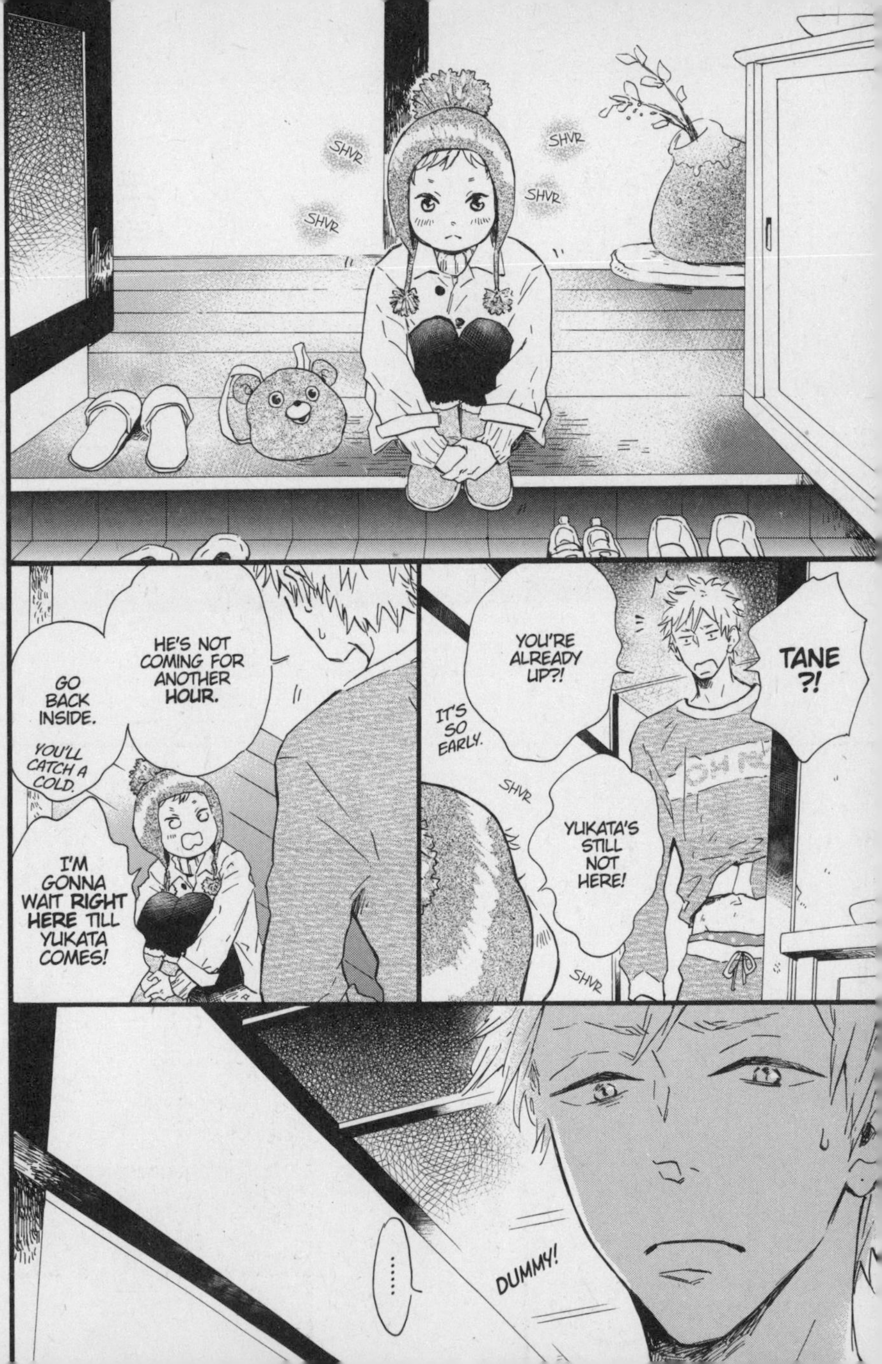
SHVR
SHVR
SHVR
SHVR
TANE?!
YOU'RE ALREADY UP?!
IT'S SO EARLY.
SHVR
YUKATA'S STILL NOT HERE!
SHVR
HE'S NOT COMING FOR ANOTHER HOUR.
GO BACK INSIDE.
YOU'LL CATCH A COLD.
I'M GONNA WAIT RIGHT HERE TILL YUKATA COMES!
DUMMY!
......

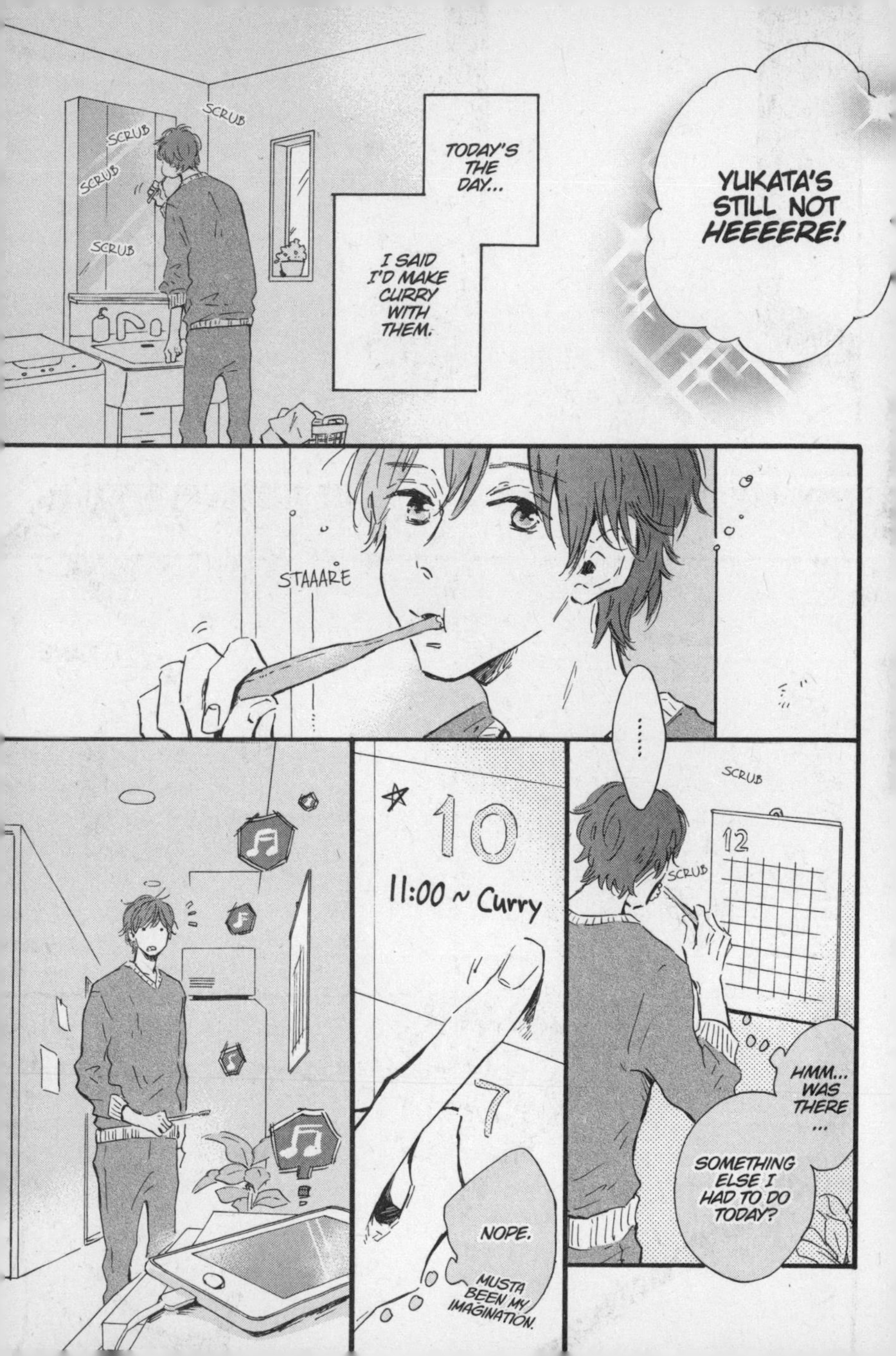
YUKATA'S STILL NOT HEEEERE!
TODAY'S THE DAY...
I SAID I'D MAKE CURRY WITH THEM.
SCRUB
SCRUB
SCRUB
SCRUB
STAAARE
......
SCRUB
12
SCRUB
HMM... WAS THERE ...
SOMETHING ELSE I HAD TO DO TODAY?
10
11:00 ~ Curry
7
NOPE.
MUSTA BEEN MY IMAGINATION.

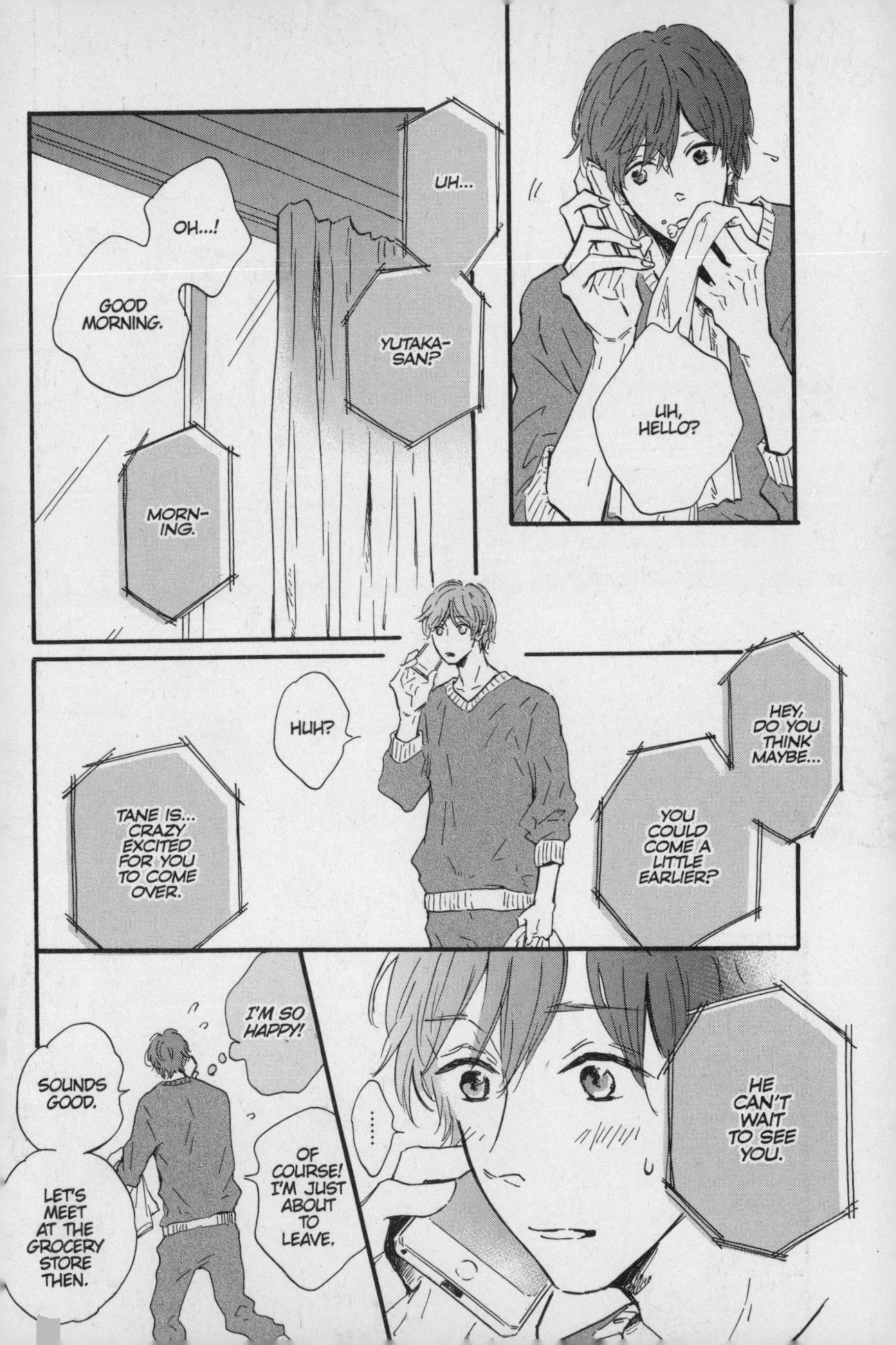
UH, HELLO?
UH...
OH...!
YUTAKA-SAN?
GOOD MORNING.
MORNING-ING.
HEY, DO YOU THINK MAYBE...
YOU COULD COME A LITTLE EARLIER?
HUH?
TANE IS... CRAZY EXCITED FOR YOU TO COME OVER.
HE CAN'T WAIT TO SEE YOU.
......
I'M SO HAPPY!
SOUNDS GOOD.
OF COURSE! I'M JUST ABOUT TO LEAVE.
LET'S MEET AT THE GROCERY STORE THEN.

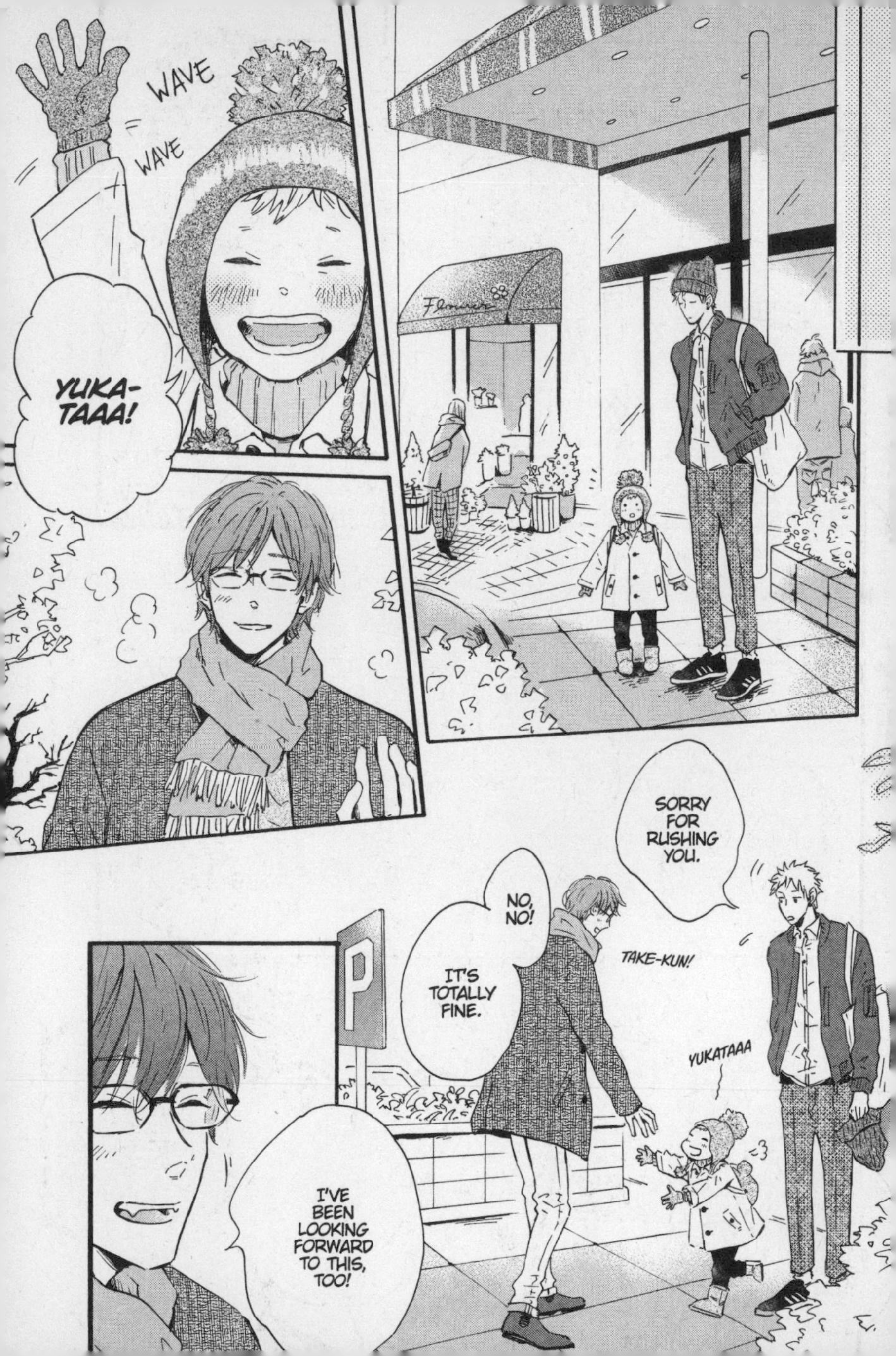
WAVE
WAVE
YUKA-TAAA!
SORRY FOR RUSHING YOU.
TAKE-KUN!
YUKATAAA
NO, NO!
IT'S TOTALLY FINE.
I'VE BEEN LOOKING FORWARD TO THIS, TOO!

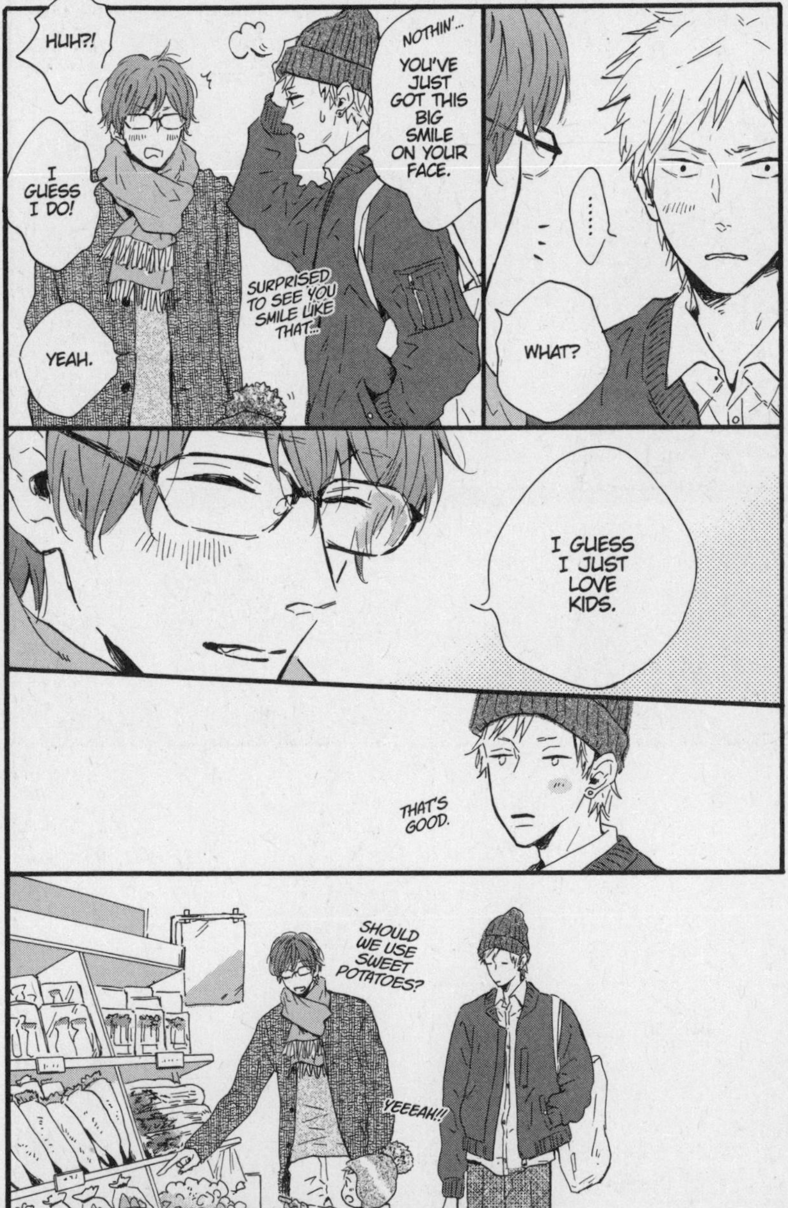
......
WHAT?
NOTHIN'...
YOU'VE JUST GOT THIS BIG SMILE ON YOUR FACE.
HUH?!
SURPRISED TO SEE YOU SMILE LIKE THAT...
I GUESS I DO!
YEAH.
I GUESS I JUST LOVE KIDS.
THAT'S GOOD.
SHOULD WE USE SWEET POTATOES?
YEEEAH!!

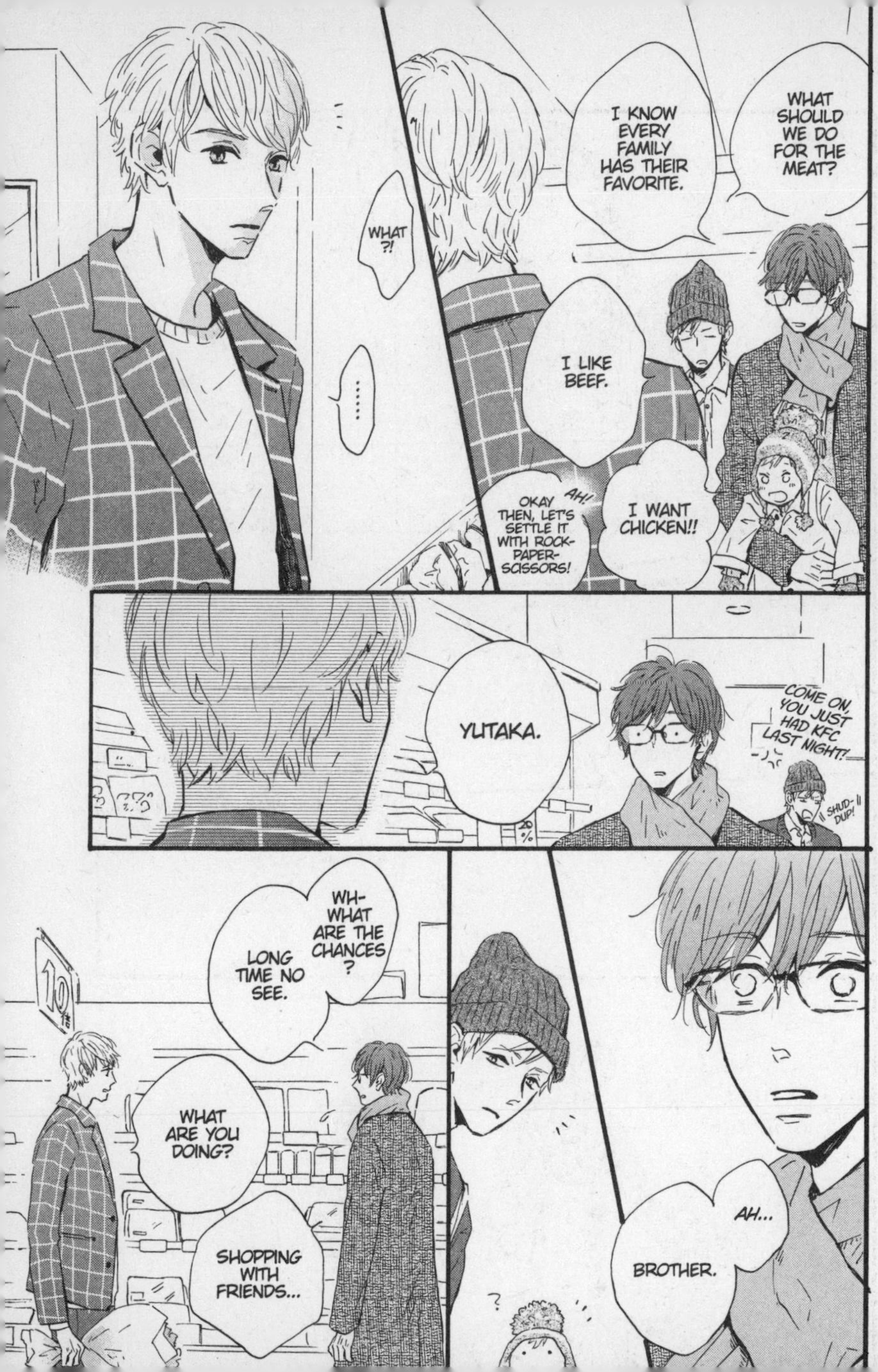
WHAT SHOULD WE DO FOR THE MEAT?
I KNOW EVERY FAMILY HAS THEIR FAVORITE.
I LIKE BEEF.
I WANT CHICKEN!!
AH! OKAY THEN, LET'S SETTLE IT WITH ROCK-PAPER-SCISSORS!
WHAT ?!
......
YUTAKA.
COME ON, YOU JUST HAD KFC LAST NIGHT!
SHUD-DUP!
AH...
BROTHER.
WH-WHAT ARE THE CHANCES?
LONG TIME NO SEE.
WHAT ARE YOU DOING?
SHOPPING WITH FRIENDS...

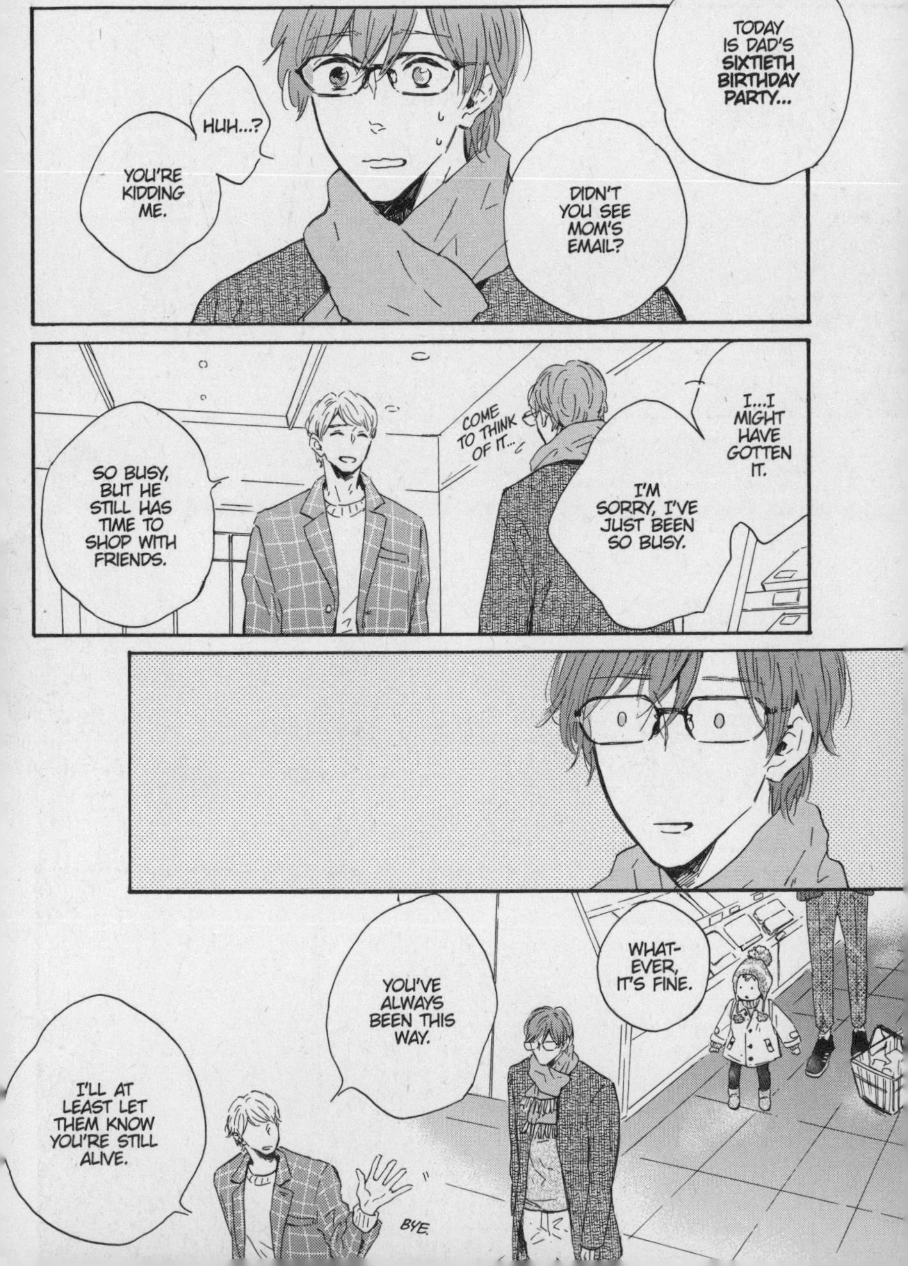
TODAY IS DAD'S SIXTIETH BIRTHDAY PARTY...
DIDN'T YOU SEE MOM'S EMAIL?
HUH...?
YOU'RE KIDDING ME.
I...I MIGHT HAVE GOTTEN IT.
I'M SORRY, I'VE JUST BEEN SO BUSY.
COME TO THINK OF IT...
SO BUSY, BUT HE STILL HAS TIME TO SHOP WITH FRIENDS.
WHAT-EVER, IT'S FINE.
YOU'VE ALWAYS BEEN THIS WAY.
I'LL AT LEAST LET THEM KNOW YOU'RE STILL ALIVE.
BYE.

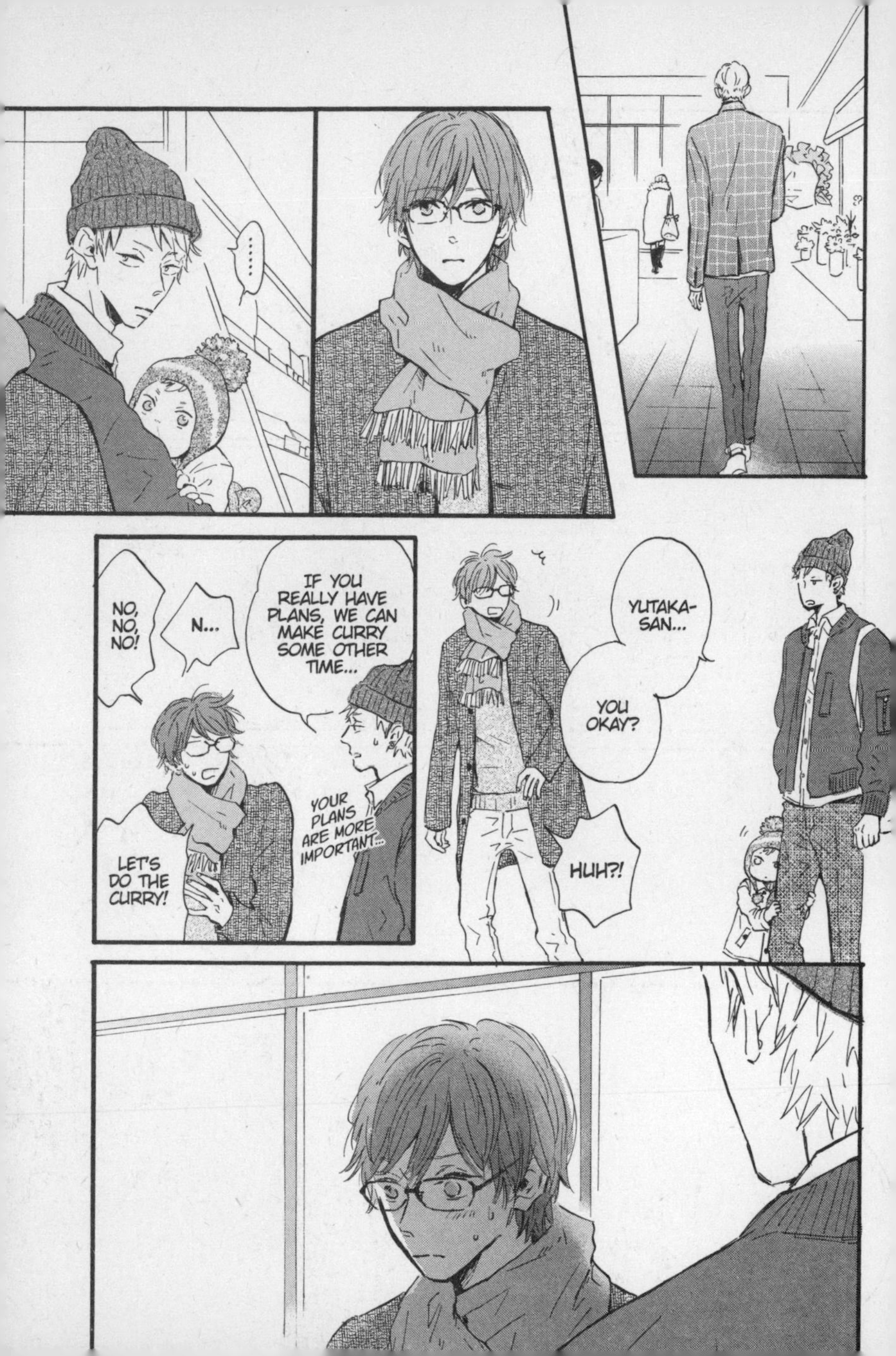
......
YUTAKA-SAN...
YOU OKAY?
HUH?!
IF YOU REALLY HAVE PLANS, WE CAN MAKE CURRY SOME OTHER TIME...
N...
NO, NO, NO!
YOUR PLANS ARE MORE IMPORTANT...
LET'S DO THE CURRY!

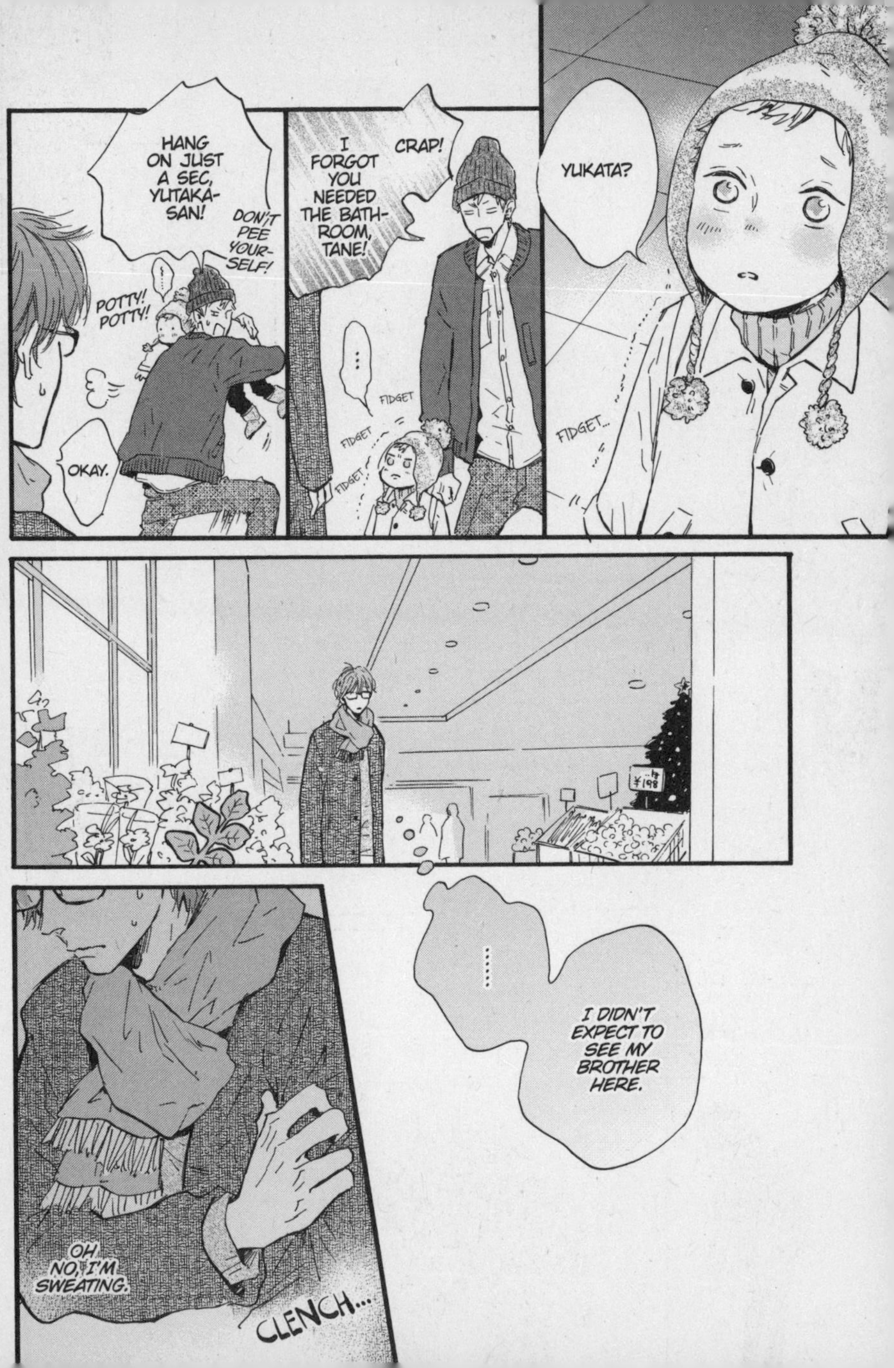
YUKATA?
FIDGET...
CRAP!
I FORGOT YOU NEEDED THE BATH-ROOM, TANE!
...
FIDGET
FIDGET
FIDGET
HANG ON JUST A SEC, YUTAKA-SAN!
DON'T PEE YOURSELF!
POTTY! POTTY!
OKAY.
¥198
......
I DIDN'T EXPECT TO SEE MY BROTHER HERE.
OH NO, I'M SWEATING.
CLENCH...

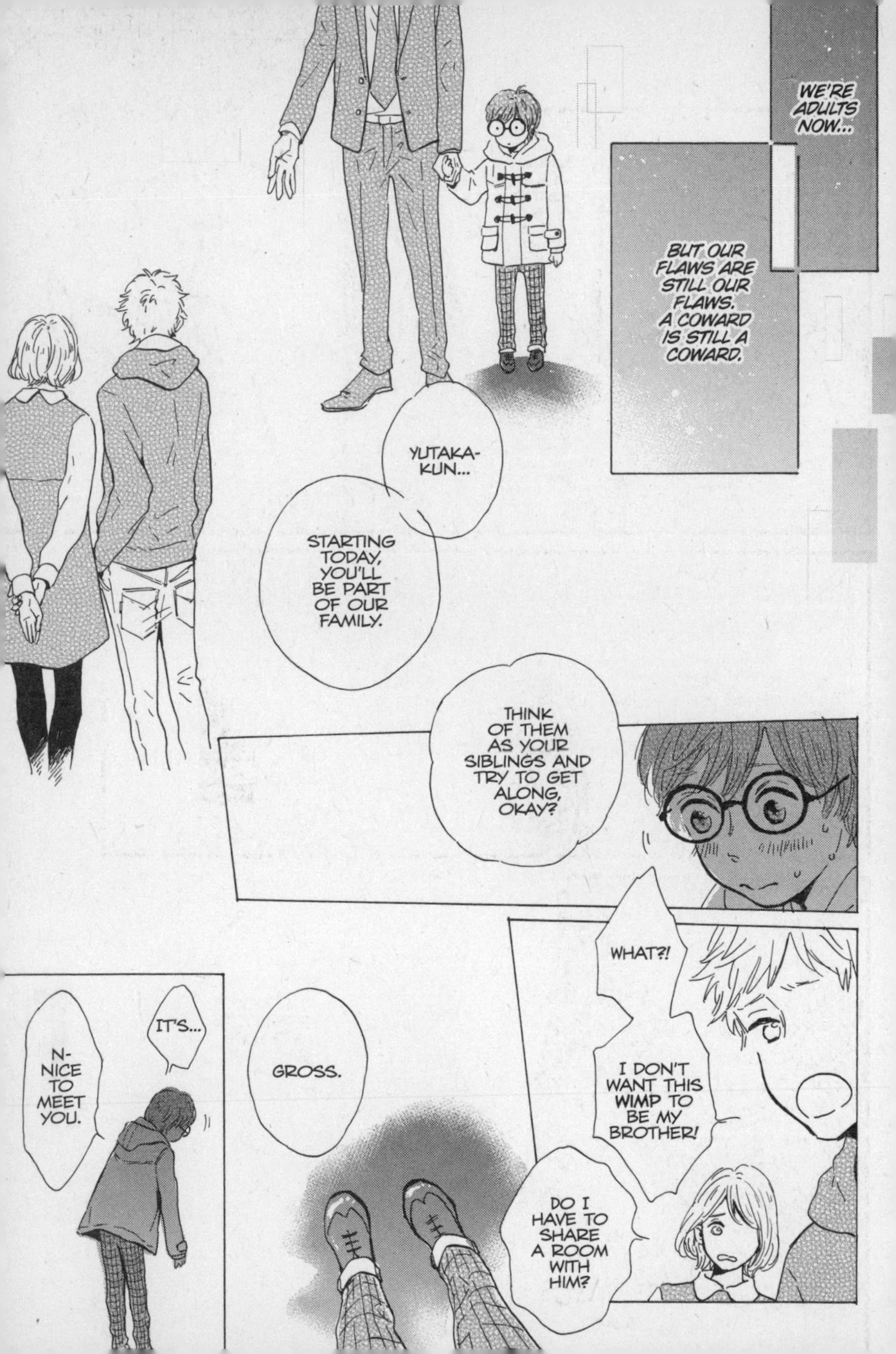
WE'RE ADULTS NOW...
BUT OUR FLAWS ARE STILL OUR FLAWS. A COWARD IS STILL A COWARD.
YUTAKA-KUN...
STARTING TODAY, YOU'LL BE PART OF OUR FAMILY.
THINK OF THEM AS YOUR SIBLINGS AND TRY TO GET ALONG, OKAY?
WHAT?!
I DON'T WANT THIS WIMP TO BE MY BROTHER!
DO I HAVE TO SHARE A ROOM WITH HIM?
GROSS.
IT'S...
N-NICE TO MEET YOU.

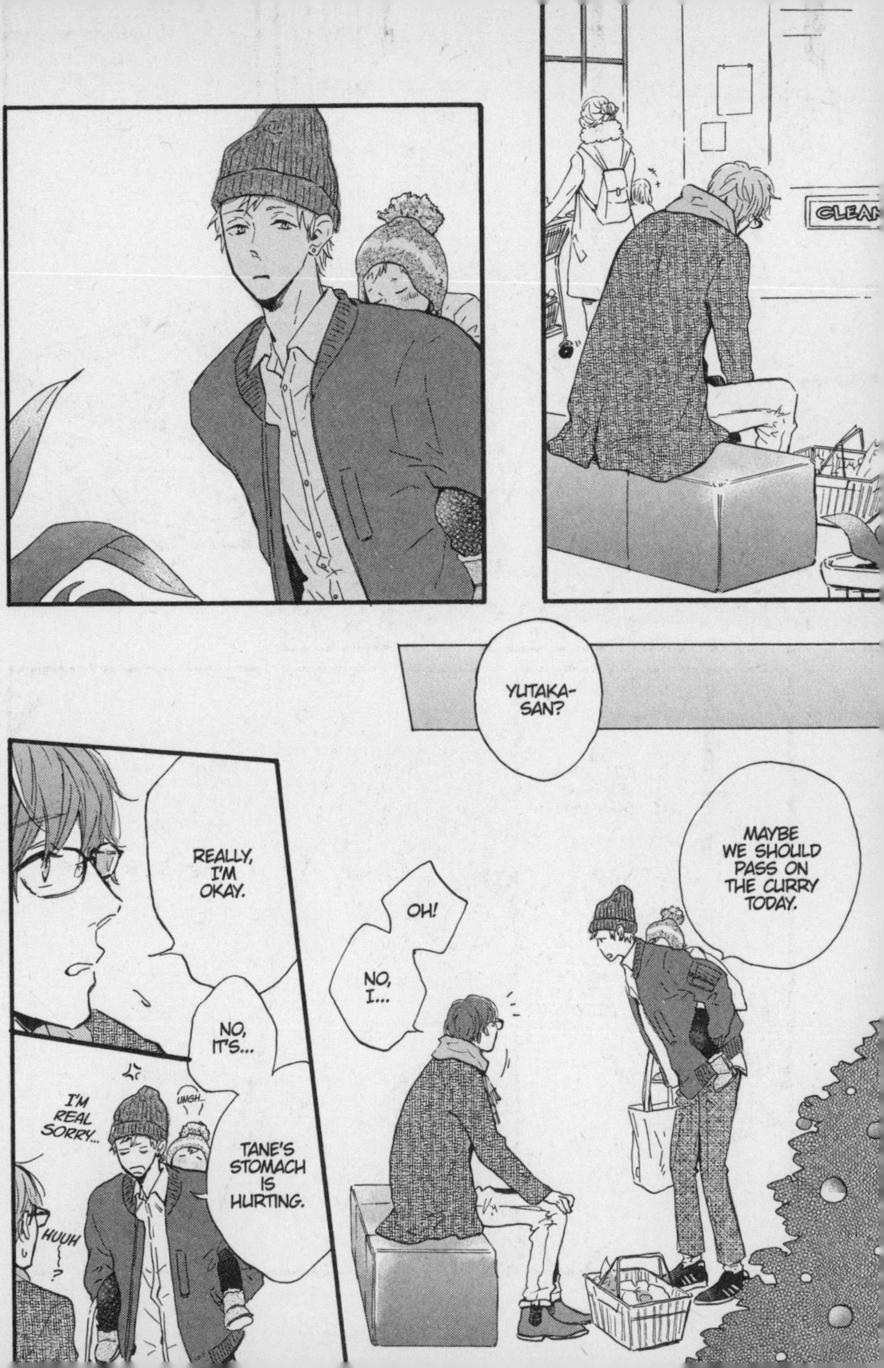
YUTAKA-SAN?
MAYBE WE SHOULD PASS ON THE CURRY TODAY.
OH!
NO, I...
REALLY, I'M OKAY.
NO, IT'S...
TANE'S STOMACH IS HURTING.
UNGH...
I'M REAL SORRY...
HUUH~?

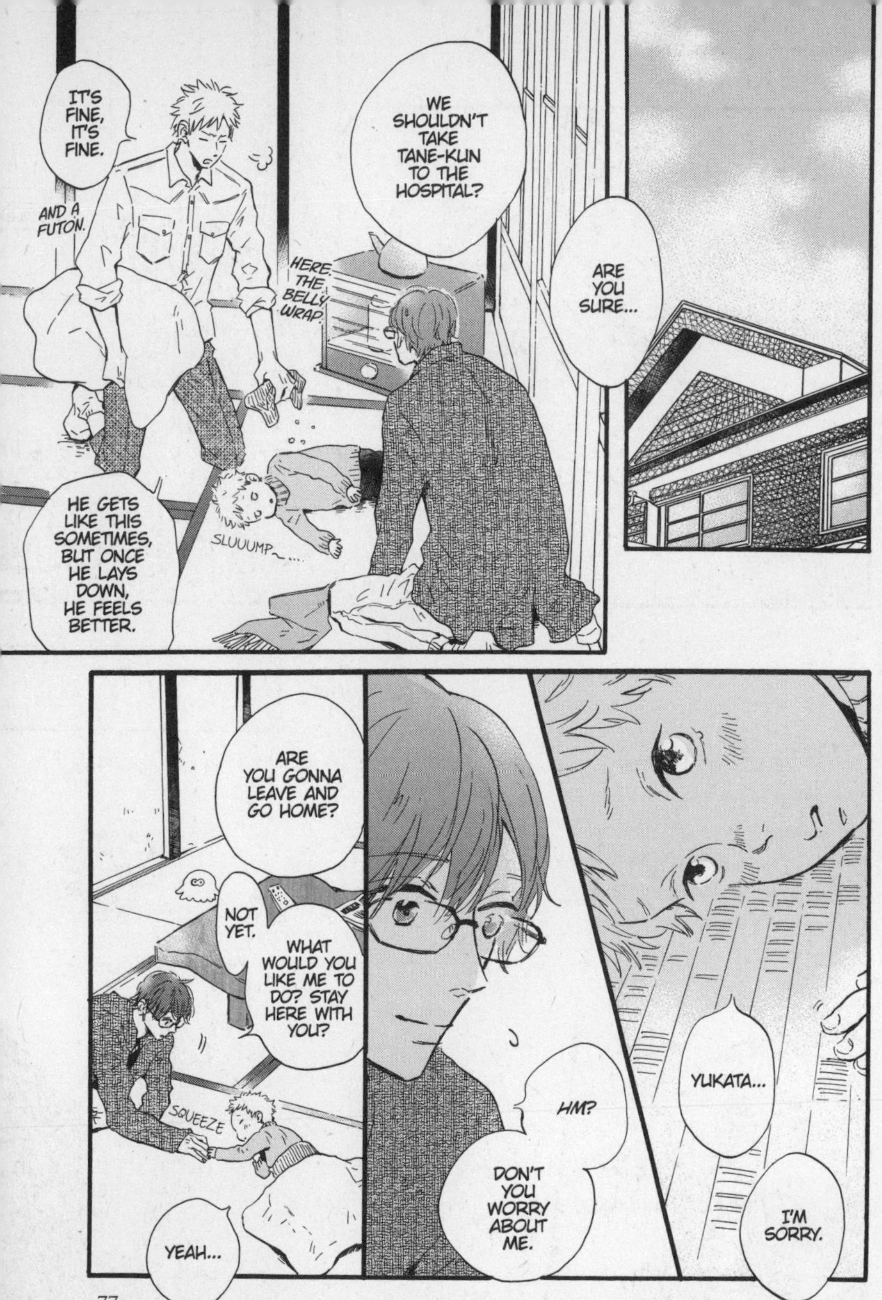
WE SHOULDN'T TAKE TANE-KUN TO THE HOSPITAL?
ARE YOU SURE...
IT'S FINE, IT'S FINE.
HERE. THE BELLY WRAP.
AND A FUTON.
HE GETS LIKE THIS SOMETIMES, BUT ONCE HE LAYS DOWN, HE FEELS BETTER.
SLUUUMP~.....
YUKATA...
I'M SORRY.
HM?
DON'T YOU WORRY ABOUT ME.
ARE YOU GONNA LEAVE AND GO HOME?
NOT YET.
WHAT WOULD YOU LIKE ME TO DO? STAY HERE WITH YOU?
SQUEEZE
YEAH...

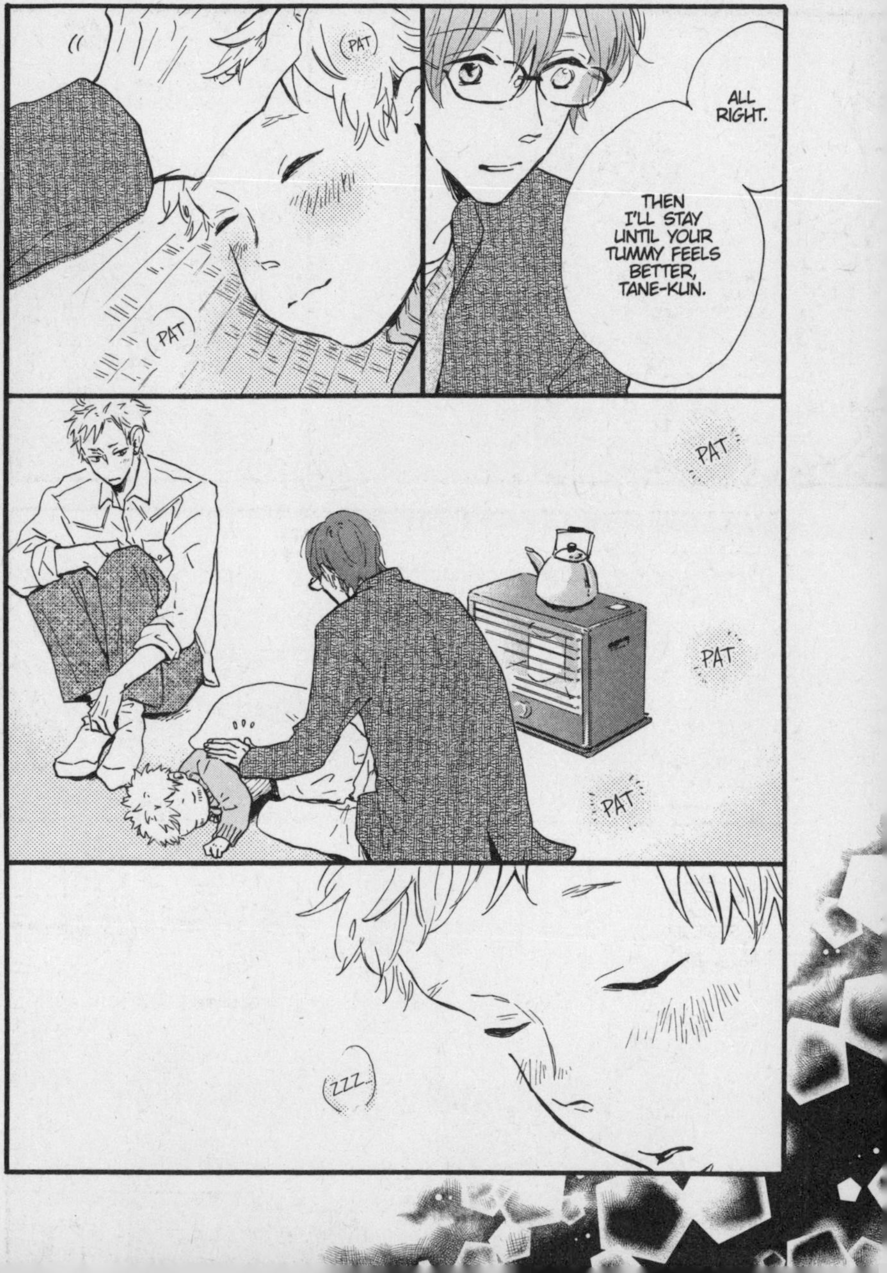
ALL RIGHT.
THEN I'LL STAY UNTIL YOUR TUMMY FEELS BETTER, TANE-KUN.
PAT
PAT
PAT
PAT
PAT
ZZZ...

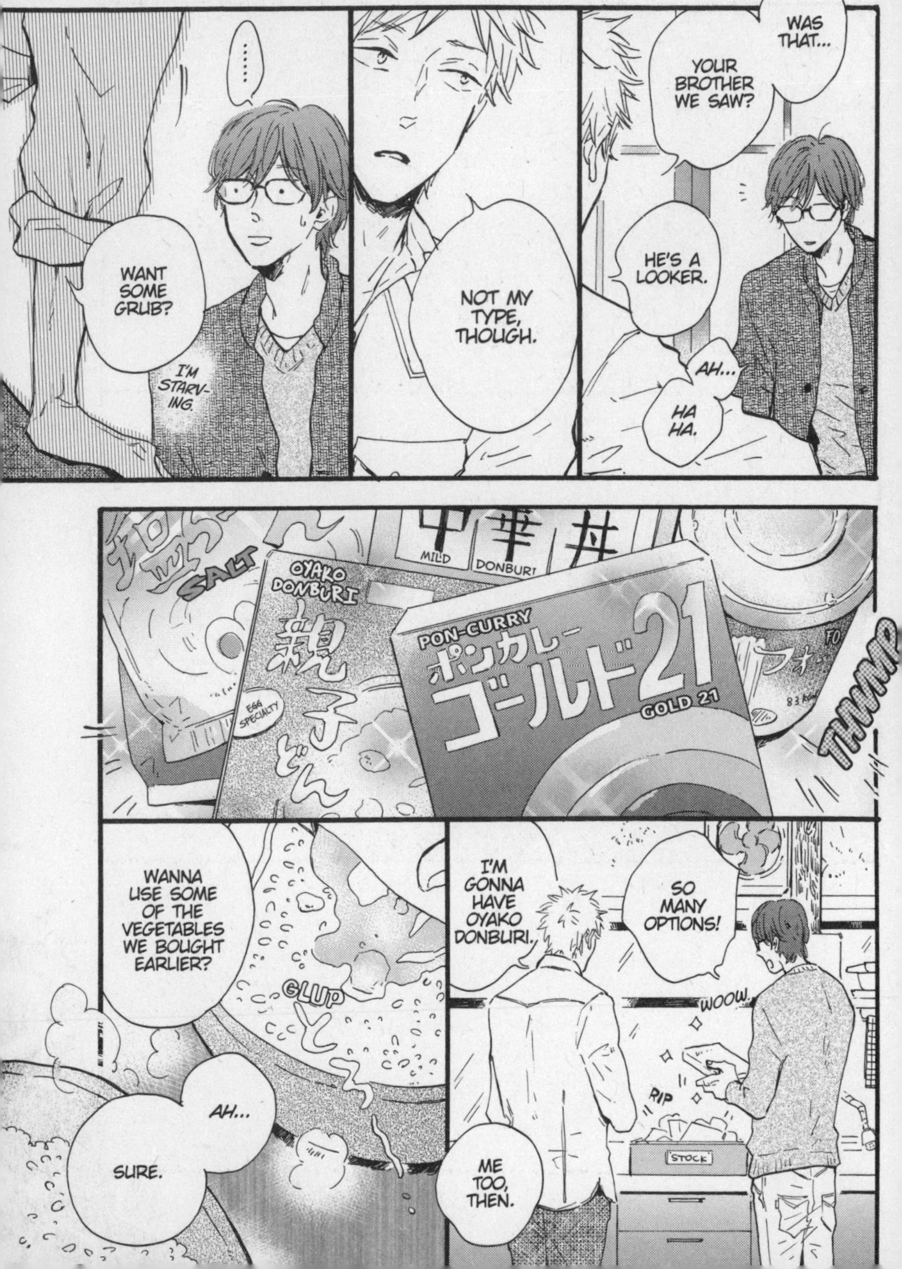
WAS THAT...
YOUR BROTHER WE SAW?
HE'S A LOOKER.
AH...
HA HA.
NOT MY TYPE, THOUGH.
......
WANT SOME GRUB?
I'M STARVING.
THUMP
中華丼
MILD
DONBURI
SALT
OYAKO DONBURI
親子どん
EGG SPECIALTY
PON-CURRY
ポンカレー ゴールド21
GOLD 21
SO MANY OPTIONS!
WOOW.
RIP
STOCK
I'M GONNA HAVE OYAKO DONBURI.
ME TOO, THEN.
WANNA USE SOME OF THE VEGETABLES WE BOUGHT EARLIER?
GLUP
AH...
SURE.

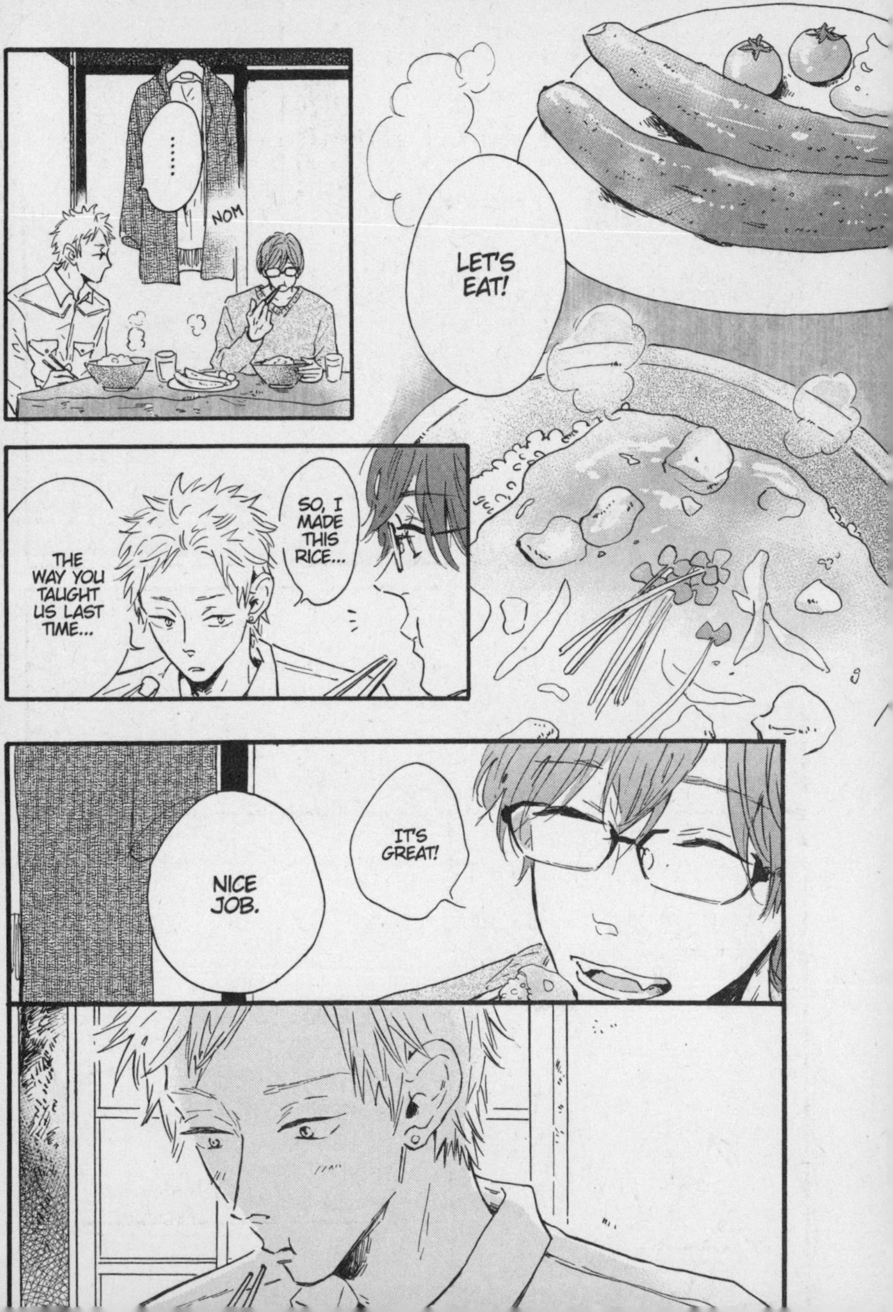
LET'S EAT!
......
NOM
SO, I MADE THIS RICE...
THE WAY YOU TAUGHT US LAST TIME...
IT'S GREAT!
NICE JOB.

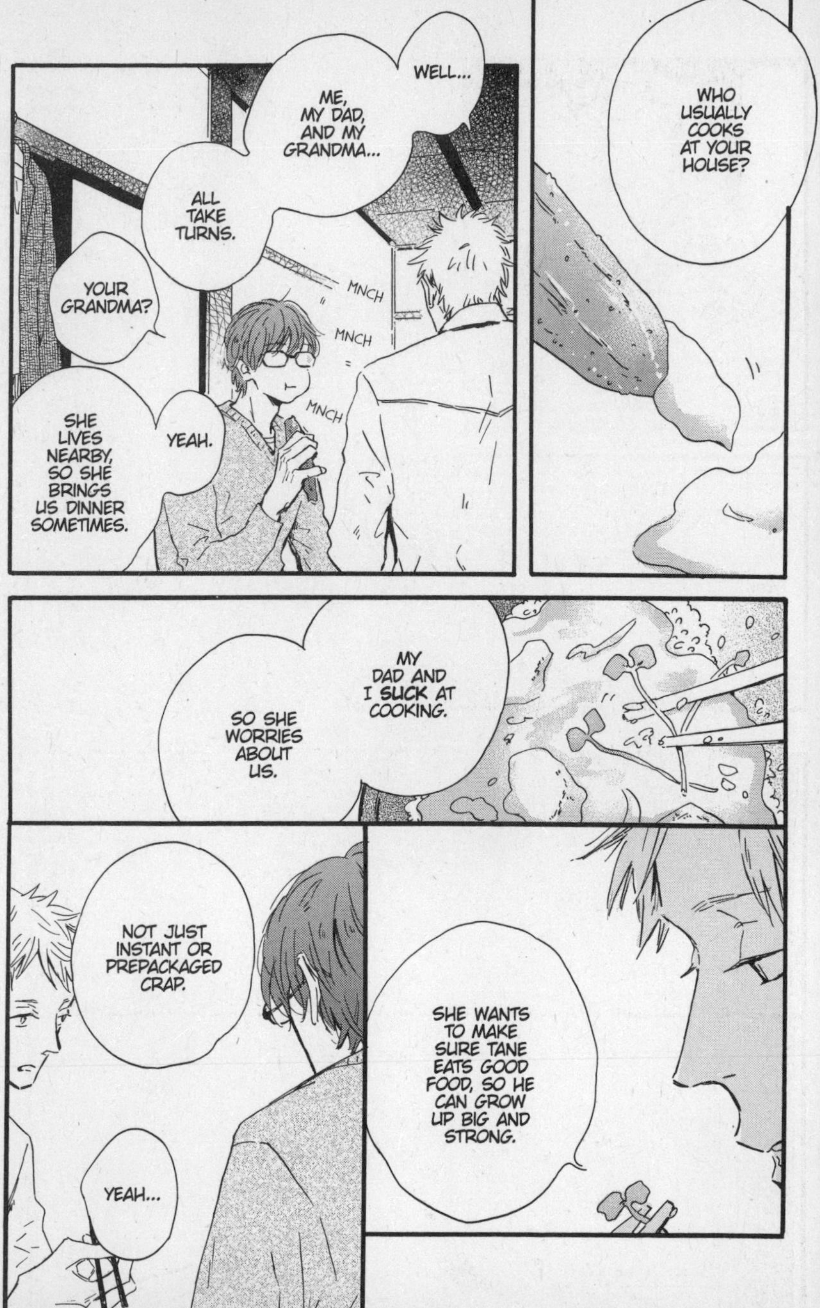
WHO USUALLY COOKS AT YOUR HOUSE?
WELL...
ME, MY DAD, AND MY GRANDMA...
ALL TAKE TURNS.
MNCH
MNCH
MNCH
YOUR GRANDMA?
YEAH.
SHE LIVES NEARBY, SO SHE BRINGS US DINNER SOMETIMES.
MY DAD AND I SUCK AT COOKING.
SO SHE WORRIES ABOUT US.
SHE WANTS TO MAKE SURE TANE EATS GOOD FOOD, SO HE CAN GROW UP BIG AND STRONG.
NOT JUST INSTANT OR PREPACKAGED CRAP.
YEAH...

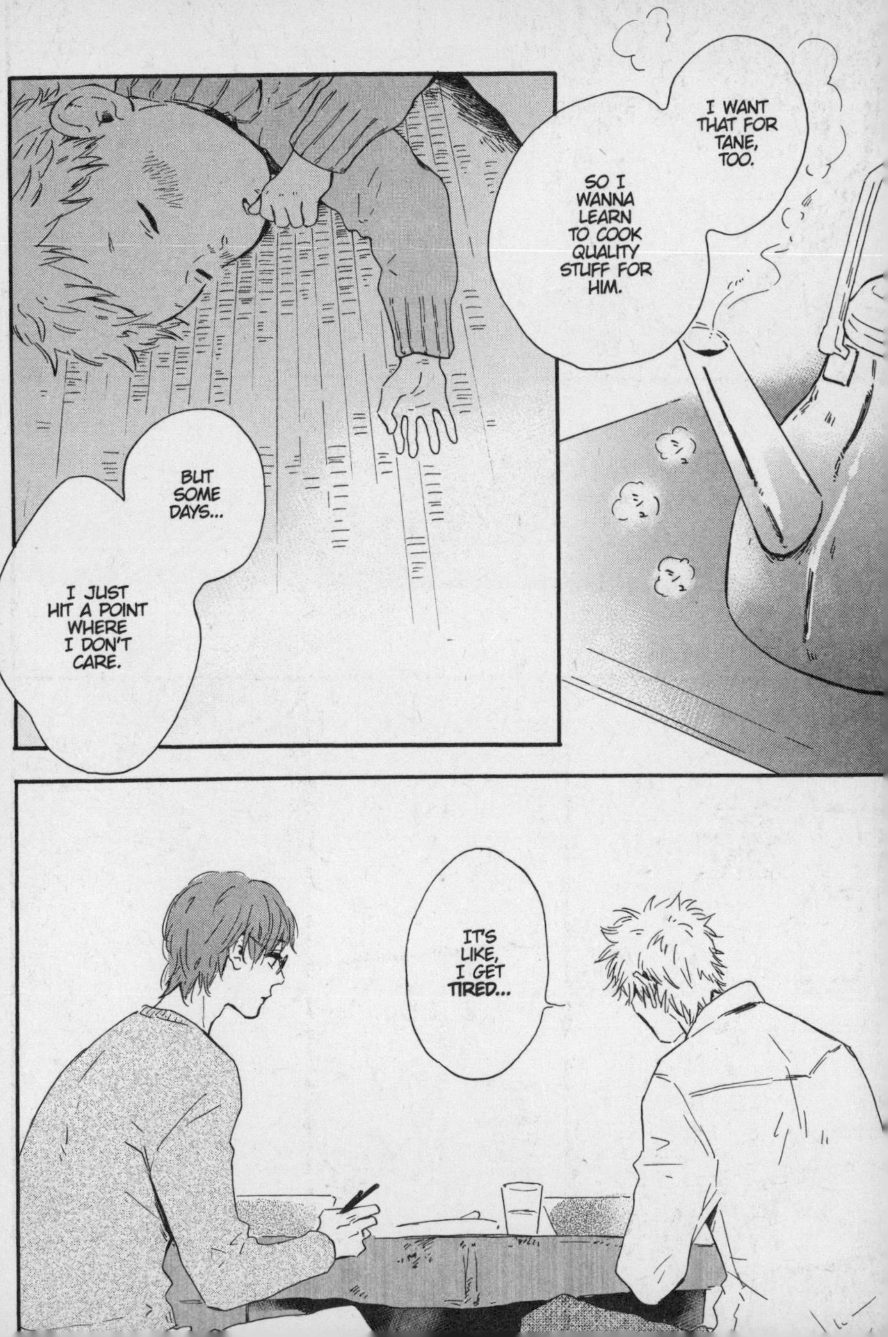
I WANT THAT FOR TANE, TOO.
SO I WANNA LEARN TO COOK QUALITY STUFF FOR HIM.
BUT SOME DAYS...
I JUST HIT A POINT WHERE I DON'T CARE.
IT'S LIKE, I GET TIRED...

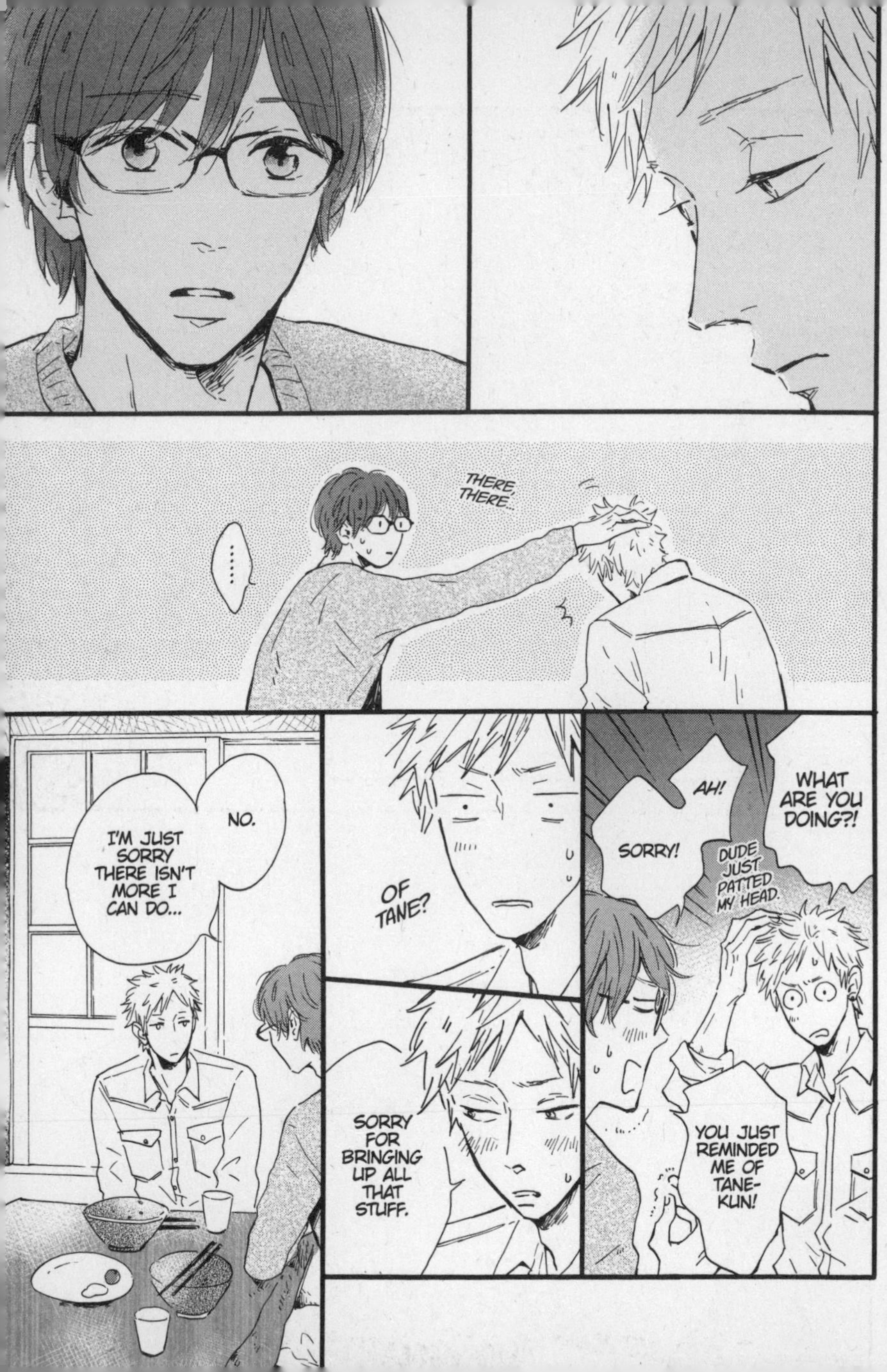
THERE, THERE...
......
WHAT ARE YOU DOING?!
AH!
DUDE JUST PATTED MY HEAD.
SORRY!
YOU JUST REMINDED ME OF TANE-KUN!
OF TANE?
SORRY FOR BRINGING UP ALL THAT STUFF.
NO.
I'M JUST SORRY THERE ISN'T MORE I CAN DO...

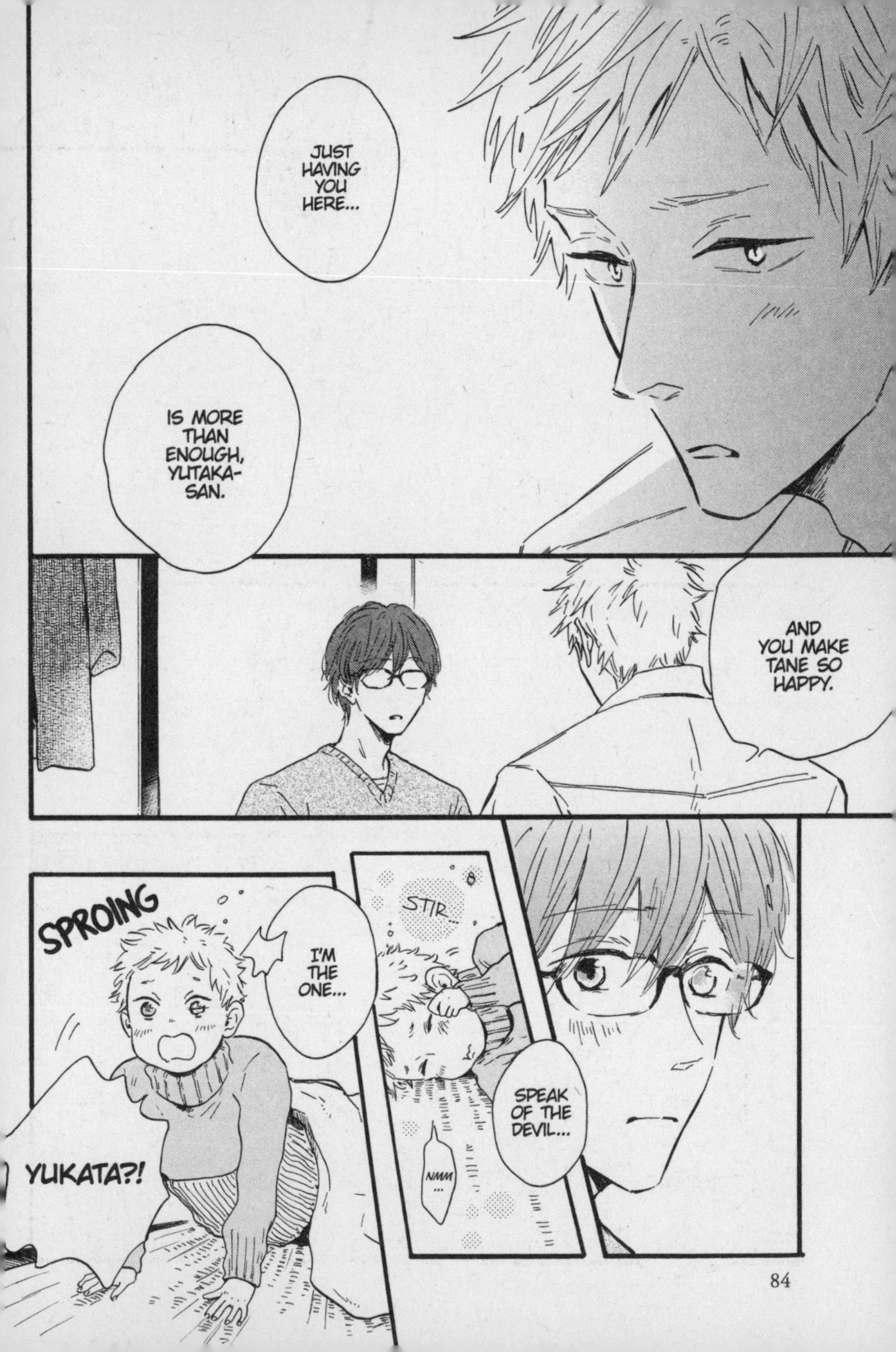
JUST HAVING YOU HERE...
IS MORE THAN ENOUGH, YUTAKA-SAN.
AND YOU MAKE TANE SO HAPPY.
SPEAK OF THE DEVIL...
STIR...
NMM...
I'M THE ONE...
SPROING
YUKATA?!

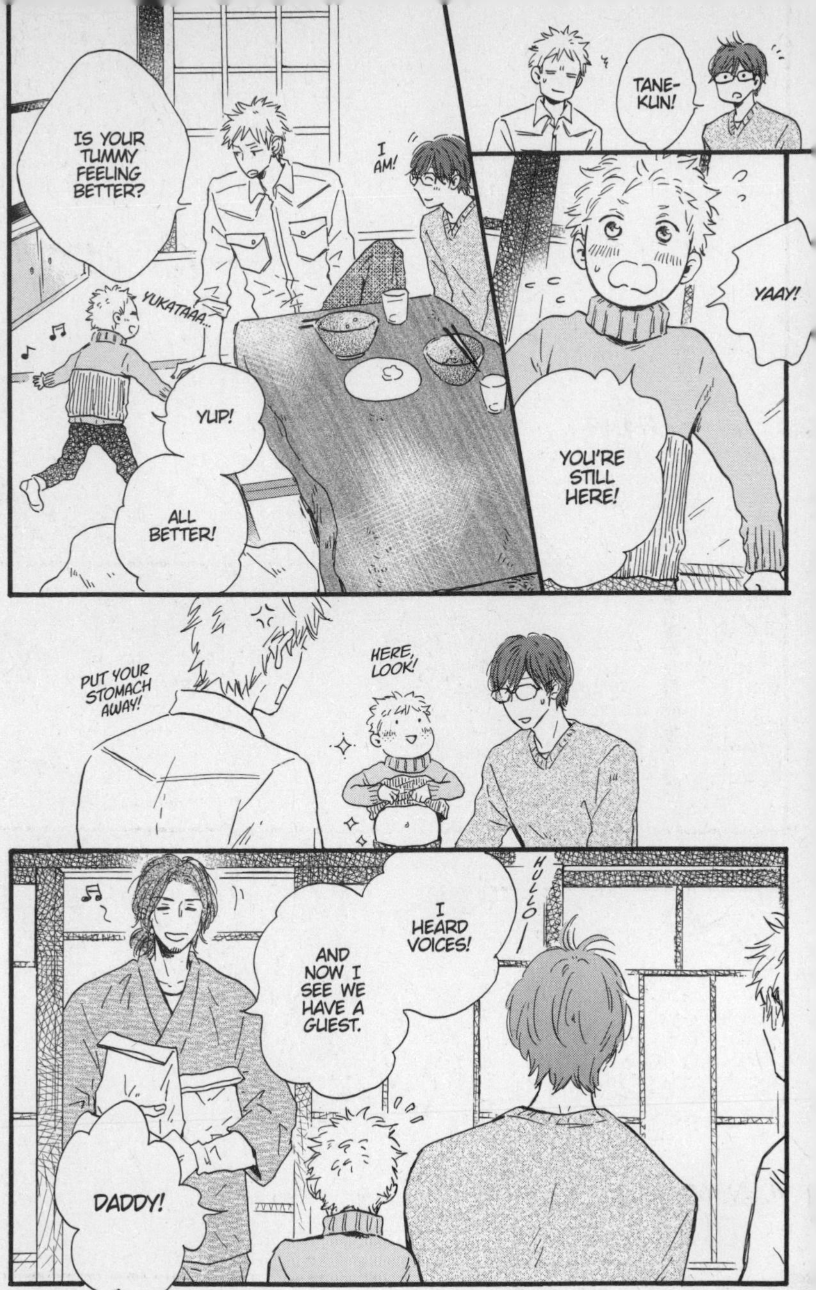
TANE-KUN!
YAAY!
YOU'RE STILL HERE!
I AM!
IS YOUR TUMMY FEELING BETTER?
YUKATAAA...
YUP!
ALL BETTER!
HERE, LOOK!
PUT YOUR STOMACH AWAY!
HULLO
I HEARD VOICES!
AND NOW I SEE WE HAVE A GUEST.
DADDY!

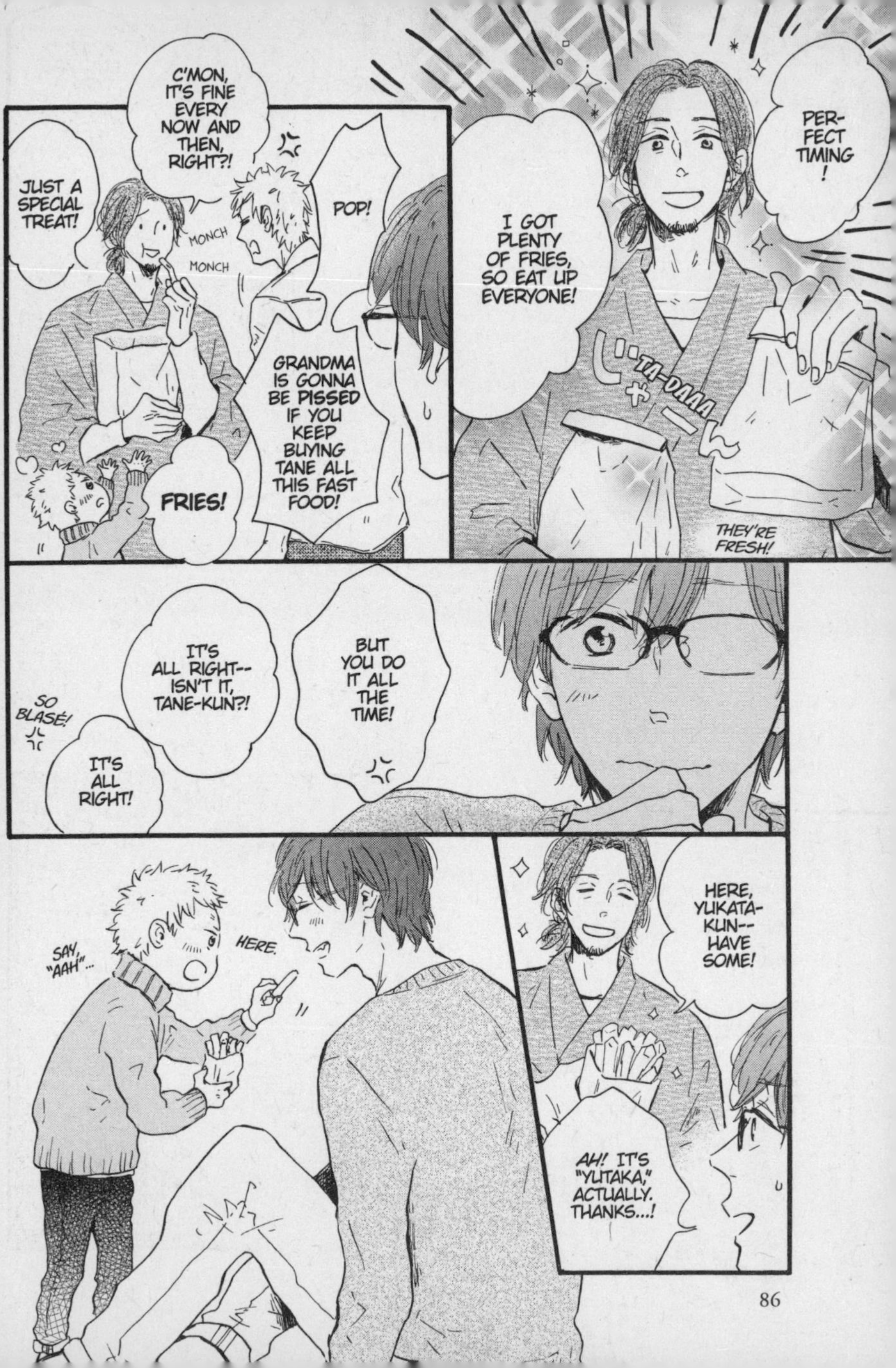
PER-FECT TIMING!
I GOT PLENTY OF FRIES, SO EAT UP EVERYONE!
じゃーん
TA-DAAA
THEY'RE FRESH!
POP!
C'MON, IT'S FINE EVERY NOW AND THEN, RIGHT?!
GRANDMA IS GONNA BE PISSED IF YOU KEEP BUYING TANE ALL THIS FAST FOOD!
JUST A SPECIAL TREAT!
MONCH
MONCH
FRIES!
BUT YOU DO IT ALL THE TIME!
IT'S ALL RIGHT-- ISN'T IT, TANE-KUN?!
SO BLASÉ!
IT'S ALL RIGHT!
HERE, YUKATA-KUN-- HAVE SOME!
AH! IT'S "YUTAKA," ACTUALLY. THANKS...!
HERE.
SAY, "AAH"...

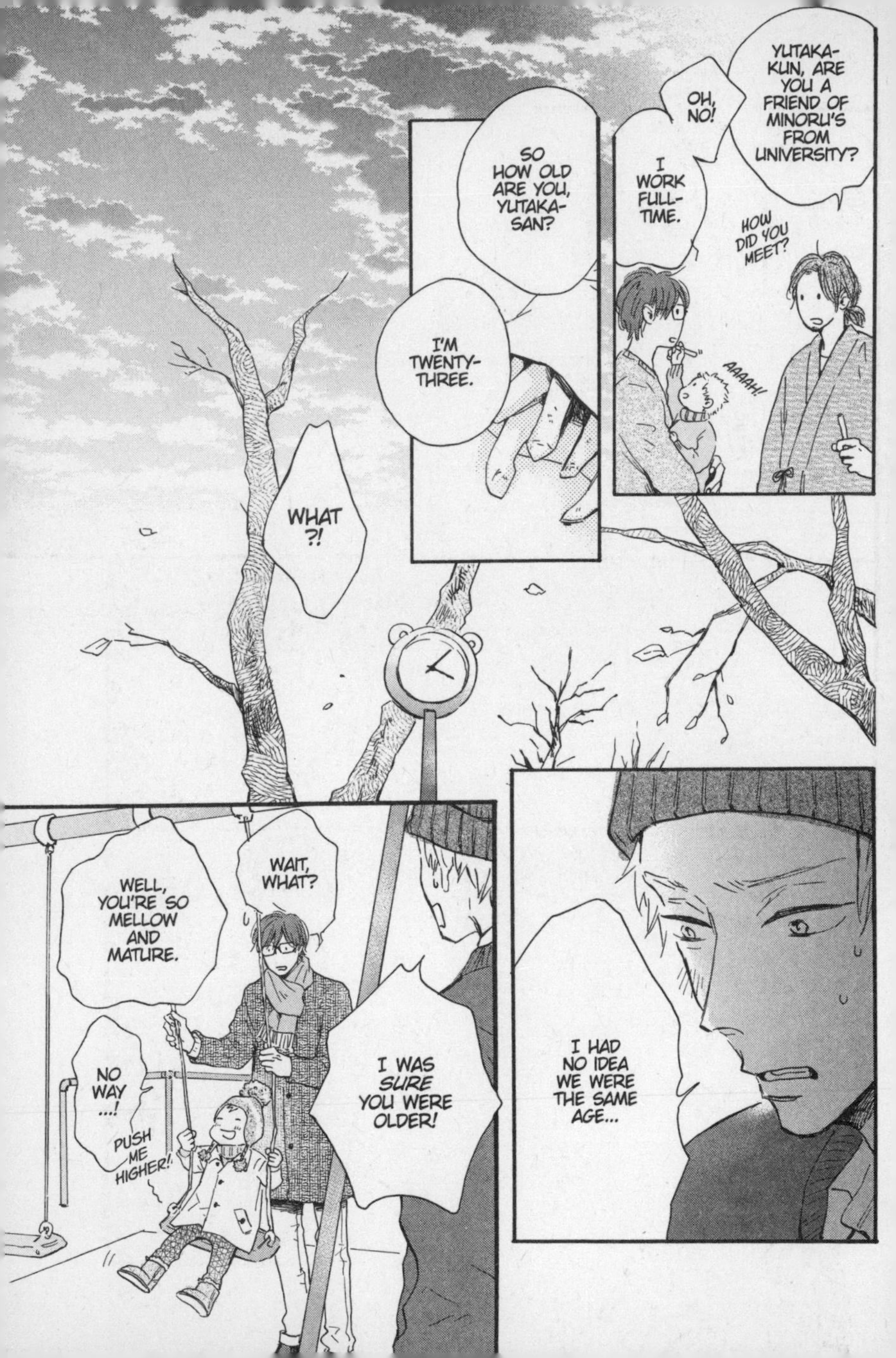
YUTAKA-KUN, ARE YOU A FRIEND OF MINORU'S FROM UNIVERSITY?
HOW DID YOU MEET?
OH, NO!
I WORK FULL-TIME.
AAAAH!
SO HOW OLD ARE YOU, YUTAKA-SAN?
I'M TWENTY-THREE.
WHAT?!
I HAD NO IDEA WE WERE THE SAME AGE...
I WAS SURE YOU WERE OLDER!
WAIT, WHAT?
WELL, YOU'RE SO MELLOW AND MATURE.
NO WAY ...!
PUSH ME HIGHER!

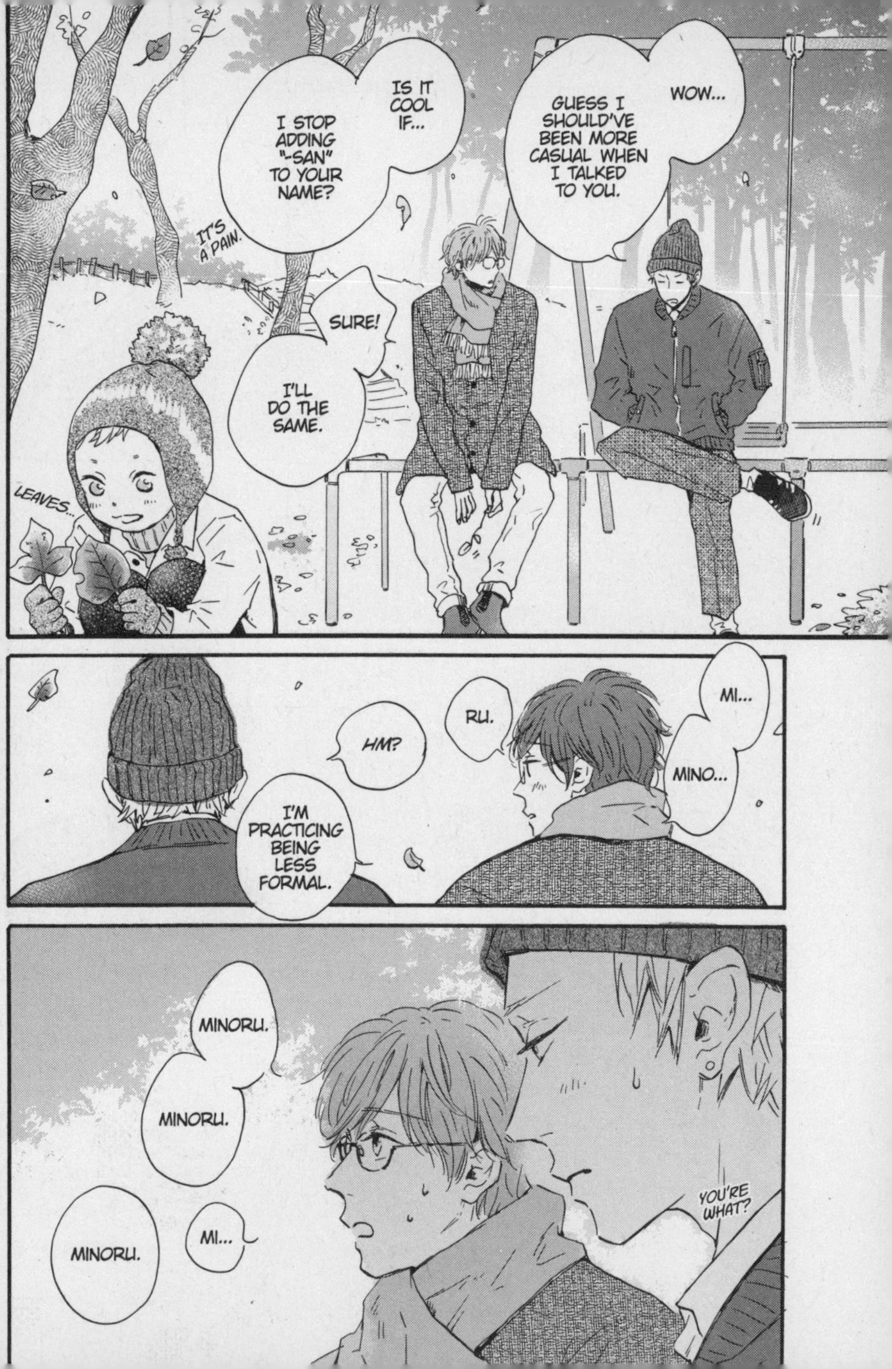
WOW...
GUESS I SHOULD'VE BEEN MORE CASUAL WHEN I TALKED TO YOU.
IS IT COOL IF...
I STOP ADDING "-SAN" TO YOUR NAME?
IT'S A PAIN.
SURE!
I'LL DO THE SAME.
LEAVES...
MI...
MINO...
RU.
HM?
I'M PRACTICING BEING LESS FORMAL.
YOU'RE WHAT?
MINORU.
MINORU.
MI...
MINORU.

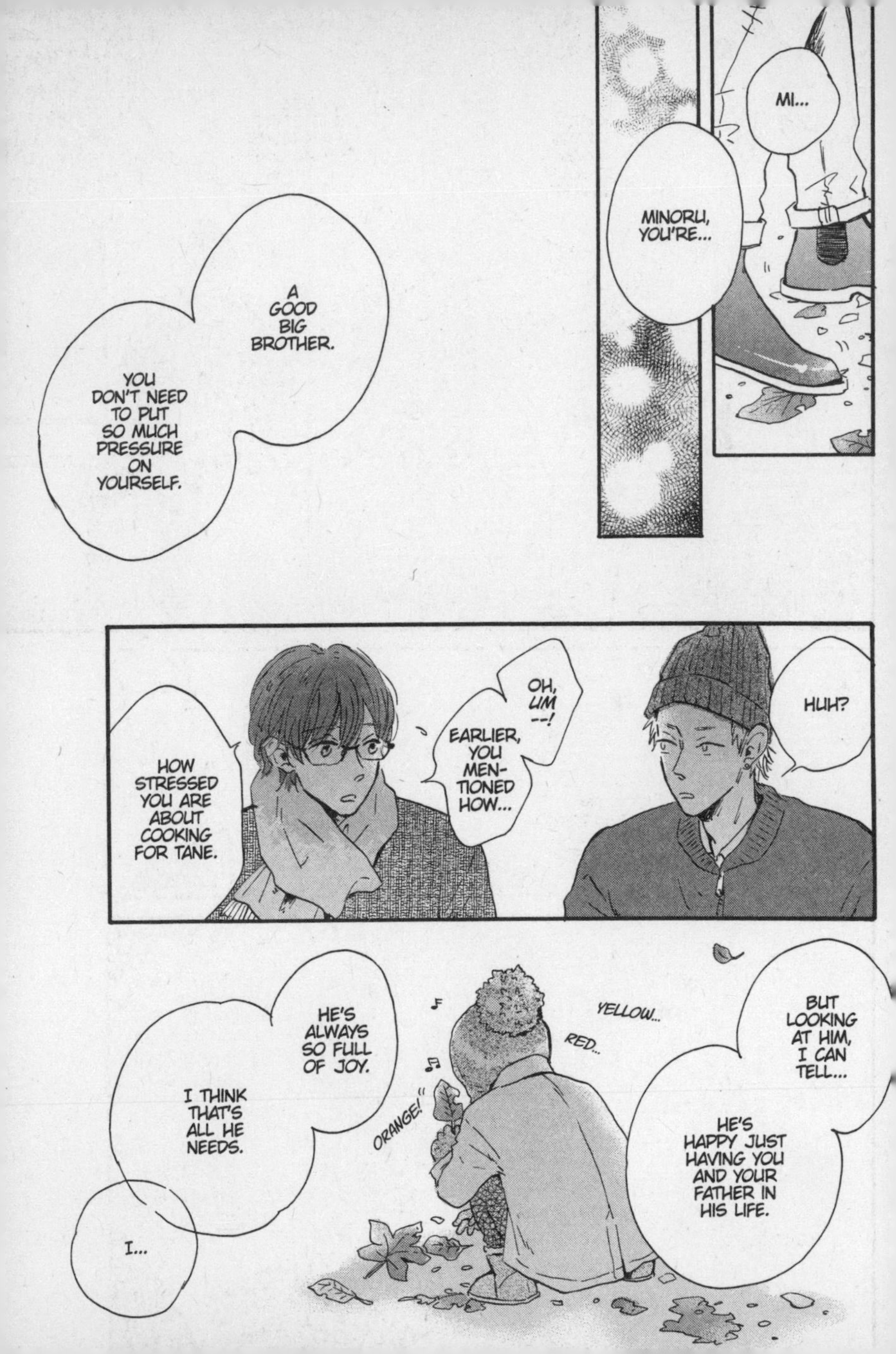

MI...
MINORU, YOU'RE...
A GOOD BIG BROTHER.
YOU DON'T NEED TO PUT SO MUCH PRESSURE ON YOURSELF.
HUH?
OH, UM --!
EARLIER, YOU MEN-TIONED HOW...
HOW STRESSED YOU ARE ABOUT COOKING FOR TANE.
BUT LOOKING AT HIM, I CAN TELL...
HE'S HAPPY JUST HAVING YOU AND YOUR FATHER IN HIS LIFE.
YELLOW...
RED...
ORANGE!
HE'S ALWAYS SO FULL OF JOY.
I THINK THAT'S ALL HE NEEDS.
I...

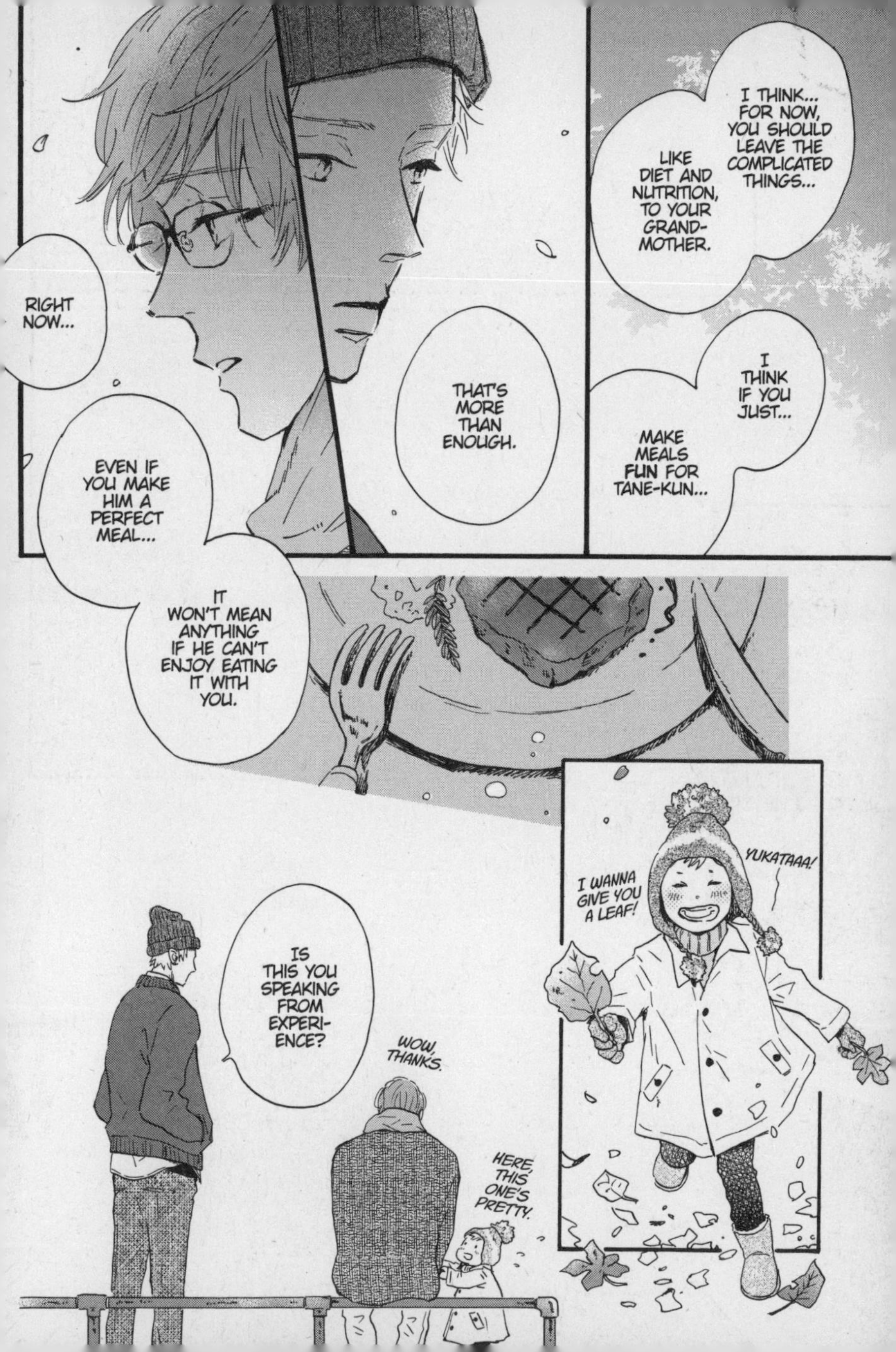
I THINK... FOR NOW, YOU SHOULD LEAVE THE COMPLICATED THINGS...
LIKE DIET AND NUTRITION, TO YOUR GRAND-MOTHER.
I THINK IF YOU JUST...
MAKE MEALS FUN FOR TANE-KUN...
RIGHT NOW...
THAT'S MORE THAN ENOUGH.
EVEN IF YOU MAKE HIM A PERFECT MEAL...
IT WON'T MEAN ANYTHING IF HE CAN'T ENJOY EATING IT WITH YOU.
YUKATAAA!
I WANNA GIVE YOU A LEAF!
IS THIS YOU SPEAKING FROM EXPERI-ENCE?
WOW, THANKS.
HERE, THIS ONE'S PRETTY.

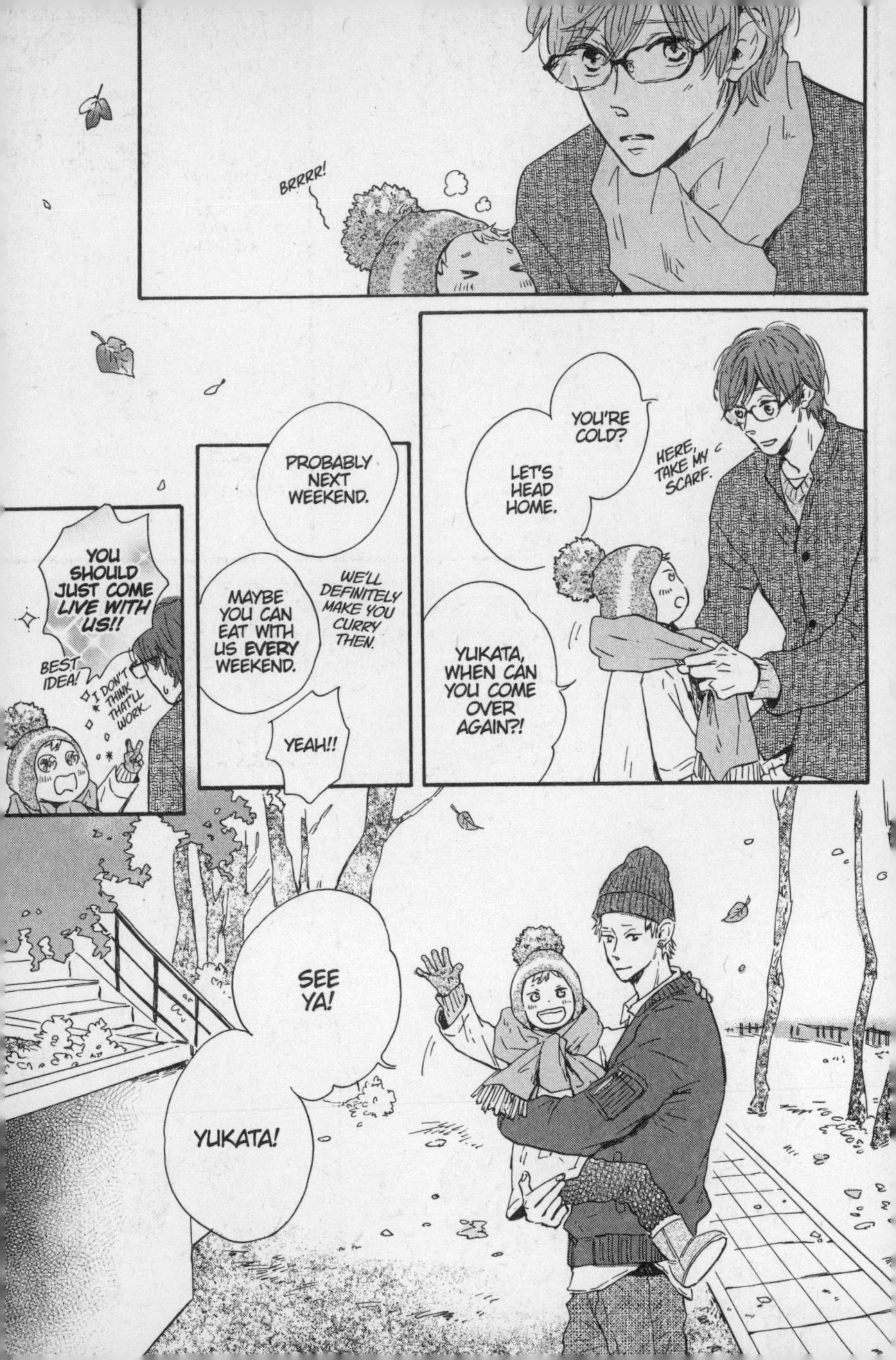
BRRRR!
YOU'RE COLD?
LET'S HEAD HOME.
HERE, TAKE MY SCARF.
YUKATA, WHEN CAN YOU COME OVER AGAIN?!
PROBABLY NEXT WEEKEND.
MAYBE YOU CAN EAT WITH US EVERY WEEKEND.
WE'LL DEFINITELY MAKE YOU CURRY THEN.
YEAH!!
YOU SHOULD JUST COME LIVE WITH US!!
BEST IDEA!
I DON'T THINK THAT'LL WORK...
SEE YA!
YUKATA!

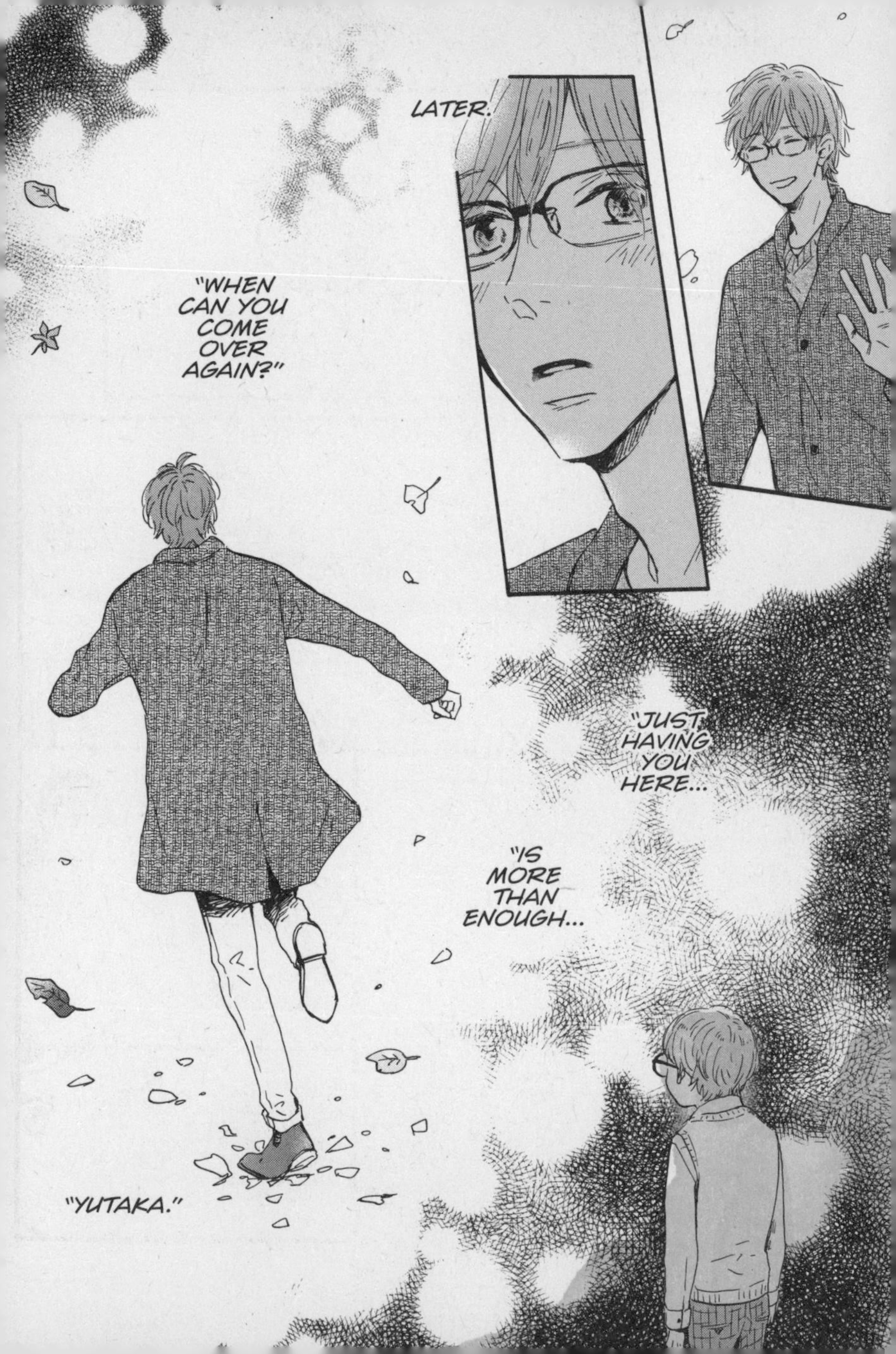
LATER.
"WHEN CAN YOU COME OVER AGAIN?"
"JUST HAVING YOU HERE...
"IS MORE THAN ENOUGH...
"YUTAKA."

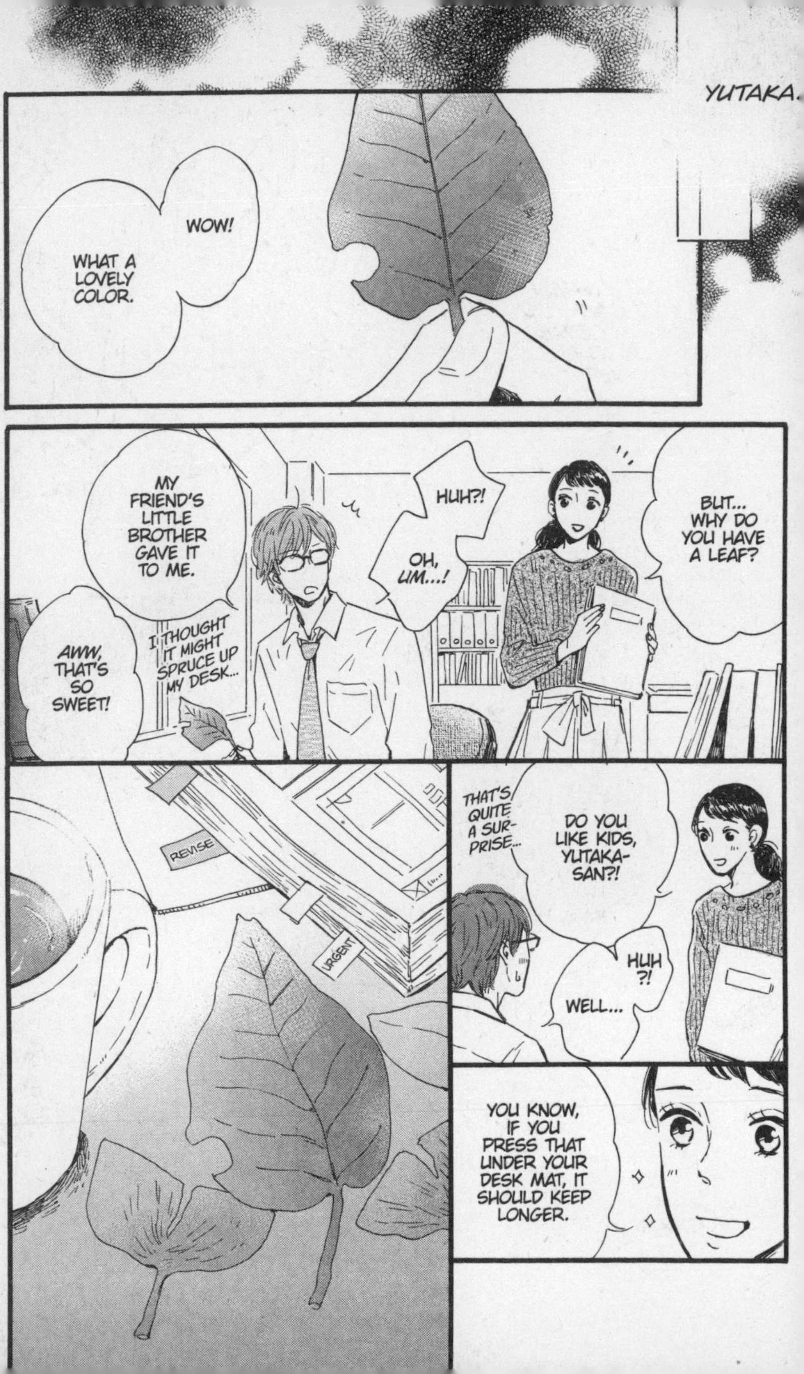
YUTAKA.
WOW!
WHAT A LOVELY COLOR.
BUT... WHY DO YOU HAVE A LEAF?
HUH?!
OH, UM...!
MY FRIEND'S LITTLE BROTHER GAVE IT TO ME.
I THOUGHT IT MIGHT SPRUCE UP MY DESK...
AWW, THAT'S SO SWEET!
DO YOU LIKE KIDS, YUTAKA-SAN?!
THAT'S QUITE A SUR-PRISE...
HUH ?!
WELL...
YOU KNOW, IF YOU PRESS THAT UNDER YOUR DESK MAT, IT SHOULD KEEP LONGER.
REVISE
URGENT

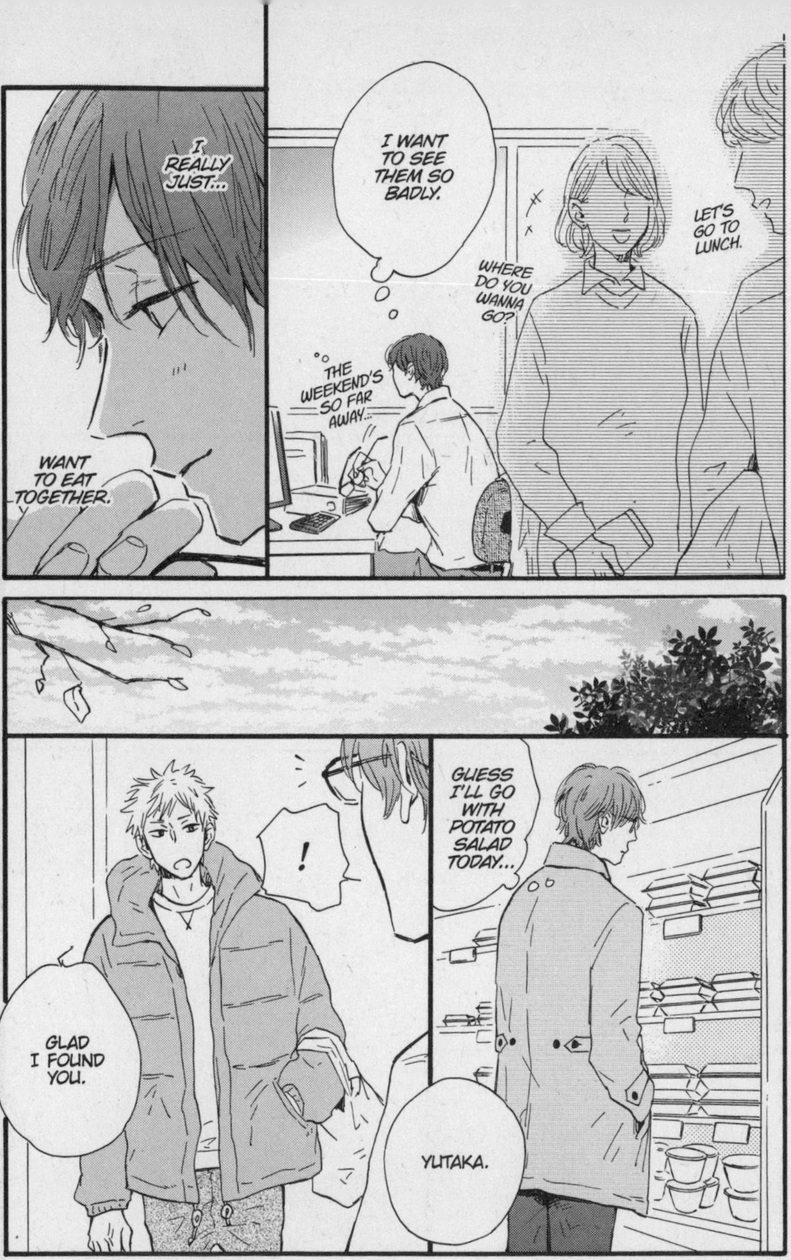
LET'S GO TO LUNCH.
WHERE DO YOU WANNA GO?
I WANT TO SEE THEM SO BADLY.
THE WEEKEND'S SO FAR AWAY...
I REALLY JUST...
WANT TO EAT TOGETHER.
GUESS I'LL GO WITH POTATO SALAD TODAY...
!
YUTAKA.
GLAD I FOUND YOU.

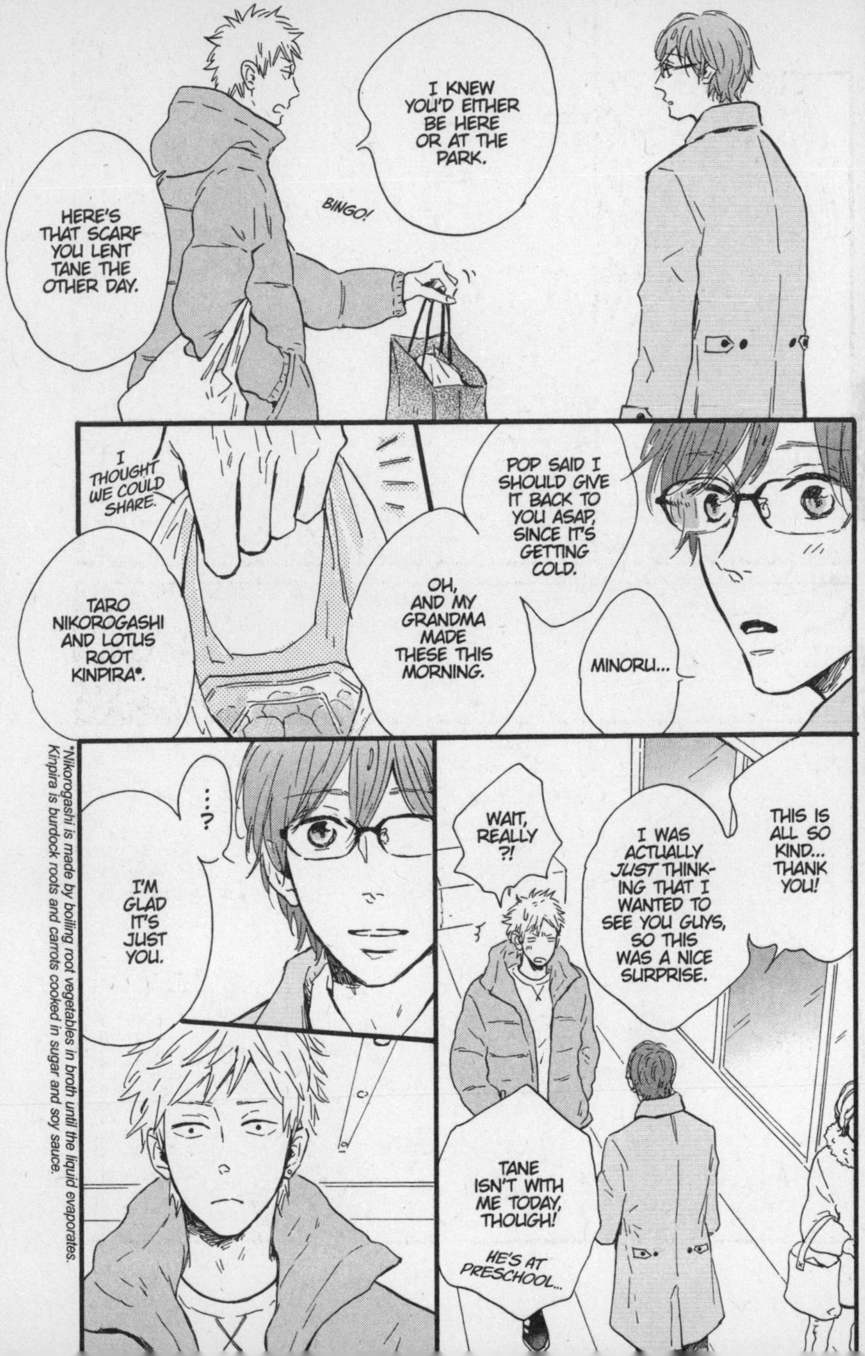
I KNEW YOU'D EITHER BE HERE OR AT THE PARK.
BINGO!
HERE'S THAT SCARF YOU LENT TANE THE OTHER DAY.
POP SAID I SHOULD GIVE IT BACK TO YOU ASAP, SINCE IT'S GETTING COLD.
MINORU...
OH, AND MY GRANDMA MADE THESE THIS MORNING.
TARO NIKOROGASHI AND LOTUS ROOT KINPIRA*.
I THOUGHT WE COULD SHARE.
THIS IS ALL SO KIND... THANK YOU!
I WAS ACTUALLY *JUST* THINKING THAT I WANTED TO SEE YOU GUYS, SO THIS WAS A NICE SURPRISE.
WAIT, REALLY ?!
TANE ISN'T WITH ME TODAY, THOUGH!
HE'S AT PRESCHOOL...
...?
I'M GLAD IT'S JUST YOU.

*Nikorogashi is made by boiling root vegetables in broth until the liquid evaporates. Kinpira is burdock roots and carrots cooked in sugar and soy sauce.

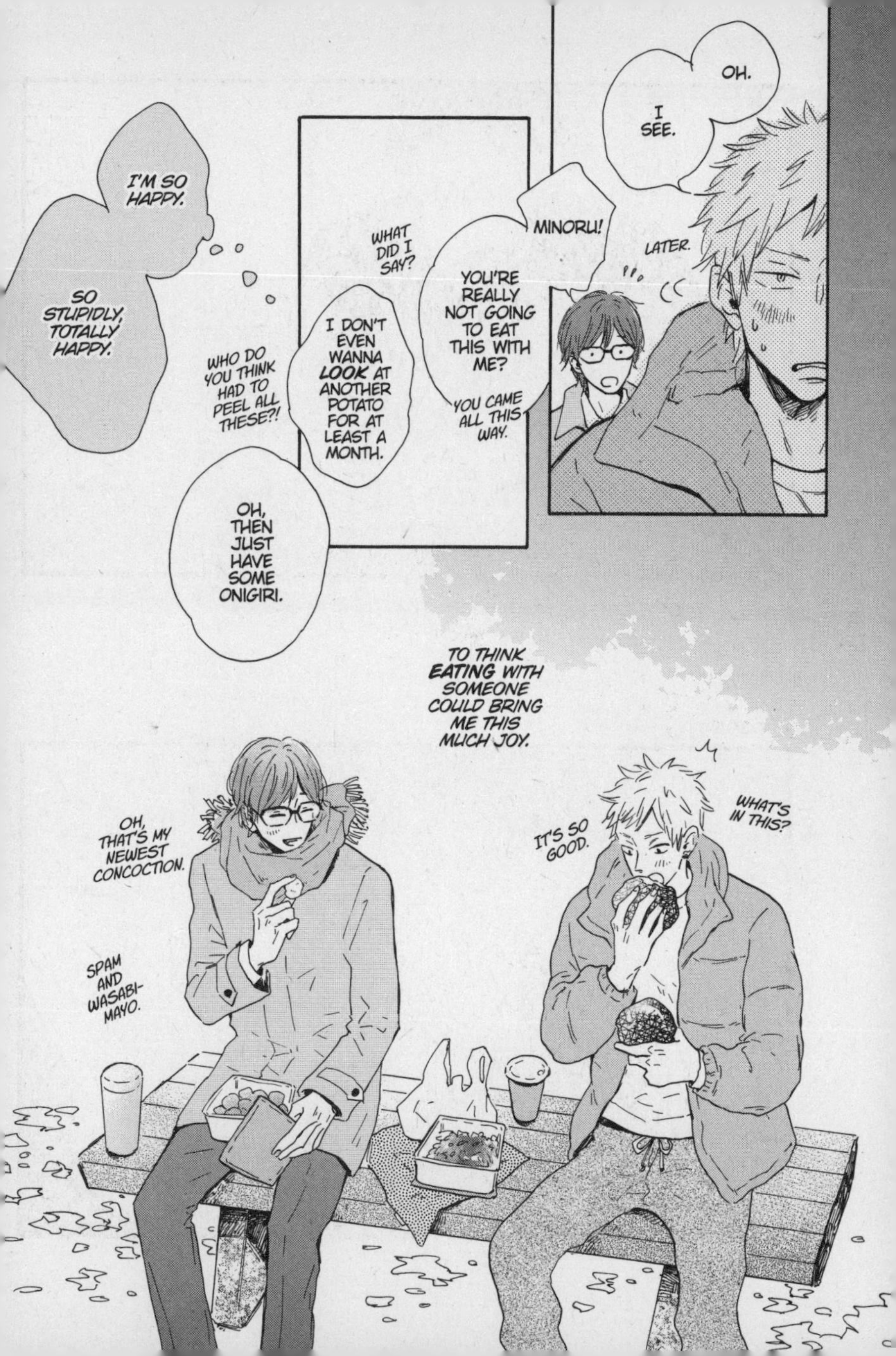
OH.
I SEE.
LATER.
MINORU!
YOU'RE REALLY NOT GOING TO EAT THIS WITH ME?
YOU CAME ALL THIS WAY.
WHAT DID I SAY?
I DON'T EVEN WANNA LOOK AT ANOTHER POTATO FOR AT LEAST A MONTH.
WHO DO YOU THINK HAD TO PEEL ALL THESE?!
OH, THEN JUST HAVE SOME ONIGIRI.
I'M SO HAPPY.
SO STUPIDLY, TOTALLY HAPPY.
TO THINK EATING WITH SOMEONE COULD BRING ME THIS MUCH JOY.
WHAT'S IN THIS?
IT'S SO GOOD.
OH, THAT'S MY NEWEST CONCOCTION.
SPAM AND WASABI-MAYO.

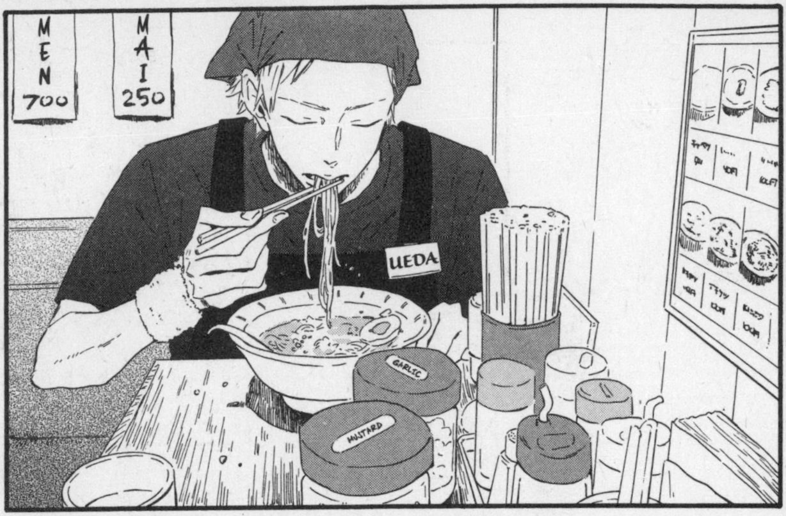
MEN 700
MAI 250
UEDA
GARLIC
MUSTARD

Chapter 3

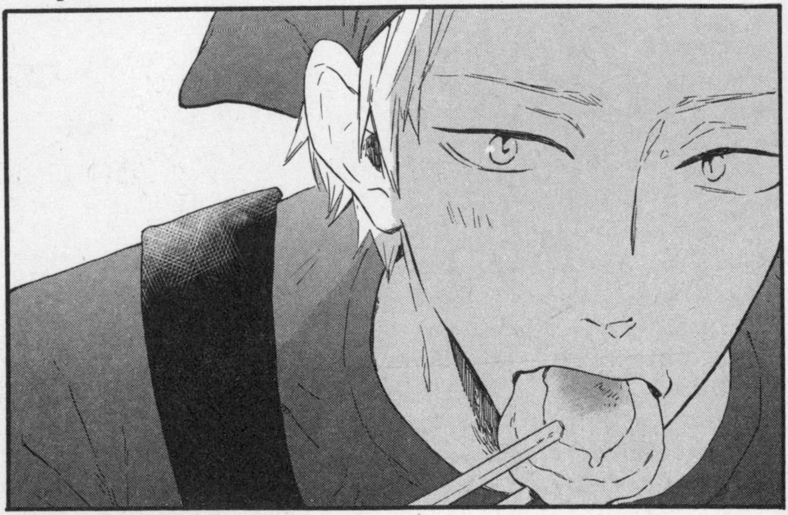

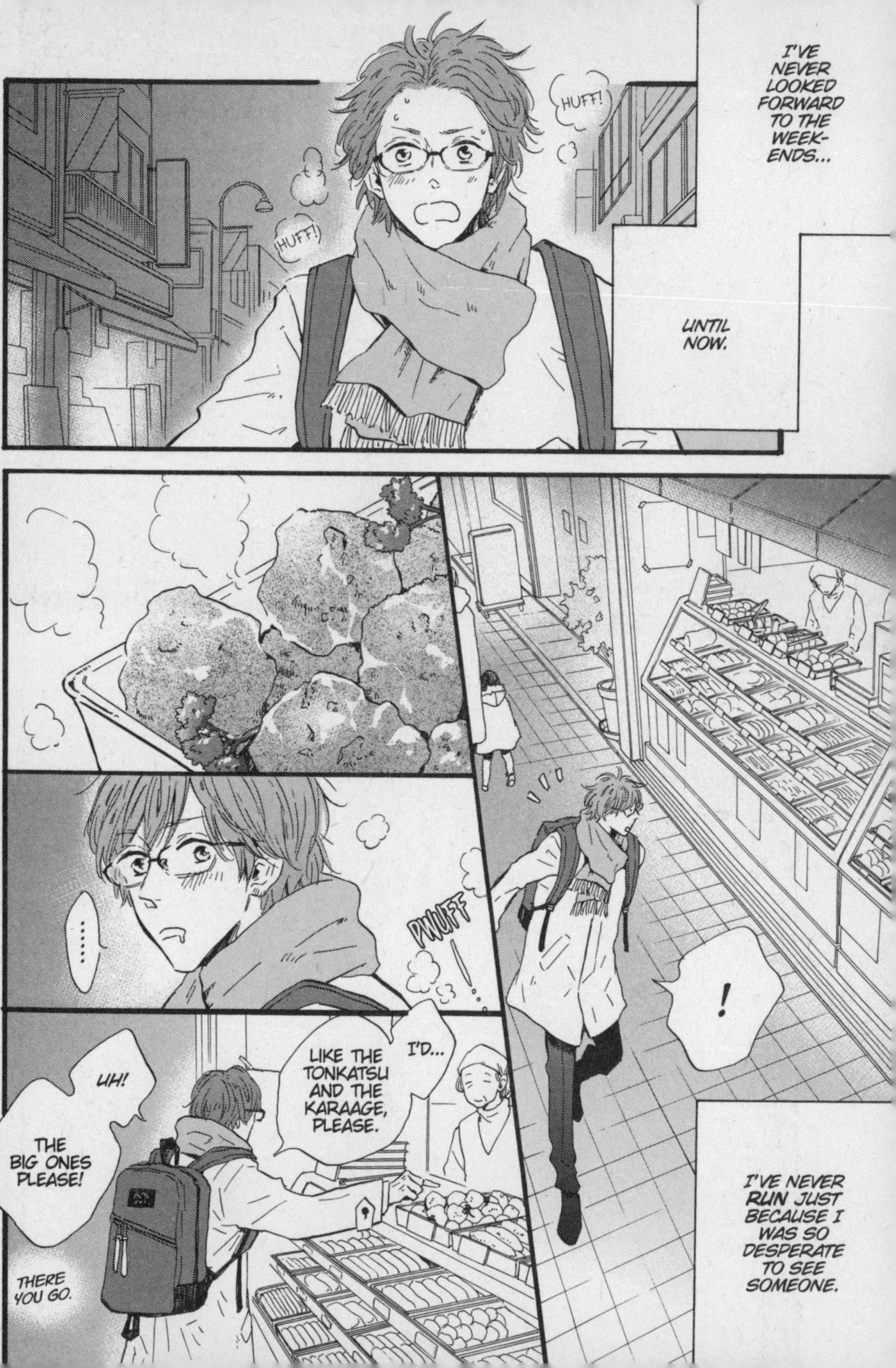
I'VE NEVER LOOKED FORWARD TO THE WEEK-ENDS...
UNTIL NOW.
HUFF!
HUFF!
!
I'VE NEVER RUN JUST BECAUSE I WAS SO DESPERATE TO SEE SOMEONE.
......
PWUFF
I'D...
LIKE THE TONKATSU AND THE KARAAGE, PLEASE.
UH!
THE BIG ONES PLEASE!
THERE YOU GO.

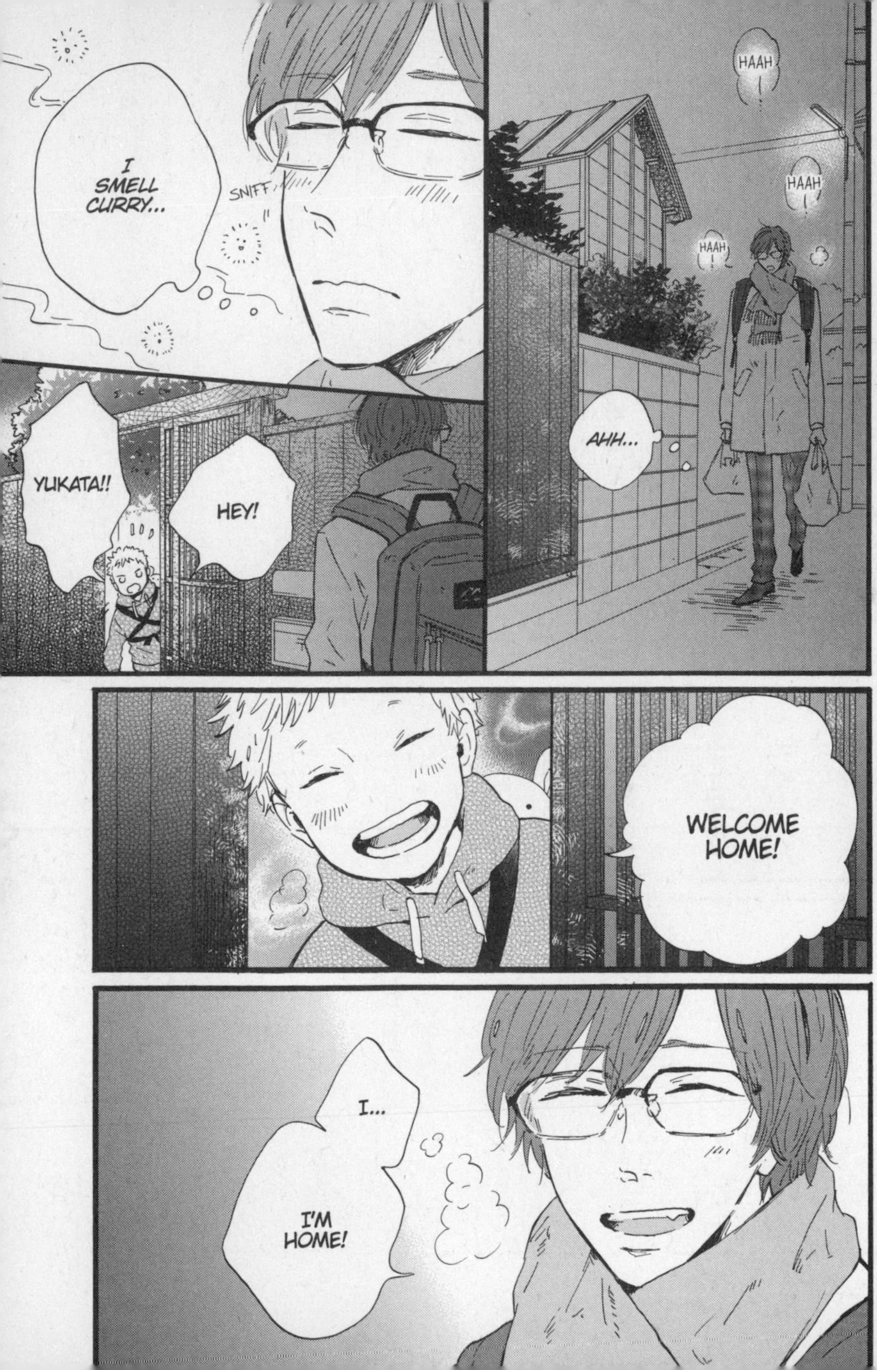
HAAH
HAAH
HAAH
AHH...
SNIFF
I SMELL CURRY...
HEY!
YUKATA!!
WELCOME HOME!
I...
I'M HOME!

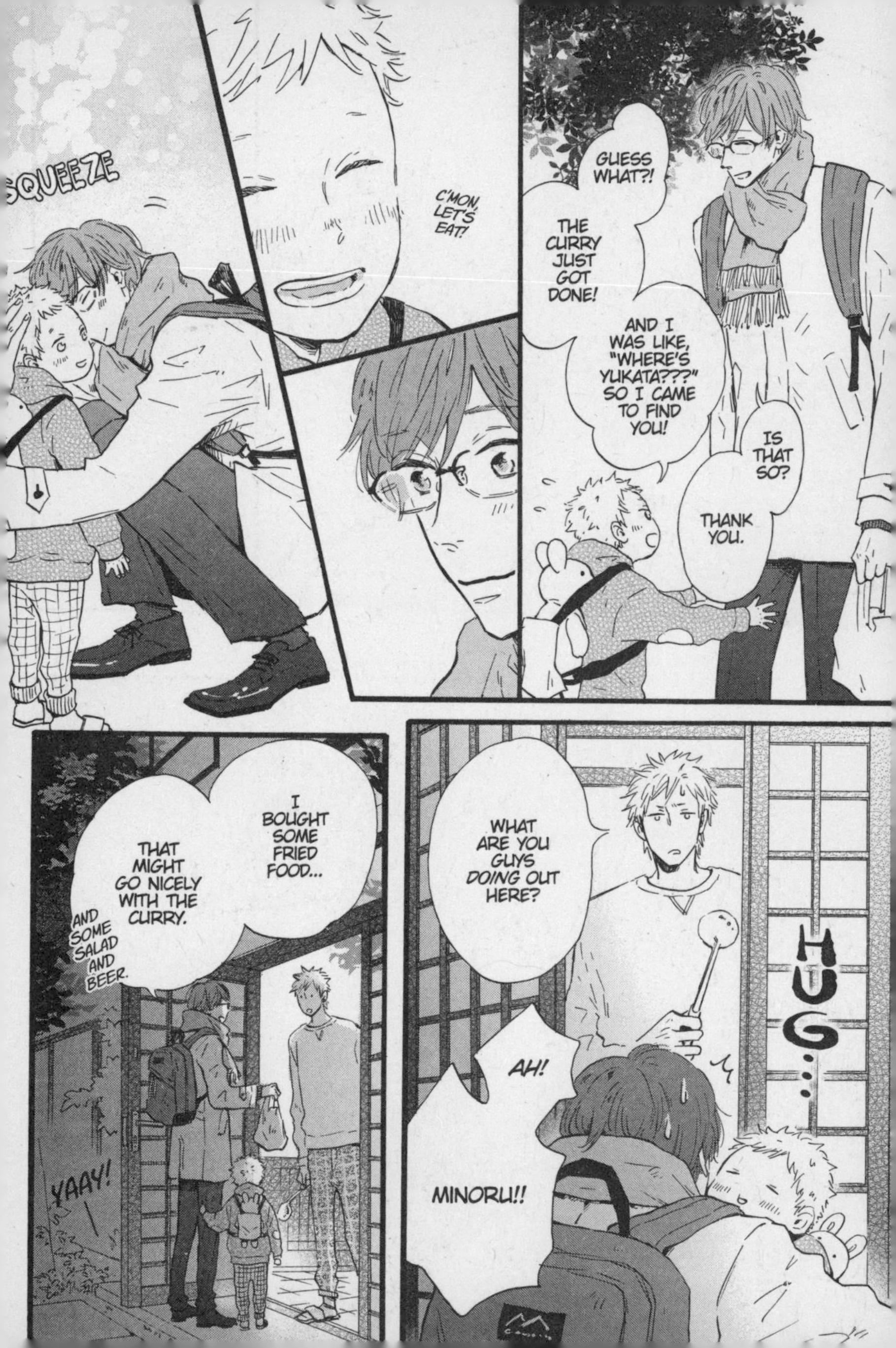
GUESS WHAT?!
THE CURRY JUST GOT DONE!
AND I WAS LIKE, "WHERE'S YUKATA???" SO I CAME TO FIND YOU!
IS THAT SO?
THANK YOU.
C'MON, LET'S EAT!
SQUEEZE
WHAT ARE YOU GUYS DOING OUT HERE?
HUG...
AH!
MINORU!!
I BOUGHT SOME FRIED FOOD...
THAT MIGHT GO NICELY WITH THE CURRY.
AND SOME SALAD AND BEER.
YAAY!

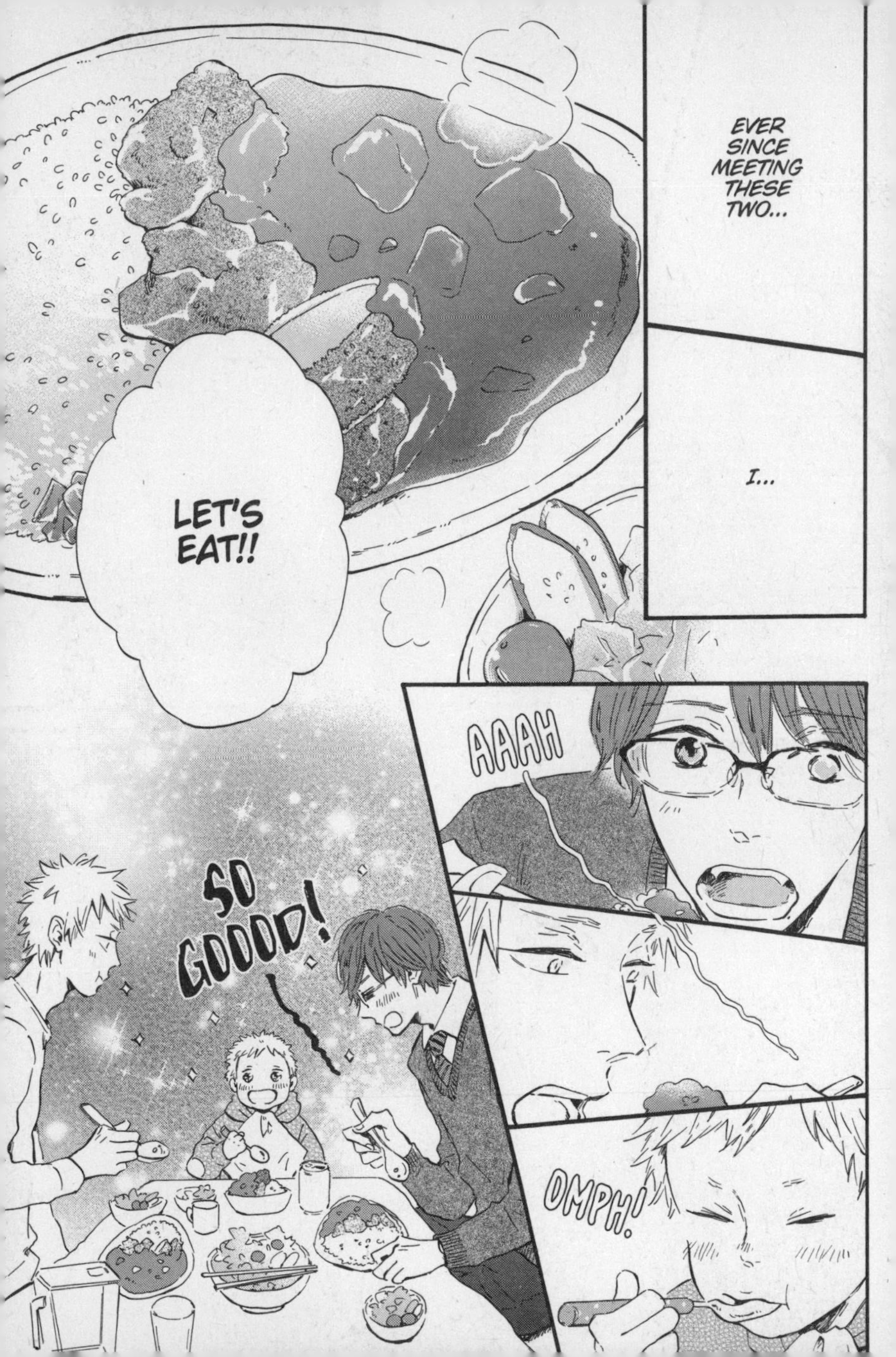
EVER SINCE MEETING THESE TWO...
I...
LET'S EAT!!
AAAH
OMPH!
SO GOOOD!

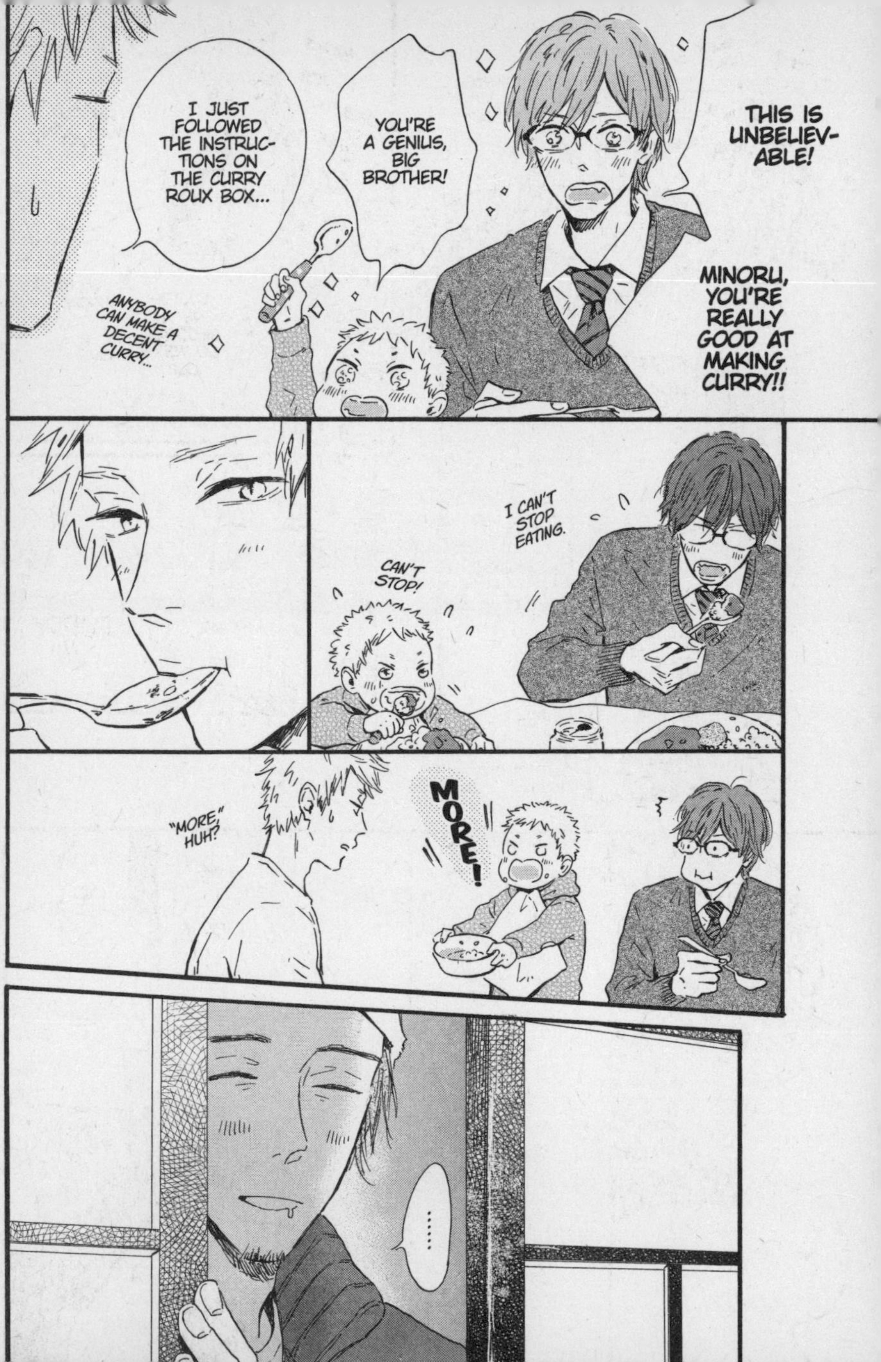
THIS IS UNBELIEV-ABLE!
MINORU, YOU'RE REALLY GOOD AT MAKING CURRY!!
YOU'RE A GENIUS, BIG BROTHER!
I JUST FOLLOWED THE INSTRUC-TIONS ON THE CURRY ROUX BOX...
ANYBODY CAN MAKE A DECENT CURRY...
I CAN'T STOP EATING.
CAN'T STOP!
MORE!
"MORE" HUH?
......

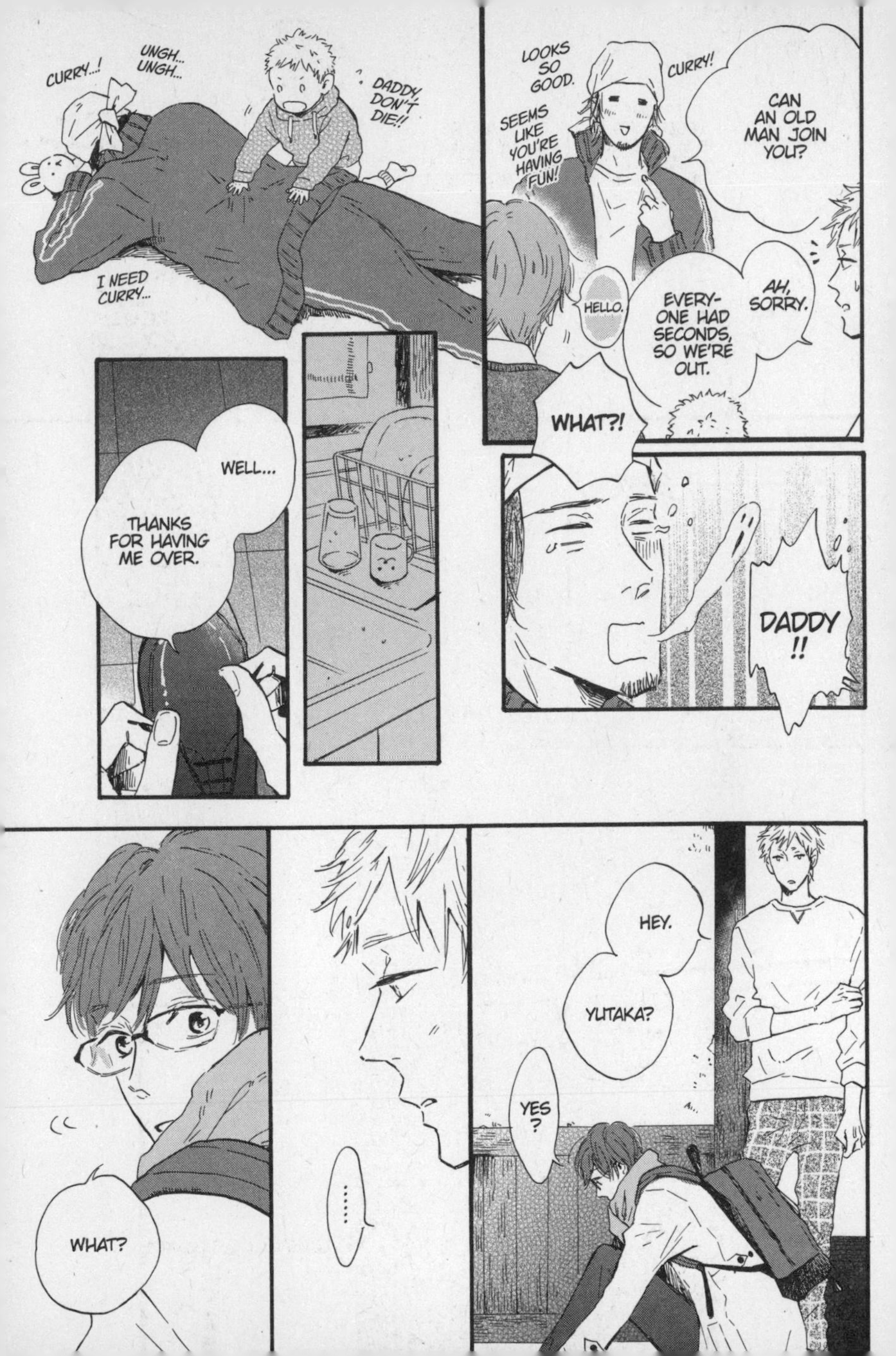
CAN AN OLD MAN JOIN YOU?
CURRY!
LOOKS SO GOOD.
SEEMS LIKE YOU'RE HAVING FUN!
AH, SORRY.
EVERY-ONE HAD SECONDS, SO WE'RE OUT.
HELLO.
WHAT?!
DADDY!!
DADDY, DON'T DIE!!
UNGH... UNGH...
CURRY...!
I NEED CURRY...
WELL...
THANKS FOR HAVING ME OVER.
HEY.
YUTAKA?
YES?
......
WHAT?

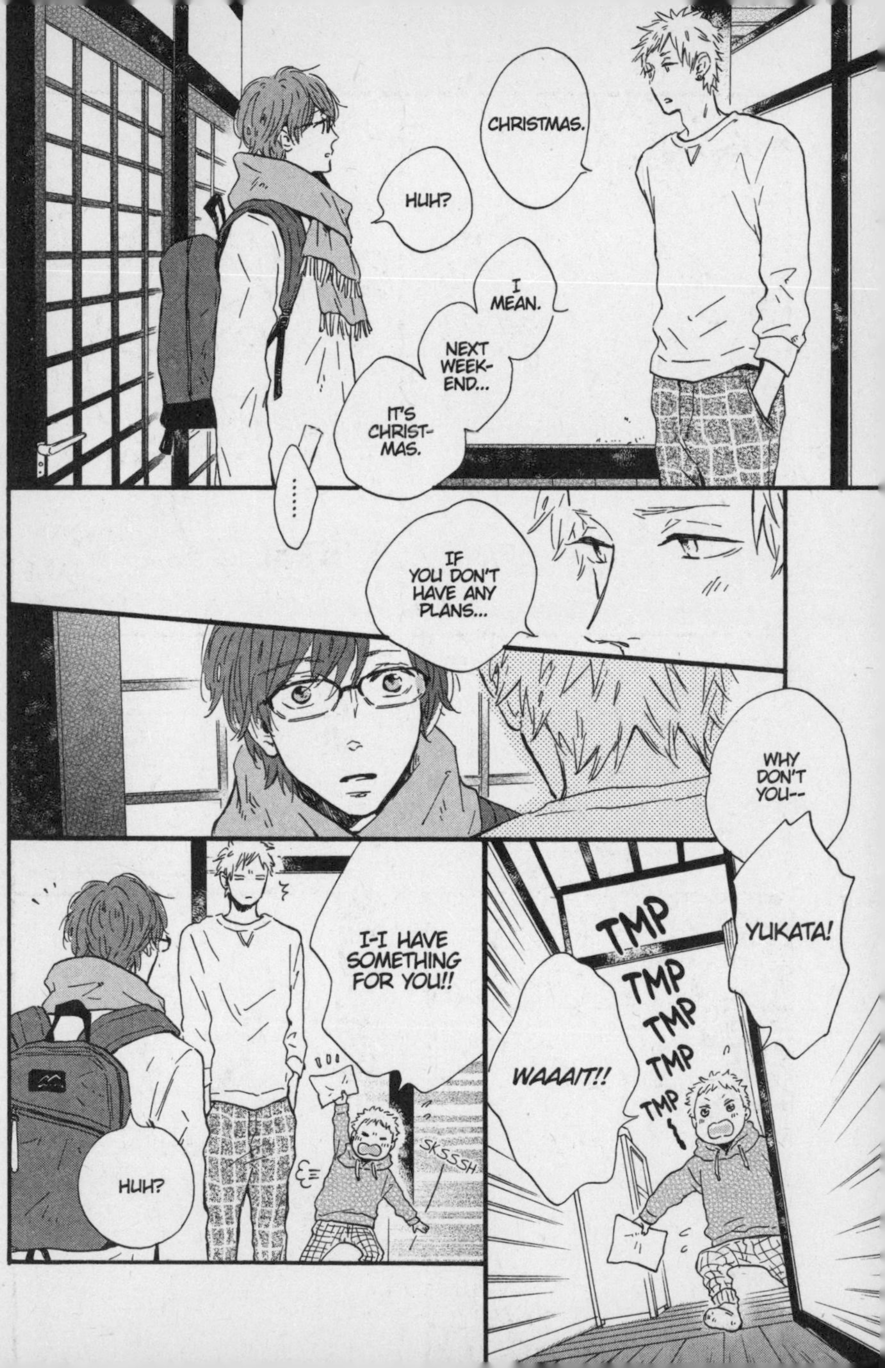
CHRISTMAS.
HUH?
I MEAN.
NEXT WEEK-END...
IT'S CHRIST-MAS.
......
IF YOU DON'T HAVE ANY PLANS...
WHY DON'T YOU--
YUKATA!
TMP TMP TMP TMP TMP
WAAAIT!!
I-I HAVE SOMETHING FOR YOU!!
SKSSSH
HUH?

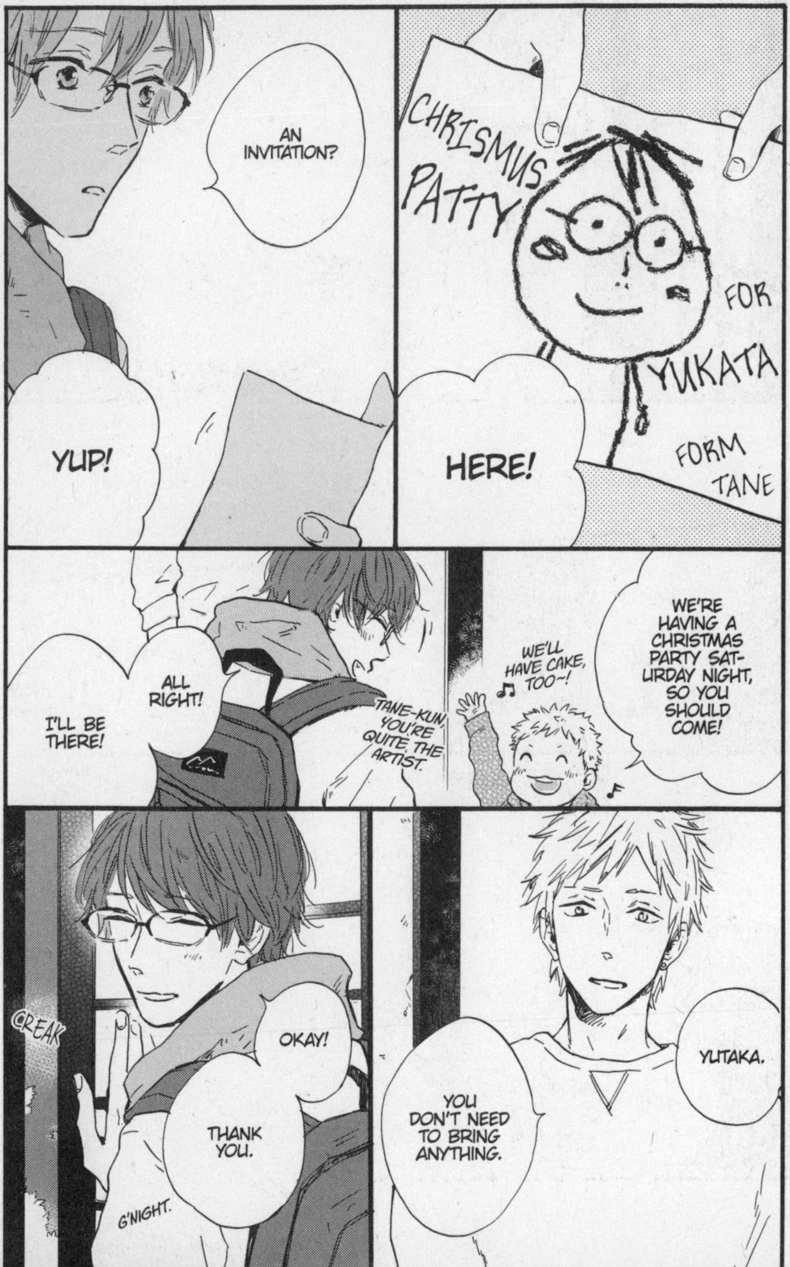
CHRISMUS PATTY
FOR YUKATA
FORM TANE
HERE!
AN INVITATION?
YUP!
WE'RE HAVING A CHRISTMAS PARTY SAT-URDAY NIGHT, SO YOU SHOULD COME!
WE'LL HAVE CAKE, TOO~!
TANE-KUN, YOU'RE QUITE THE ARTIST.
ALL RIGHT!
I'LL BE THERE!
YUTAKA.
YOU DON'T NEED TO BRING ANYTHING.
OKAY!
THANK YOU.
CREAK
G'NIGHT.

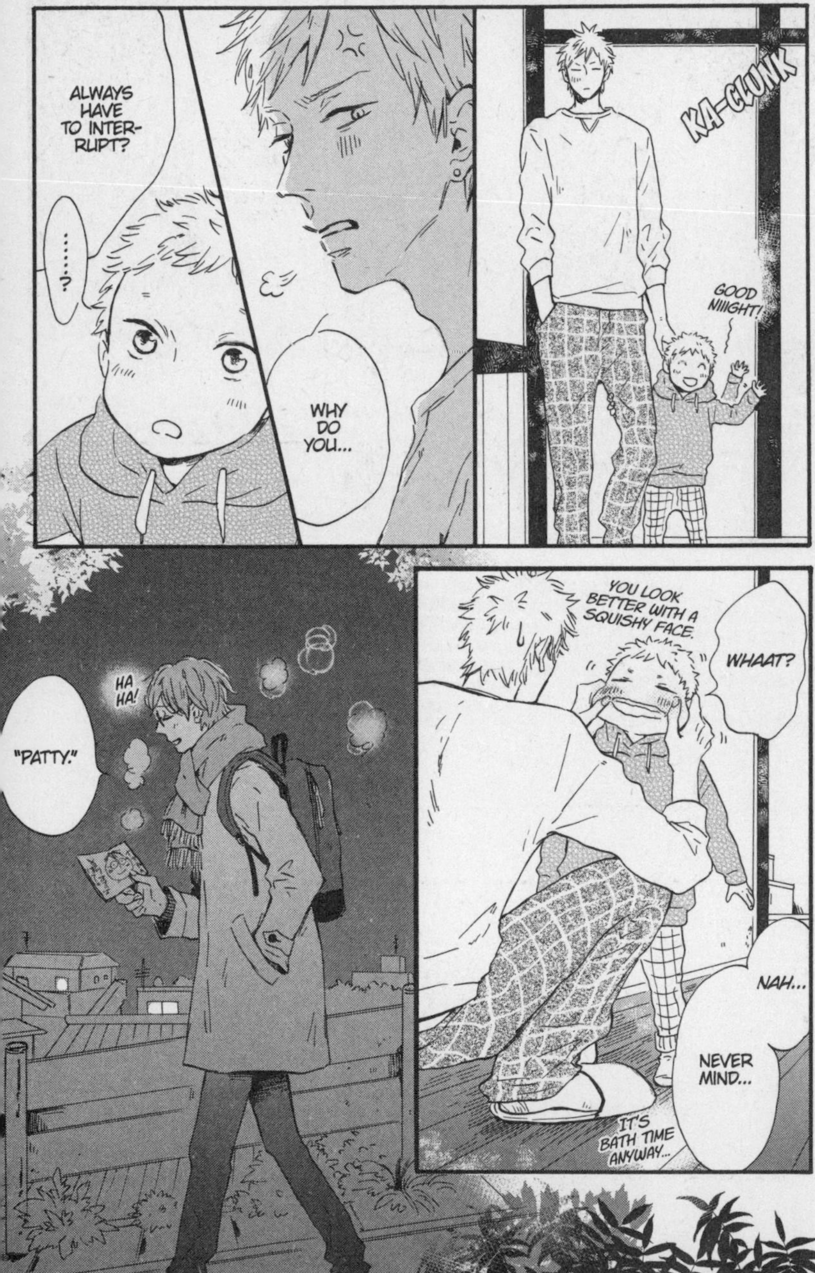

KA-CLUNK
GOOD NIIIGHT!
WHY DO YOU...
ALWAYS HAVE TO INTER-RUPT?
......?
YOU LOOK BETTER WITH A SQUISHY FACE.
WHAAT?
NAH...
NEVER MIND...
IT'S BATH TIME ANYWAY...
HA HA!
"PATTY."

I'M SO EXCITED!

THIS MIGHT BE THE FIRST TIME I'VE HAD PLANS ON CHRISTMAS...

HUFF!

I DON'T THINK...

I'VE EVER BEEN THIS CLOSE TO ANYONE.

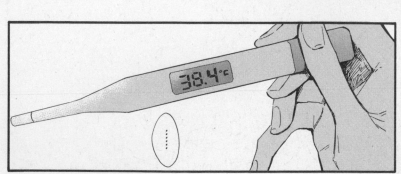

38.4℃

.....

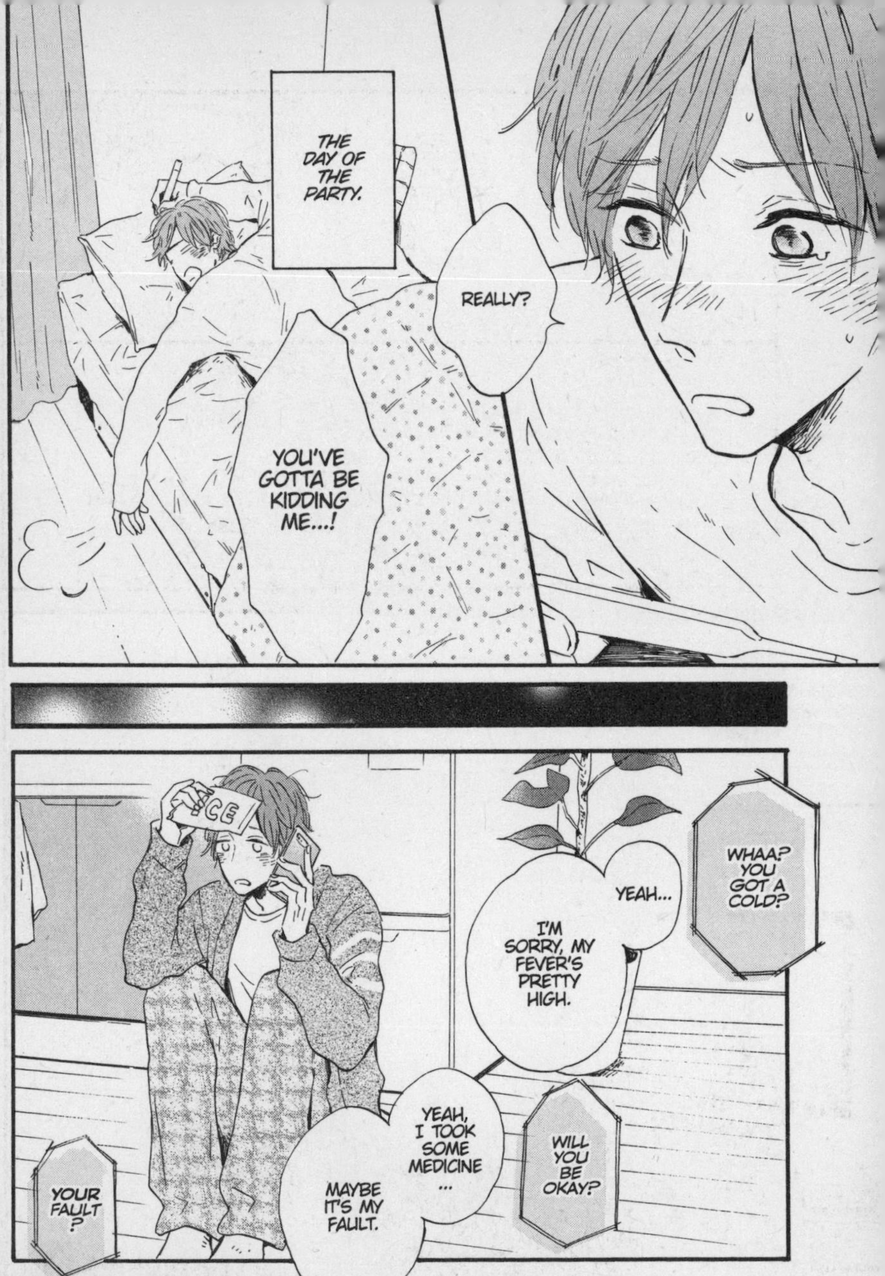
REALLY?
THE DAY OF THE PARTY.
YOU'VE GOTTA BE KIDDING ME...!
WHAA? YOU GOT A COLD?
YEAH...
I'M SORRY, MY FEVER'S PRETTY HIGH.
WILL YOU BE OKAY?
YEAH, I TOOK SOME MEDICINE ...
MAYBE IT'S MY FAULT.
YOUR FAULT?

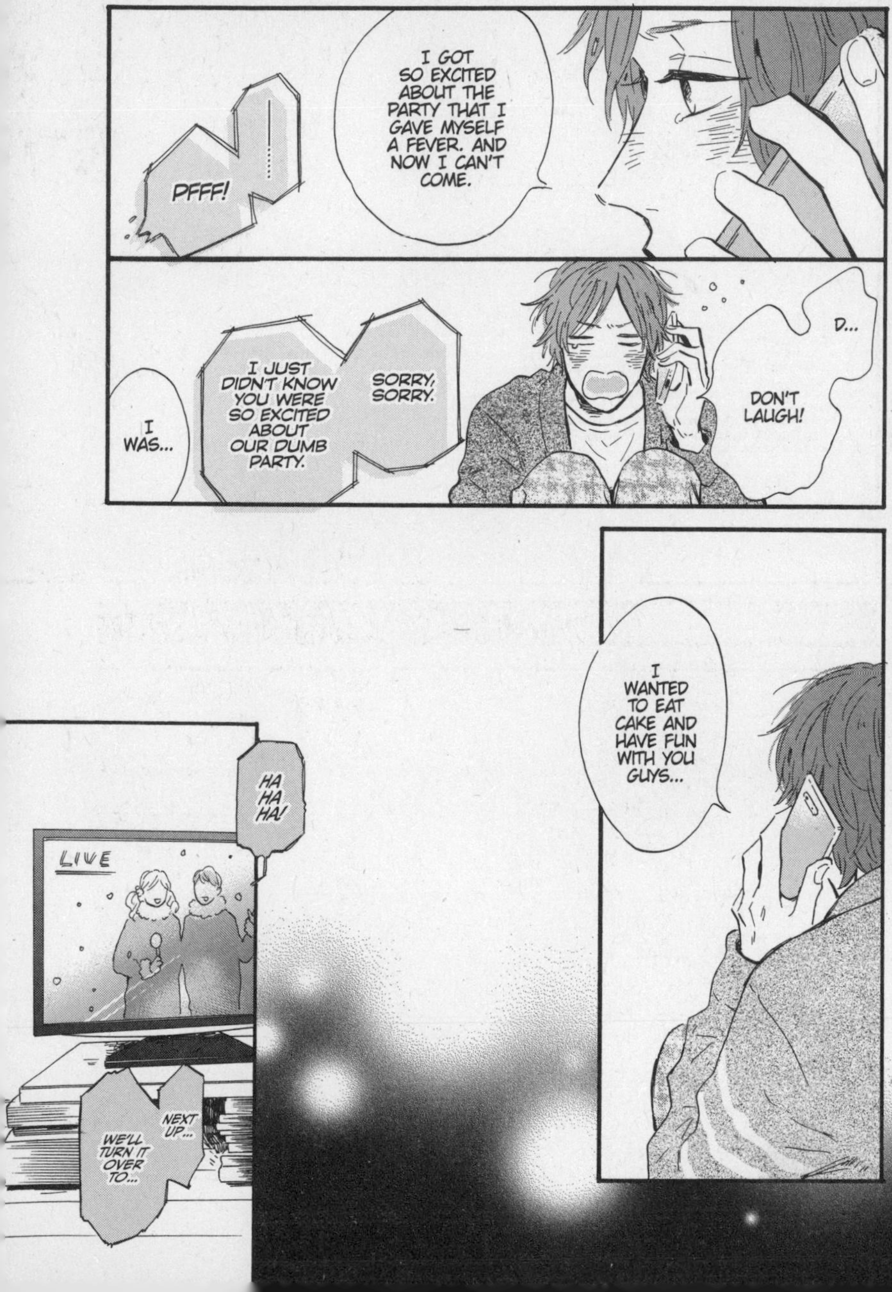
I GOT SO EXCITED ABOUT THE PARTY THAT I GAVE MYSELF A FEVER. AND NOW I CAN'T COME.
......
PFFF!
D...
DON'T LAUGH!
SORRY, SORRY.
I JUST DIDN'T KNOW YOU WERE SO EXCITED ABOUT OUR DUMB PARTY.
I WAS...
I WANTED TO EAT CAKE AND HAVE FUN WITH YOU GUYS...
HA HA HA!
LIVE
NEXT UP...
WE'LL TURN IT OVER TO...

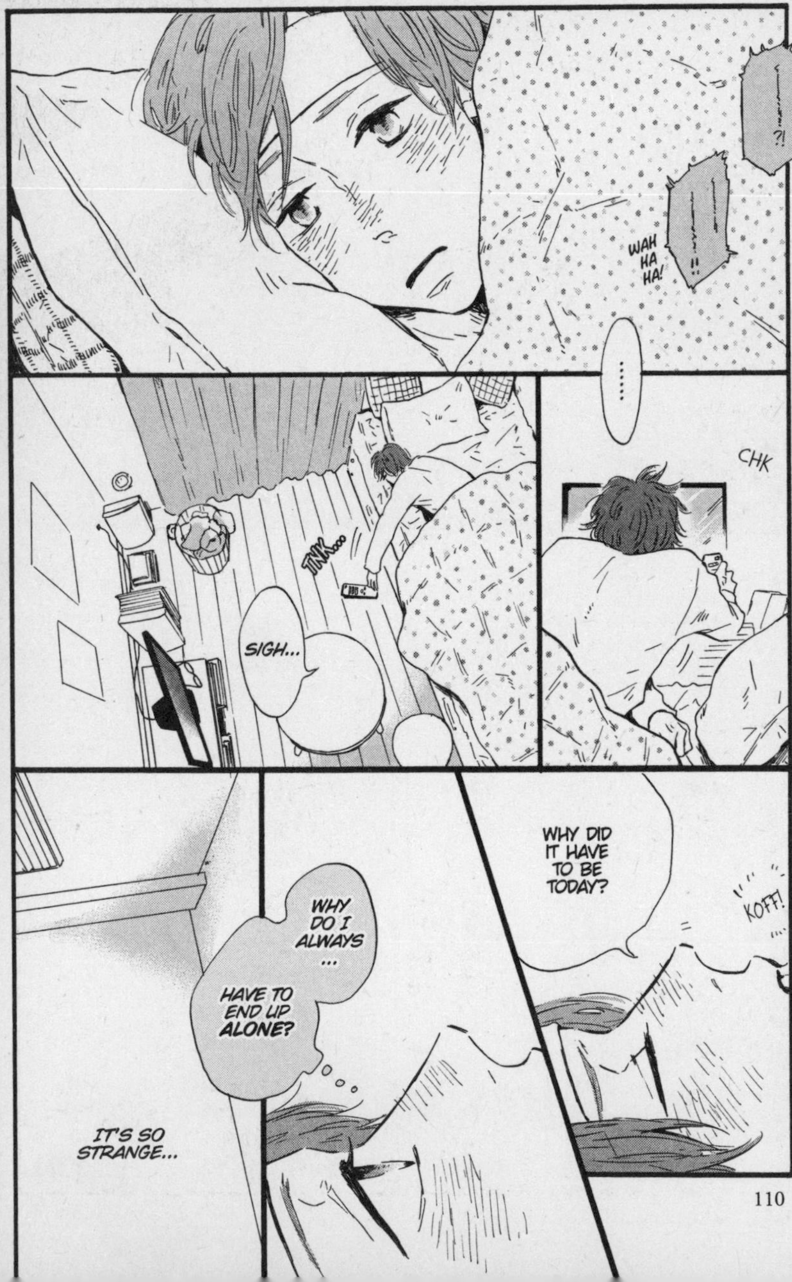

—?!
—!!
WAH HA HA!
......
CHK
TNK...
SIGH...
WHY DID IT HAVE TO BE TODAY?
KOFF!
WHY DO I ALWAYS ... HAVE TO END UP ALONE?
IT'S SO STRANGE...

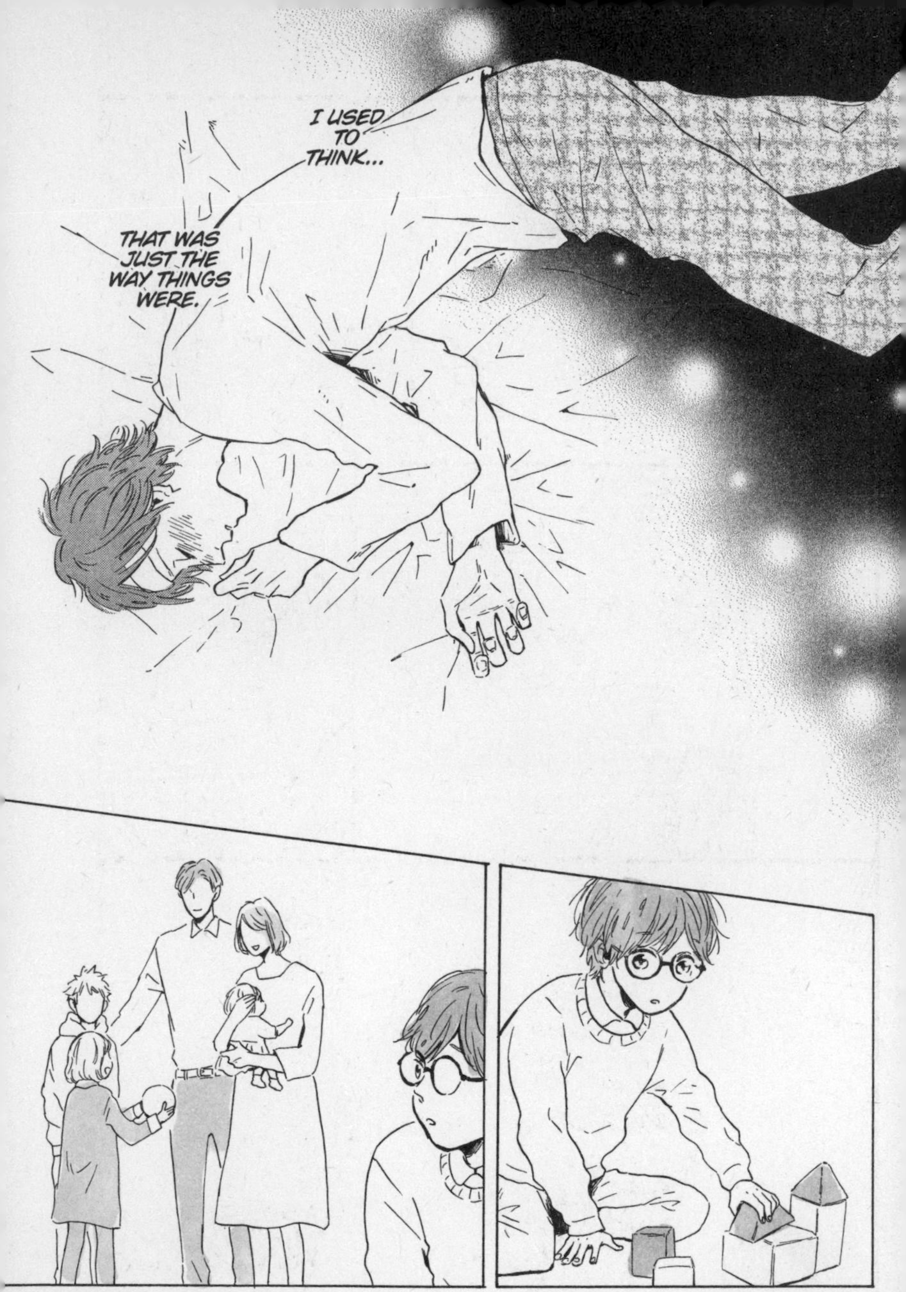
I USED TO THINK...
THAT WAS JUST THE WAY THINGS WERE.

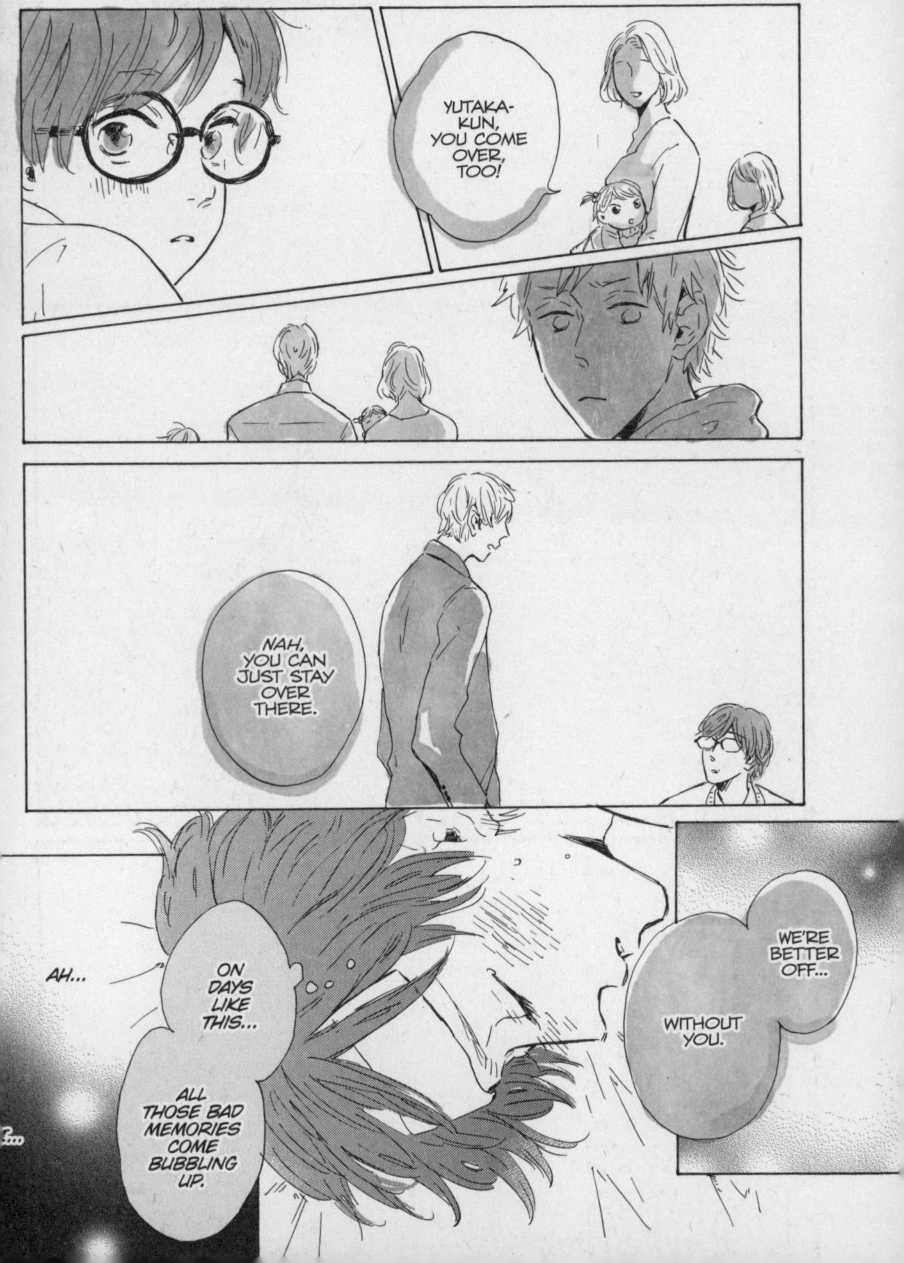
YUTAKA-KUN, YOU COME OVER, TOO!
NAH, YOU CAN JUST STAY OVER THERE.
WE'RE BETTER OFF...
WITHOUT YOU.
AH...
ON DAYS LIKE THIS...
ALL THOSE BAD MEMORIES COME BUBBLING UP.

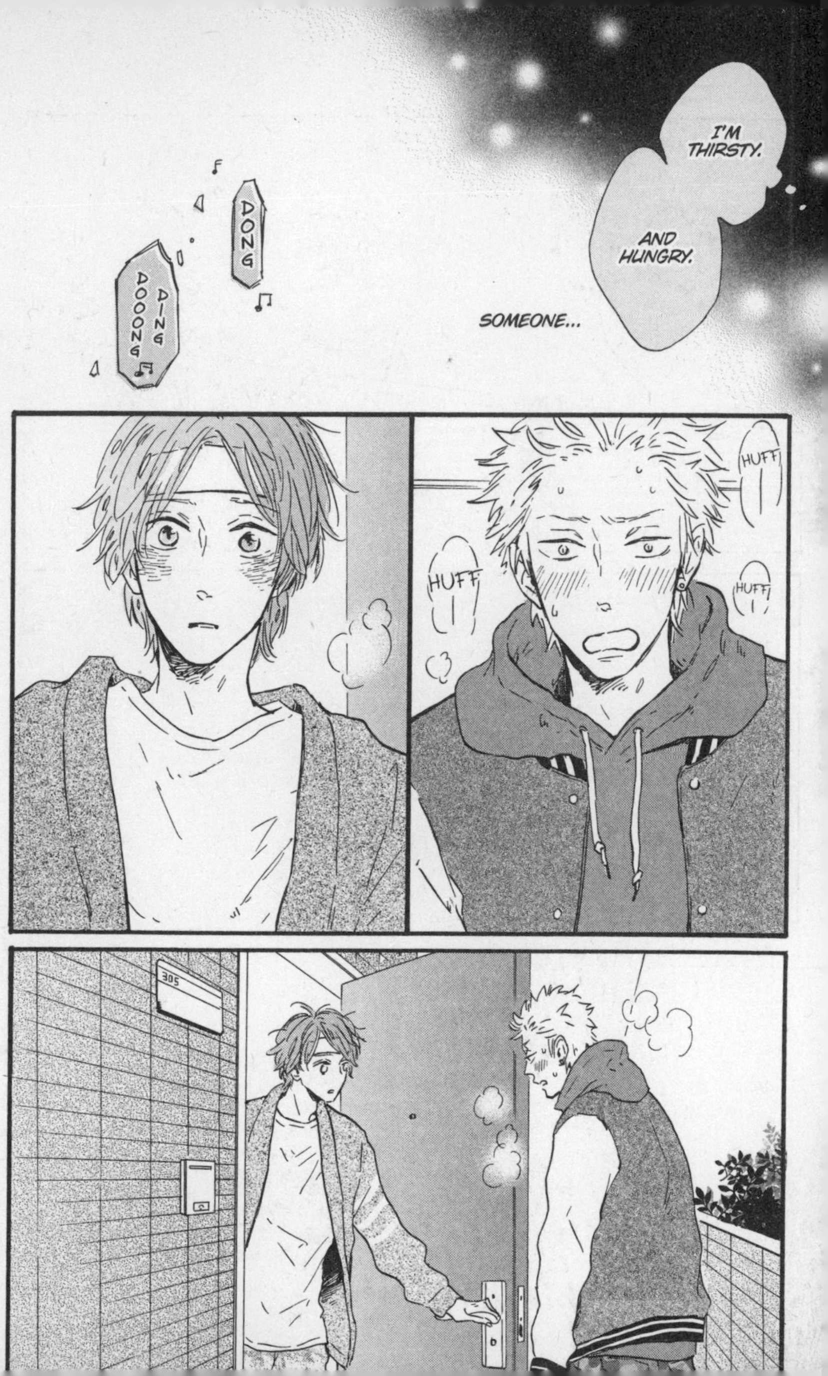
I'M THIRSTY.
AND HUNGRY.
SOMEONE...
DONG
DING DOOOONG
HUFF
HUFF
HUFF

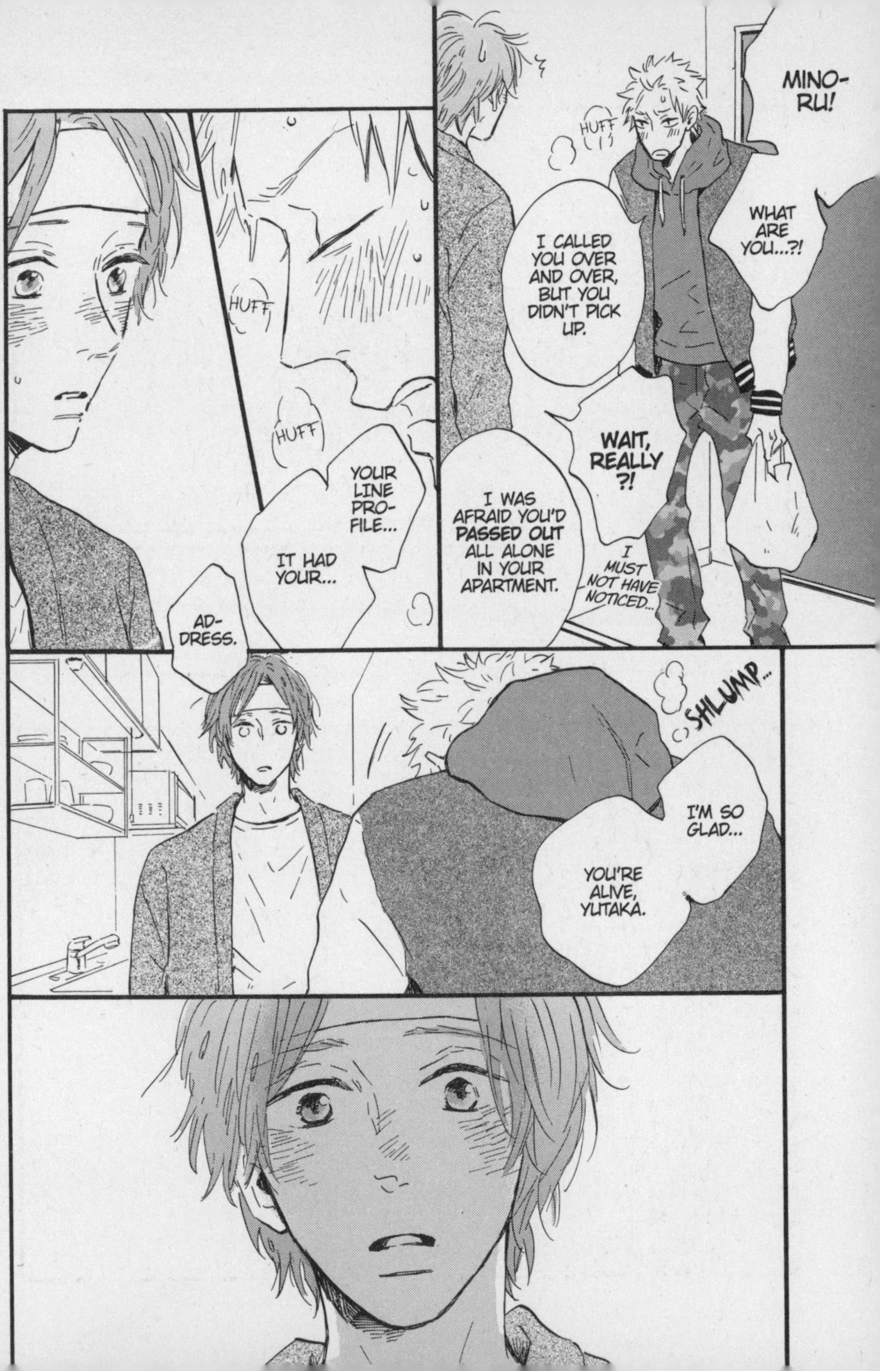
MINO-RU!
HUFF
WHAT ARE YOU...?!
I CALLED YOU OVER AND OVER, BUT YOU DIDN'T PICK UP.
WAIT, REALLY?!
I MUST NOT HAVE NOTICED...
I WAS AFRAID YOU'D PASSED OUT ALL ALONE IN YOUR APARTMENT.
HUFF
HUFF
YOUR LINE PRO-FILE...
IT HAD YOUR...
AD-DRESS.
SHLUMP...
I'M SO GLAD...
YOU'RE ALIVE, YUTAKA.

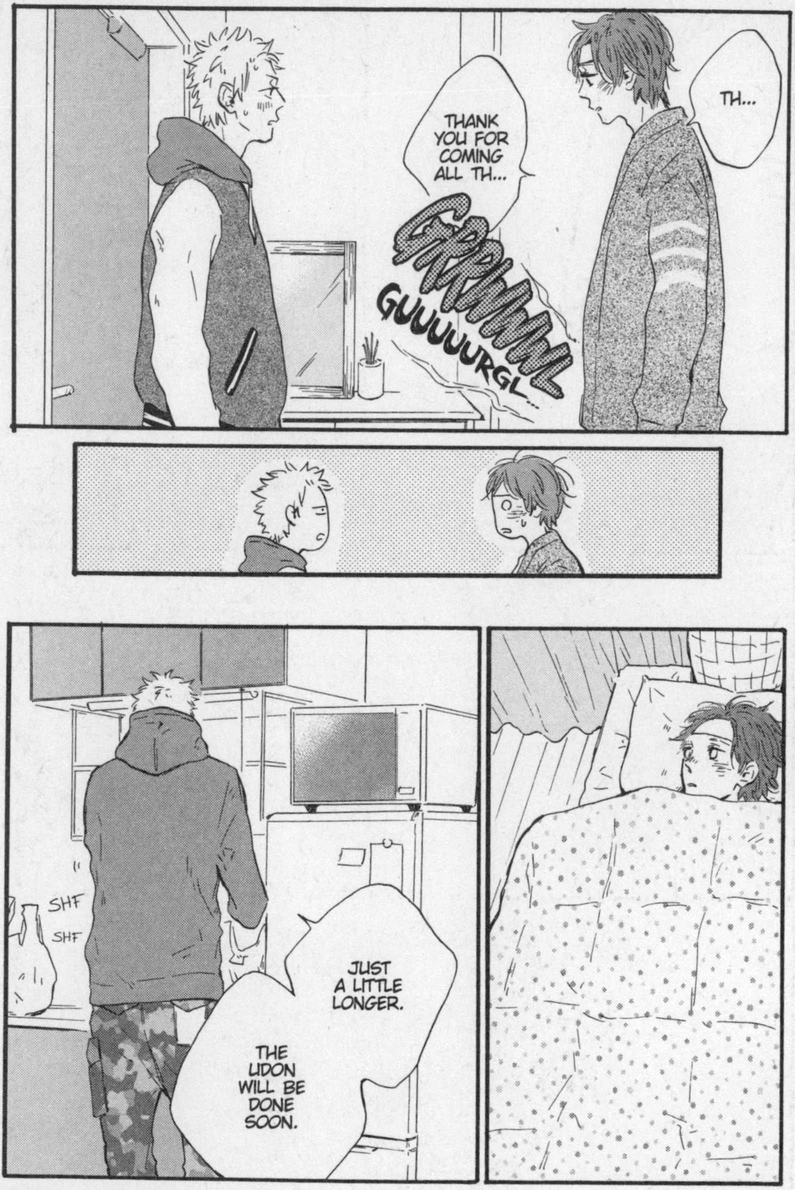
TH...
THANK YOU FOR COMING ALL TH...
GRRWWWL
GUUUUUURGL...
JUST A LITTLE LONGER.
THE UDON WILL BE DONE SOON.
SHF
SHF

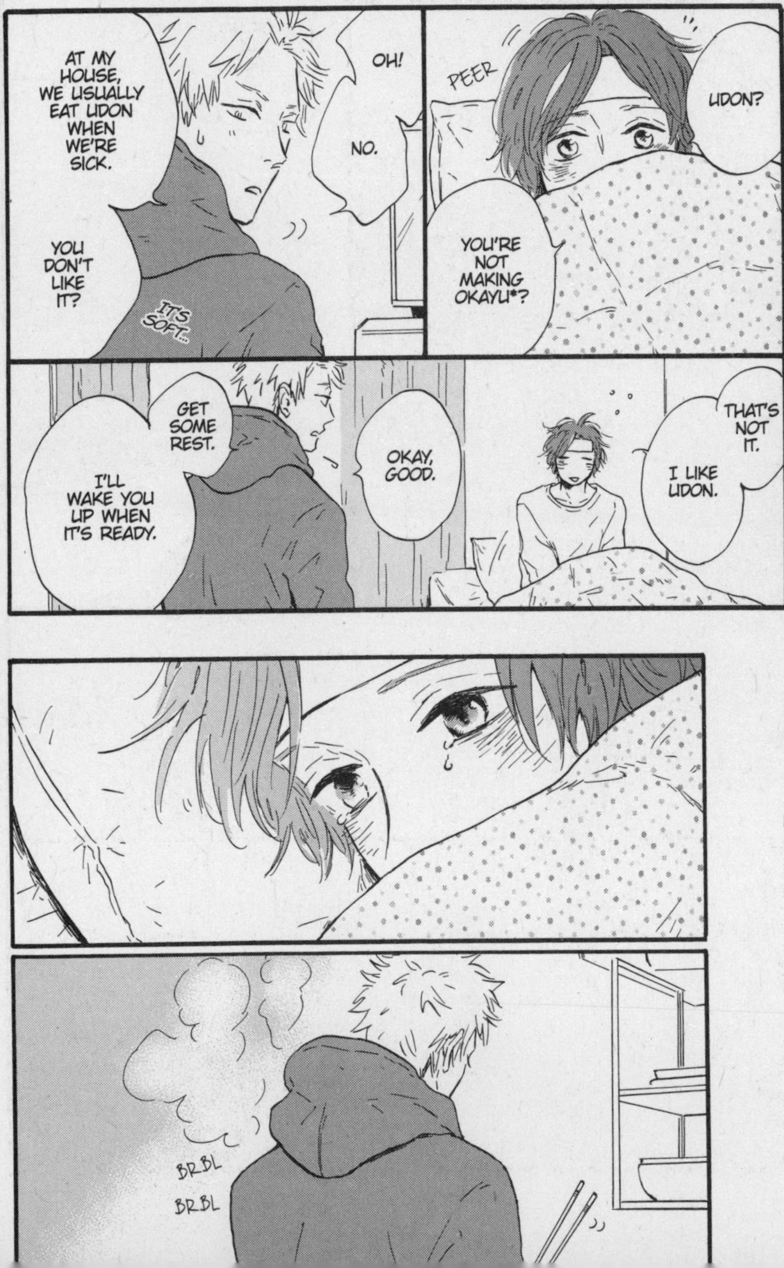
PEER
UDON?
YOU'RE NOT MAKING OKAYU*?
OH!
NO.
AT MY HOUSE, WE USUALLY EAT UDON WHEN WE'RE SICK.
YOU DON'T LIKE IT?
IT'S SOFT...
THAT'S NOT IT.
I LIKE UDON.
OKAY, GOOD.
GET SOME REST.
I'LL WAKE YOU UP WHEN IT'S READY.
BRBL
BRBL

*A type of rice porridge that is often eaten by people when they're sick.

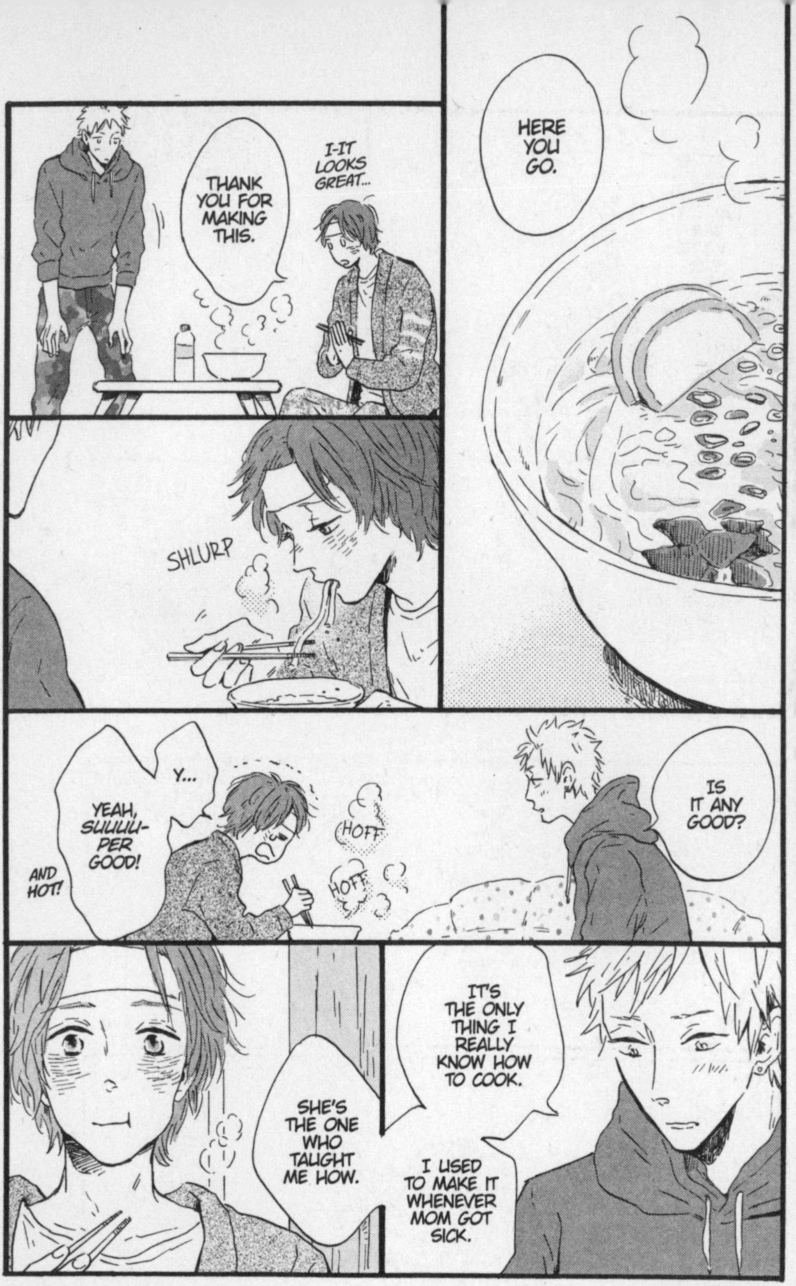
HERE YOU GO.
I-IT LOOKS GREAT...
THANK YOU FOR MAKING THIS.
SHLURP
IS IT ANY GOOD?
HOFF
HOFF
Y...
YEAH, SUUUUU-PER GOOD!
AND HOT!
IT'S THE ONLY THING I REALLY KNOW HOW TO COOK.
I USED TO MAKE IT WHENEVER MOM GOT SICK.
SHE'S THE ONE WHO TAUGHT ME HOW.

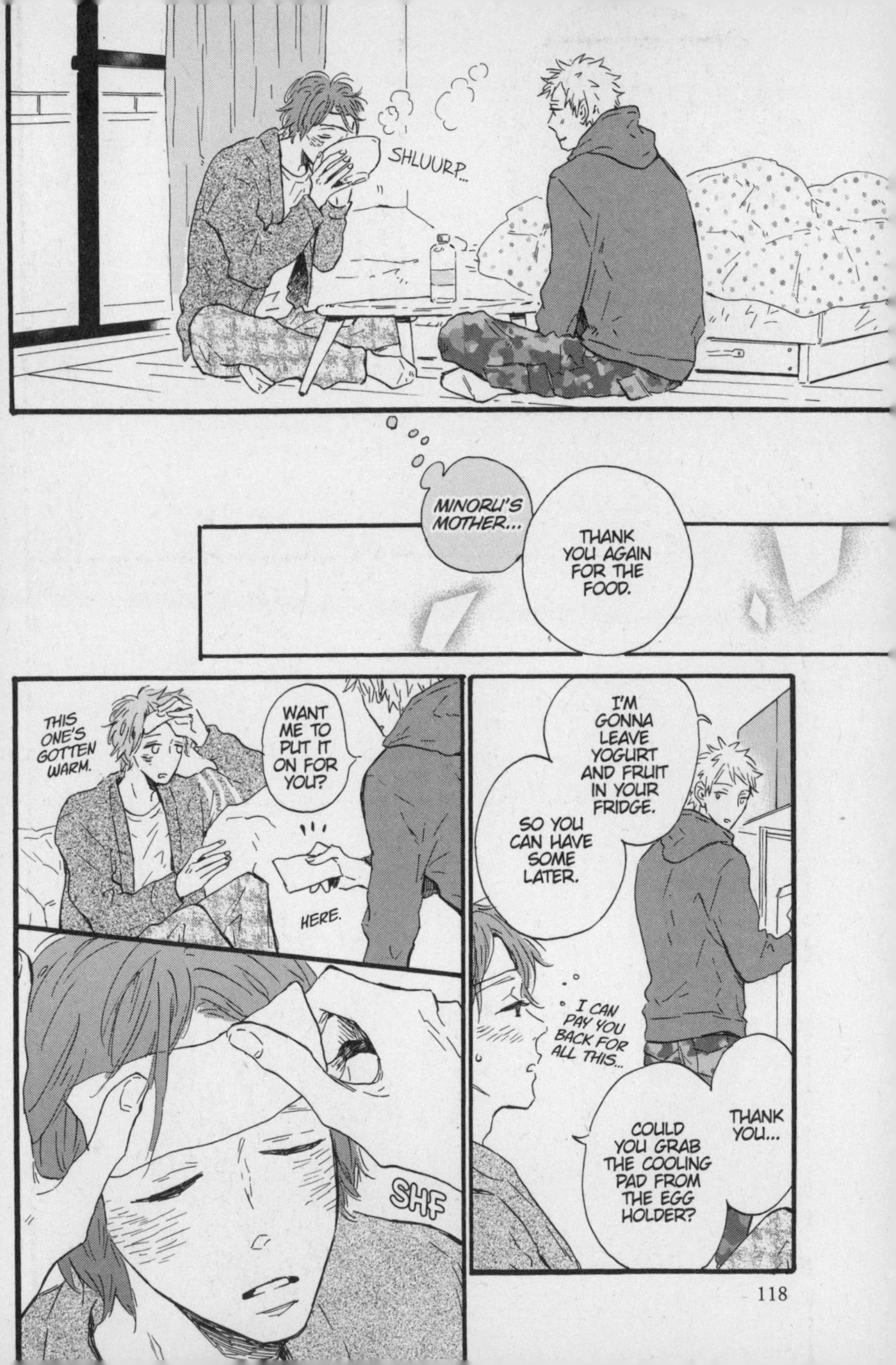
SHLUURP...
THANK YOU AGAIN FOR THE FOOD.
MINORU'S MOTHER...
I'M GONNA LEAVE YOGURT AND FRUIT IN YOUR FRIDGE.
SO YOU CAN HAVE SOME LATER.
I CAN PAY YOU BACK FOR ALL THIS...
THANK YOU...
COULD YOU GRAB THE COOLING PAD FROM THE EGG HOLDER?
WANT ME TO PUT IT ON FOR YOU?
THIS ONE'S GOTTEN WARM.
HERE.
SHF

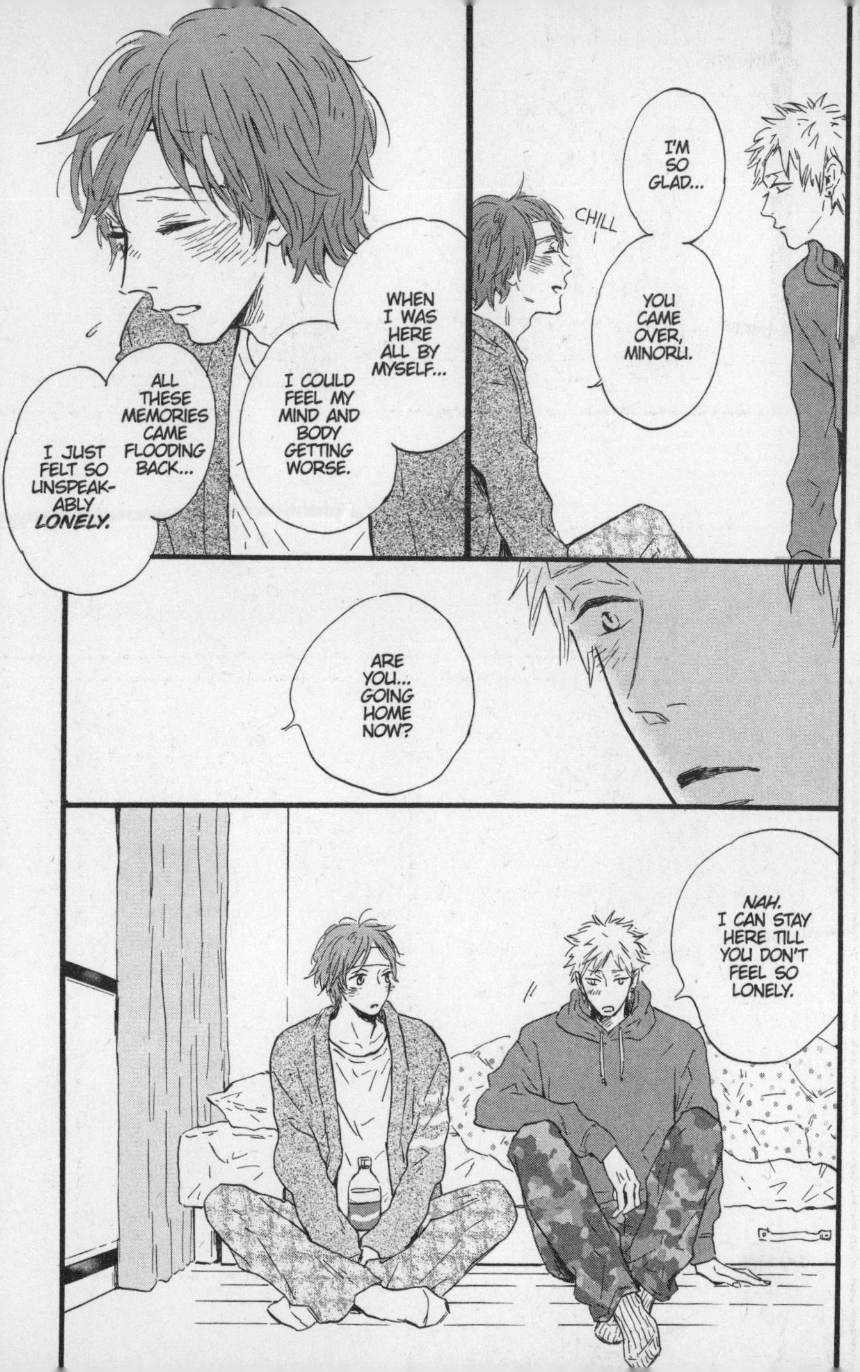
I'M SO GLAD...
CHILL
YOU CAME OVER, MINORU.
WHEN I WAS HERE ALL BY MYSELF...
I COULD FEEL MY MIND AND BODY GETTING WORSE.
ALL THESE MEMORIES CAME FLOODING BACK...
I JUST FELT SO UNSPEAKABLY *LONELY.*
ARE YOU... GOING HOME NOW?
NAH. I CAN STAY HERE TILL YOU DON'T FEEL SO LONELY.

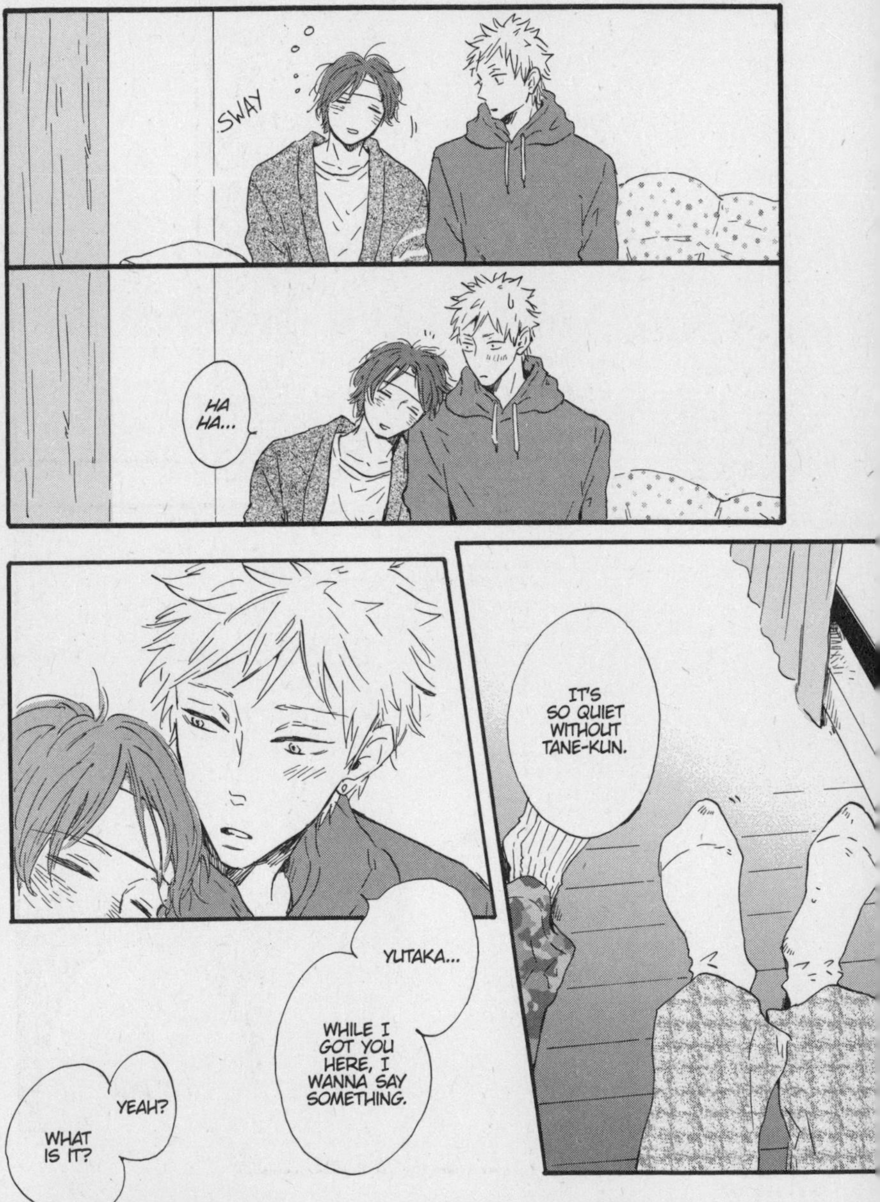
SWAY
HA HA...
IT'S SO QUIET WITHOUT TANE-KUN.
YUTAKA...
WHILE I GOT YOU HERE, I WANNA SAY SOMETHING.
YEAH?
WHAT IS IT?

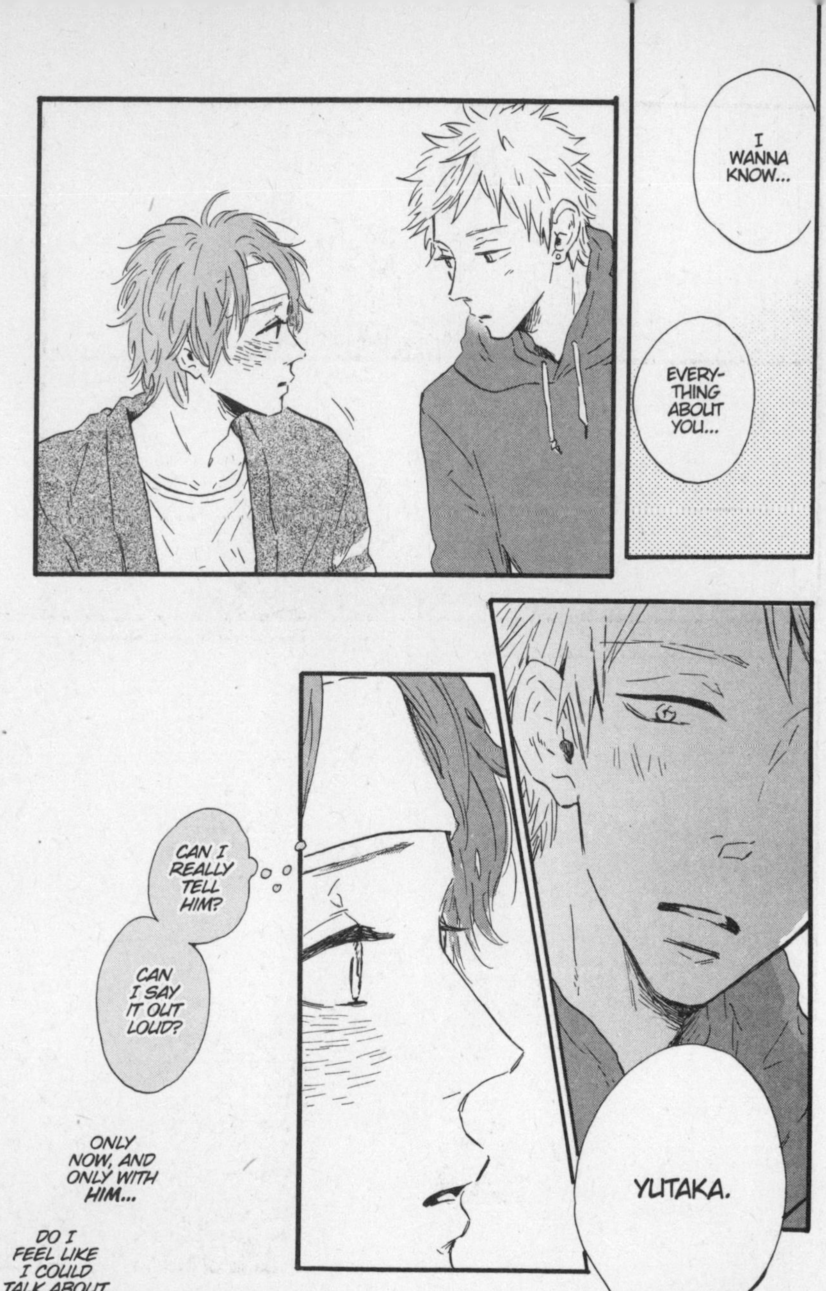
I WANNA KNOW...
EVERYTHING ABOUT YOU...
YUTAKA.
CAN I REALLY TELL HIM?
CAN I SAY IT OUT LOUD?
ONLY NOW, AND ONLY WITH HIM...
DO I FEEL LIKE I COULD TALK ABOUT IT.

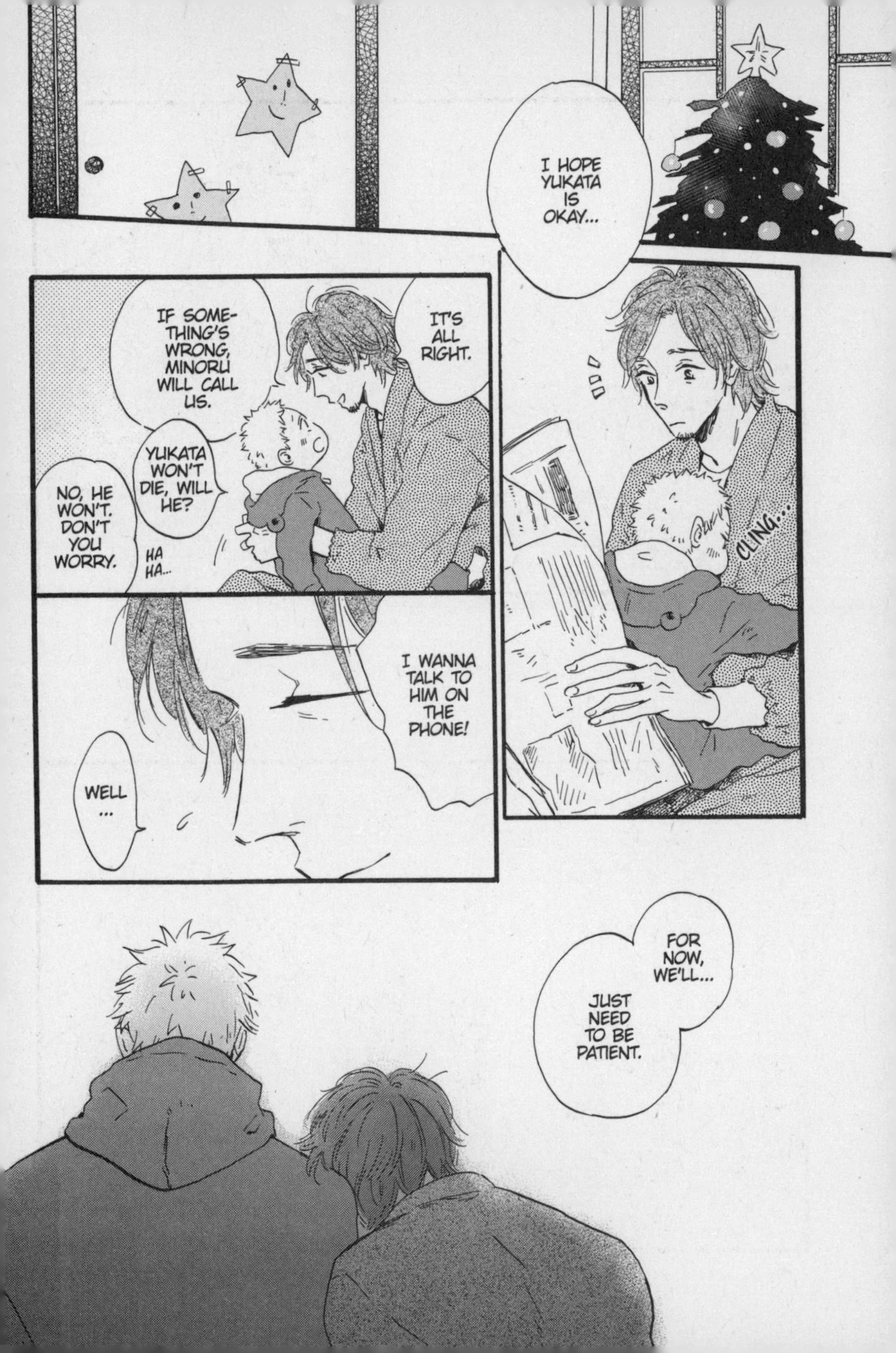
I HOPE YUKATA IS OKAY...
CLING...
IT'S ALL RIGHT.
IF SOME-THING'S WRONG, MINORU WILL CALL US.
YUKATA WON'T DIE, WILL HE?
HA HA...
NO, HE WON'T. DON'T YOU WORRY.
I WANNA TALK TO HIM ON THE PHONE!
WELL ...
FOR NOW, WE'LL...
JUST NEED TO BE PATIENT.

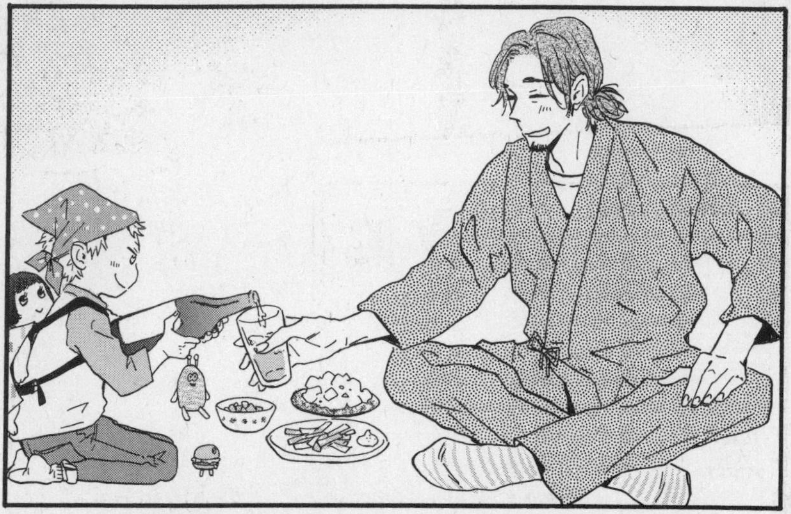

Chapter 4

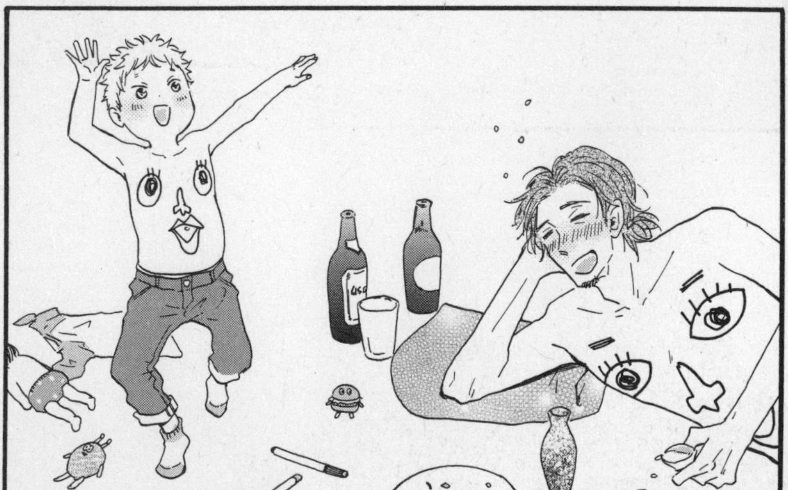

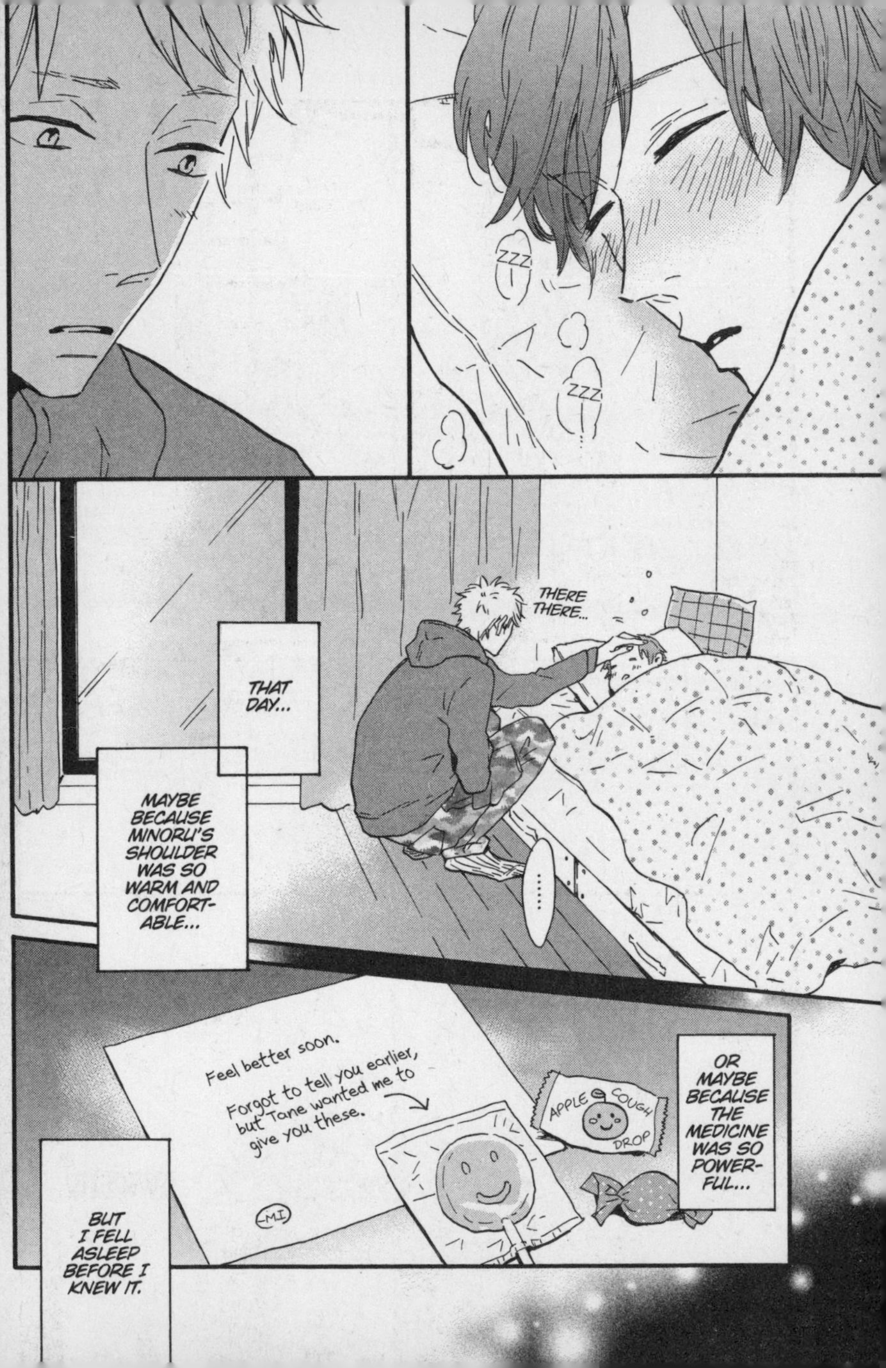
ZZZ
ZZZ
THERE THERE...
THAT DAY...
......
MAYBE BECAUSE MINORU'S SHOULDER WAS SO WARM AND COMFORTABLE...
OR MAYBE BECAUSE THE MEDICINE WAS SO POWERFUL...
Feel better soon.
Forgot to tell you earlier, but Tane wanted me to give you these.
APPLE COUGH DROP
-MI
BUT I FELL ASLEEP BEFORE I KNEW IT.

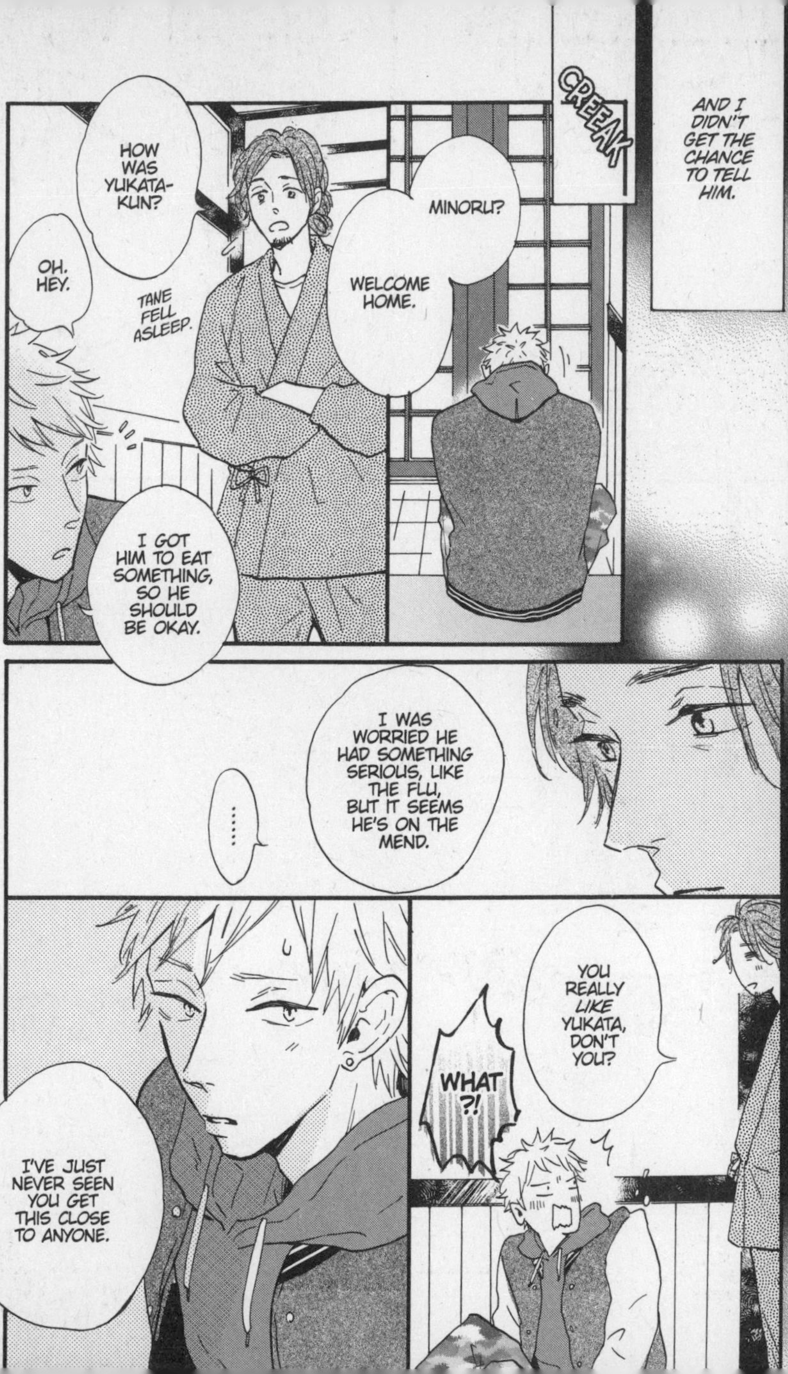
AND I DIDN'T GET THE CHANCE TO TELL HIM.
CREEAK
MINORU?
WELCOME HOME.
HOW WAS YUKATA-KUN?
OH. HEY.
TANE FELL ASLEEP.
I GOT HIM TO EAT SOMETHING, SO HE SHOULD BE OKAY.
I WAS WORRIED HE HAD SOMETHING SERIOUS, LIKE THE FLU, BUT IT SEEMS HE'S ON THE MEND.
......
YOU REALLY LIKE YUKATA, DON'T YOU?
WHAT?!
I'VE JUST NEVER SEEN YOU GET THIS CLOSE TO ANYONE.

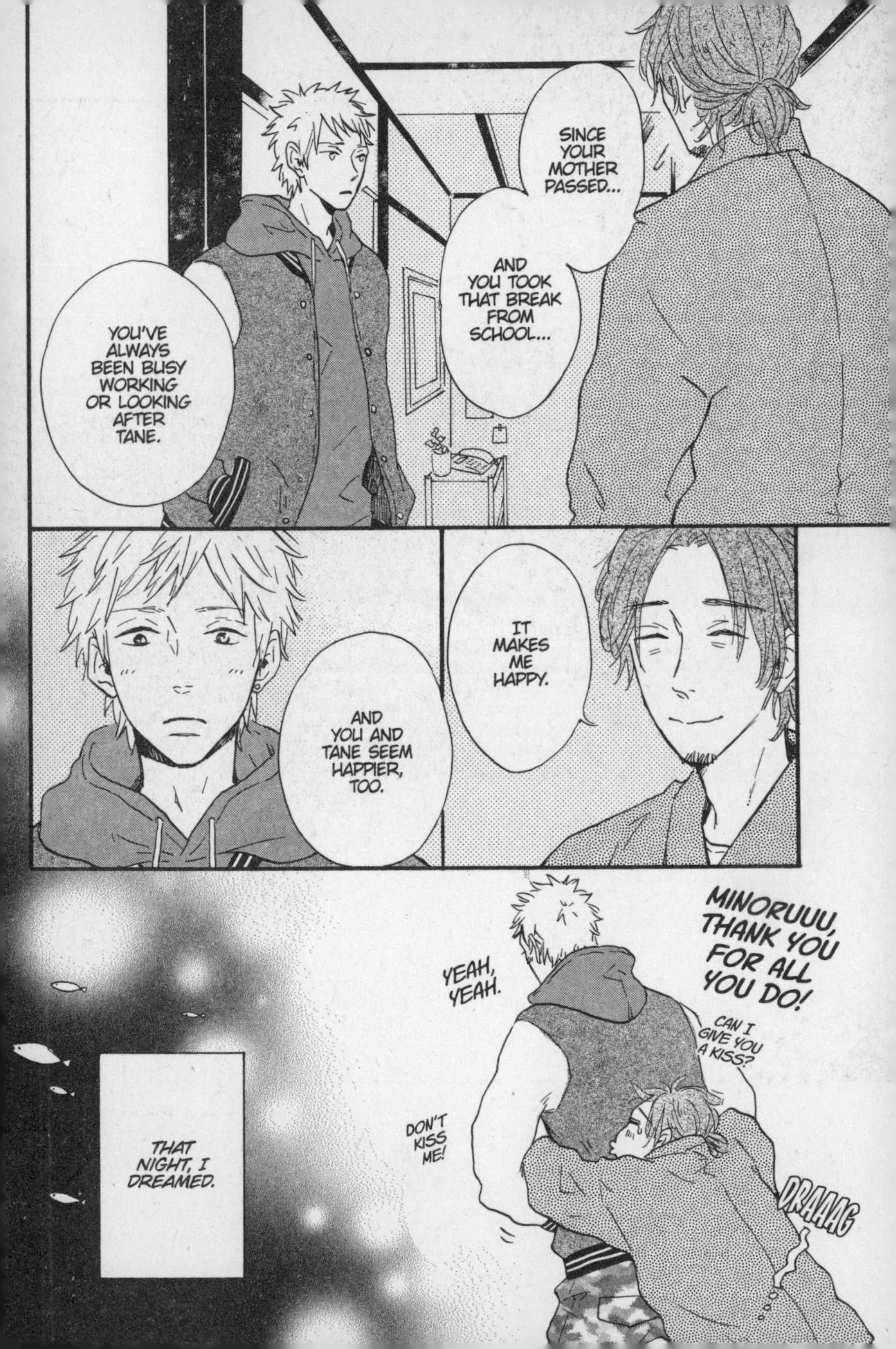
SINCE YOUR MOTHER PASSED...
AND YOU TOOK THAT BREAK FROM SCHOOL...
YOU'VE ALWAYS BEEN BUSY WORKING OR LOOKING AFTER TANE.
IT MAKES ME HAPPY.
AND YOU AND TANE SEEM HAPPIER, TOO.
MINORUUU, THANK YOU FOR ALL YOU DO!
CAN I GIVE YOU A KISS?
YEAH, YEAH.
DON'T KISS ME!
DRAAAG
THAT NIGHT, I DREAMED.

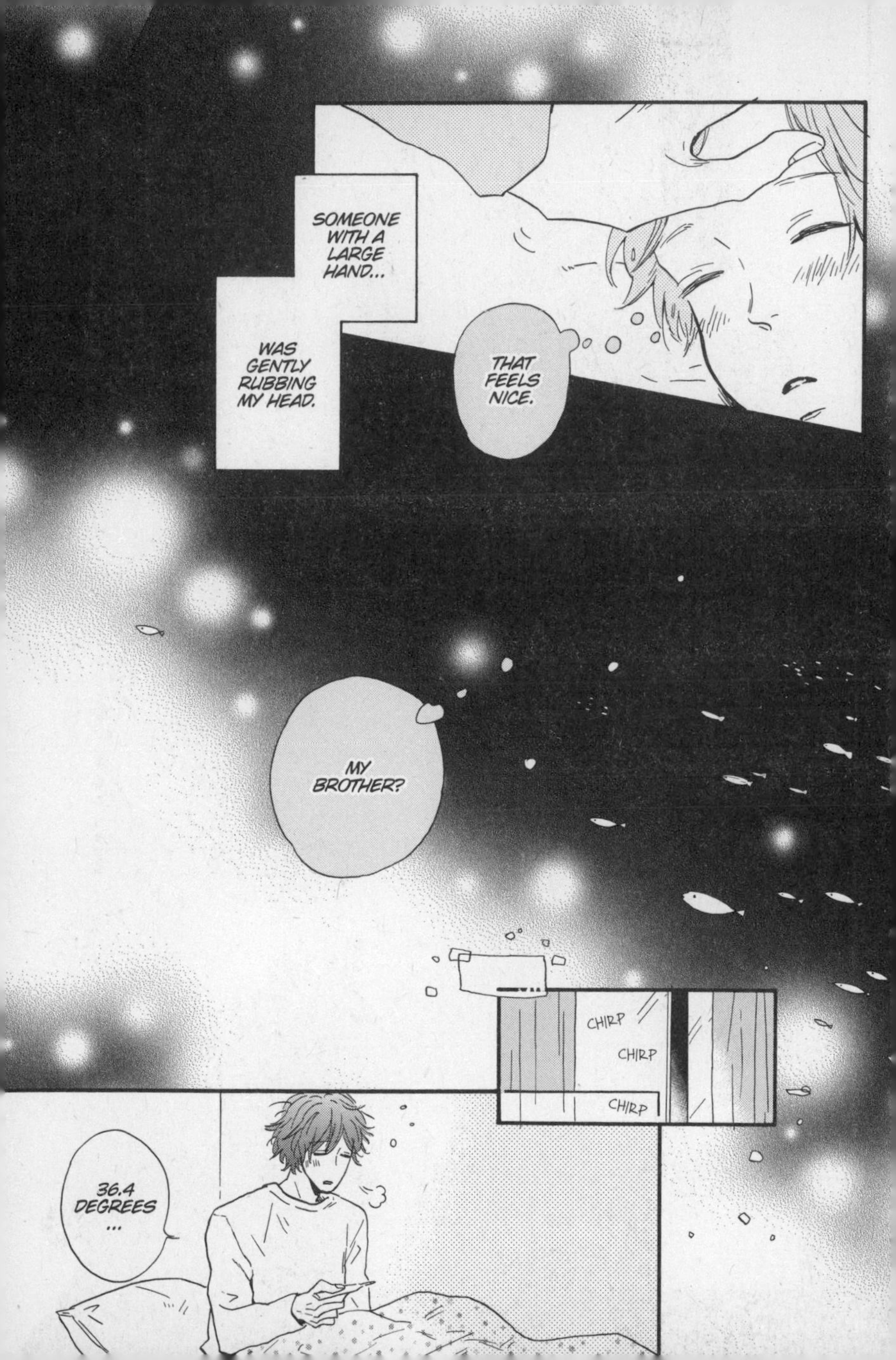
SOMEONE WITH A LARGE HAND...
WAS GENTLY RUBBING MY HEAD.
THAT FEELS NICE.
MY BROTHER?
CHIRP
CHIRP
CHIRP
36.4 DEGREES ...

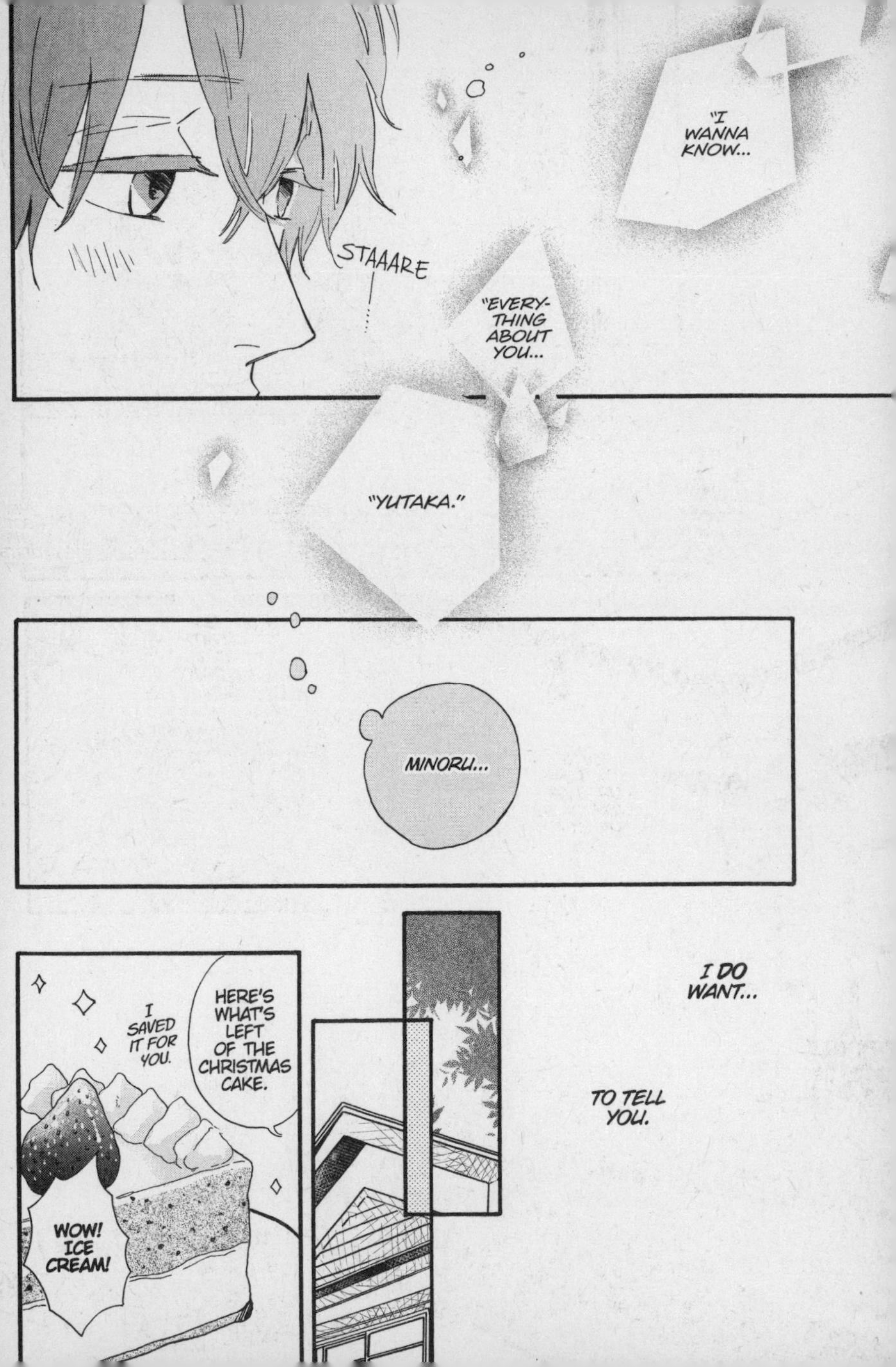
"I WANNA KNOW...
"EVERYTHING ABOUT YOU...
STAAARE
"YUTAKA."
MINORU...
I DO WANT...
TO TELL YOU.
HERE'S WHAT'S LEFT OF THE CHRISTMAS CAKE.
I SAVED IT FOR YOU.
WOW! ICE CREAM!

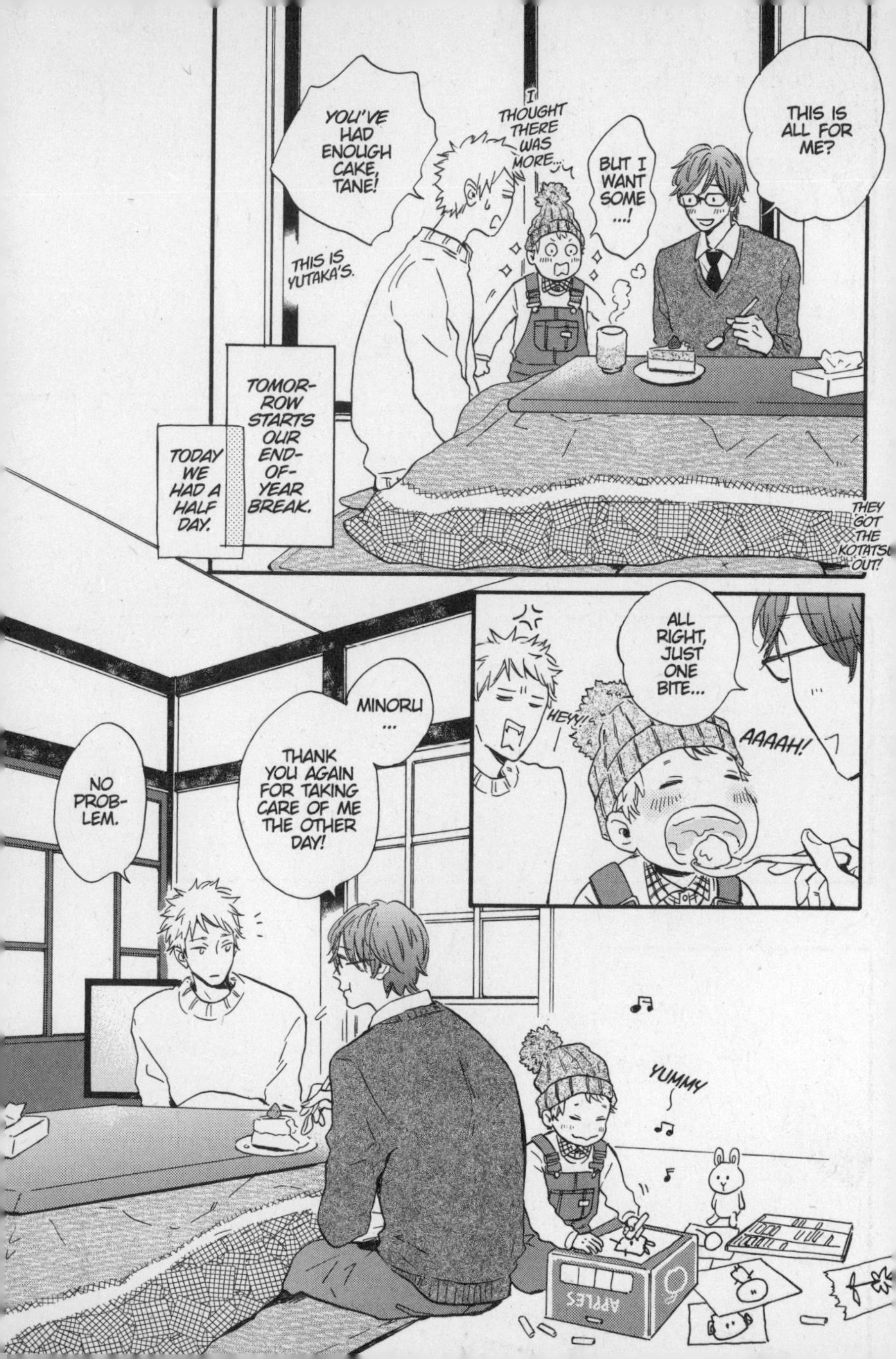
THEY GOT THE KOTATSU OUT!
THIS IS ALL FOR ME?
BUT I WANT SOME ...!
I THOUGHT THERE WAS MORE...
YOU'VE HAD ENOUGH CAKE, TANE!
THIS IS YUTAKA'S.
TOMORROW STARTS OUR END-OF-YEAR BREAK.
TODAY WE HAD A HALF DAY.
ALL RIGHT, JUST ONE BITE...
AAAAH!
HEY!!
MINORU ...
THANK YOU AGAIN FOR TAKING CARE OF ME THE OTHER DAY!
NO PROBLEM.
YUMMY
APPLES

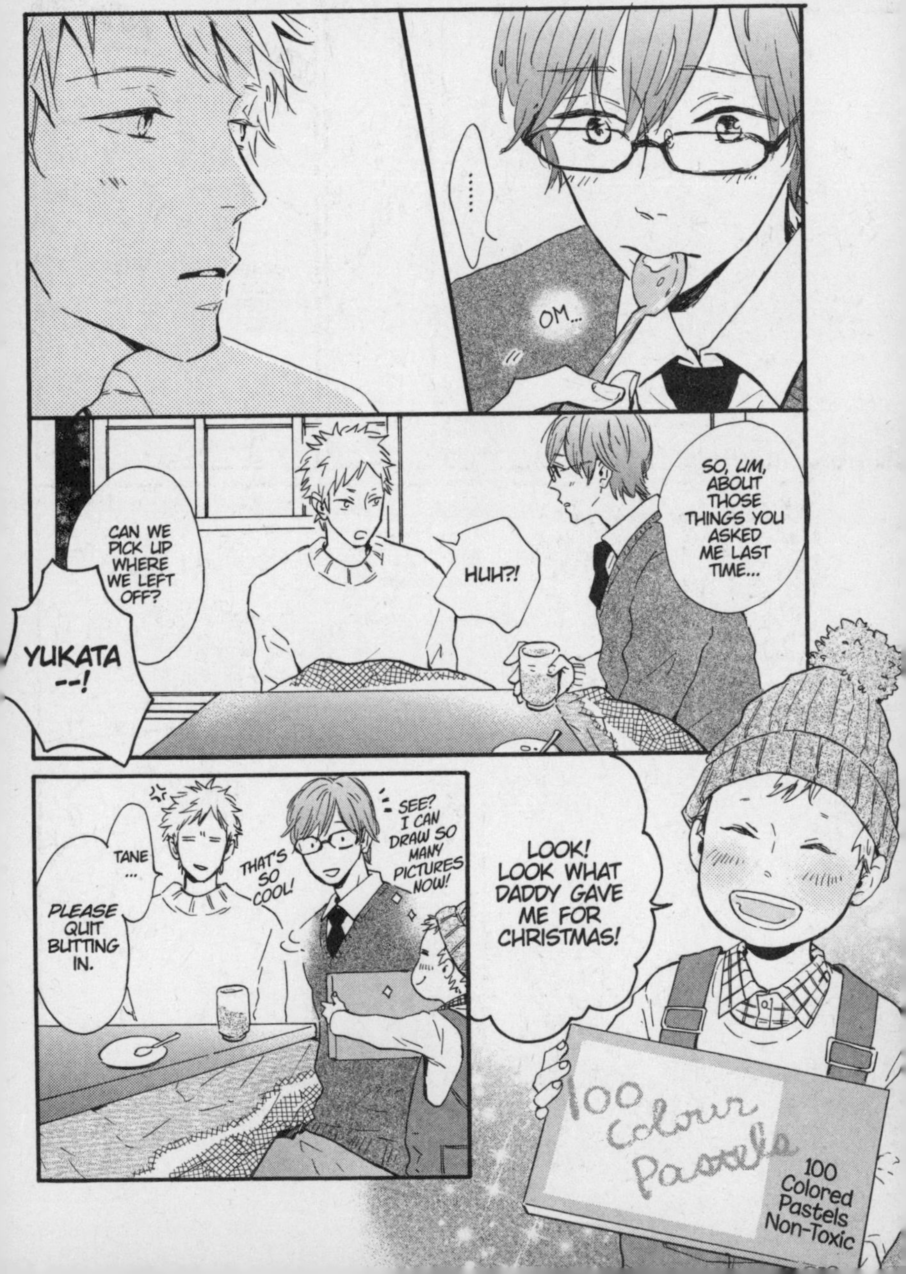
......
OM...
SO, UM, ABOUT THOSE THINGS YOU ASKED ME LAST TIME...
HUH?!
CAN WE PICK UP WHERE WE LEFT OFF?
YUKATA--!
LOOK! LOOK WHAT DADDY GAVE ME FOR CHRISTMAS!
100 Colour Pastels
100 Colored Pastels Non-Toxic
SEE? I CAN DRAW SO MANY PICTURES NOW!
THAT'S SO COOL!
TANE... PLEASE QUIT BUTTING IN.

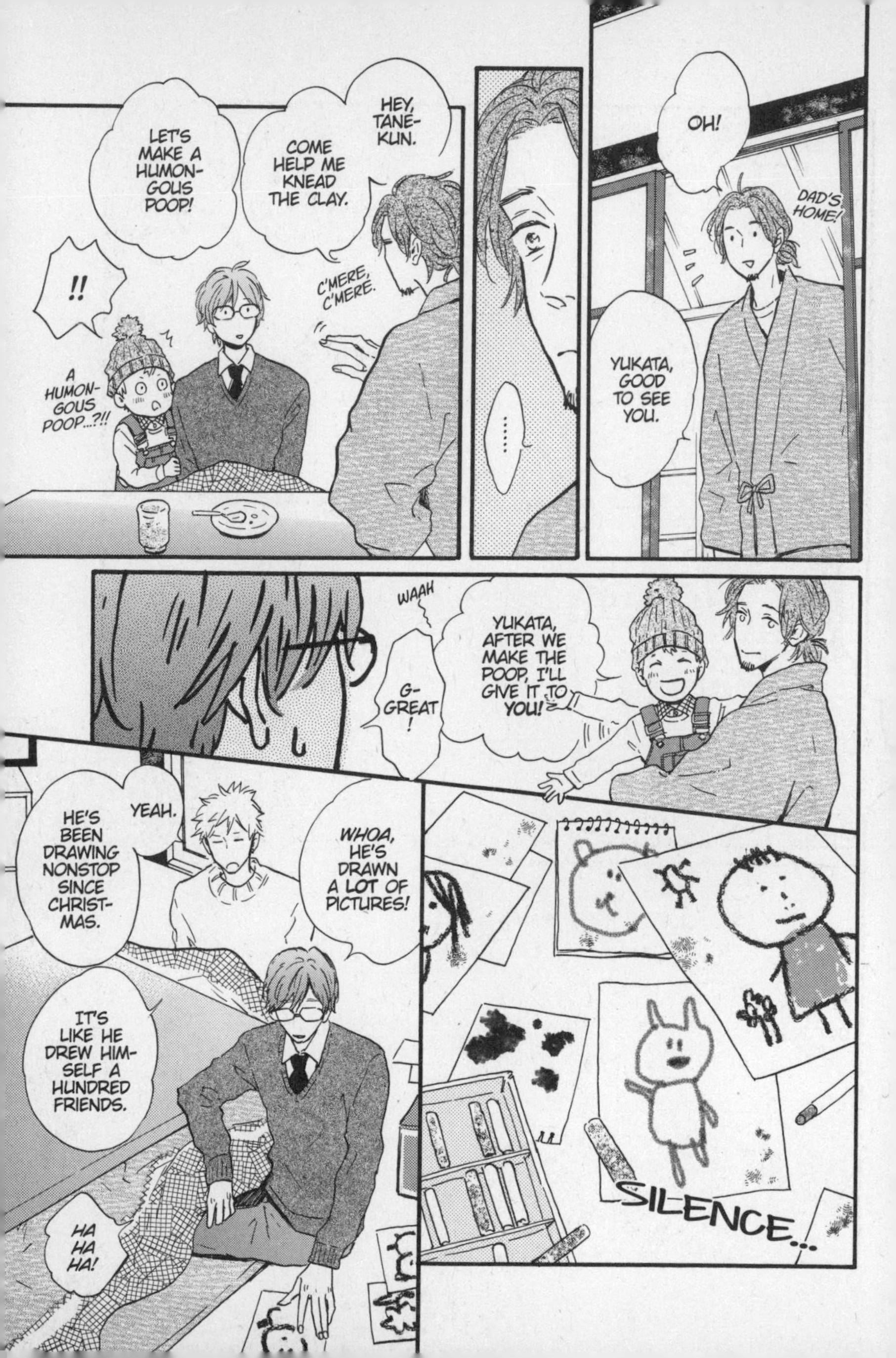
OH!
DAD'S HOME!
YUKATA, GOOD TO SEE YOU.
......
HEY, TANE-KUN.
COME HELP ME KNEAD THE CLAY.
LET'S MAKE A HUMONGOUS POOP!
C'MERE, C'MERE.
!!
A HUMONGOUS POOP...?!!
YUKATA, AFTER WE MAKE THE POOP, I'LL GIVE IT TO YOU!
WAAH
G-GREAT!
SILENCE...
WHOA, HE'S DRAWN A LOT OF PICTURES!
YEAH.
HE'S BEEN DRAWING NONSTOP SINCE CHRISTMAS.
IT'S LIKE HE DREW HIMSELF A HUNDRED FRIENDS.
HA HA HA!

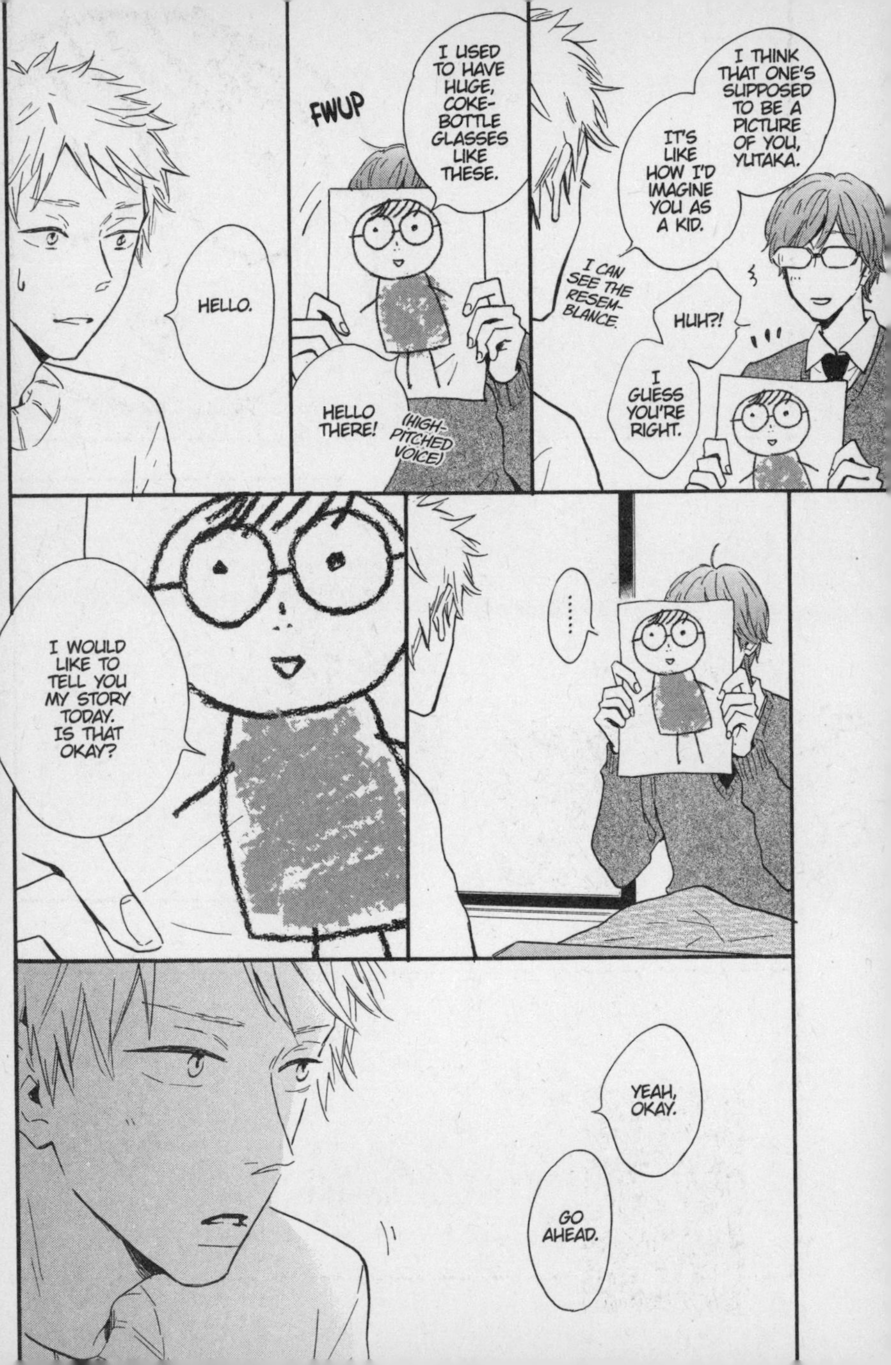
I THINK THAT ONE'S SUPPOSED TO BE A PICTURE OF YOU, YUTAKA.
IT'S LIKE HOW I'D IMAGINE YOU AS A KID.
I CAN SEE THE RESEM-BLANCE.
HUH?!
I GUESS YOU'RE RIGHT.
I USED TO HAVE HUGE, COKE-BOTTLE GLASSES LIKE THESE.
FWUP
HELLO THERE!
(HIGH-PITCHED VOICE)
HELLO.
......
I WOULD LIKE TO TELL YOU MY STORY TODAY. IS THAT OKAY?
YEAH, OKAY.
GO AHEAD.

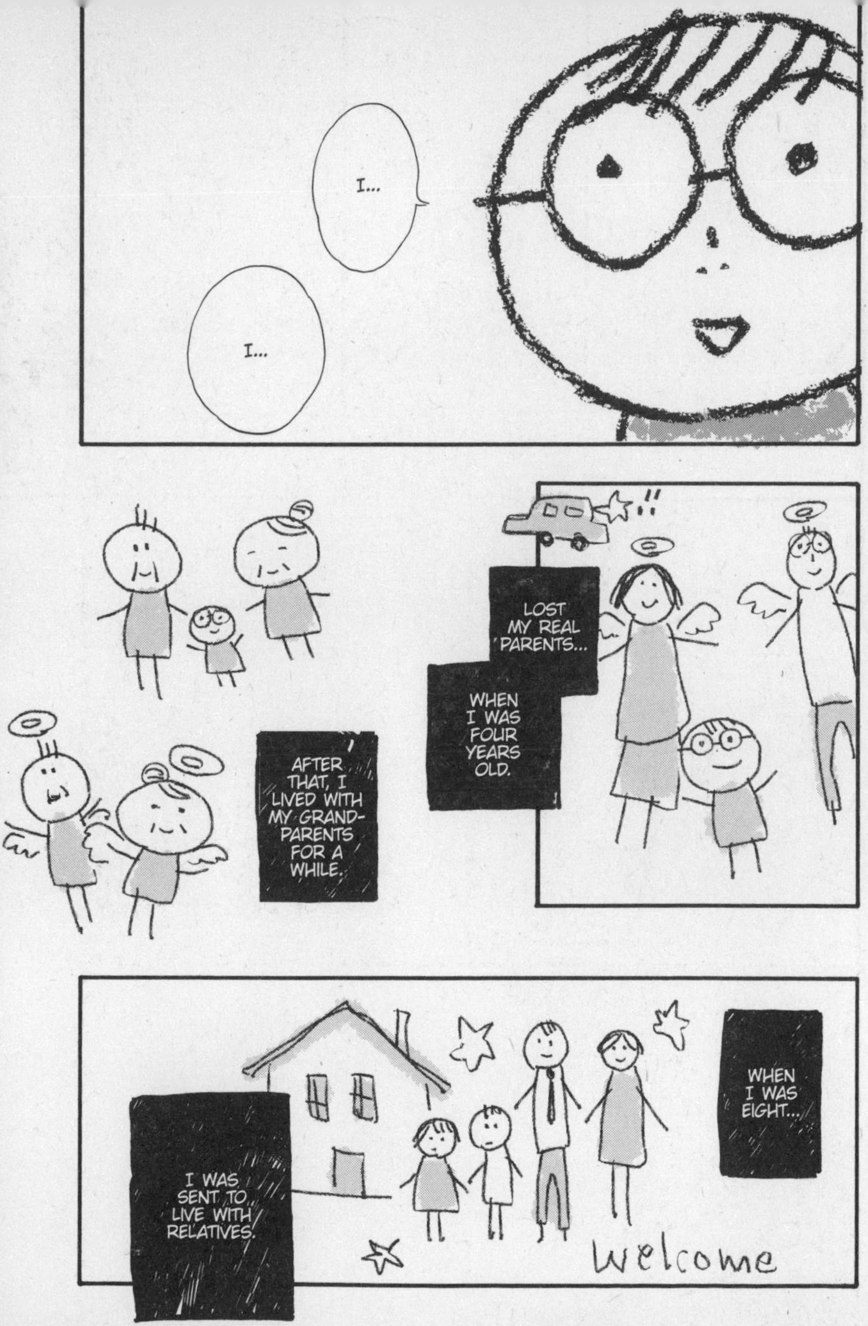
I...
I...
LOST MY REAL PARENTS...
WHEN I WAS FOUR YEARS OLD.
AFTER THAT, I LIVED WITH MY GRAND-PARENTS FOR A WHILE.
WHEN I WAS EIGHT...
I WAS SENT TO LIVE WITH RELATIVES.
welcome

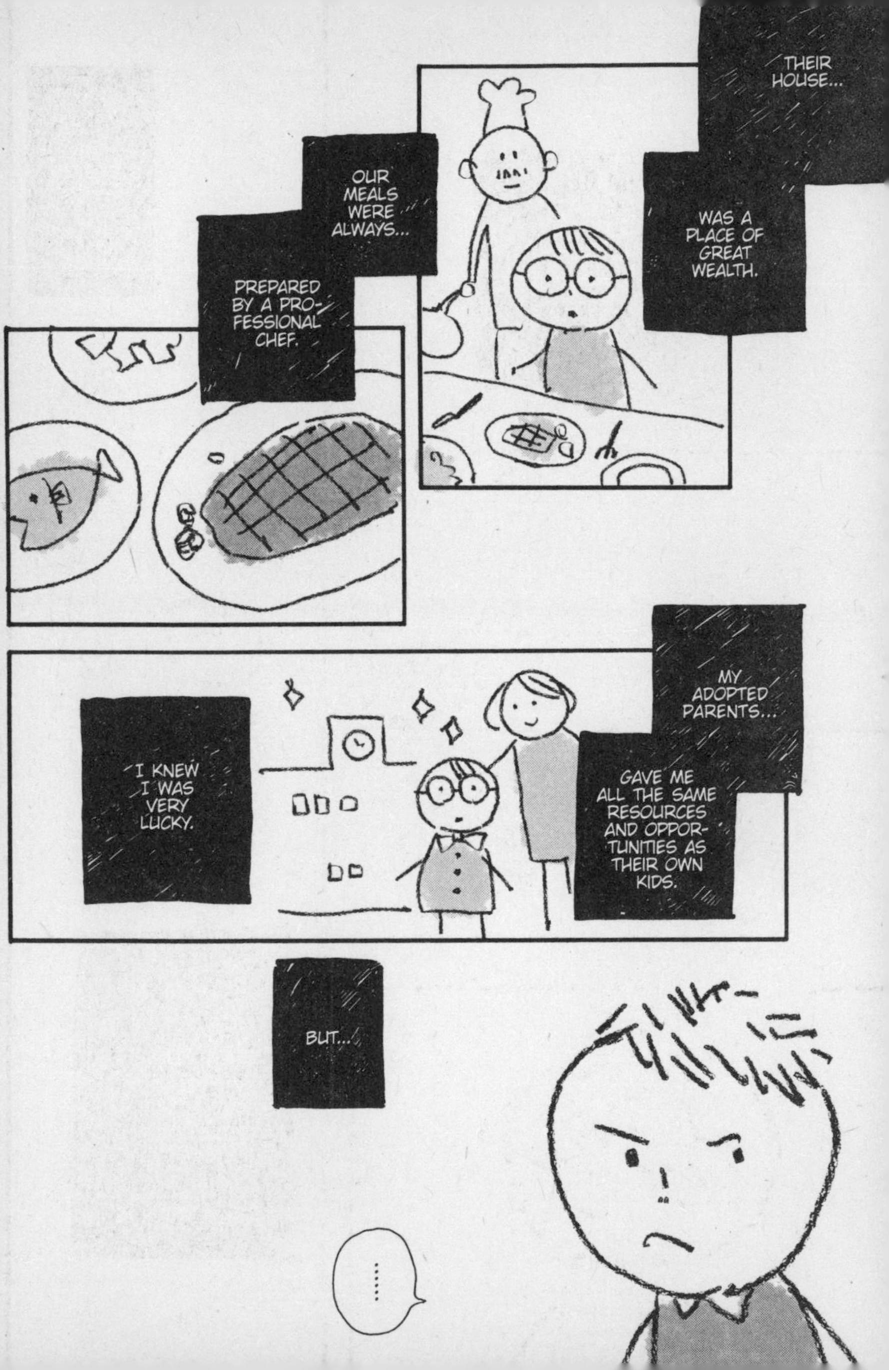
THEIR HOUSE...
WAS A PLACE OF GREAT WEALTH.
OUR MEALS WERE ALWAYS...
PREPARED BY A PROFESSIONAL CHEF.
MY ADOPTED PARENTS...
GAVE ME ALL THE SAME RESOURCES AND OPPORTUNITIES AS THEIR OWN KIDS.
I KNEW I WAS VERY LUCKY.
BUT...
......

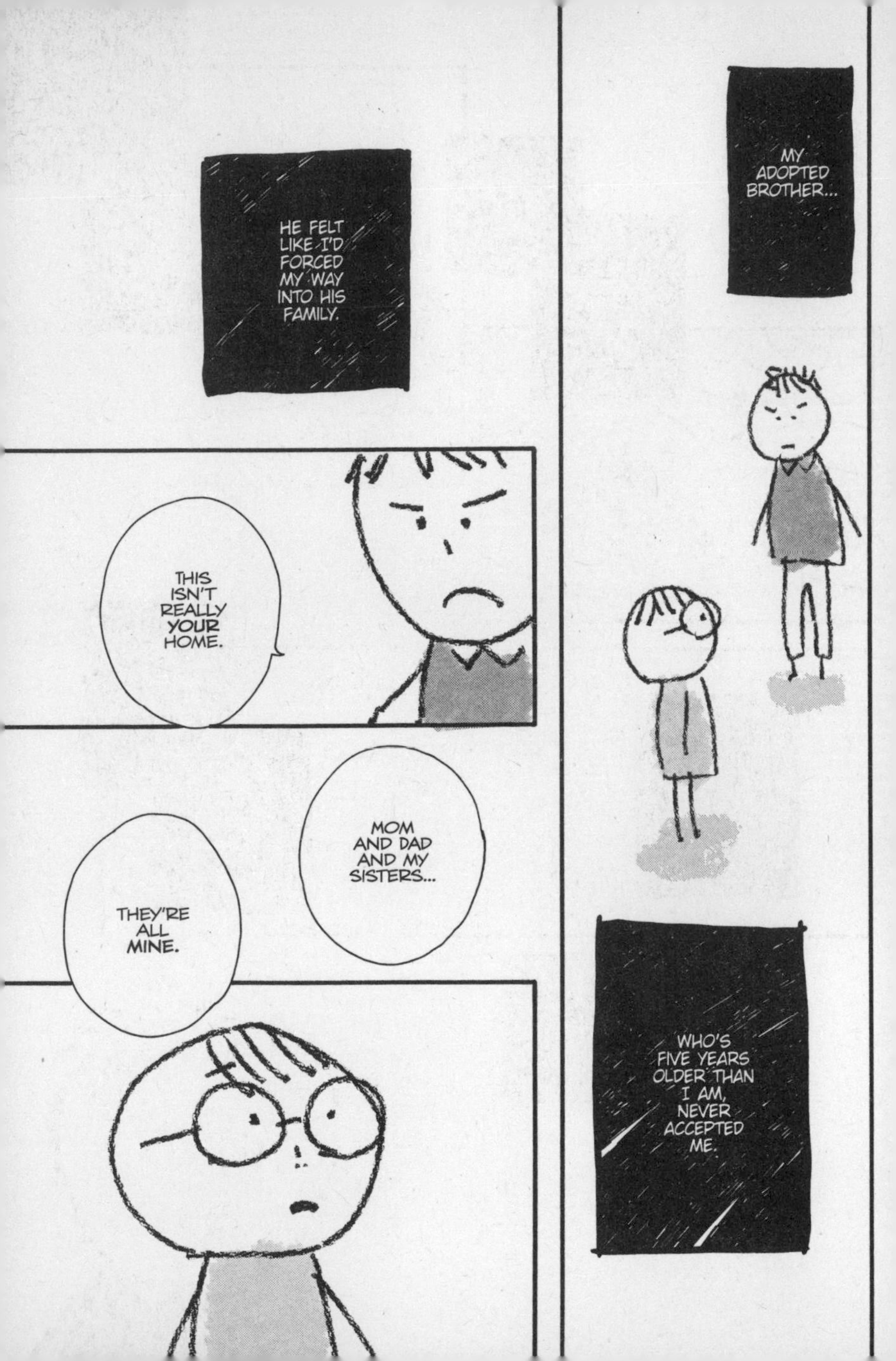
MY ADOPTED BROTHER...
WHO'S FIVE YEARS OLDER THAN I AM, NEVER ACCEPTED ME.
HE FELT LIKE I'D FORCED MY WAY INTO HIS FAMILY.
THIS ISN'T REALLY YOUR HOME.
MOM AND DAD AND MY SISTERS...
THEY'RE ALL MINE.

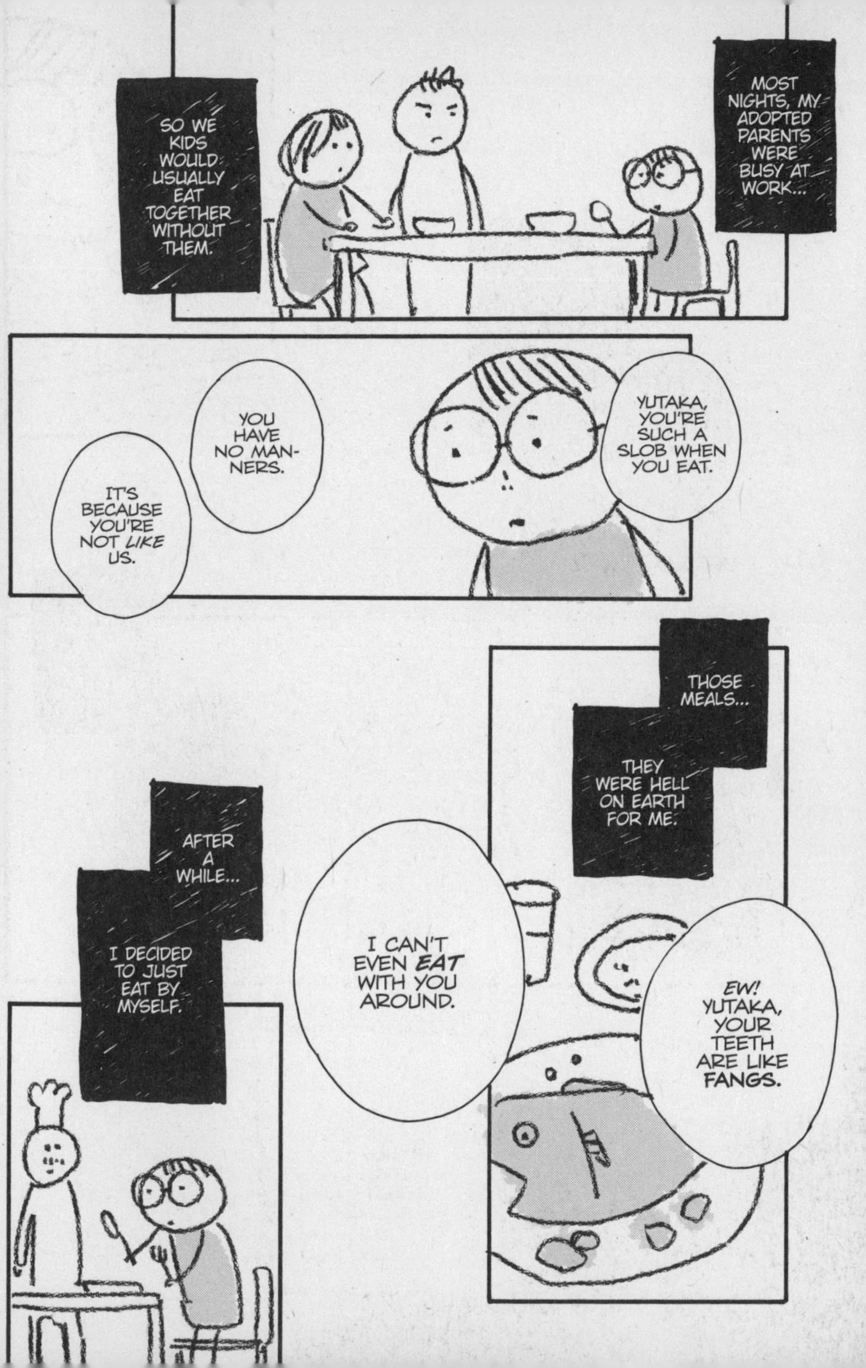
MOST NIGHTS, MY ADOPTED PARENTS WERE BUSY AT WORK...
SO WE KIDS WOULD USUALLY EAT TOGETHER WITHOUT THEM.
YUTAKA, YOU'RE SUCH A SLOB WHEN YOU EAT.
YOU HAVE NO MAN-NERS.
IT'S BECAUSE YOU'RE NOT *LIKE* US.
THOSE MEALS...
THEY WERE HELL ON EARTH FOR ME.
EW! YUTAKA, YOUR TEETH ARE LIKE **FANGS.**
I CAN'T EVEN ***EAT*** WITH YOU AROUND.
AFTER A WHILE...
I DECIDED TO JUST EAT BY MYSELF.

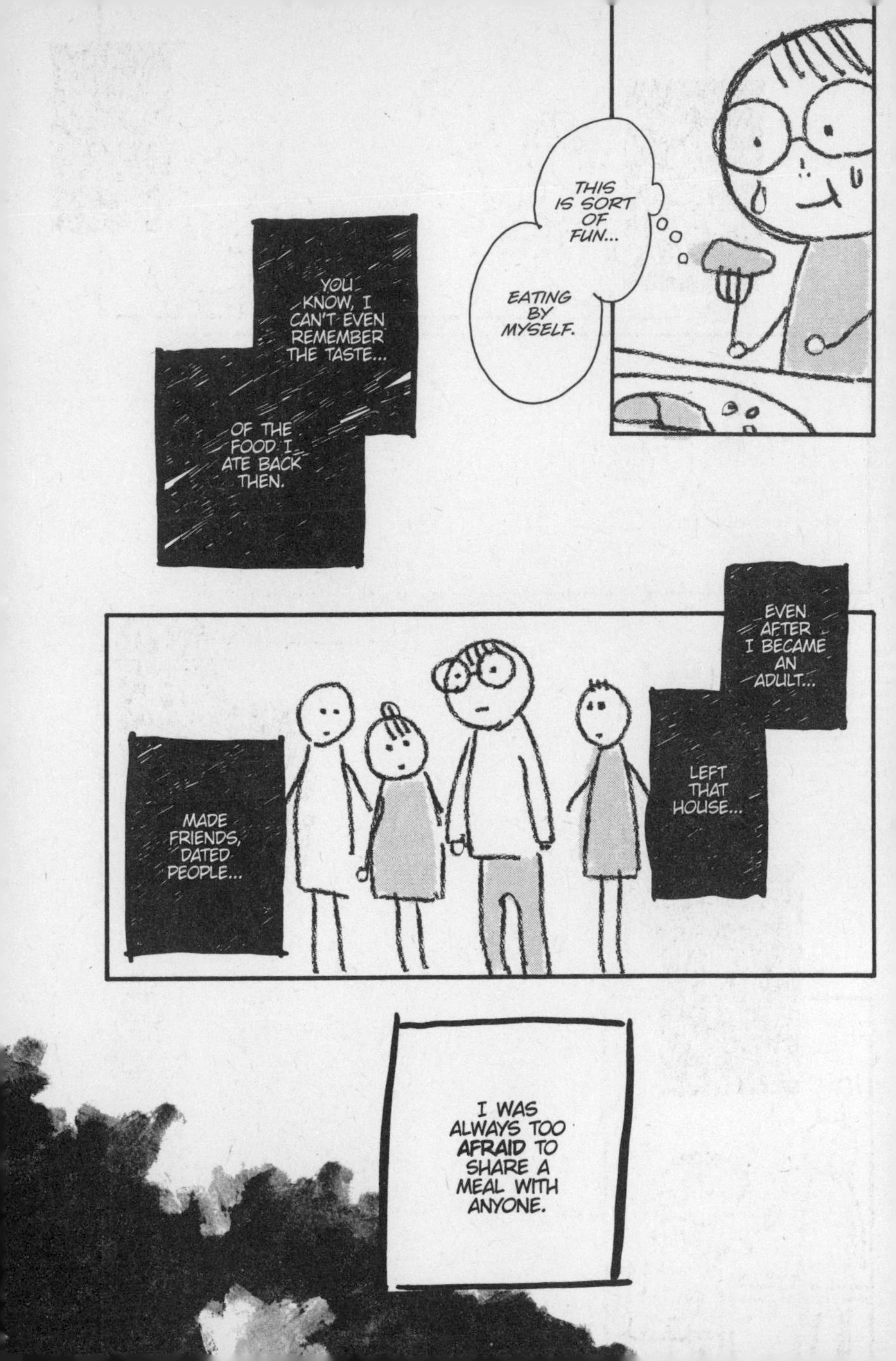
THIS IS SORT OF FUN...
EATING BY MYSELF.
YOU KNOW, I CAN'T EVEN REMEMBER THE TASTE...
OF THE FOOD I ATE BACK THEN.
EVEN AFTER I BECAME AN ADULT...
LEFT THAT HOUSE...
MADE FRIENDS, DATED PEOPLE...
I WAS ALWAYS TOO **AFRAID** TO SHARE A MEAL WITH ANYONE.

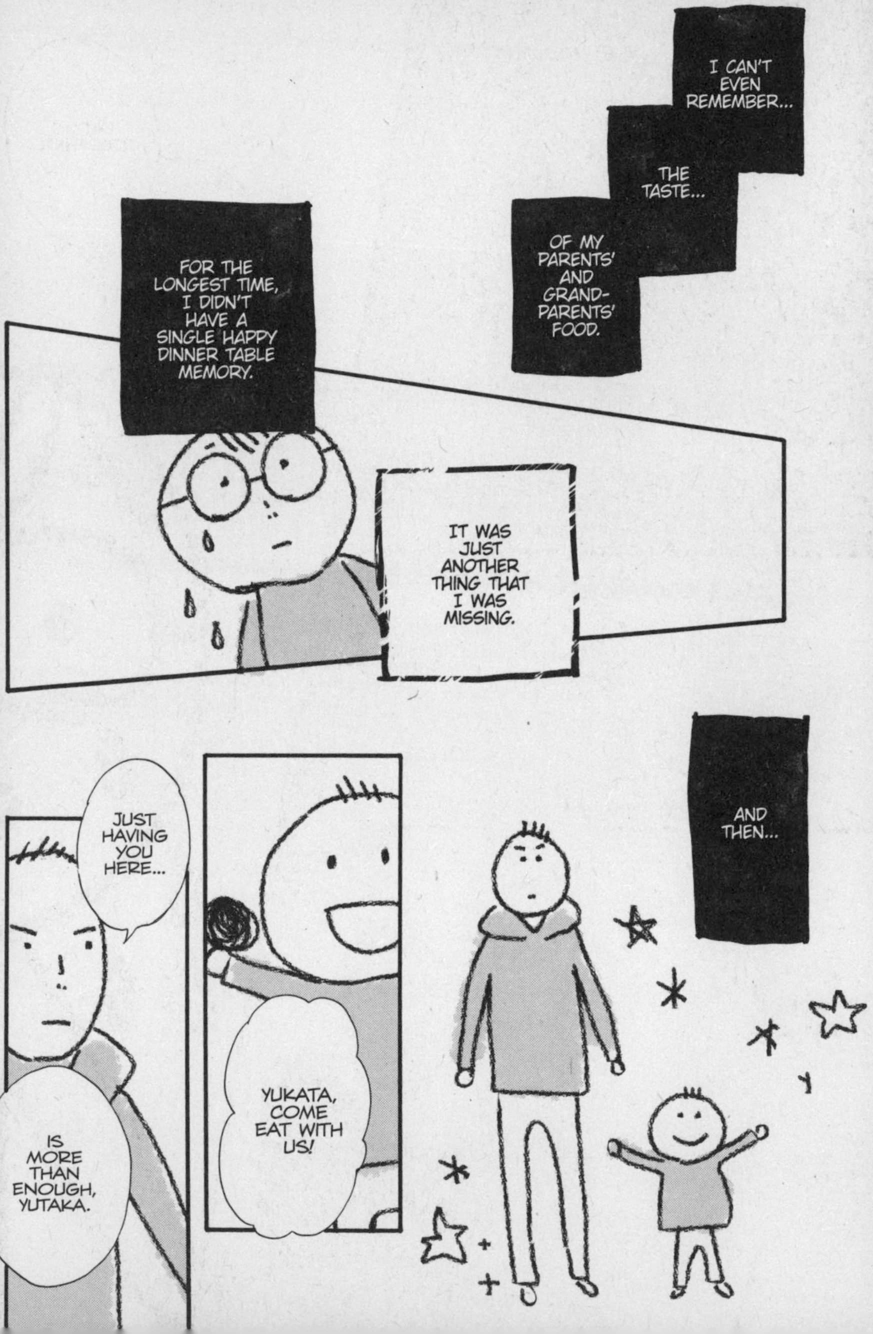
I CAN'T EVEN REMEMBER...
THE TASTE...
OF MY PARENTS' AND GRAND-PARENTS' FOOD.
FOR THE LONGEST TIME, I DIDN'T HAVE A SINGLE HAPPY DINNER TABLE MEMORY.
IT WAS JUST ANOTHER THING THAT I WAS MISSING.
AND THEN...
YUKATA, COME EAT WITH US!
JUST HAVING YOU HERE...
IS MORE THAN ENOUGH, YUTAKA.

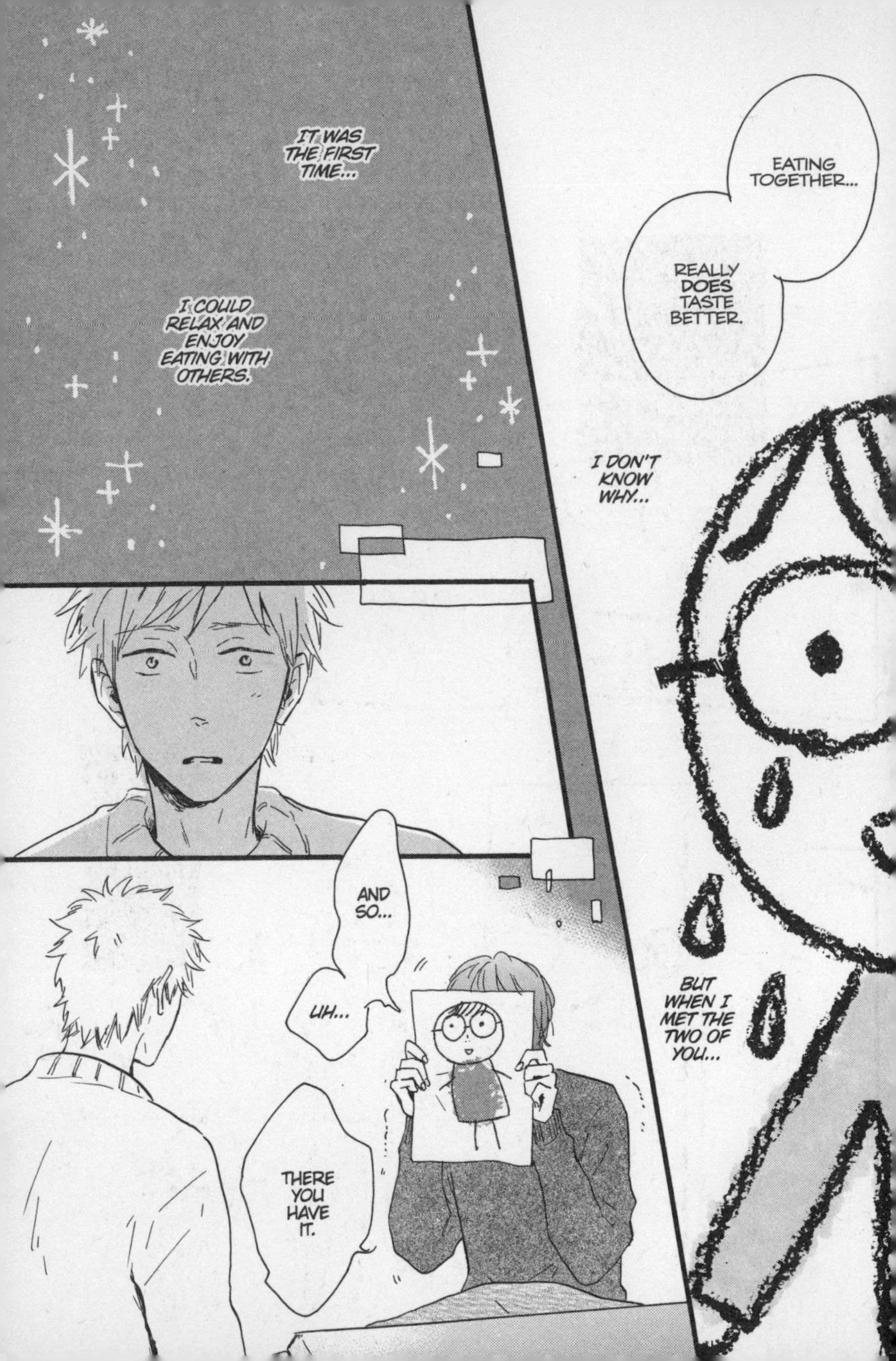
EATING TOGETHER...
REALLY DOES TASTE BETTER.
I DON'T KNOW WHY...
BUT WHEN I MET THE TWO OF YOU...
IT WAS THE FIRST TIME...
I COULD RELAX AND ENJOY EATING WITH OTHERS.
AND SO...
UH...
THERE YOU HAVE IT.

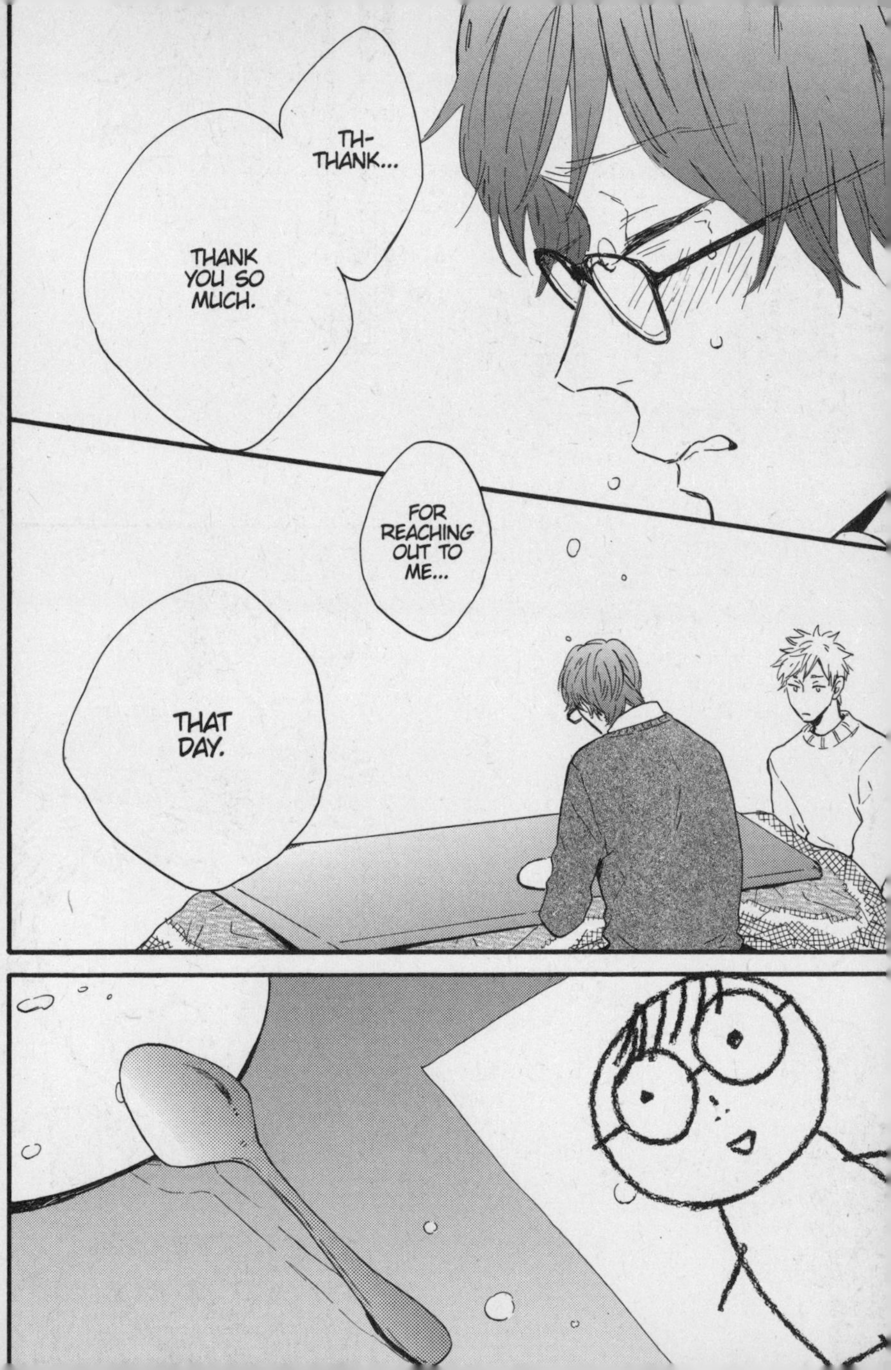
TH-
THANK...
THANK YOU SO MUCH.
FOR REACHING OUT TO ME...
THAT DAY.

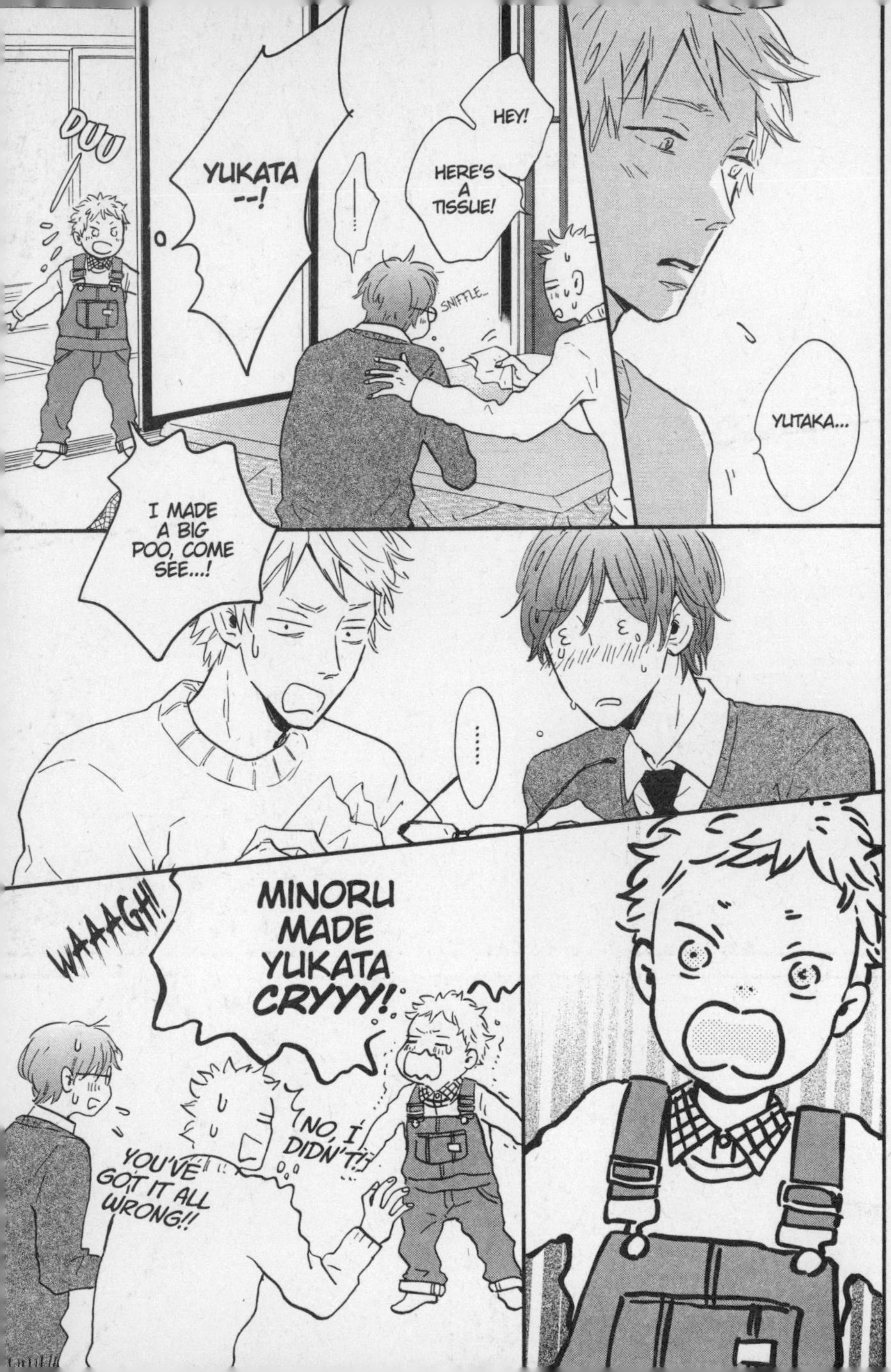
YUTAKA...
HEY!
HERE'S A TISSUE!
SNIFFLE...
...
YUKATA --!
DUU
I MADE A BIG POO, COME SEE...!
......
WAAAGH!
MINORU MADE YUKATA CRYYY!
NO, I DIDN'T!
YOU'VE GOT IT ALL WRONG!!

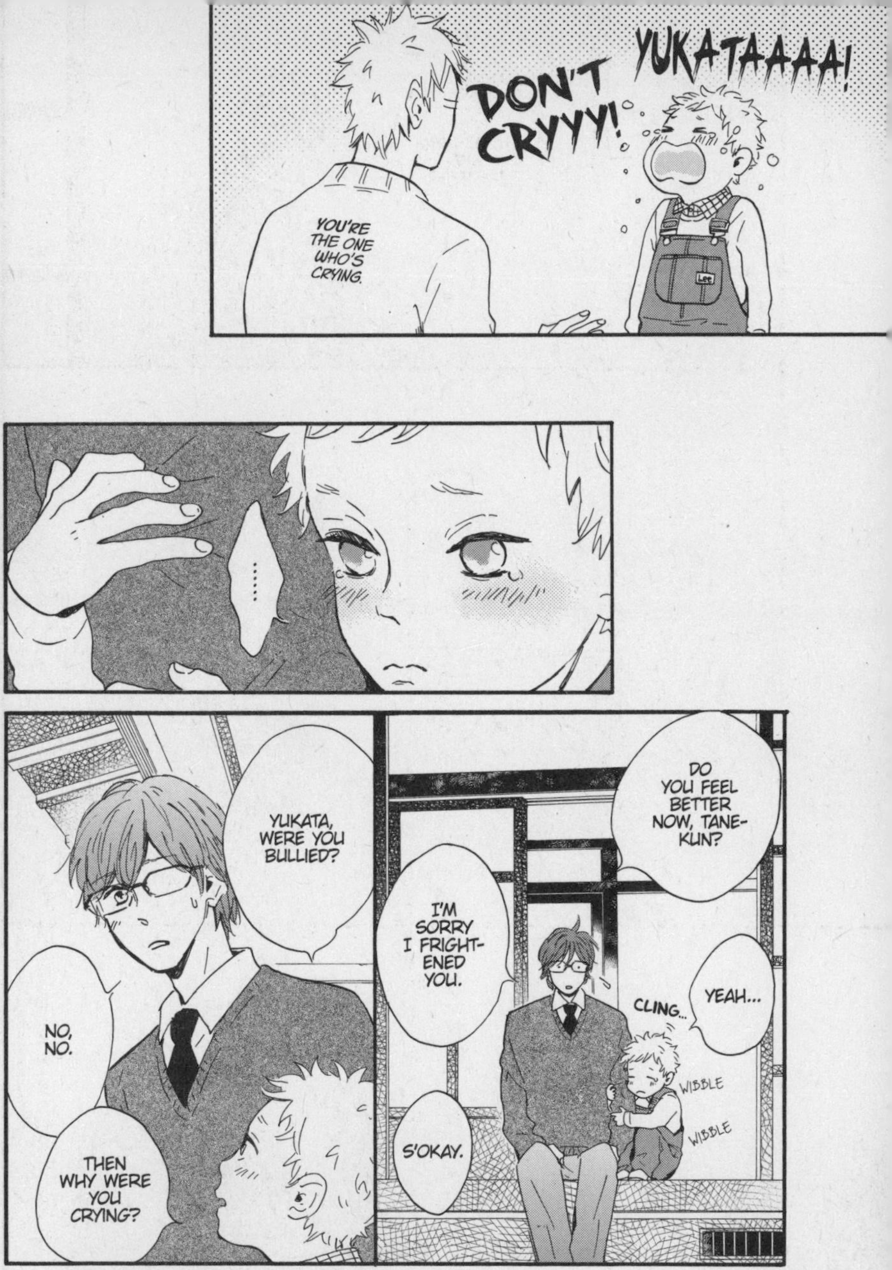
YUKATAAAA!
DON'T CRYYY!
YOU'RE THE ONE WHO'S CRYING.
......
DO YOU FEEL BETTER NOW, TANE-KUN?
YEAH...
CLING...
I'M SORRY I FRIGHT-ENED YOU.
WIBBLE
WIBBLE
S'OKAY.
YUKATA, WERE YOU BULLIED?
NO, NO.
THEN WHY WERE YOU CRYING?

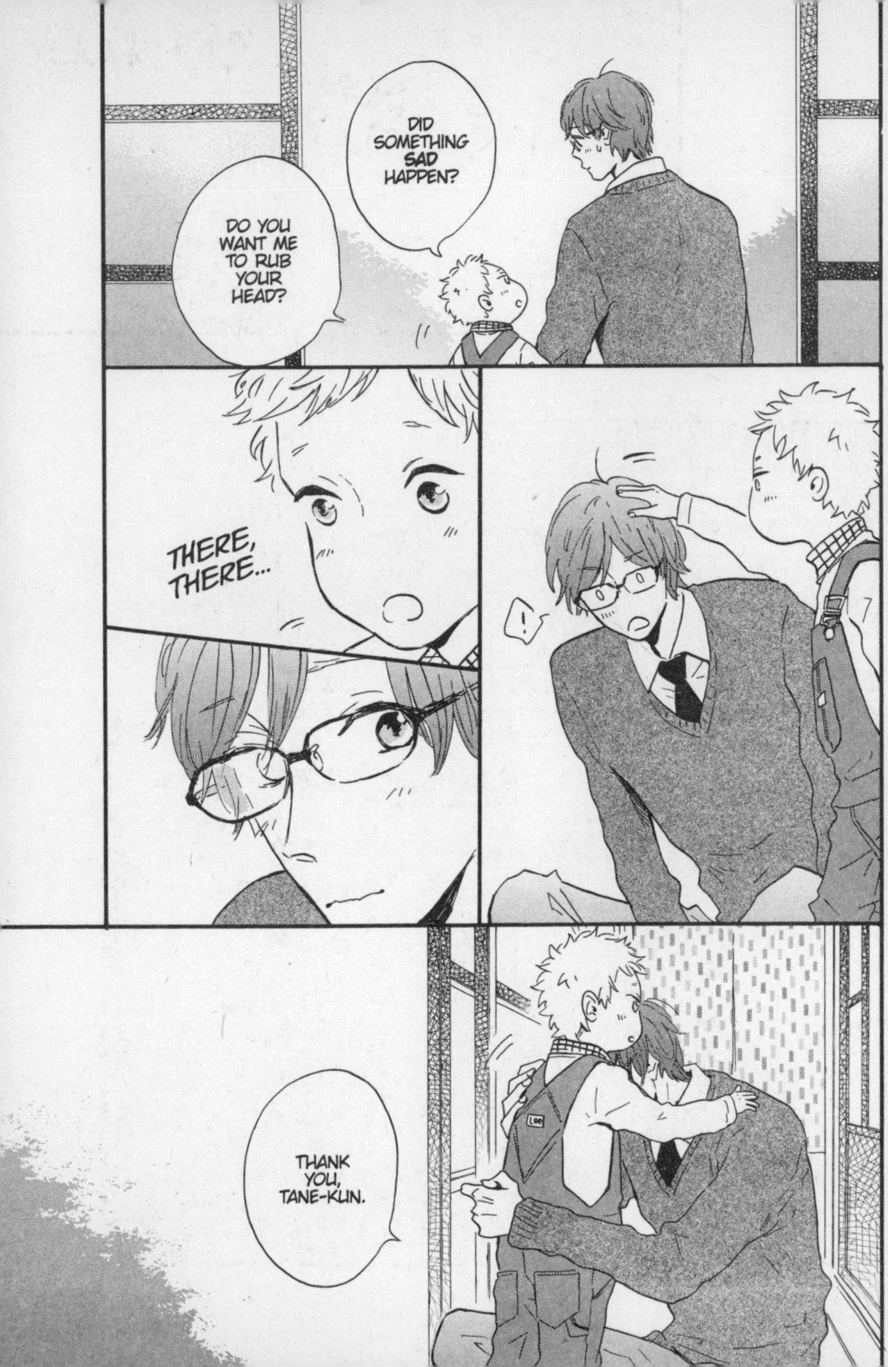
DID SOMETHING SAD HAPPEN?
DO YOU WANT ME TO RUB YOUR HEAD?
!
THERE, THERE...
THANK YOU, TANE-KUN.

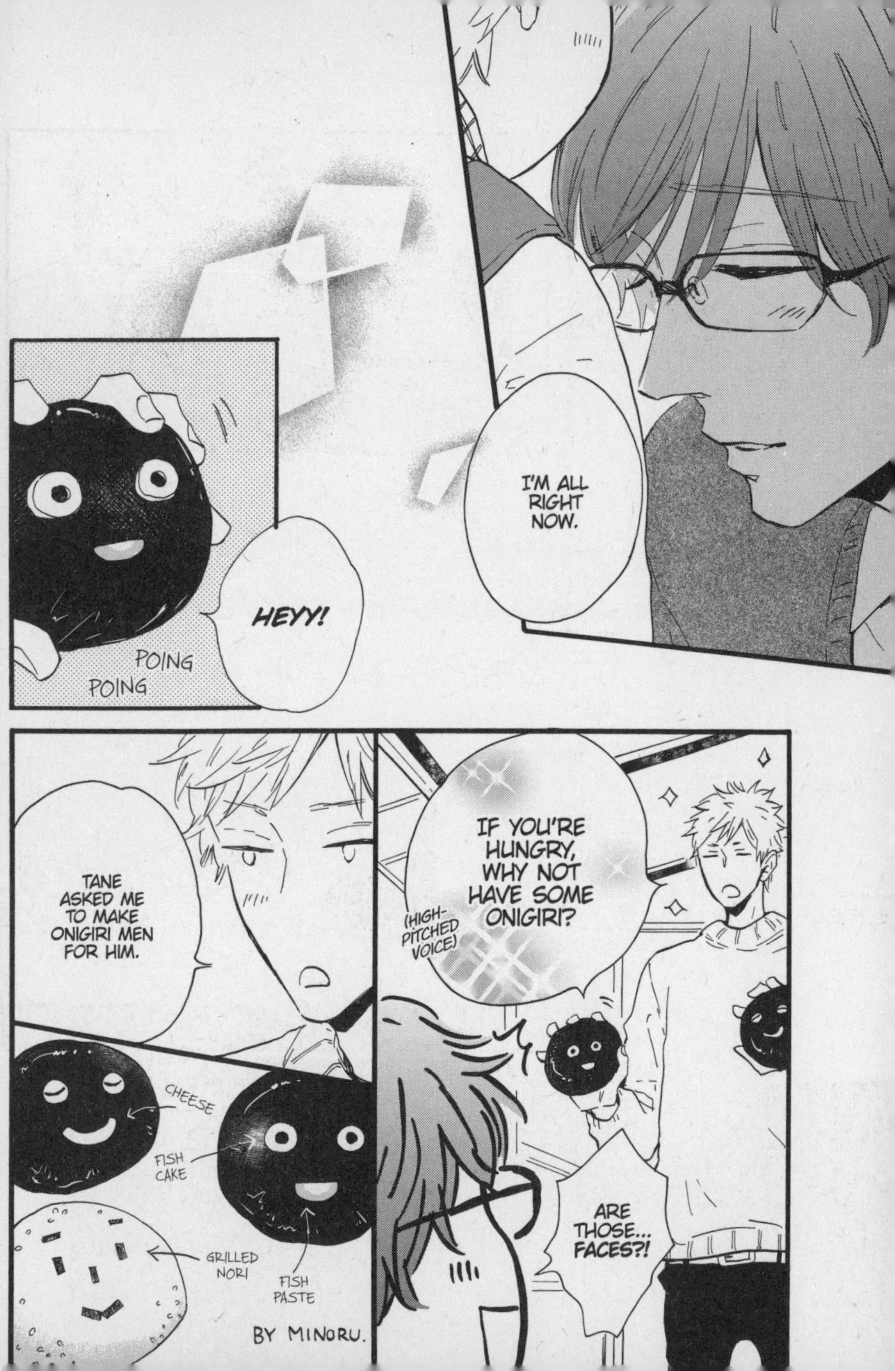
I'M ALL RIGHT NOW.
HEYY!
POING POING
IF YOU'RE HUNGRY, WHY NOT HAVE SOME ONIGIRI?
(HIGH-PITCHED VOICE)
ARE THOSE... FACES?!
TANE ASKED ME TO MAKE ONIGIRI MEN FOR HIM.
CHEESE
FISH CAKE
GRILLED NORI
FISH PASTE
BY MINORU.

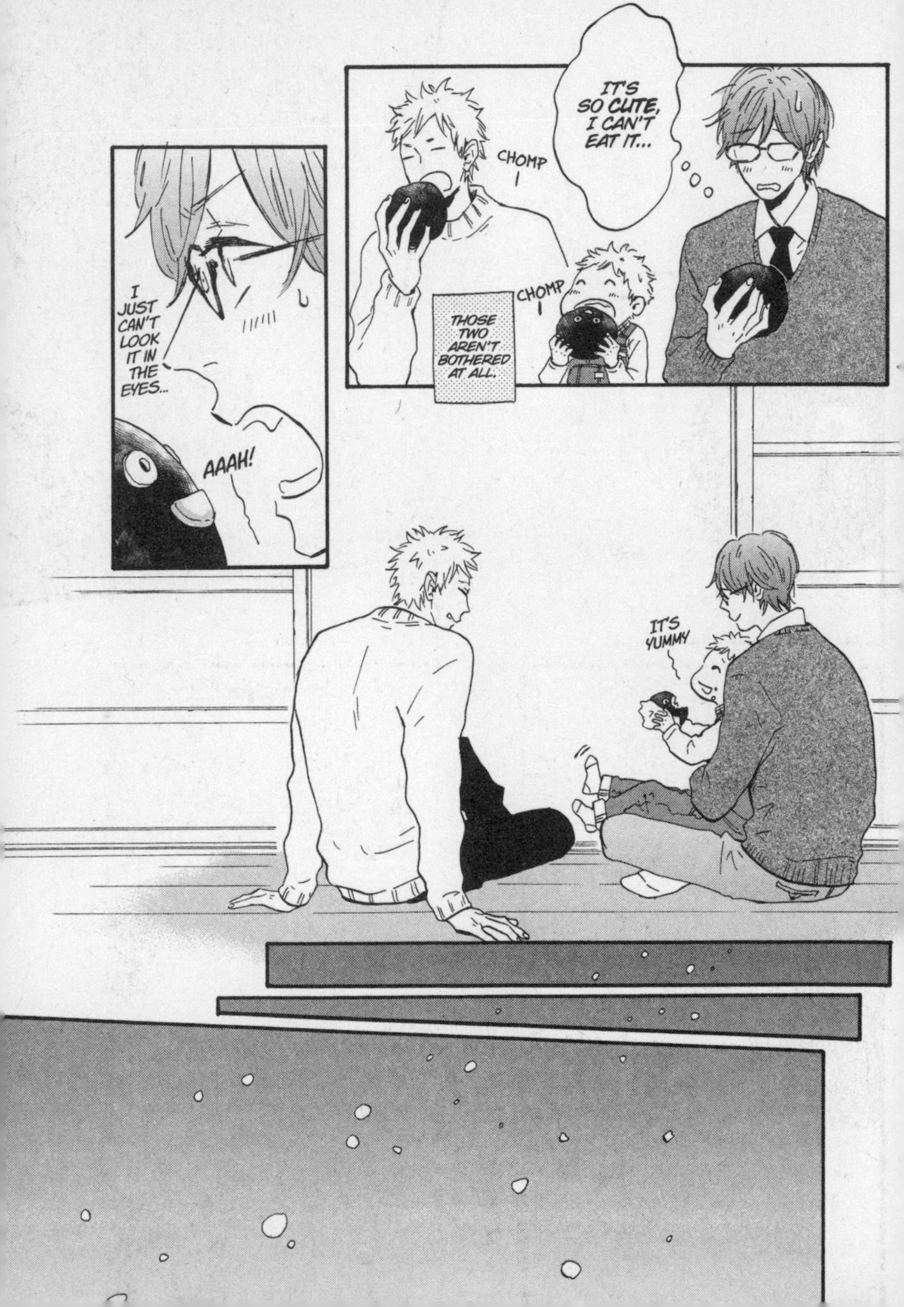
IT'S SO CUTE, I CAN'T EAT IT...
CHOMP
CHOMP
THOSE TWO AREN'T BOTHERED AT ALL.
I JUST CAN'T LOOK IT IN THE EYES...
AAAH!
IT'S YUMMY

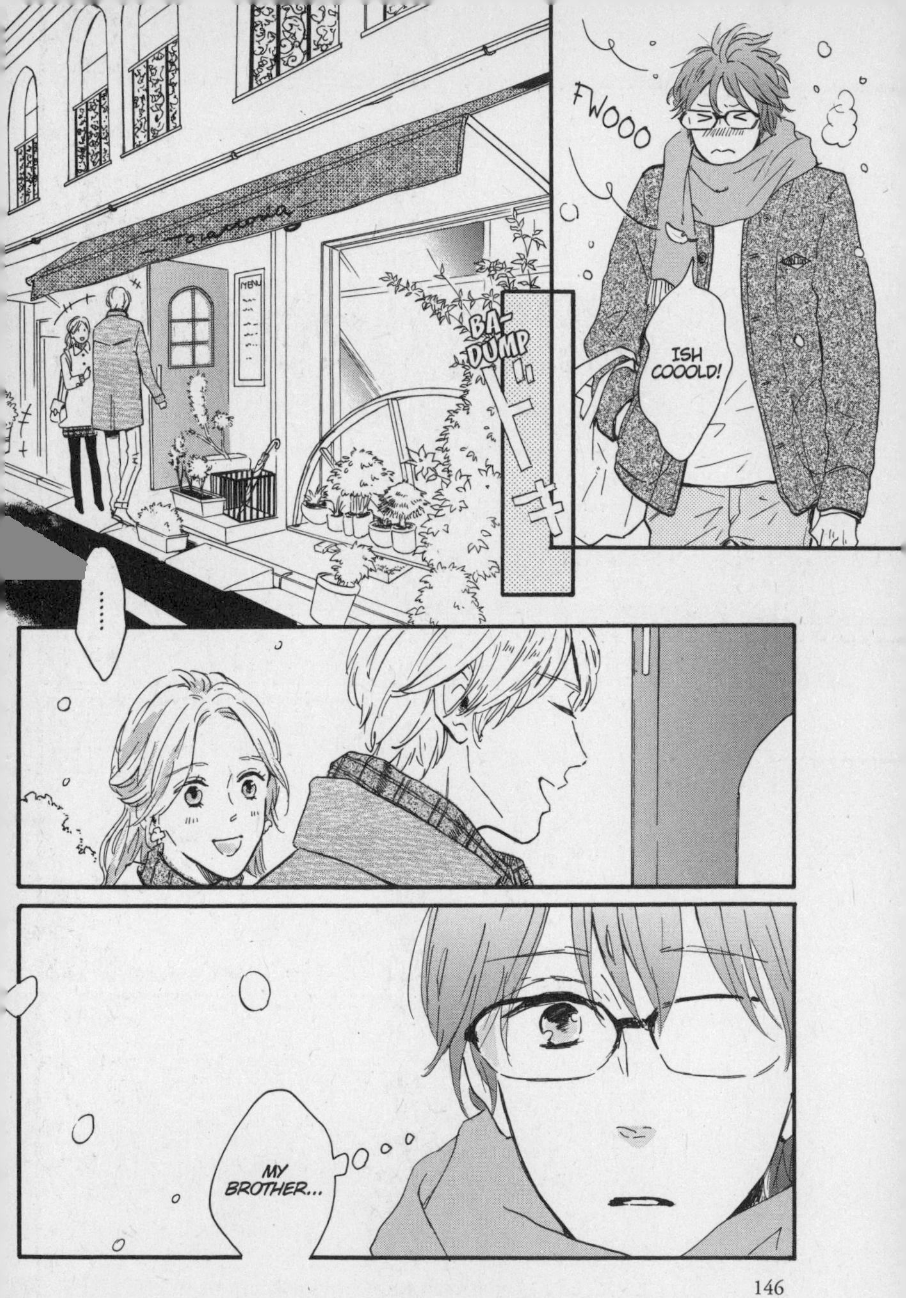
FWOOO
ISH COOOLD!
BA-DUMP
MENU
......
MY BROTHER...

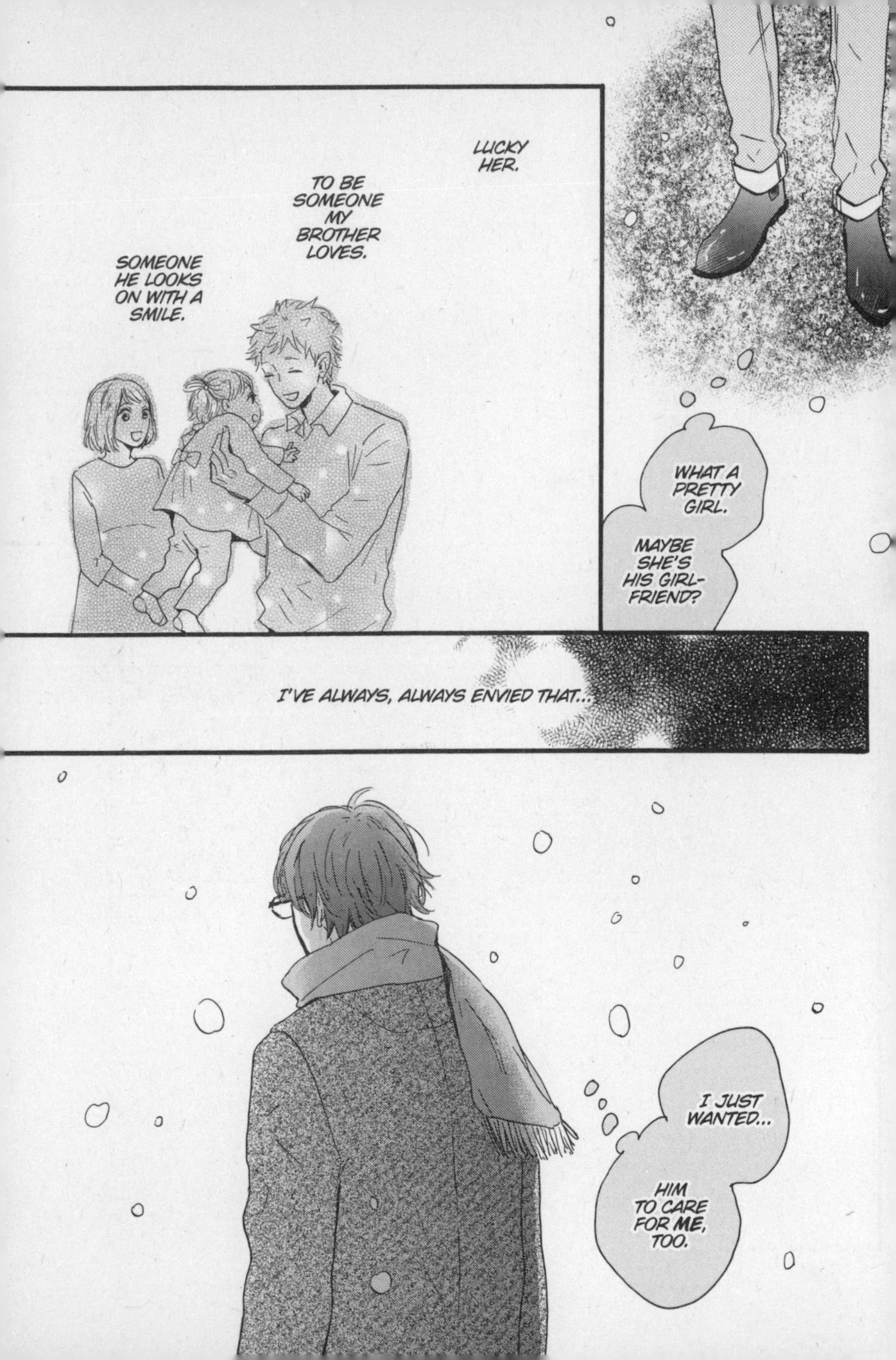
WHAT A PRETTY GIRL.
MAYBE SHE'S HIS GIRL-FRIEND?
LUCKY HER.
TO BE SOMEONE MY BROTHER LOVES.
SOMEONE HE LOOKS ON WITH A SMILE.
I'VE ALWAYS, ALWAYS ENVIED THAT...
I JUST WANTED...
HIM TO CARE FOR ME, TOO.

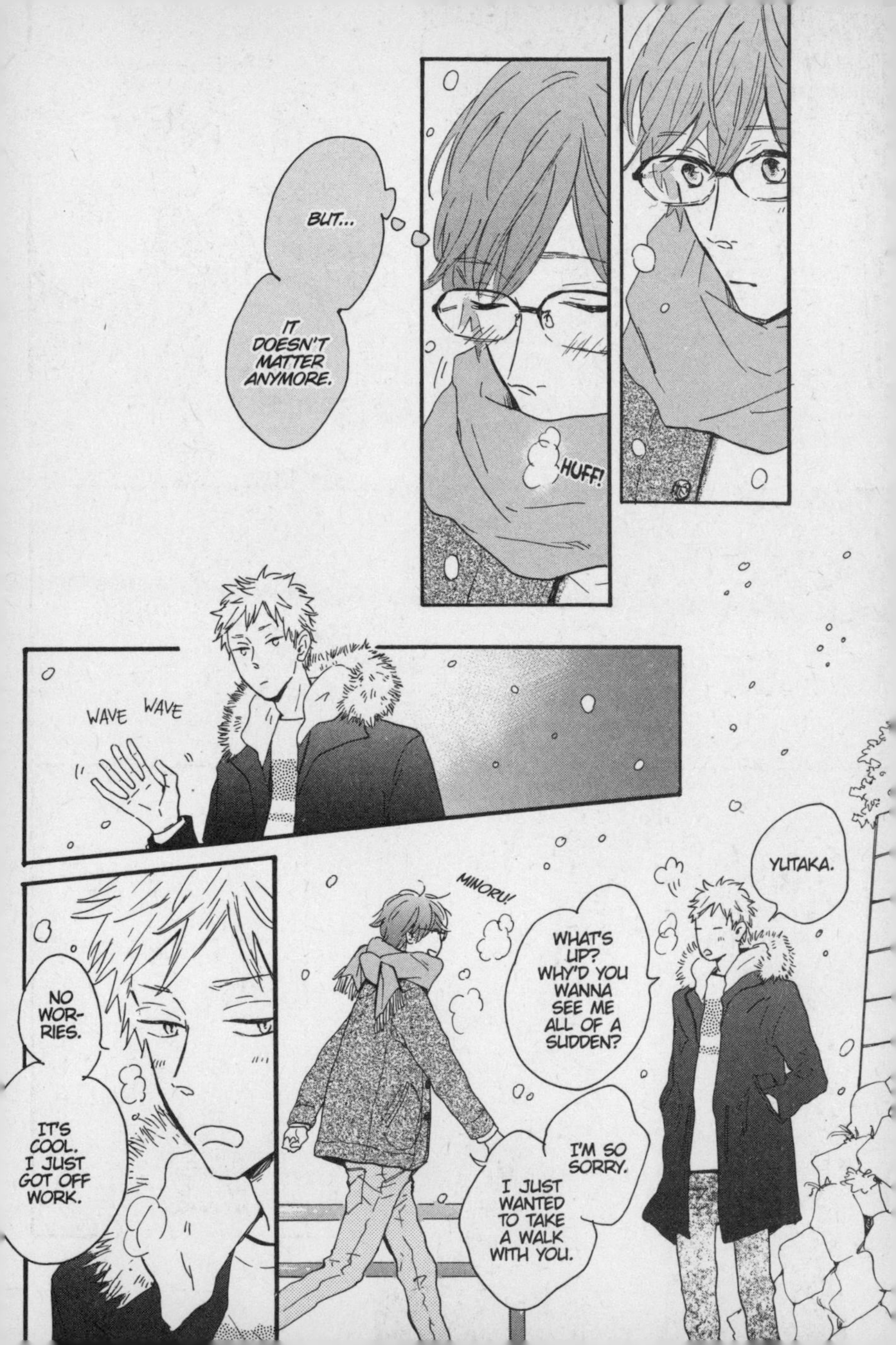
HUFF!
BUT...
IT DOESN'T MATTER ANYMORE.
WAVE WAVE
YUTAKA.
MINORU!
WHAT'S UP? WHY'D YOU WANNA SEE ME ALL OF A SUDDEN?
I'M SO SORRY.
I JUST WANTED TO TAKE A WALK WITH YOU.
NO WOR-RIES.
IT'S COOL. I JUST GOT OFF WORK.

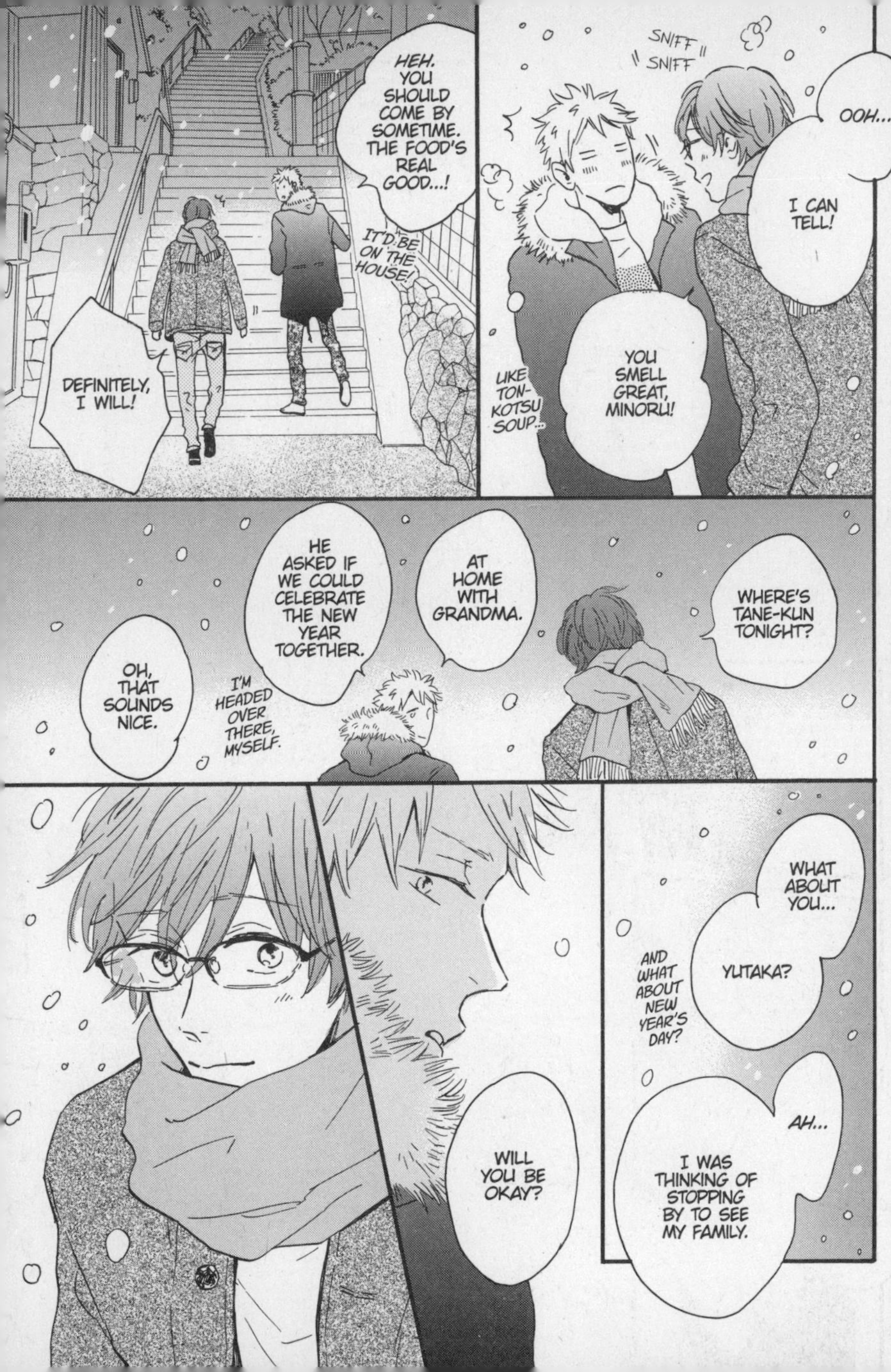
SNIFF SNIFF
OOH...
I CAN TELL!
YOU SMELL GREAT, MINORU!
LIKE TON-KOTSU SOUP...
HEH. YOU SHOULD COME BY SOMETIME. THE FOOD'S REAL GOOD...!
IT'D BE ON THE HOUSE!
DEFINITELY, I WILL!
WHERE'S TANE-KUN TONIGHT?
AT HOME WITH GRANDMA.
HE ASKED IF WE COULD CELEBRATE THE NEW YEAR TOGETHER.
I'M HEADED OVER THERE, MYSELF.
OH, THAT SOUNDS NICE.
WHAT ABOUT YOU...
YUTAKA?
AND WHAT ABOUT NEW YEAR'S DAY?
AH...
I WAS THINKING OF STOPPING BY TO SEE MY FAMILY.
WILL YOU BE OKAY?

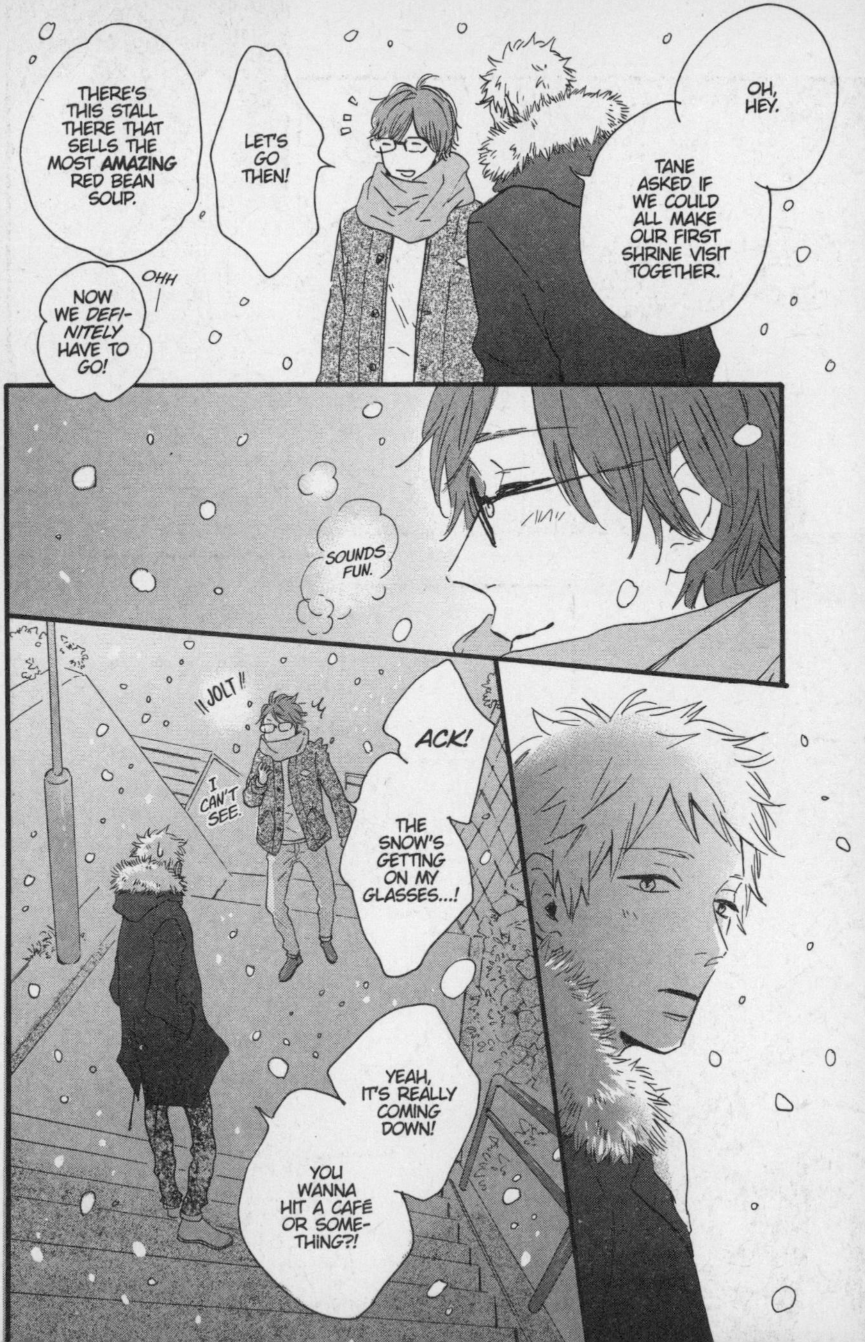
OH, HEY.
TANE ASKED IF WE COULD ALL MAKE OUR FIRST SHRINE VISIT TOGETHER.
LET'S GO THEN!
THERE'S THIS STALL THERE THAT SELLS THE MOST **AMAZING** RED BEAN SOUP.
OHH
NOW WE *DEFINITELY* HAVE TO GO!
SOUNDS FUN.
!! JOLT !!
I CAN'T SEE.
ACK!
THE SNOW'S GETTING ON MY GLASSES...!
YEAH, IT'S REALLY COMING DOWN!
YOU WANNA HIT A CAFÉ OR SOMETHING?!

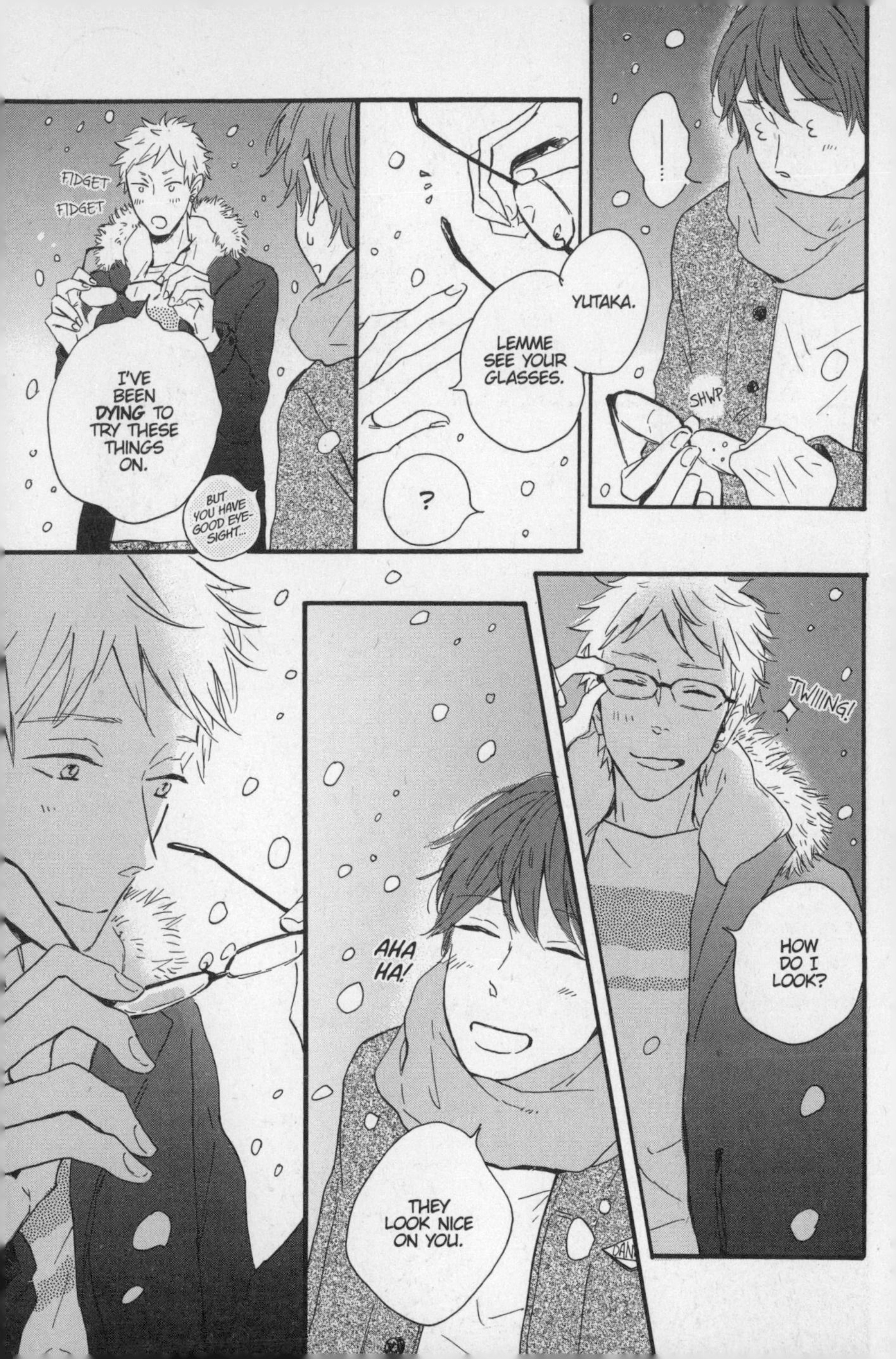
...!
SHWP
YUTAKA.
LEMME SEE YOUR GLASSES.
?
FIDGET FIDGET
I'VE BEEN DYING TO TRY THESE THINGS ON.
BUT YOU HAVE GOOD EYE-SIGHT...
TWIIING!
HOW DO I LOOK?
AHA HA!
THEY LOOK NICE ON YOU.

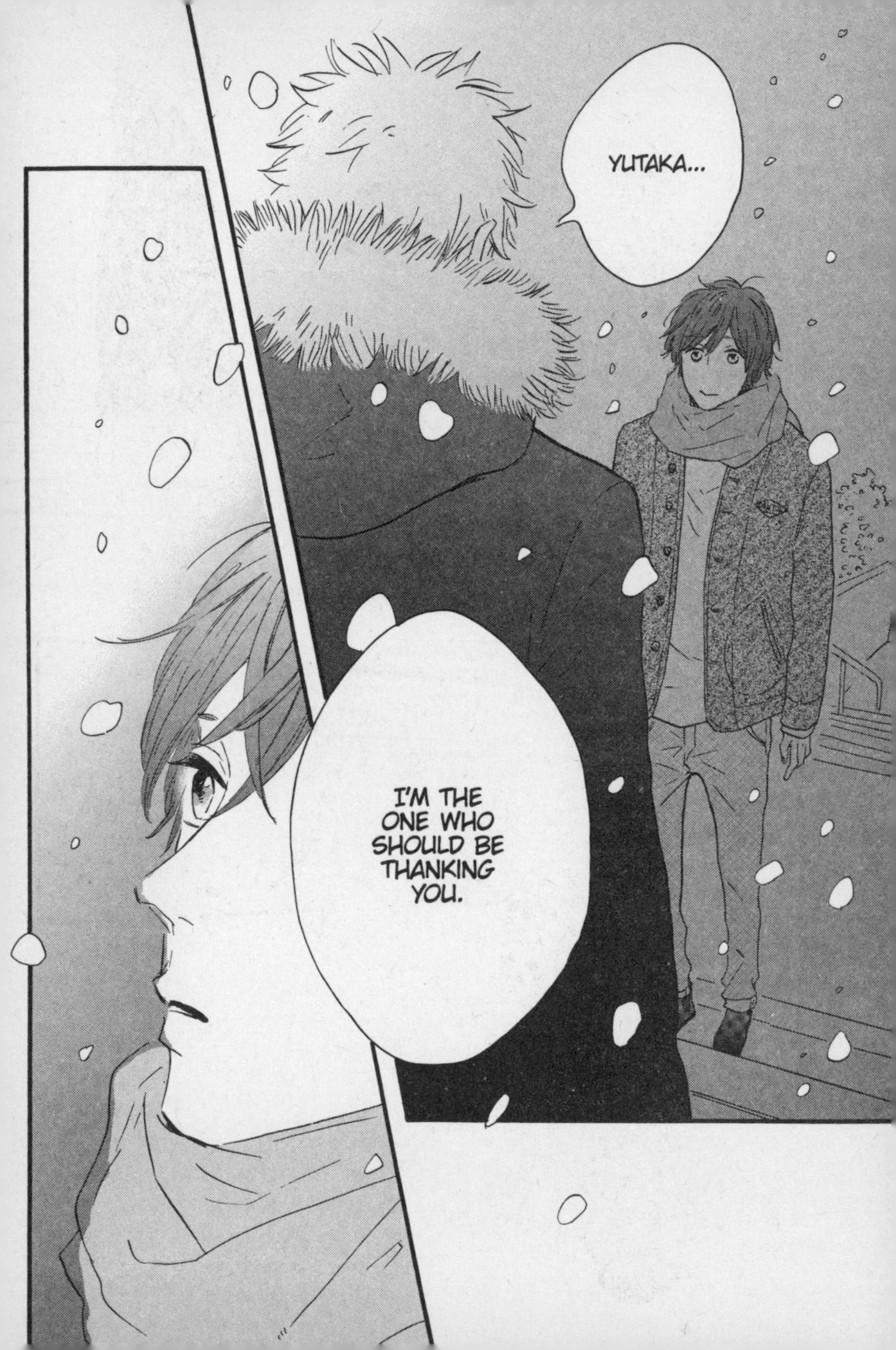
YUTAKA...
I'M THE ONE WHO SHOULD BE THANKING YOU.

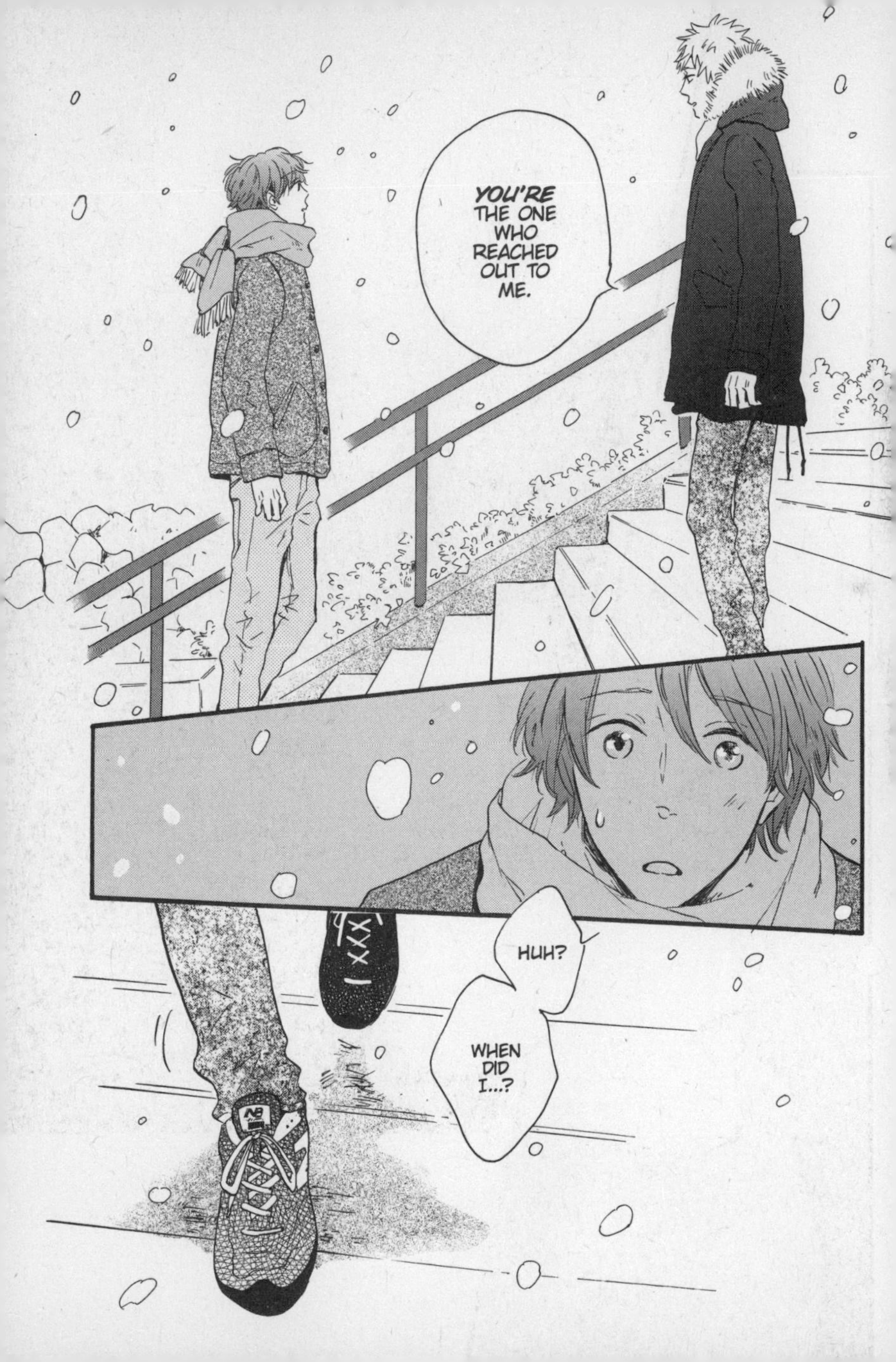
YOU'RE THE ONE WHO REACHED OUT TO ME.
HUH?
WHEN DID I...?

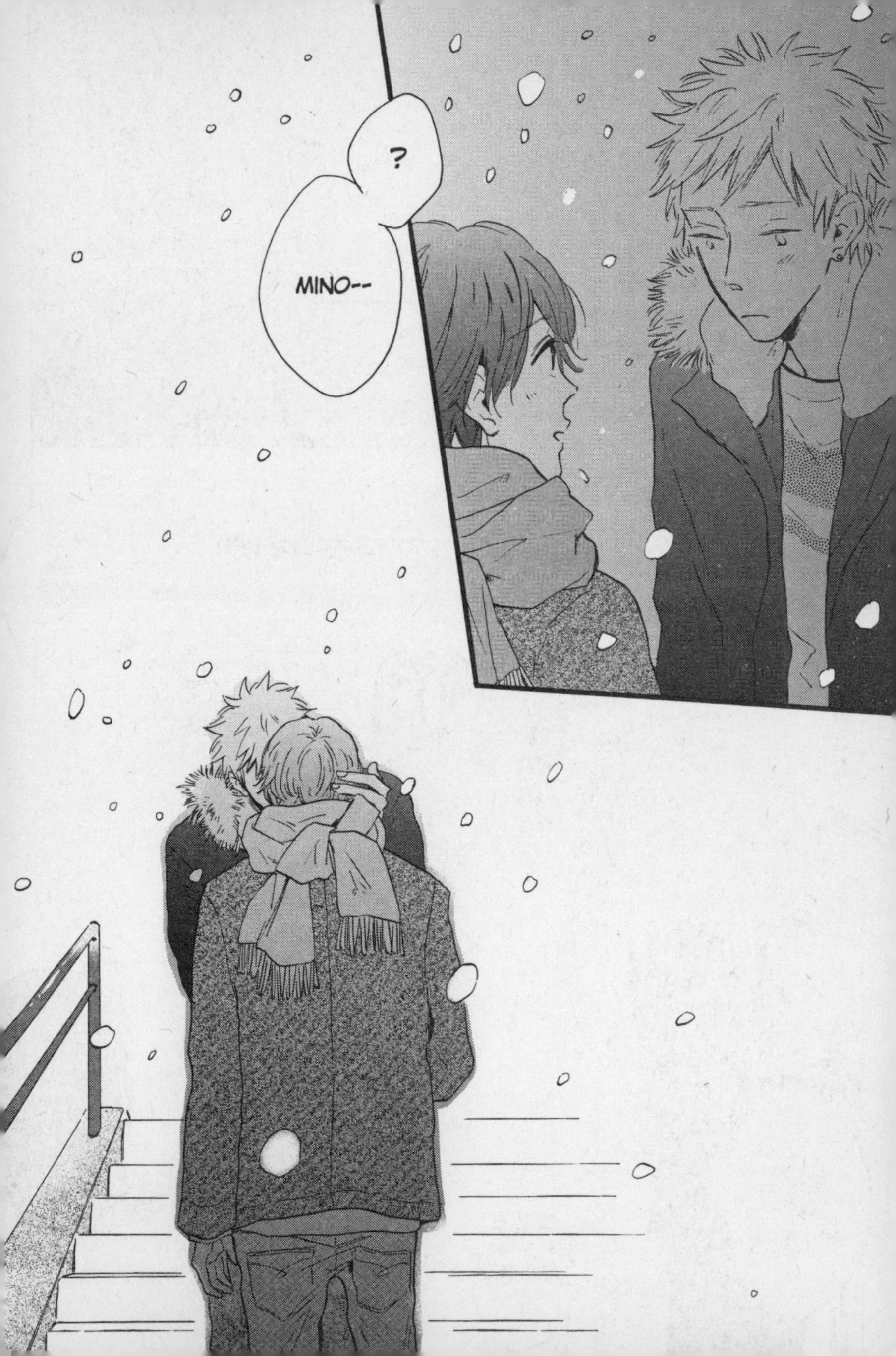
?
MINO--

Chapter 5

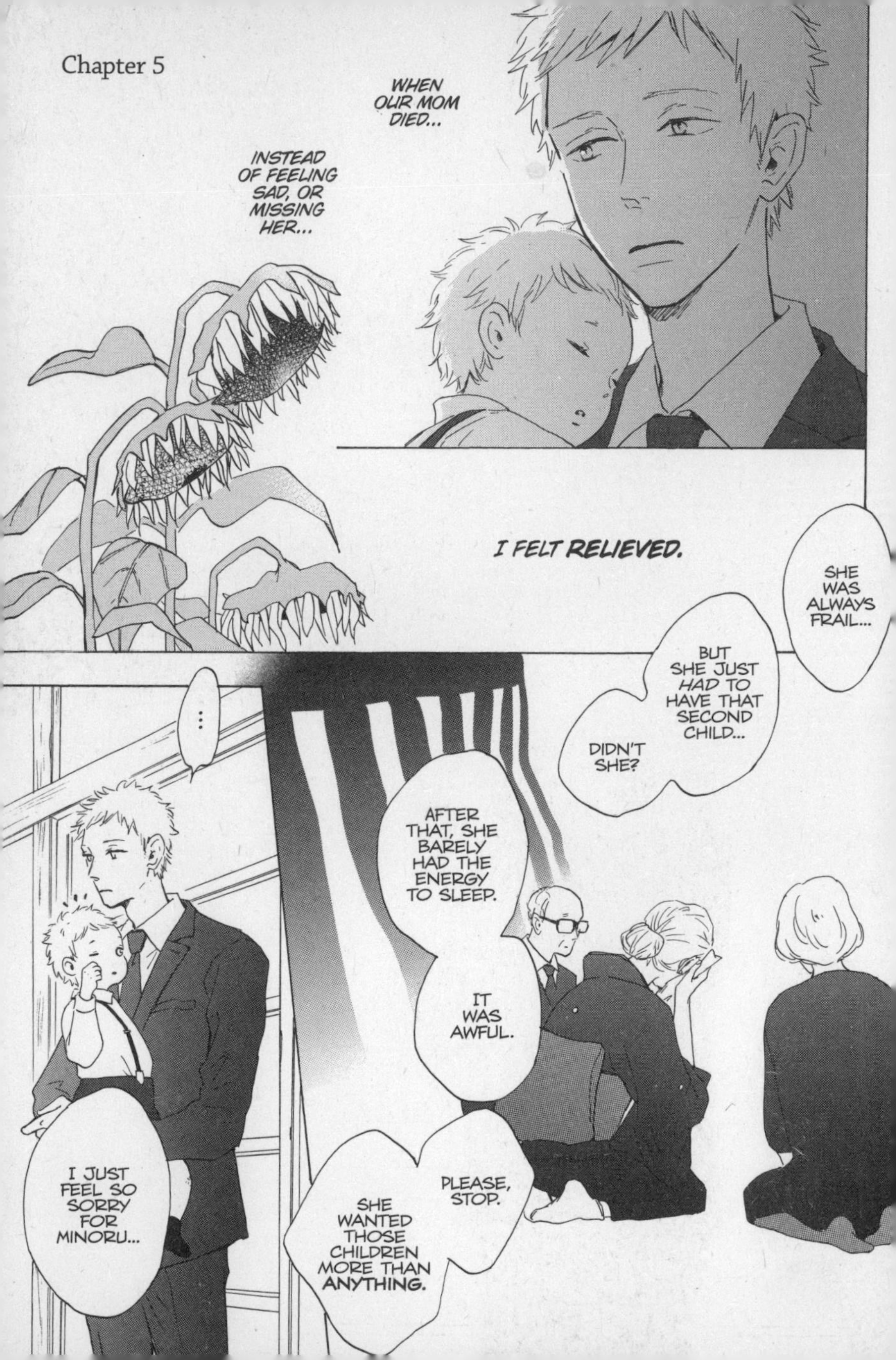

WHEN OUR MOM DIED...
INSTEAD OF FEELING SAD, OR MISSING HER...
I FELT RELIEVED.
SHE WAS ALWAYS FRAIL...
BUT SHE JUST HAD TO HAVE THAT SECOND CHILD...
DIDN'T SHE?
AFTER THAT, SHE BARELY HAD THE ENERGY TO SLEEP.
IT WAS AWFUL.
PLEASE, STOP.
SHE WANTED THOSE CHILDREN MORE THAN ANYTHING.
...
I JUST FEEL SO SORRY FOR MINORU...

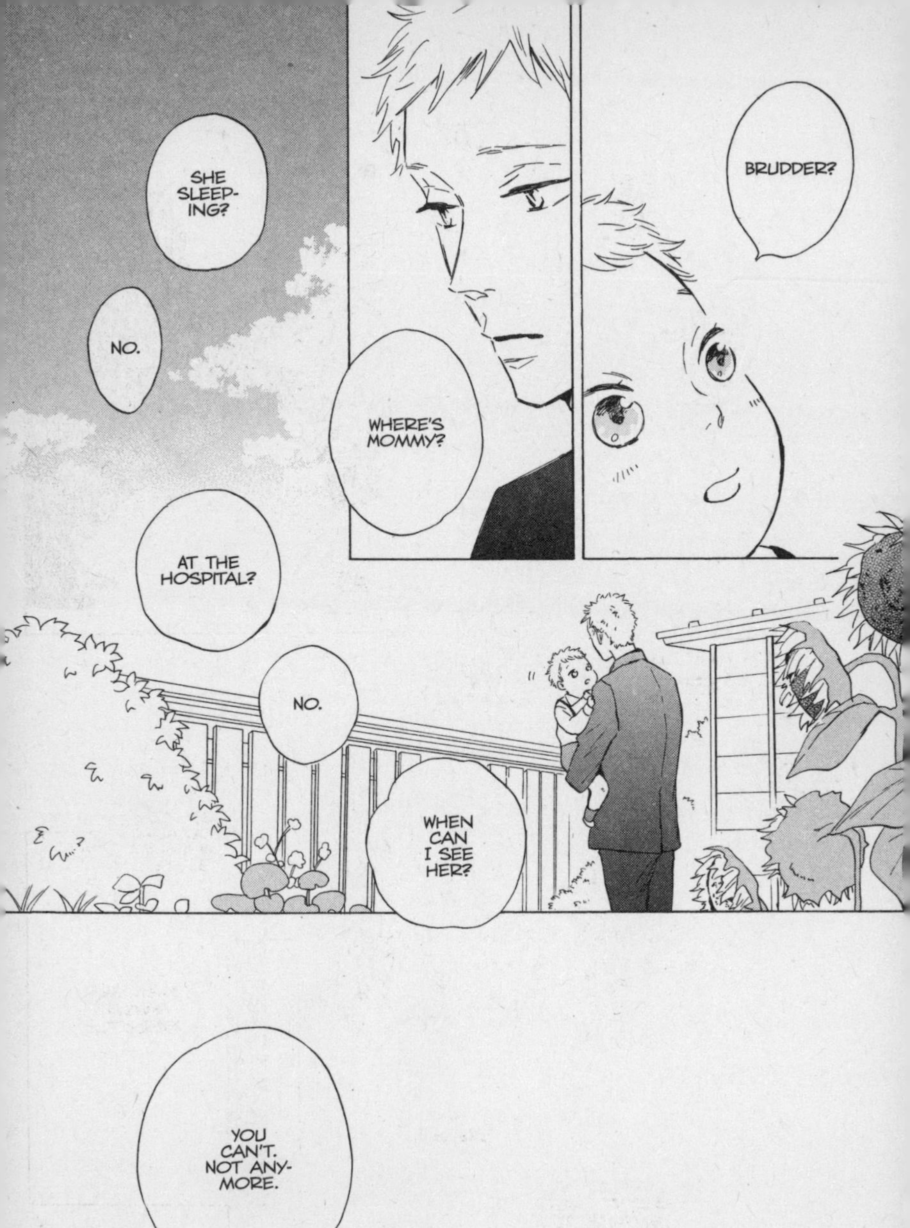
BRUDDER?
WHERE'S MOMMY?
SHE SLEEP-ING?
NO.
AT THE HOSPITAL?
NO.
WHEN CAN I SEE HER?
YOU CAN'T. NOT ANY-MORE.

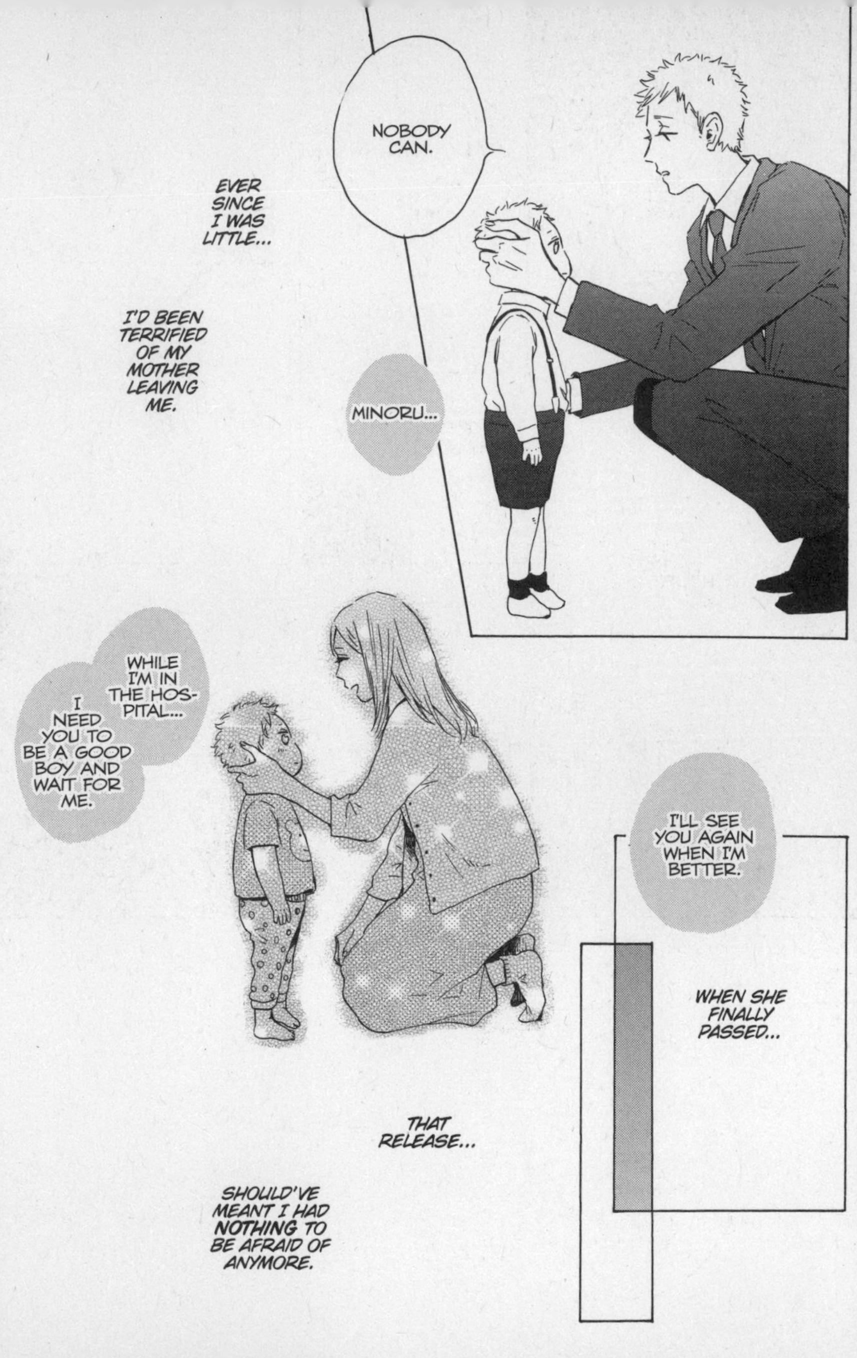
NOBODY CAN.
MINORU...
EVER SINCE I WAS LITTLE...
I'D BEEN TERRIFIED OF MY MOTHER LEAVING ME.
WHILE I'M IN THE HOS-PITAL...
I NEED YOU TO BE A GOOD BOY AND WAIT FOR ME.
I'LL SEE YOU AGAIN WHEN I'M BETTER.
WHEN SHE FINALLY PASSED...
THAT RELEASE...
SHOULD'VE MEANT I HAD **NOTHING** TO BE AFRAID OF ANYMORE.

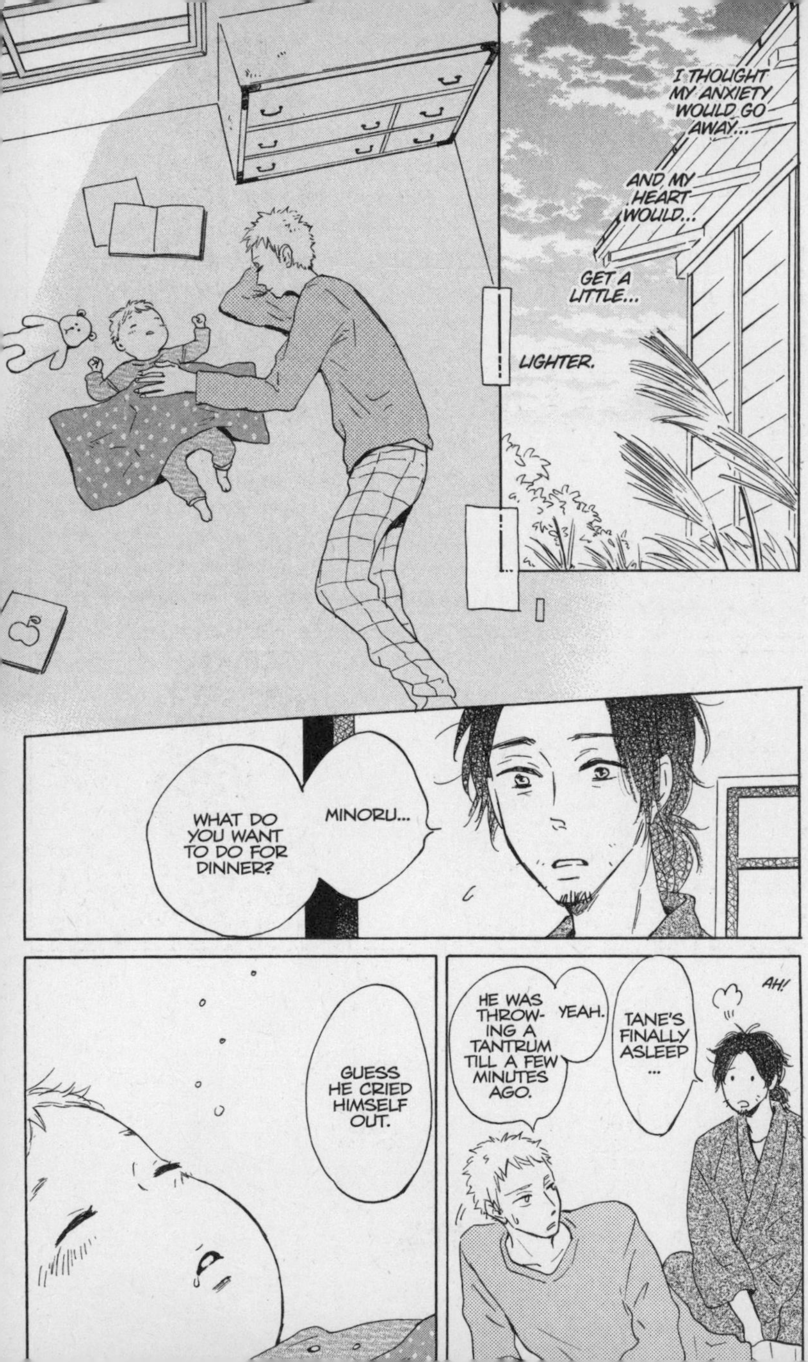

I THOUGHT MY ANXIETY WOULD GO AWAY...
AND, MY HEART WOULD...
GET A LITTLE...
LIGHTER.
MINORU...
WHAT DO YOU WANT TO DO FOR DINNER?
AH!
TANE'S FINALLY ASLEEP ...
YEAH.
HE WAS THROWING A TANTRUM TILL A FEW MINUTES AGO.
GUESS HE CRIED HIMSELF OUT.

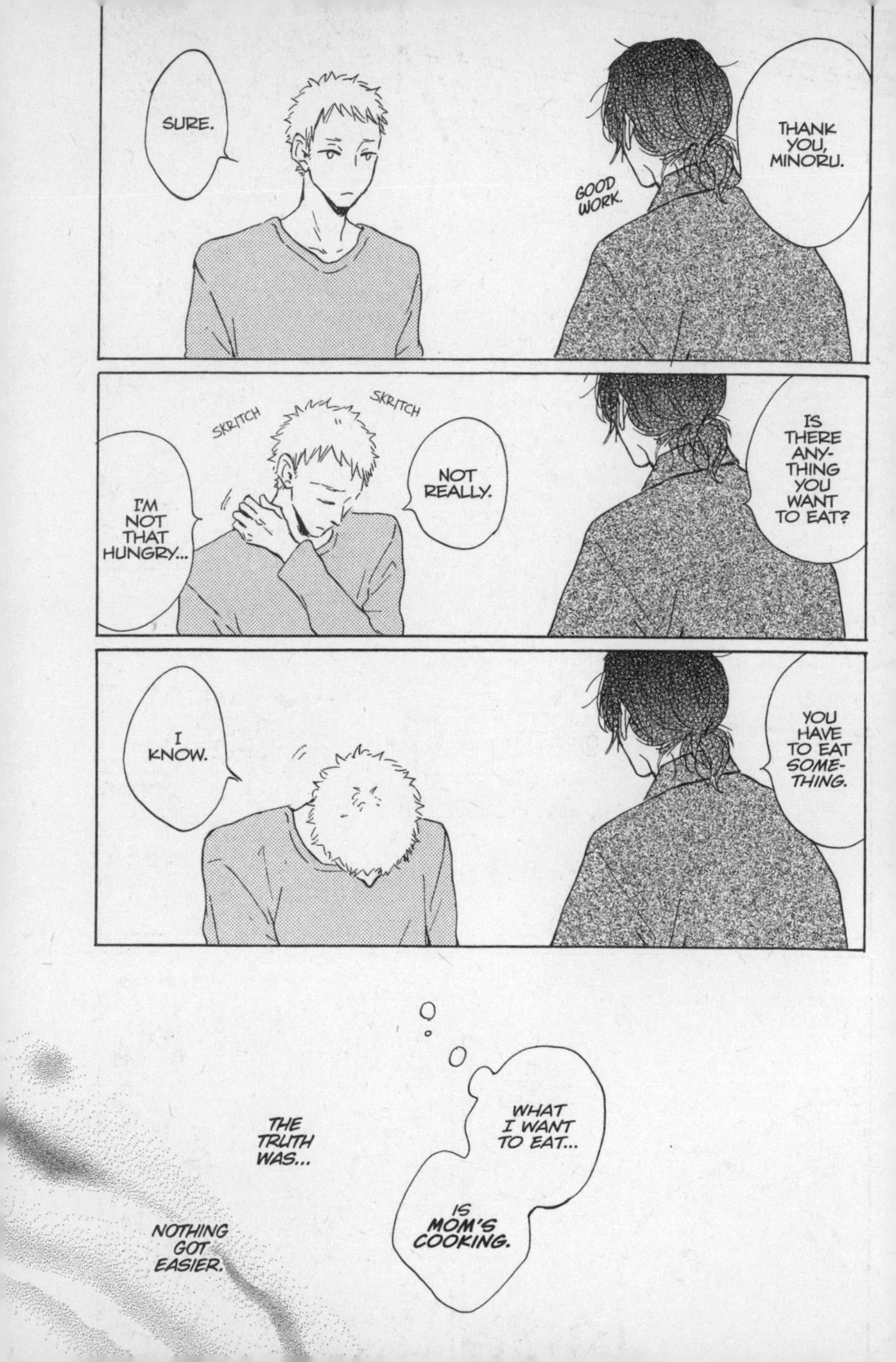
THANK YOU, MINORU.
GOOD WORK.
SURE.
IS THERE ANY-THING YOU WANT TO EAT?
SKRITCH
NOT REALLY.
SKRITCH
I'M NOT THAT HUNGRY...
YOU HAVE TO EAT SOME-THING.
I KNOW.
WHAT I WANT TO EAT...
IS MOM'S COOKING.
THE TRUTH WAS...
NOTHING GOT EASIER.

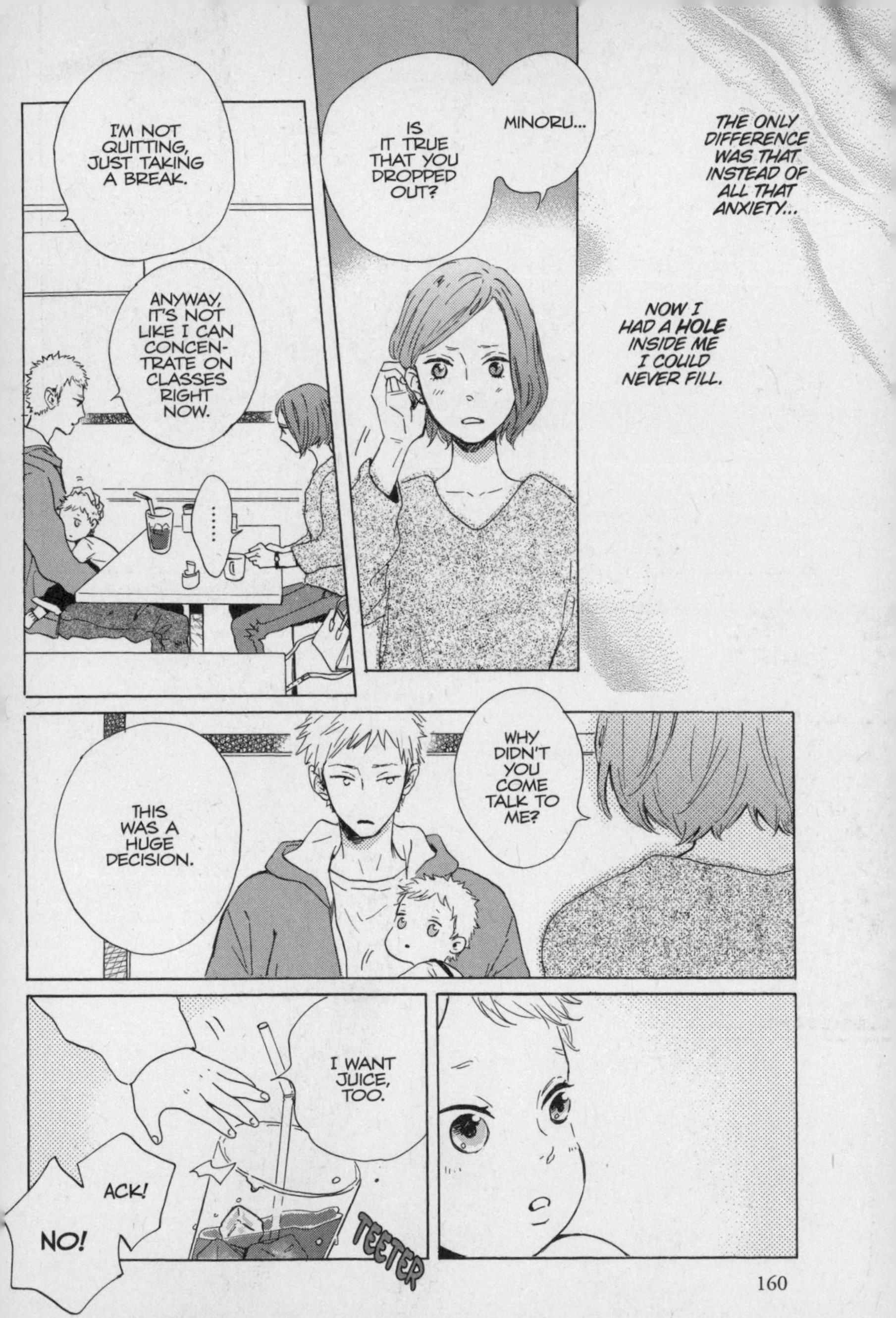
THE ONLY DIFFERENCE WAS THAT INSTEAD OF ALL THAT ANXIETY...
NOW I HAD A **HOLE** INSIDE ME I COULD NEVER FILL.
MINORU...
IS IT TRUE THAT YOU DROPPED OUT?
I'M NOT QUITTING, JUST TAKING A BREAK.
ANYWAY, IT'S NOT LIKE I CAN CONCEN-TRATE ON CLASSES RIGHT NOW.
......
WHY DIDN'T YOU COME TALK TO ME?
THIS WAS A HUGE DECISION.
I WANT JUICE, TOO.
ACK!
TEETER
NO!

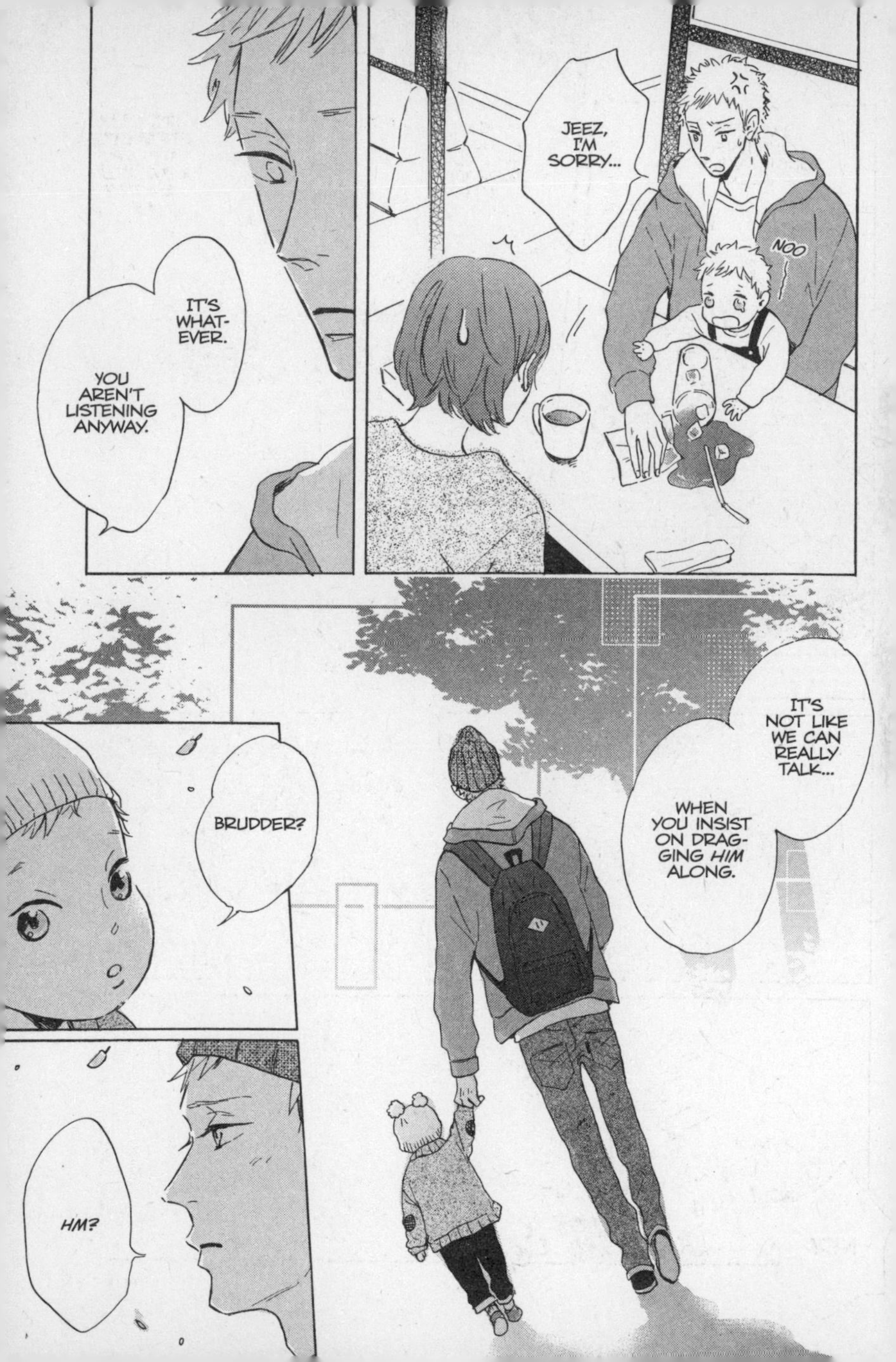
JEEZ, I'M SORRY...
NOO
IT'S WHATEVER.
YOU AREN'T LISTENING ANYWAY.
IT'S NOT LIKE WE CAN REALLY TALK...
WHEN YOU INSIST ON DRAGGING *HIM* ALONG.
BRUDDER?
HM?

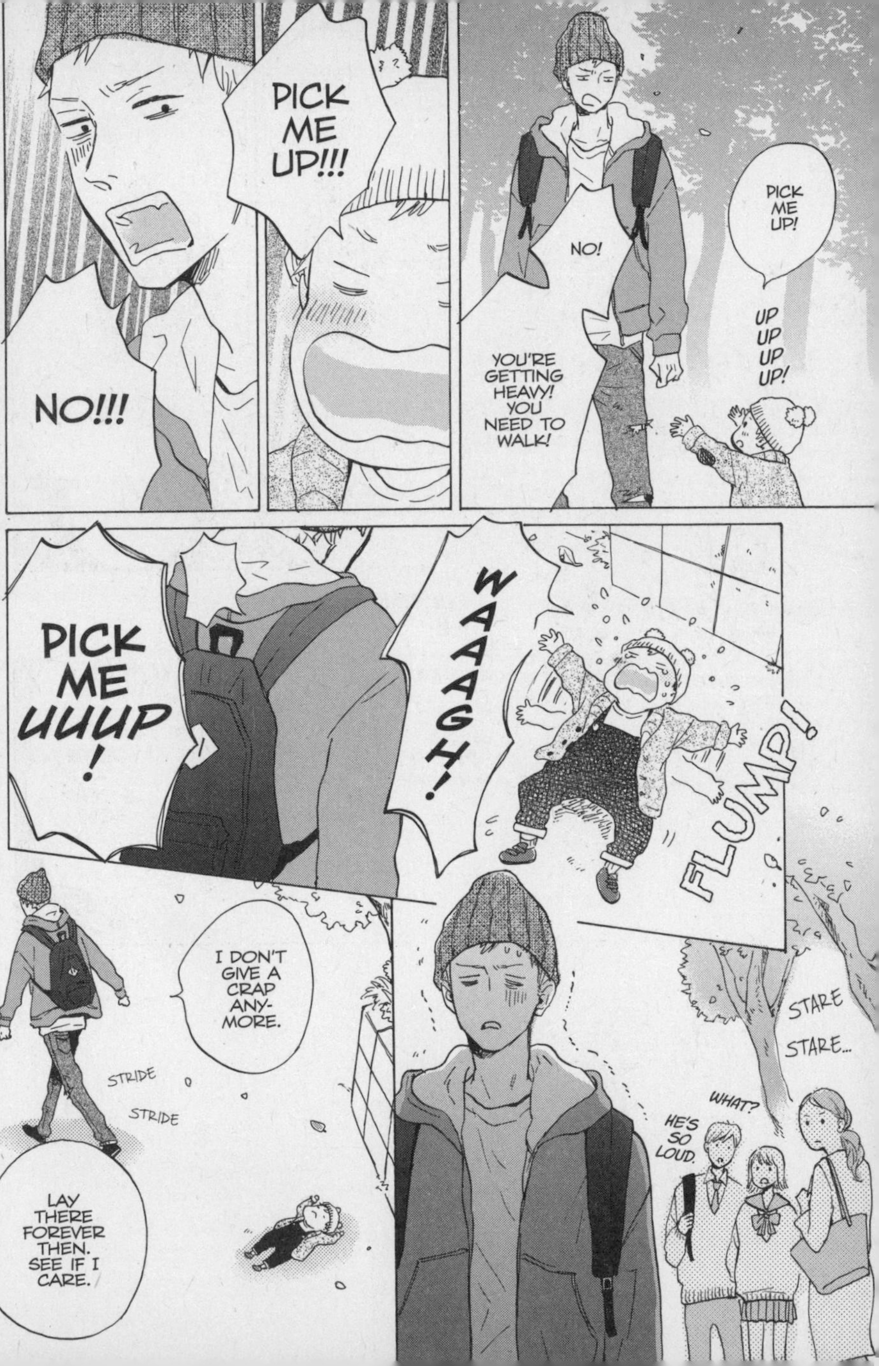
PICK ME UP!
NO!
UP UP UP UP!
YOU'RE GETTING HEAVY! YOU NEED TO WALK!
PICK ME UP!!!
NO!!!
WAAAAGH!
FLUMP!
PICK ME UUUP!
STARE
STARE...
WHAT?
HE'S SO LOUD.
I DON'T GIVE A CRAP ANY-MORE.
STRIDE
STRIDE
LAY THERE FOREVER THEN. SEE IF I CARE.

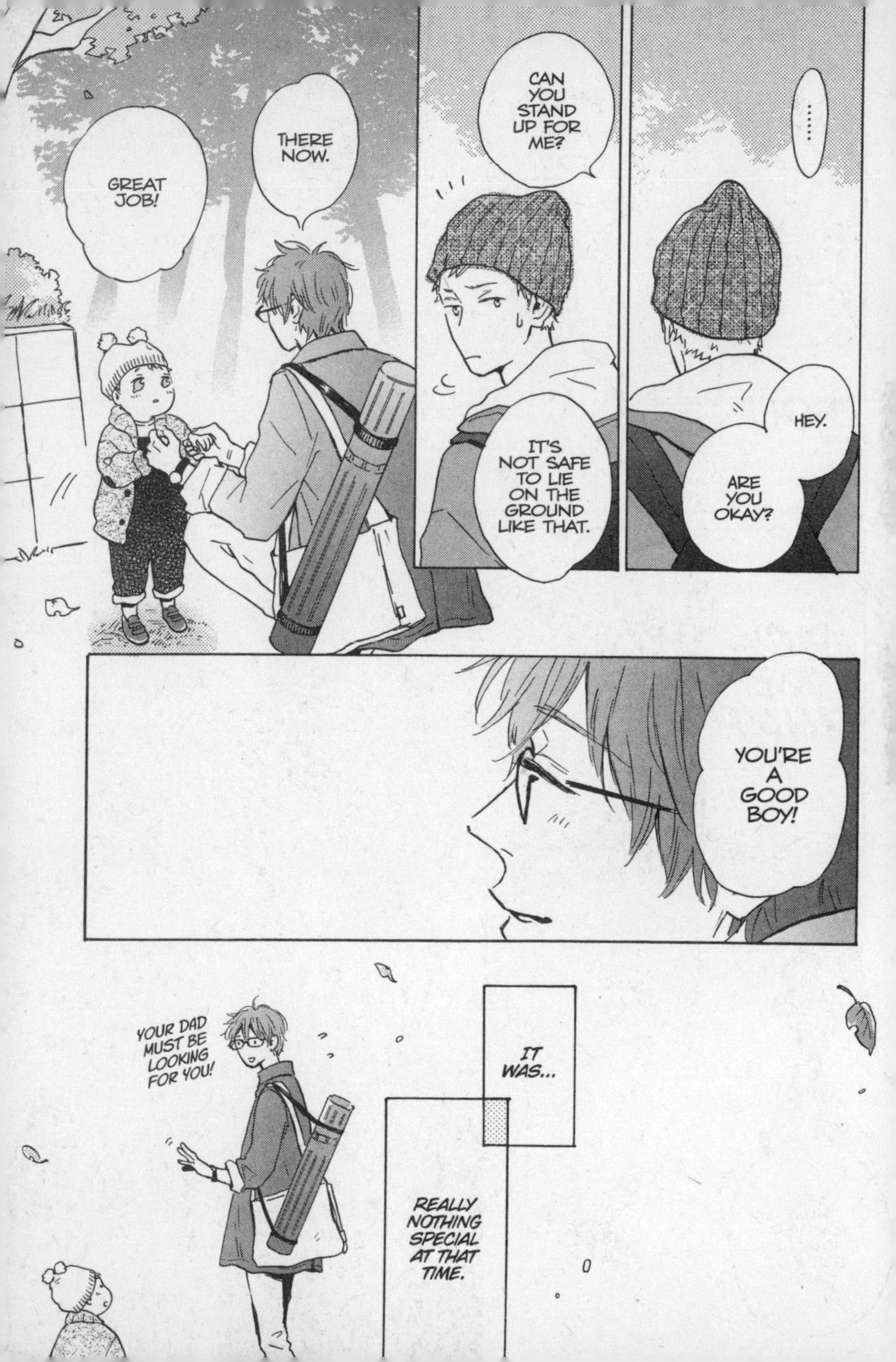
......
HEY.
ARE YOU OKAY?
CAN YOU STAND UP FOR ME?
IT'S NOT SAFE TO LIE ON THE GROUND LIKE THAT.
THERE NOW.
GREAT JOB!
YOU'RE A GOOD BOY!
IT WAS...
REALLY NOTHING SPECIAL AT THAT TIME.
YOUR DAD MUST BE LOOKING FOR YOU!

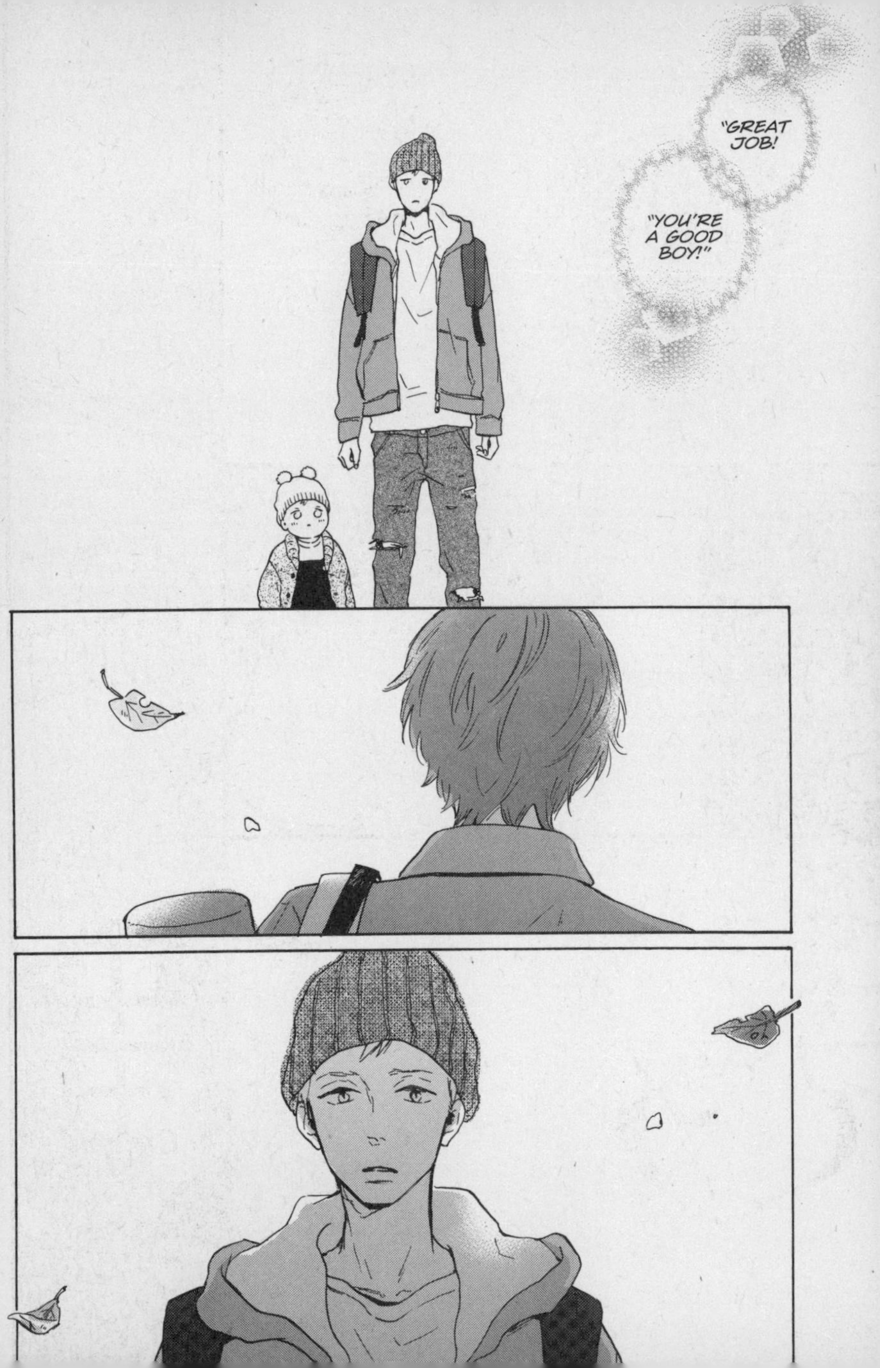
"GREAT JOB!
"YOU'RE A GOOD BOY!"

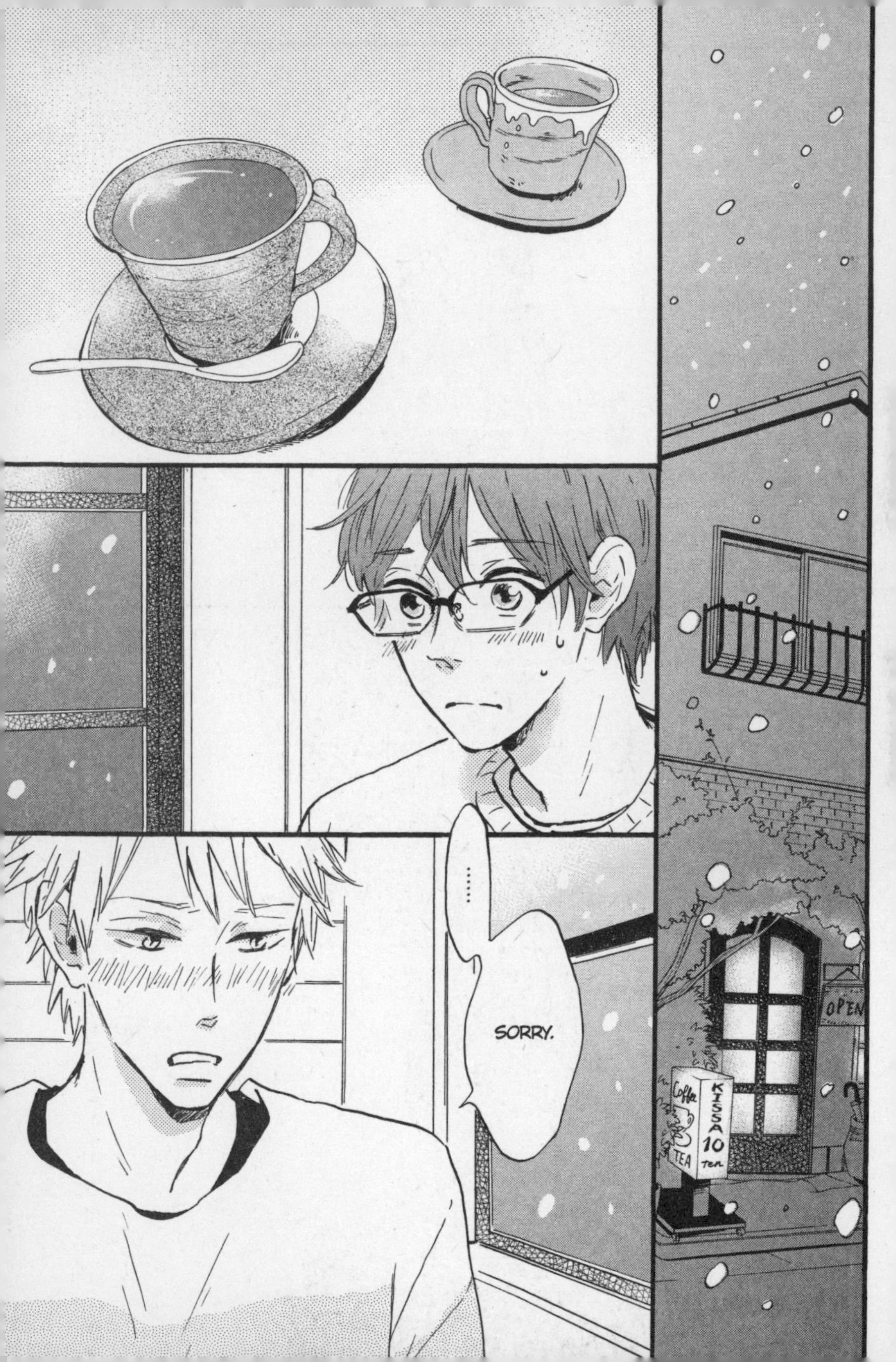
OPEN
Coffee
TEA
KISSA
10
ten
......
SORRY.

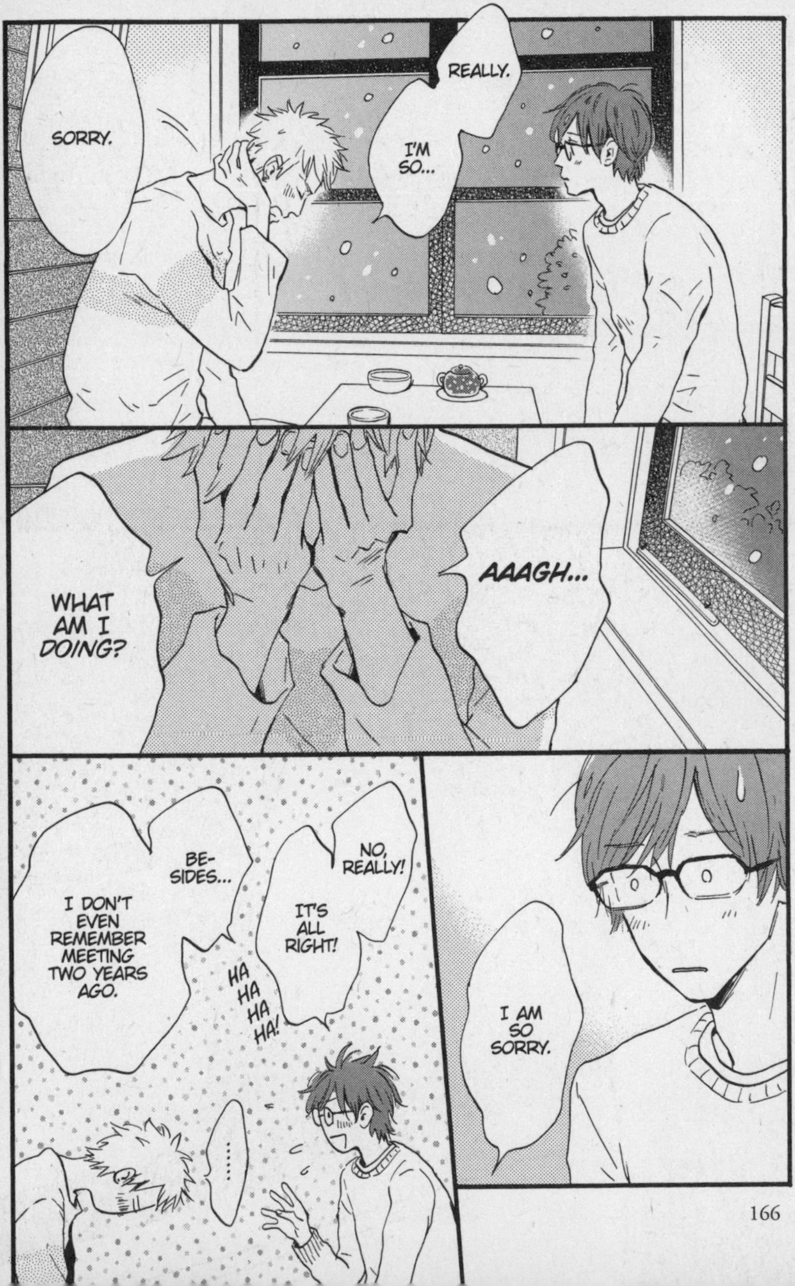
REALLY.
I'M SO...
SORRY.
AAAGH...
WHAT AM I DOING?
I AM SO SORRY.
NO, REALLY!
IT'S ALL RIGHT!
HA HA HA HA!
BE- SIDES...
I DON'T EVEN REMEMBER MEETING TWO YEARS AGO.
......

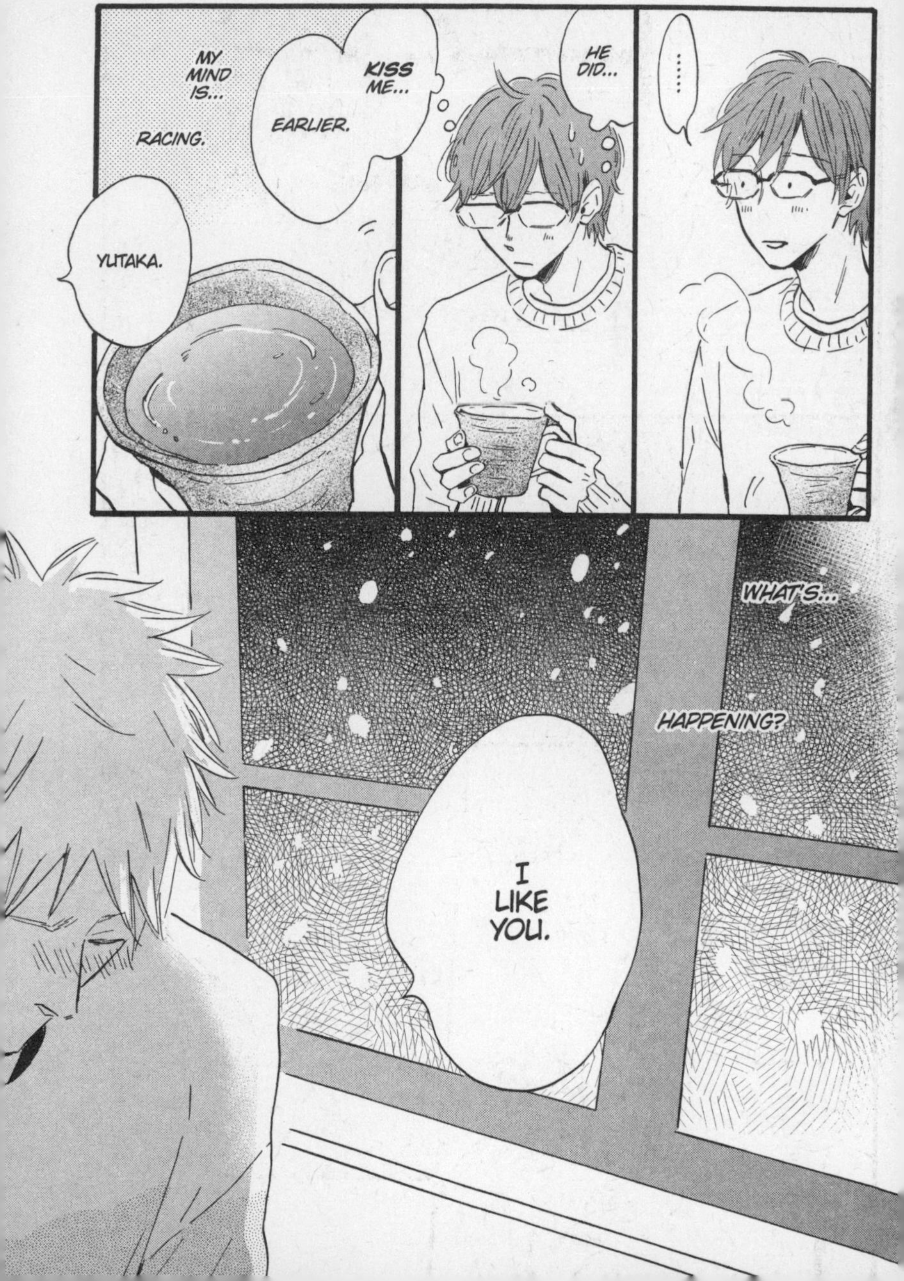
......
HE DID...
KISS ME... EARLIER.
MY MIND IS... RACING.
YUTAKA.
WHAT'S... HAPPENING?
I LIKE YOU.

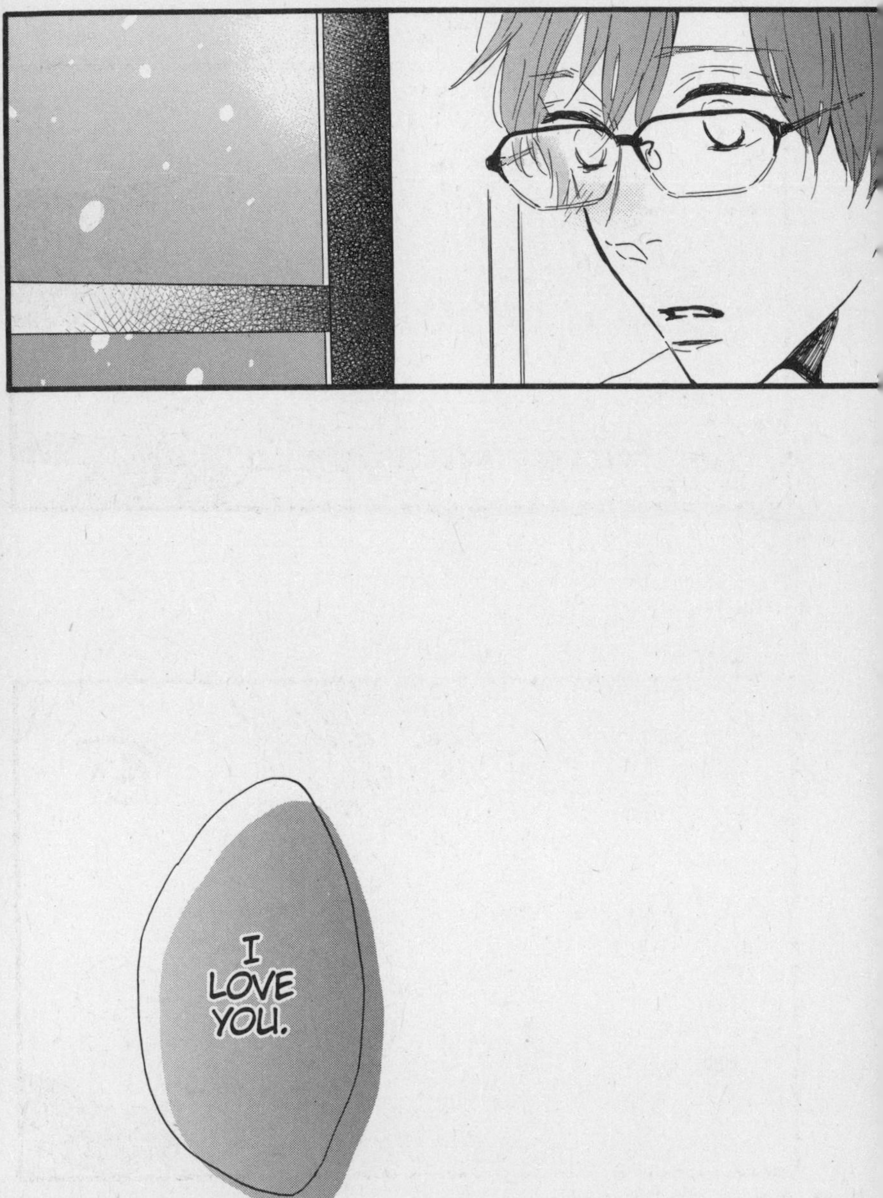
I LOVE YOU.

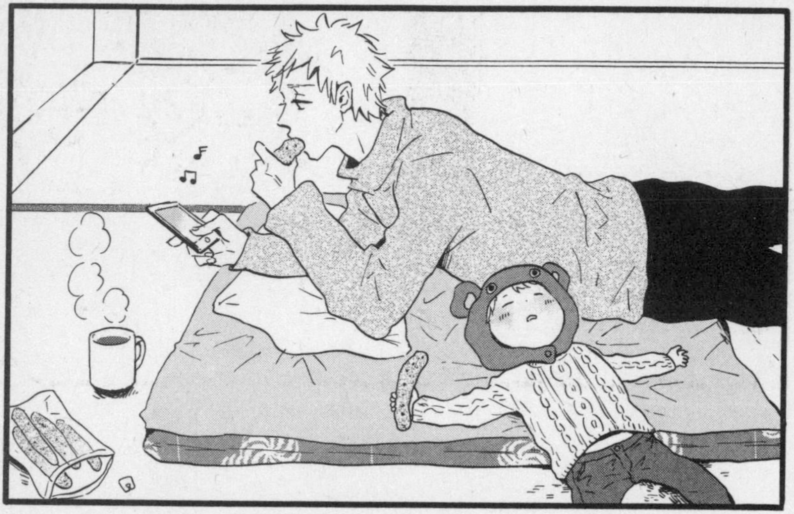

Chapter 6

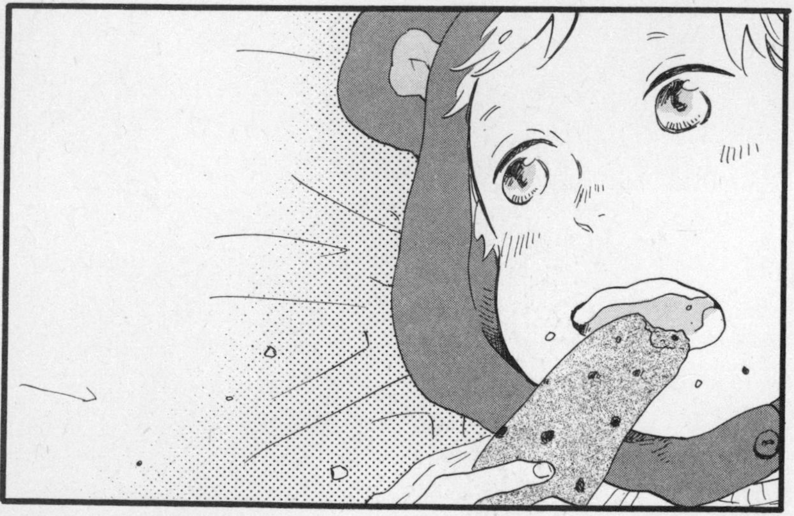

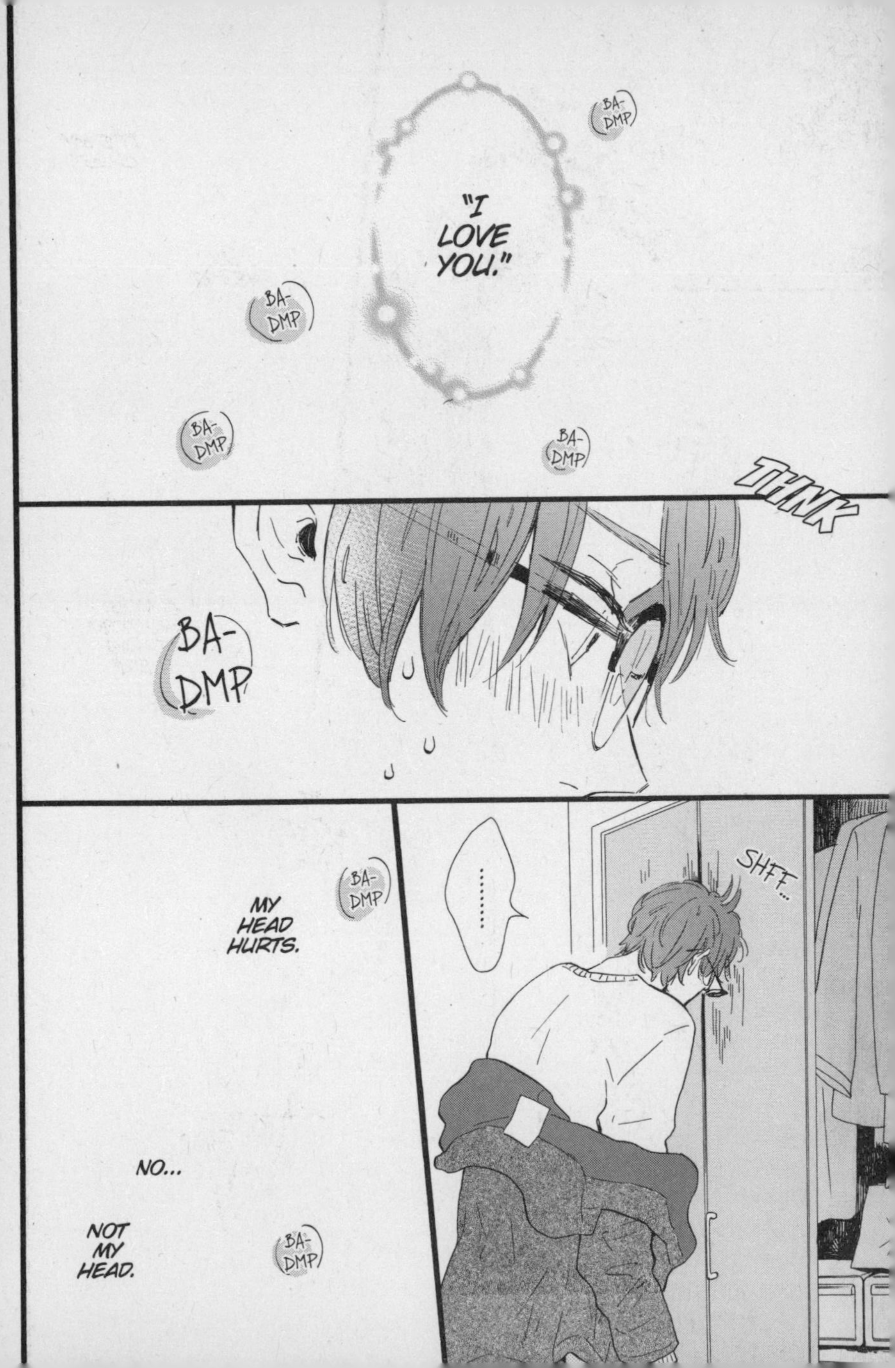
BA-DMP
"I LOVE YOU."
BA-DMP
BA-DMP
BA-DMP
THNK
BA-DMP
SHFF...
......
BA-DMP
MY HEAD HURTS.
NO...
NOT MY HEAD.
BA-DMP

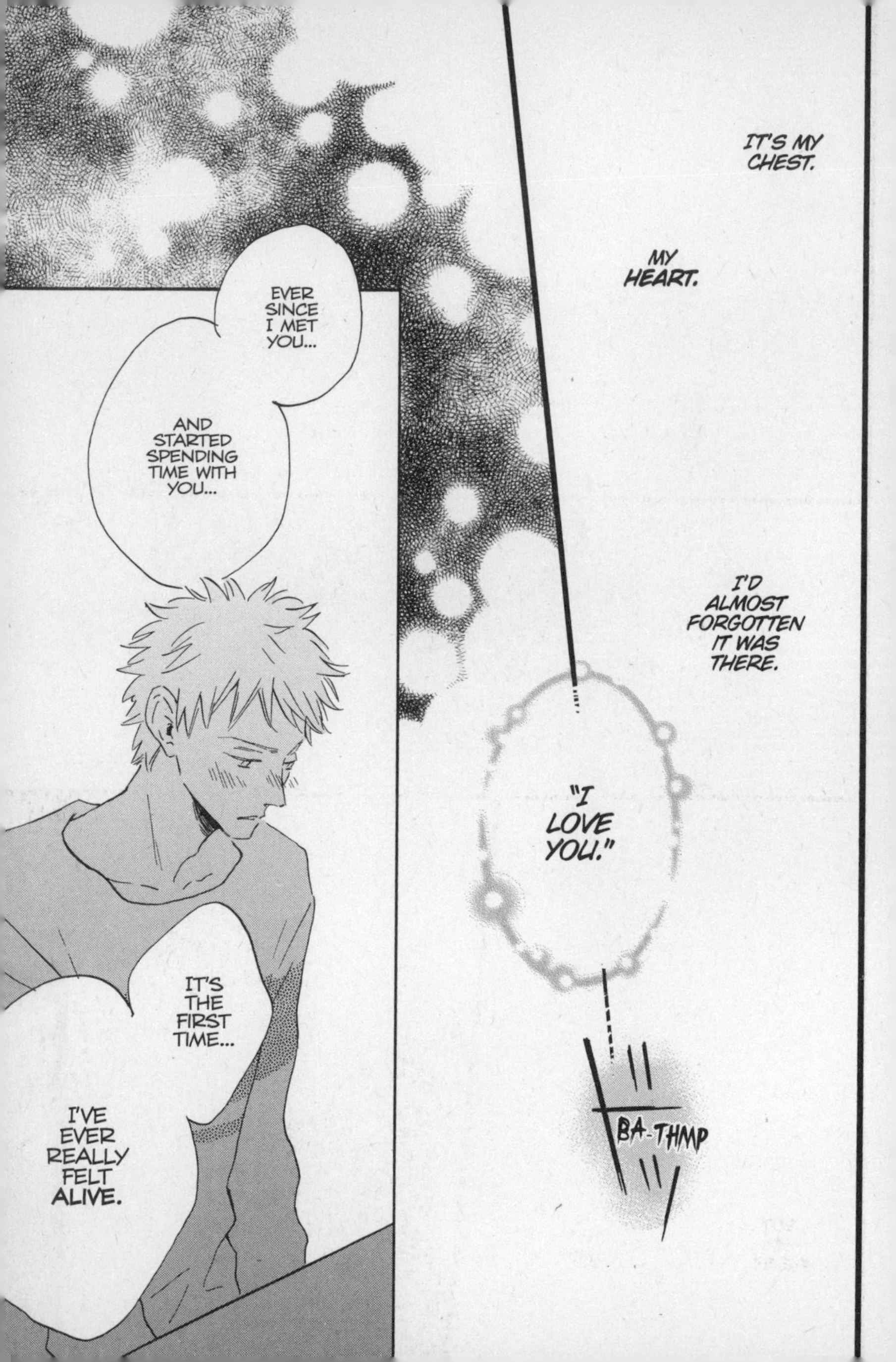
IT'S MY CHEST.
MY HEART.
I'D ALMOST FORGOTTEN IT WAS THERE.
"I LOVE YOU."
BA-THMP
EVER SINCE I MET YOU...
AND STARTED SPENDING TIME WITH YOU...
IT'S THE FIRST TIME...
I'VE EVER REALLY FELT ALIVE.

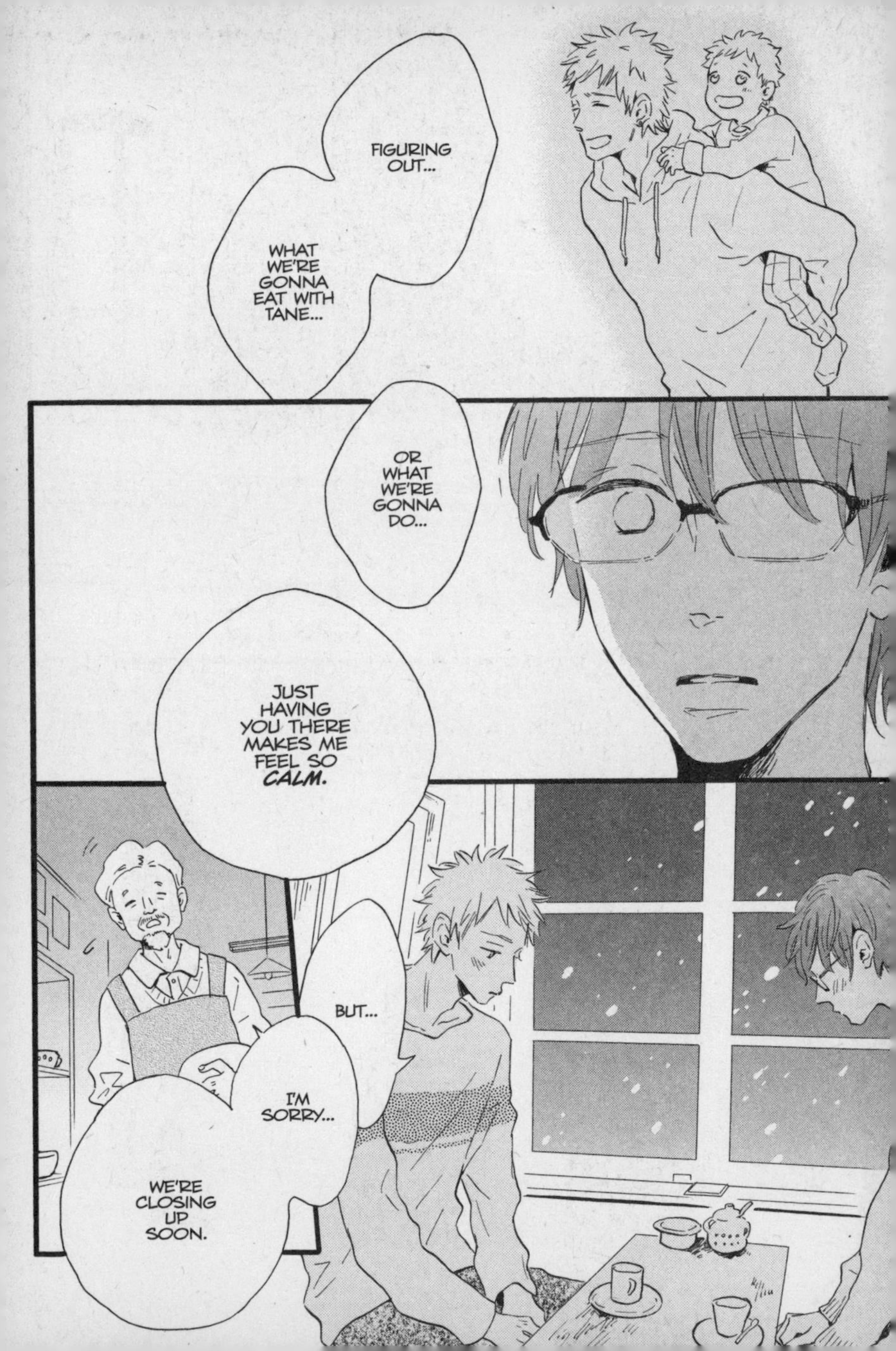
FIGURING OUT...
WHAT WE'RE GONNA EAT WITH TANE...
OR WHAT WE'RE GONNA DO...
JUST HAVING YOU THERE MAKES ME FEEL SO CALM.
BUT...
I'M SORRY...
WE'RE CLOSING UP SOON.

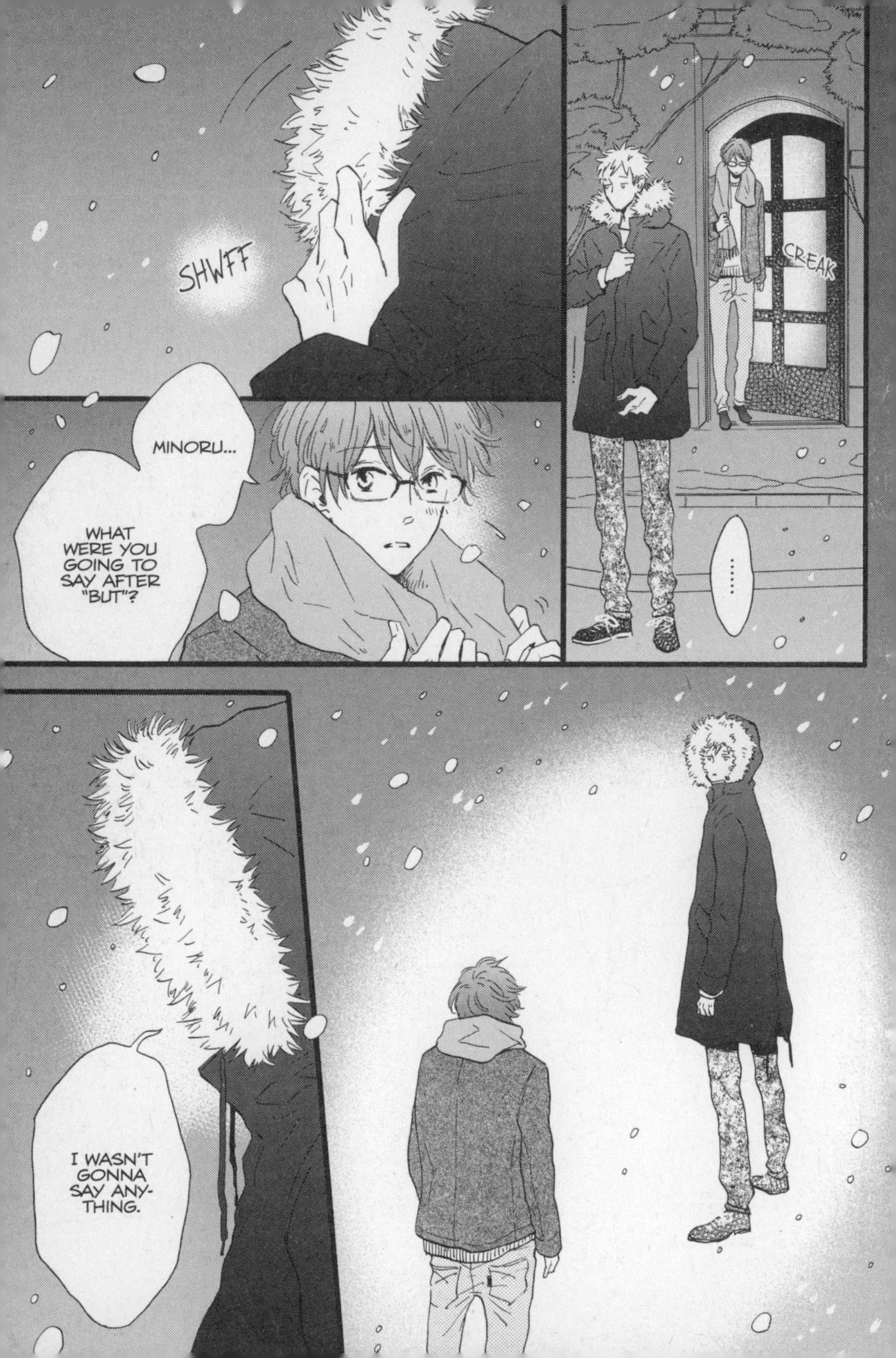
CR-EAK
......
SHWFF
MINORU...
WHAT WERE YOU GOING TO SAY AFTER "BUT"?
I WASN'T GONNA SAY ANYTHING.

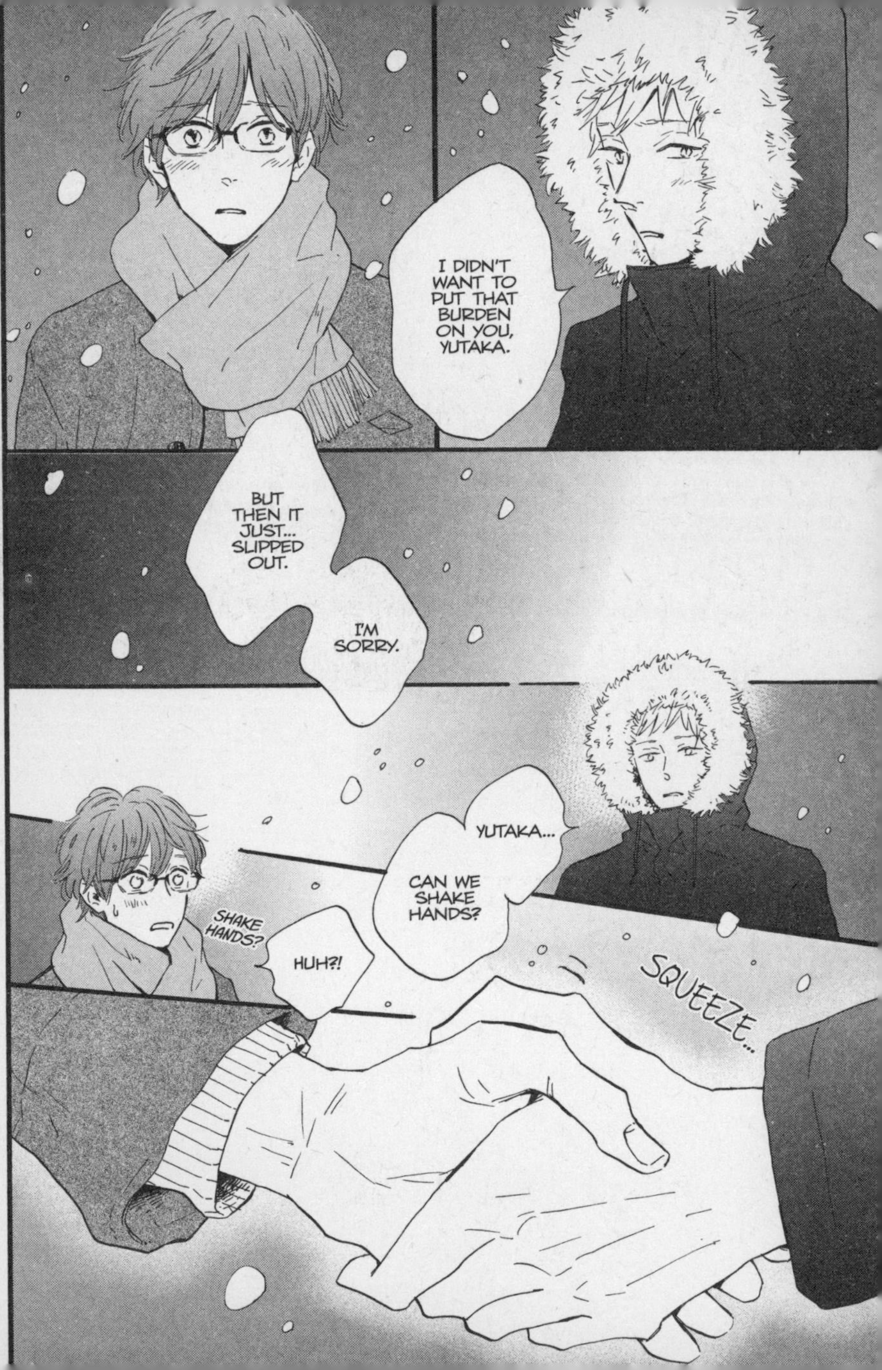
I DIDN'T WANT TO PUT THAT BURDEN ON YOU, YUTAKA.
BUT THEN IT JUST... SLIPPED OUT.
I'M SORRY.
YUTAKA...
CAN WE SHAKE HANDS?
HUH?!
SHAKE HANDS?
SQUEEZE...

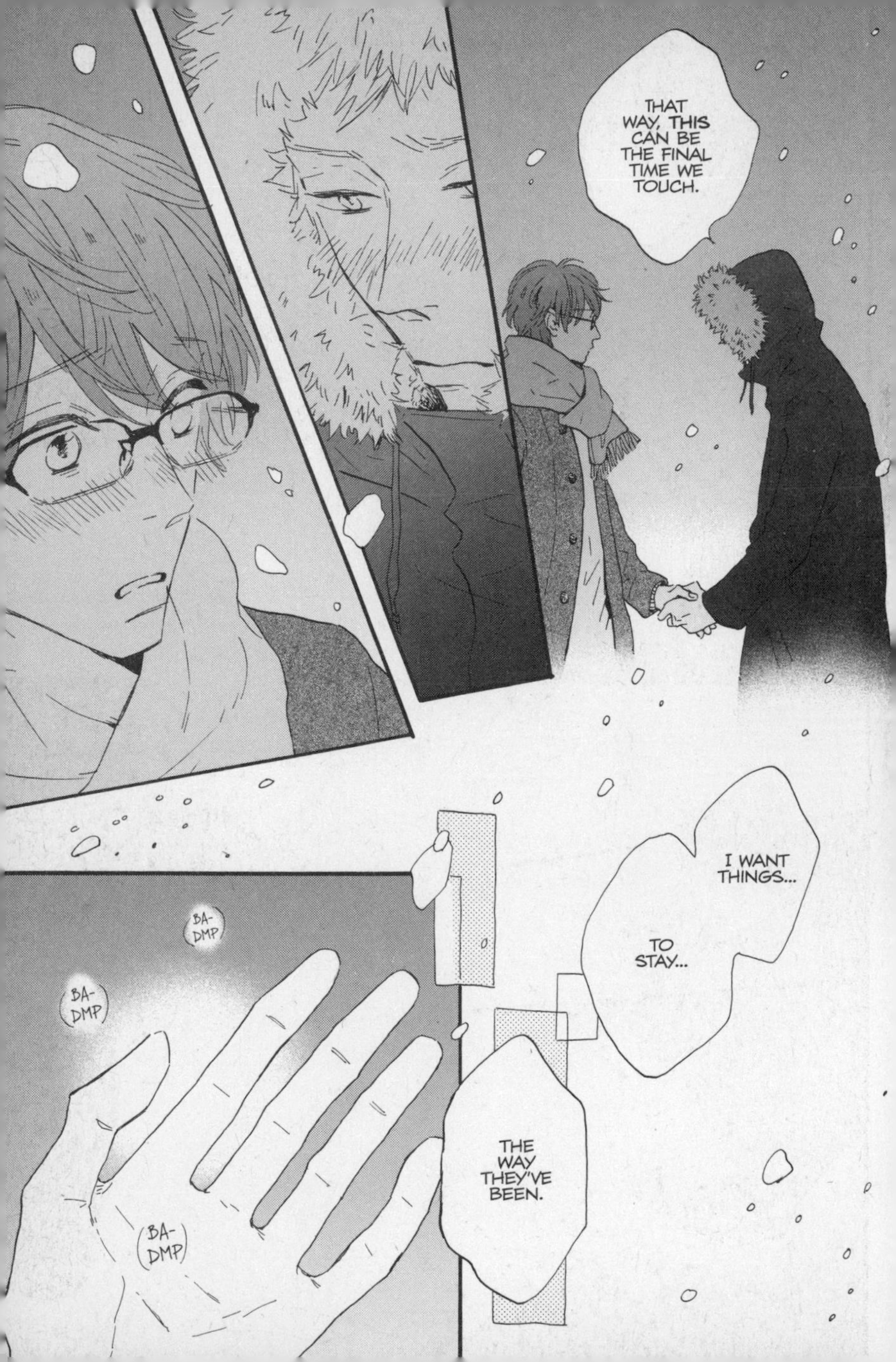
THAT WAY, THIS CAN BE THE FINAL TIME WE TOUCH.
I WANT THINGS...
TO STAY...
THE WAY THEY'VE BEEN.
BA-DMP
BA-DMP
BA-DMP

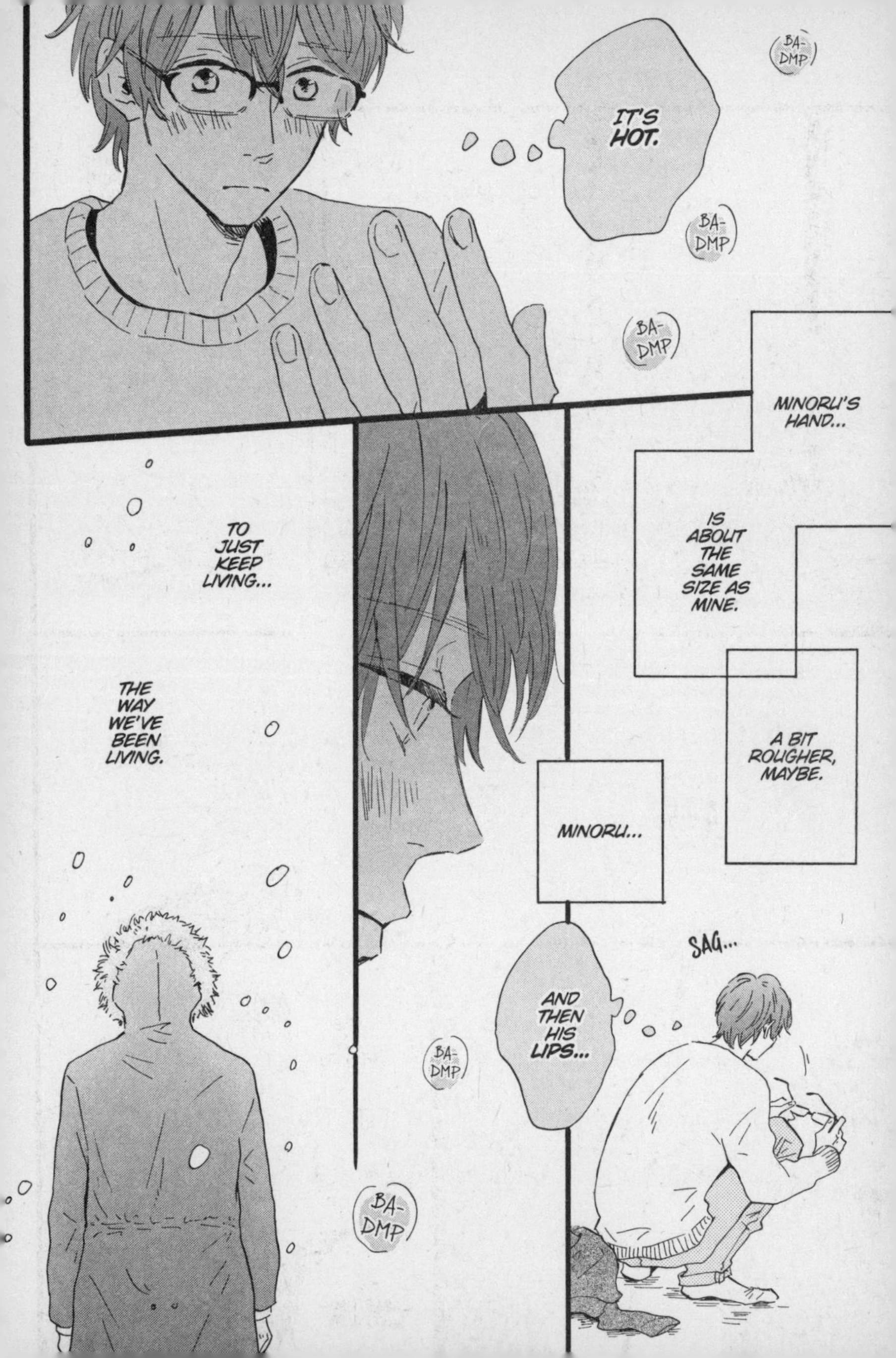
BA-DMP
IT'S HOT.
BA-DMP
BA-DMP
MINORU'S HAND...
IS ABOUT THE SAME SIZE AS MINE.
A BIT ROUGHER, MAYBE.
MINORU...
SAG...
AND THEN HIS LIPS...
BA-DMP
BA-DMP
TO JUST KEEP LIVING...
THE WAY WE'VE BEEN LIVING.

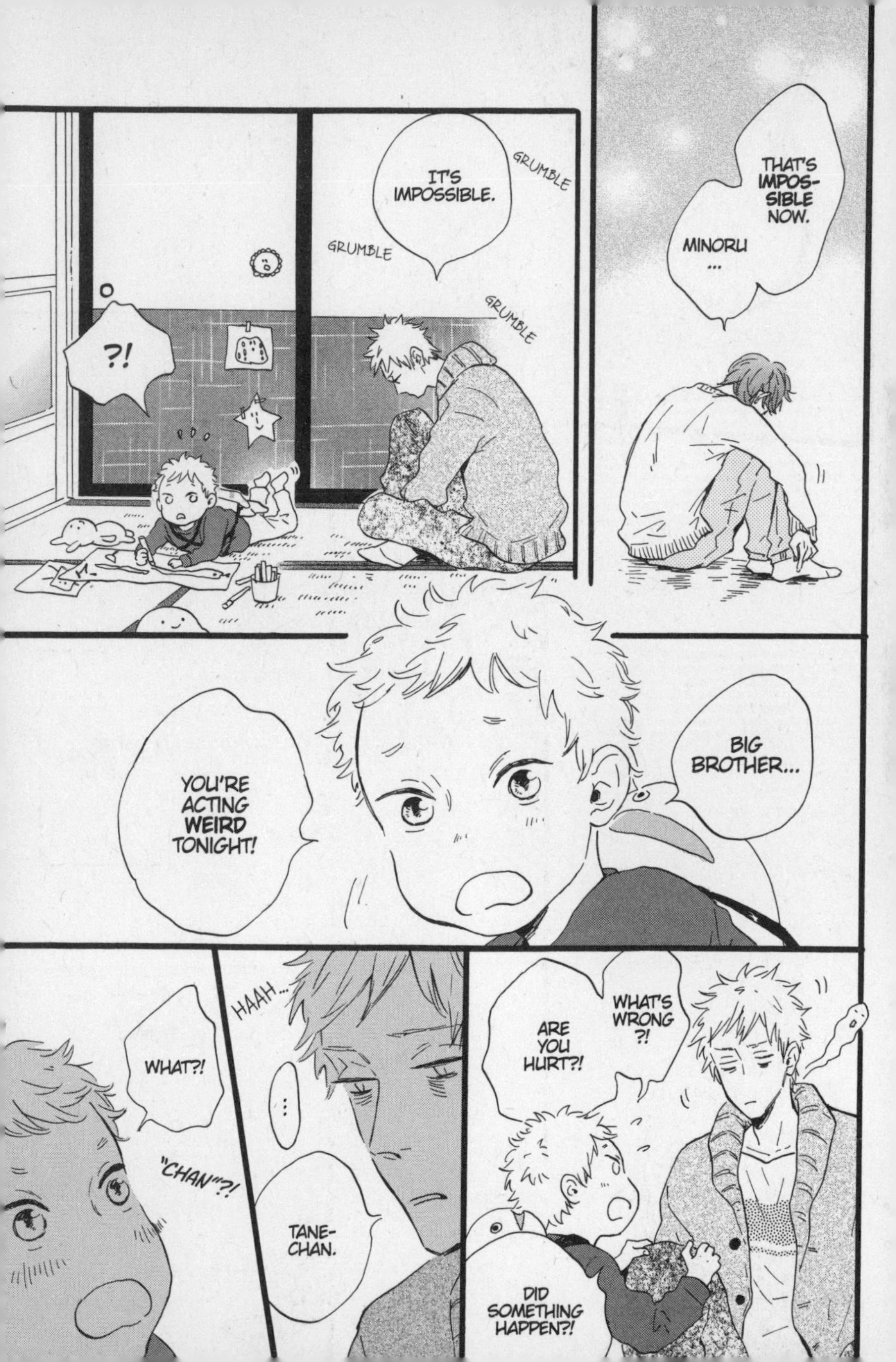
THAT'S IMPOSSIBLE NOW.
MINORU...
IT'S IMPOSSIBLE.
GRUMBLE
GRUMBLE
GRUMBLE
?!
BIG BROTHER...
YOU'RE ACTING WEIRD TONIGHT!
WHAT'S WRONG?!
ARE YOU HURT?!
DID SOMETHING HAPPEN?!
HAAH...
...
TANE-CHAN.
WHAT?!
"CHAN"?!

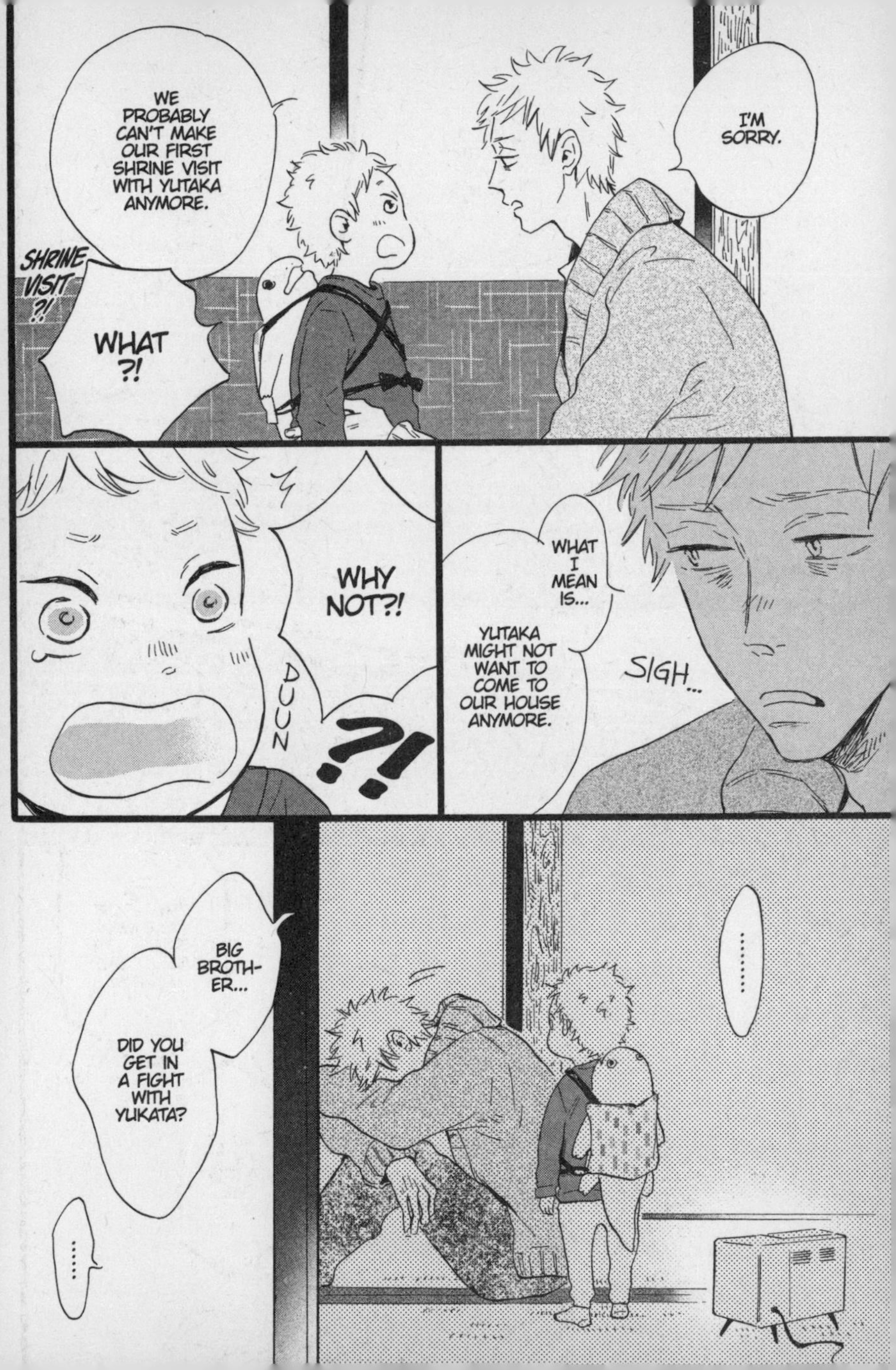

I'M SORRY.
WE PROBABLY CAN'T MAKE OUR FIRST SHRINE VISIT WITH YUTAKA ANYMORE.
SHRINE VISIT ?!
WHAT ?!
WHAT I MEAN IS...
YUTAKA MIGHT NOT WANT TO COME TO OUR HOUSE ANYMORE.
SIGH...
WHY NOT?!
DUUN
?!
......
BIG BROTHER...
DID YOU GET IN A FIGHT WITH YUKATA?
......

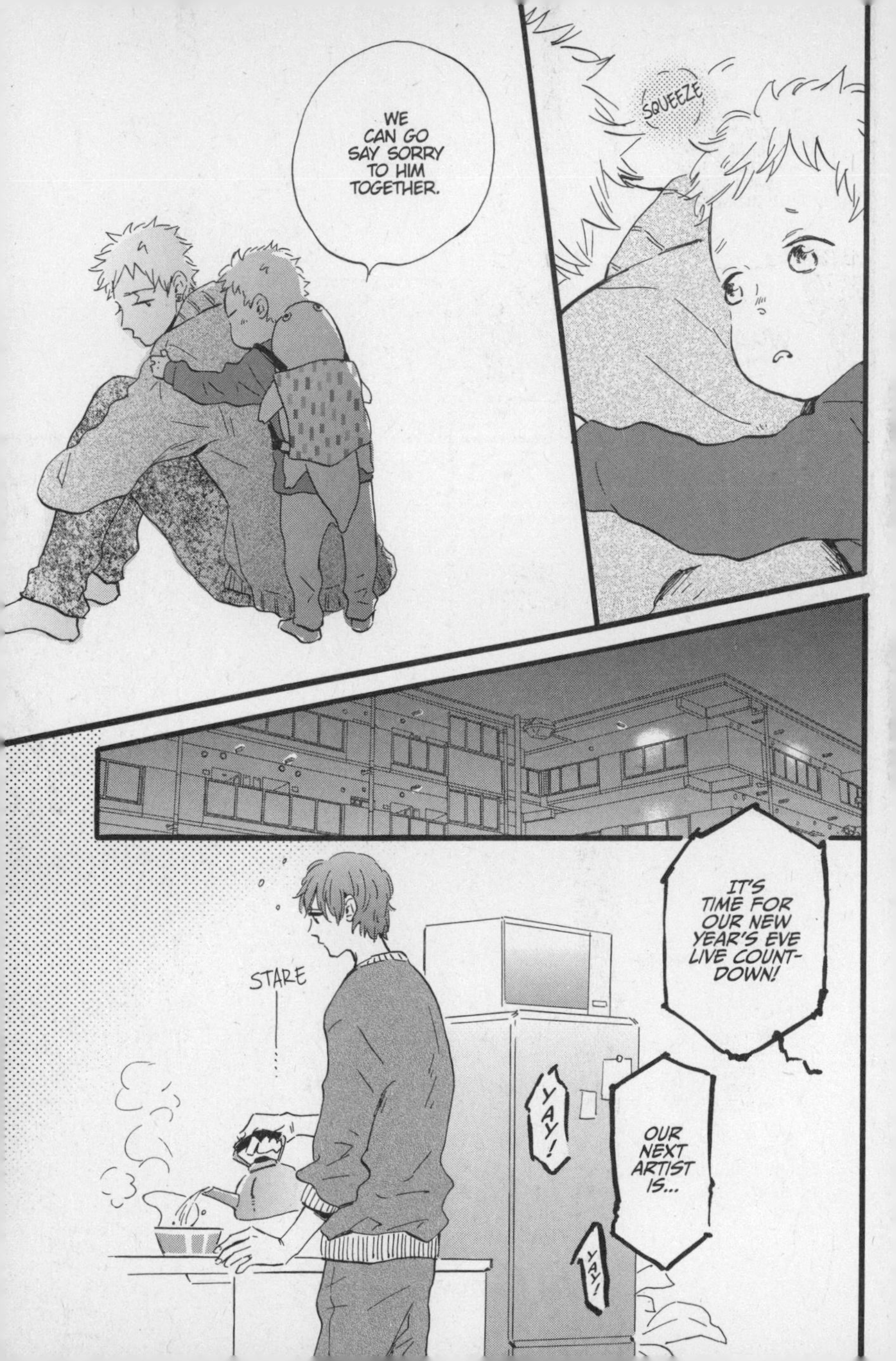
SQUEEZE
WE CAN GO SAY SORRY TO HIM TOGETHER.
IT'S TIME FOR OUR NEW YEAR'S EVE LIVE COUNT-DOWN!
OUR NEXT ARTIST IS...
YAY!
YAY!
STARE

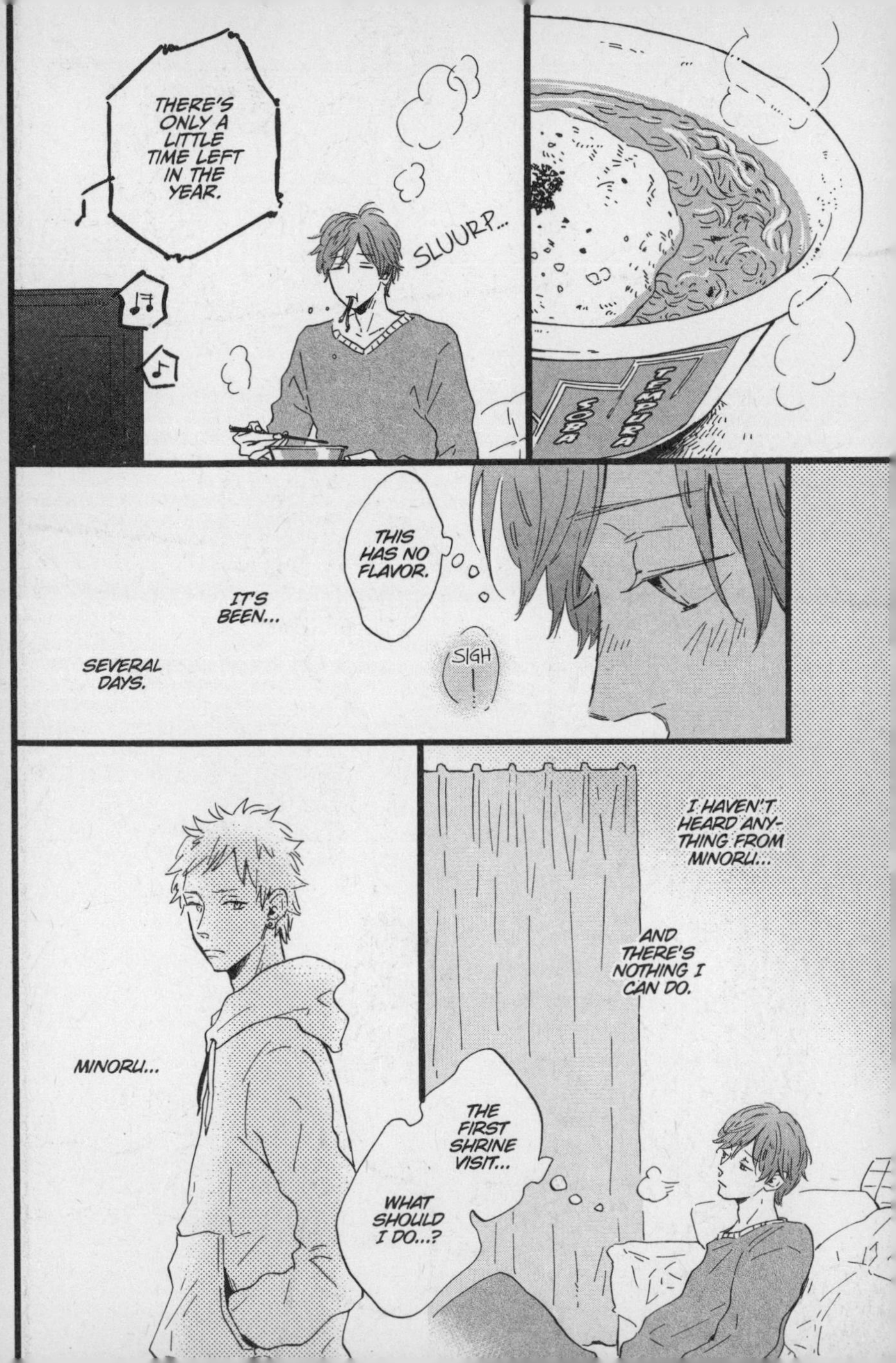
TEMPURA SOBA
THERE'S ONLY A LITTLE TIME LEFT IN THE YEAR.
SLUURP...
THIS HAS NO FLAVOR.
SIGH...
IT'S BEEN...
SEVERAL DAYS.
I HAVEN'T HEARD ANYTHING FROM MINORU...
AND THERE'S NOTHING I CAN DO.
THE FIRST SHRINE VISIT...
WHAT SHOULD I DO...?
MINORU...

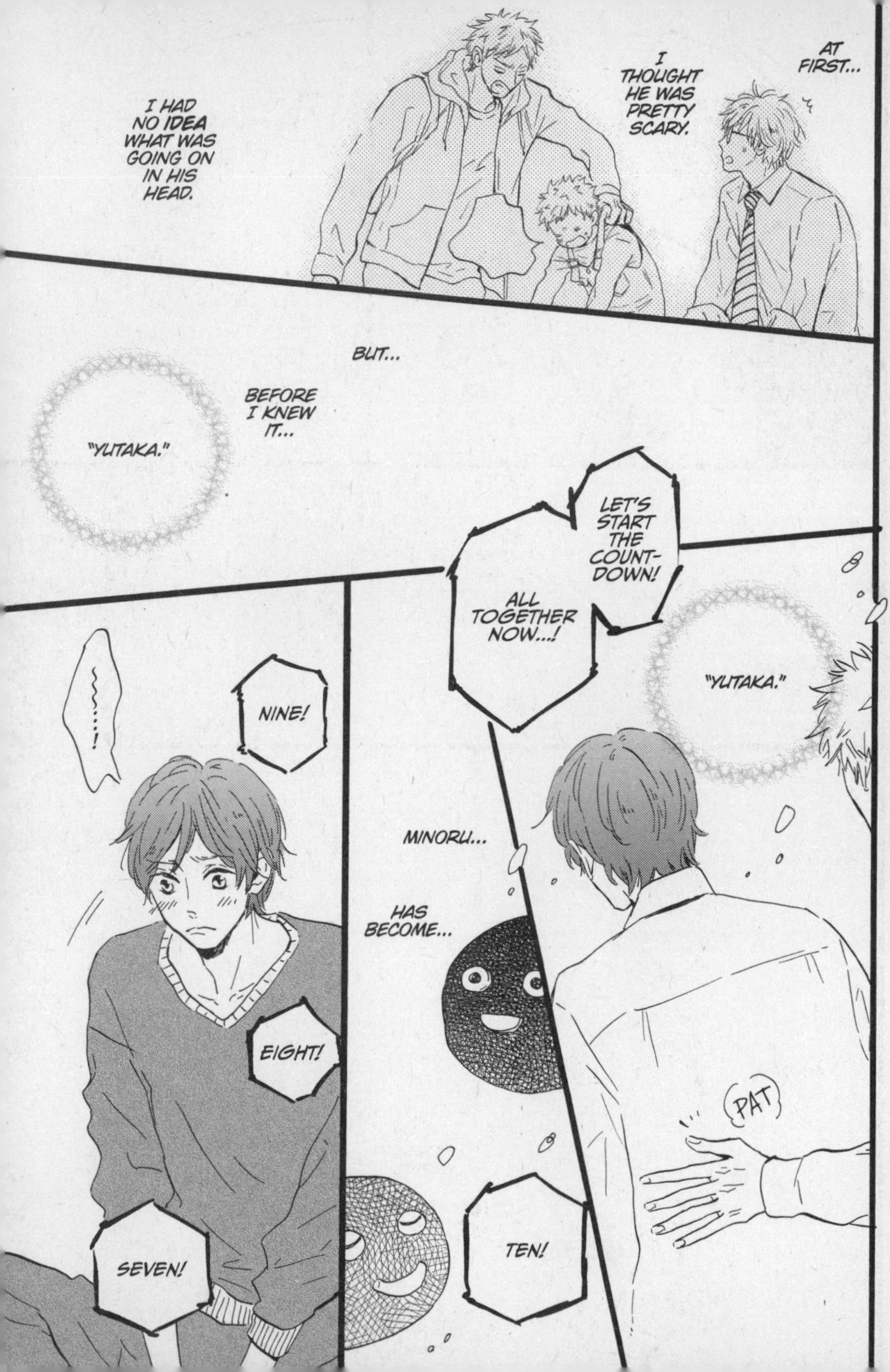
AT FIRST...
I THOUGHT HE WAS PRETTY SCARY.
I HAD NO IDEA WHAT WAS GOING ON IN HIS HEAD.
BUT...
BEFORE I KNEW IT...
"YUTAKA."
LET'S START THE COUNT-DOWN!
ALL TOGETHER NOW...!
"YUTAKA."
MINORU...
HAS BECOME...
PAT
TEN!
......!
NINE!
EIGHT!
SEVEN!

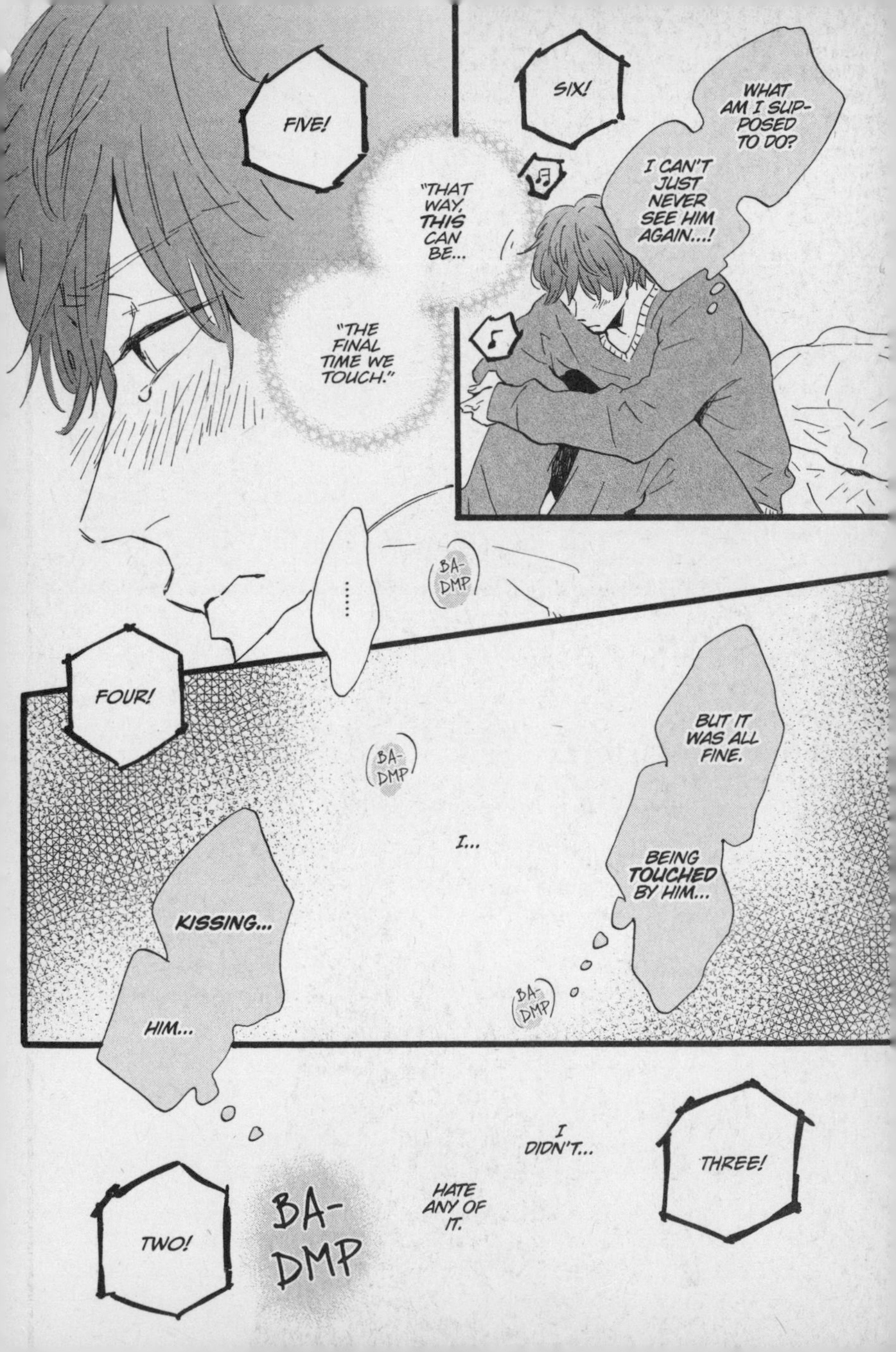
SIX!
WHAT AM I SUPPOSED TO DO?
I CAN'T JUST NEVER SEE HIM AGAIN...!
FIVE!
"THAT WAY, THIS CAN BE...
"THE FINAL TIME WE TOUCH."
......
BA-DMP
FOUR!
BUT IT WAS ALL FINE.
BEING TOUCHED BY HIM...
BA-DMP
I...
BA-DMP
KISSING...
HIM...
THREE!
I DIDN'T...
HATE ANY OF IT.
BA-DMP
TWO!

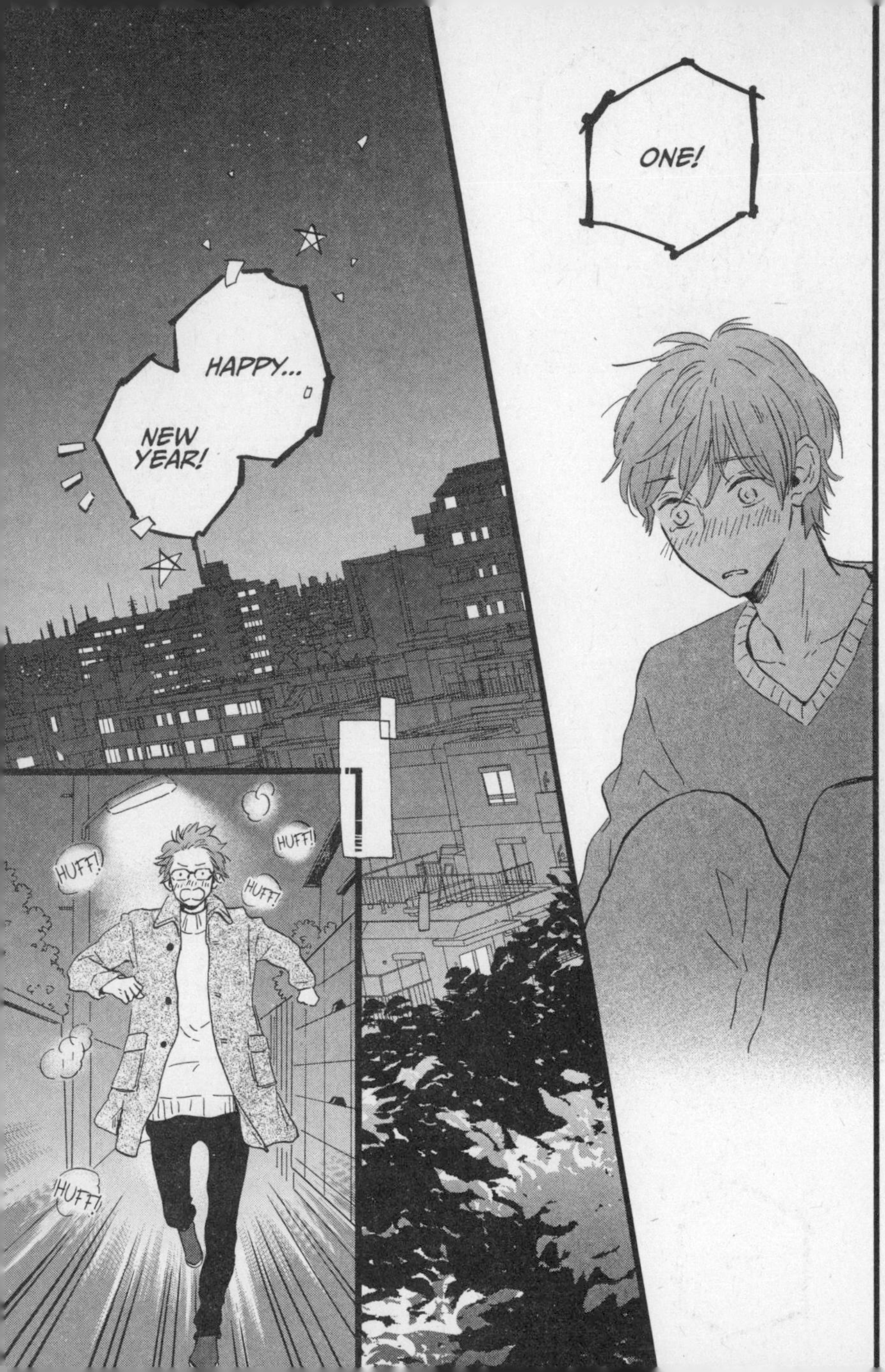
ONE!
HAPPY...
NEW YEAR!
HUFF!
HUFF!
HUFF!
HUFF!

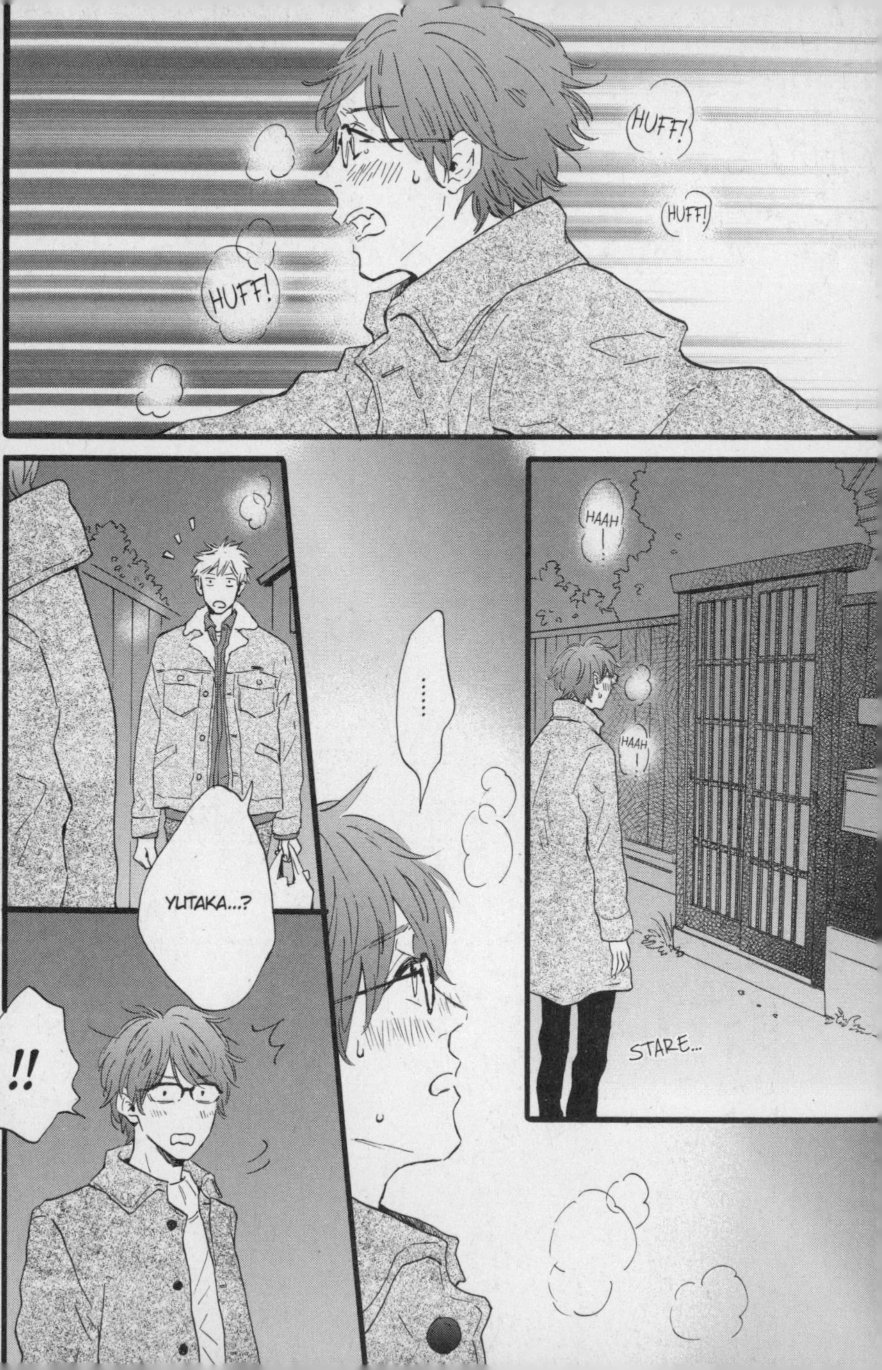
HUFF!
HUFF!
HUFF!
HAAH!
HAAH!
STARE...
......
YUTAKA...?
!!

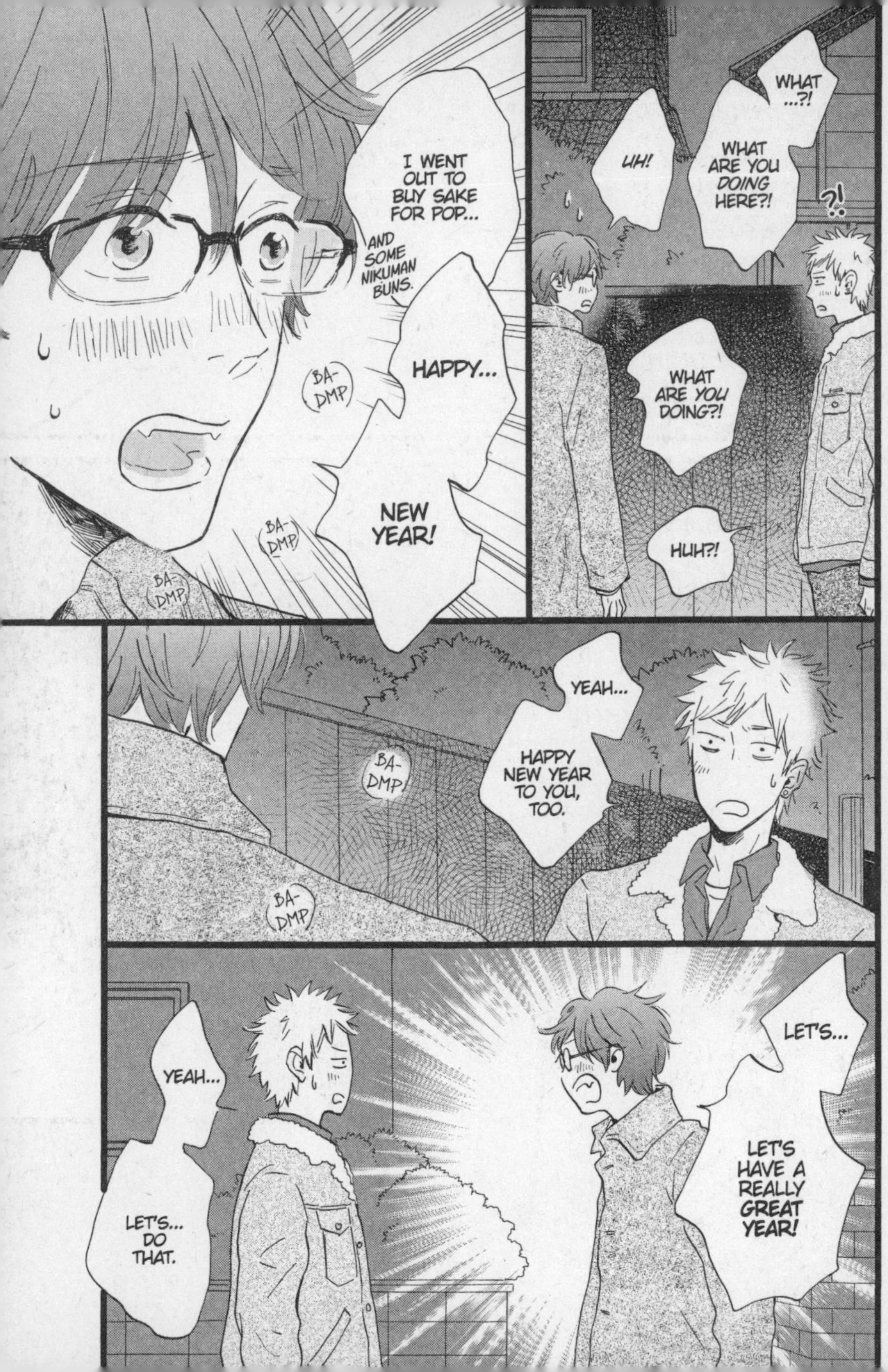
WHAT ...?!
WHAT ARE YOU DOING HERE?!
?!
UH!
WHAT ARE YOU DOING?!
HUH?!
I WENT OUT TO BUY SAKE FOR POP...
AND SOME NIKUMAN BUNS.
BA-DMP
HAPPY...
NEW YEAR!
BA-DMP
BA-DMP
YEAH...
HAPPY NEW YEAR TO YOU, TOO.
BA-DMP
BA-DMP
LET'S...
LET'S HAVE A REALLY GREAT YEAR!
YEAH...
LET'S... DO THAT.

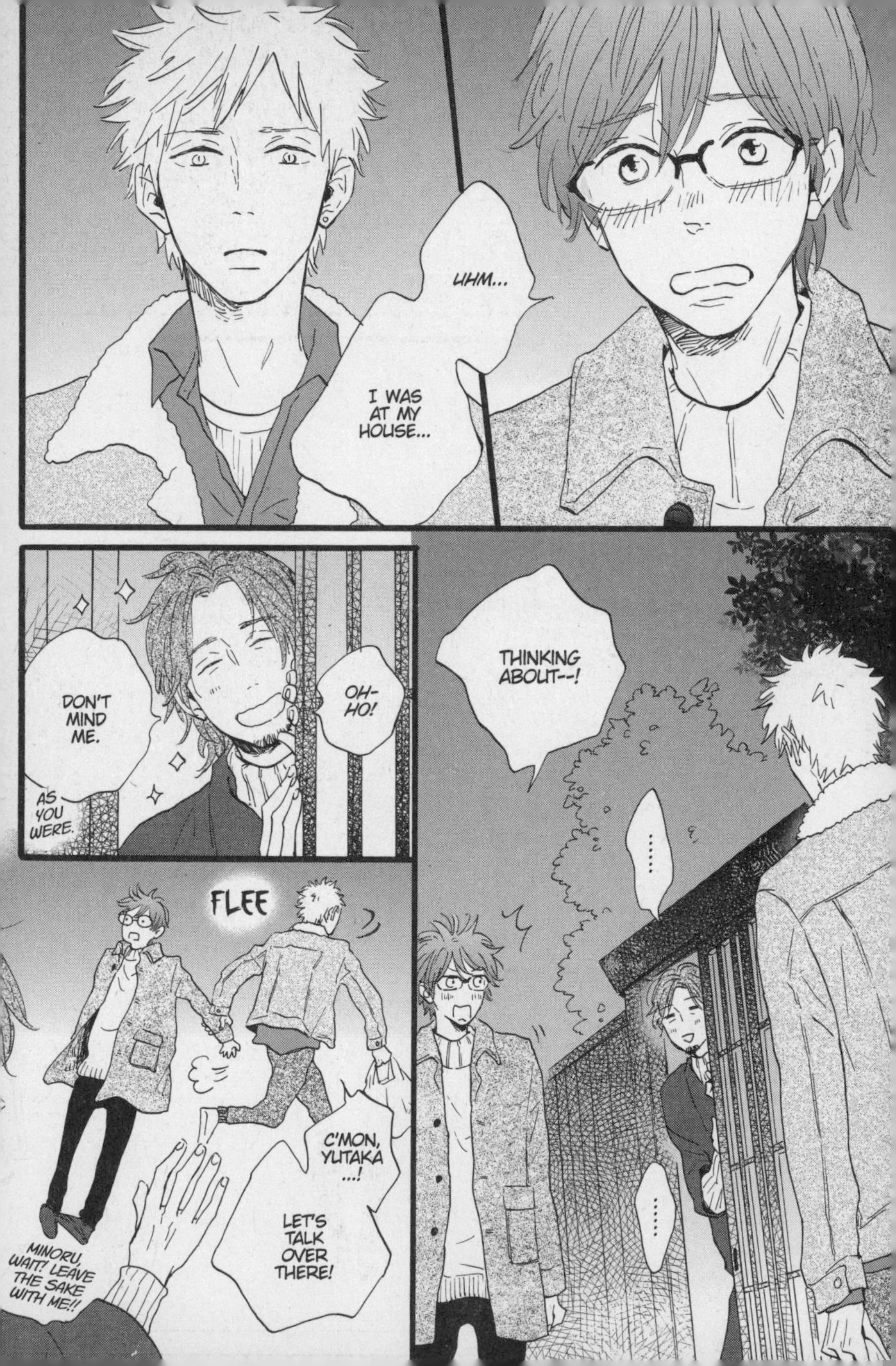
UHM...
I WAS AT MY HOUSE...
THINKING ABOUT--!
......
......
OH-HO!
DON'T MIND ME.
AS YOU WERE.
FLEE
C'MON, YUTAKA ...!
LET'S TALK OVER THERE!
MINORU, WAIT! LEAVE THE SAKE WITH ME!!

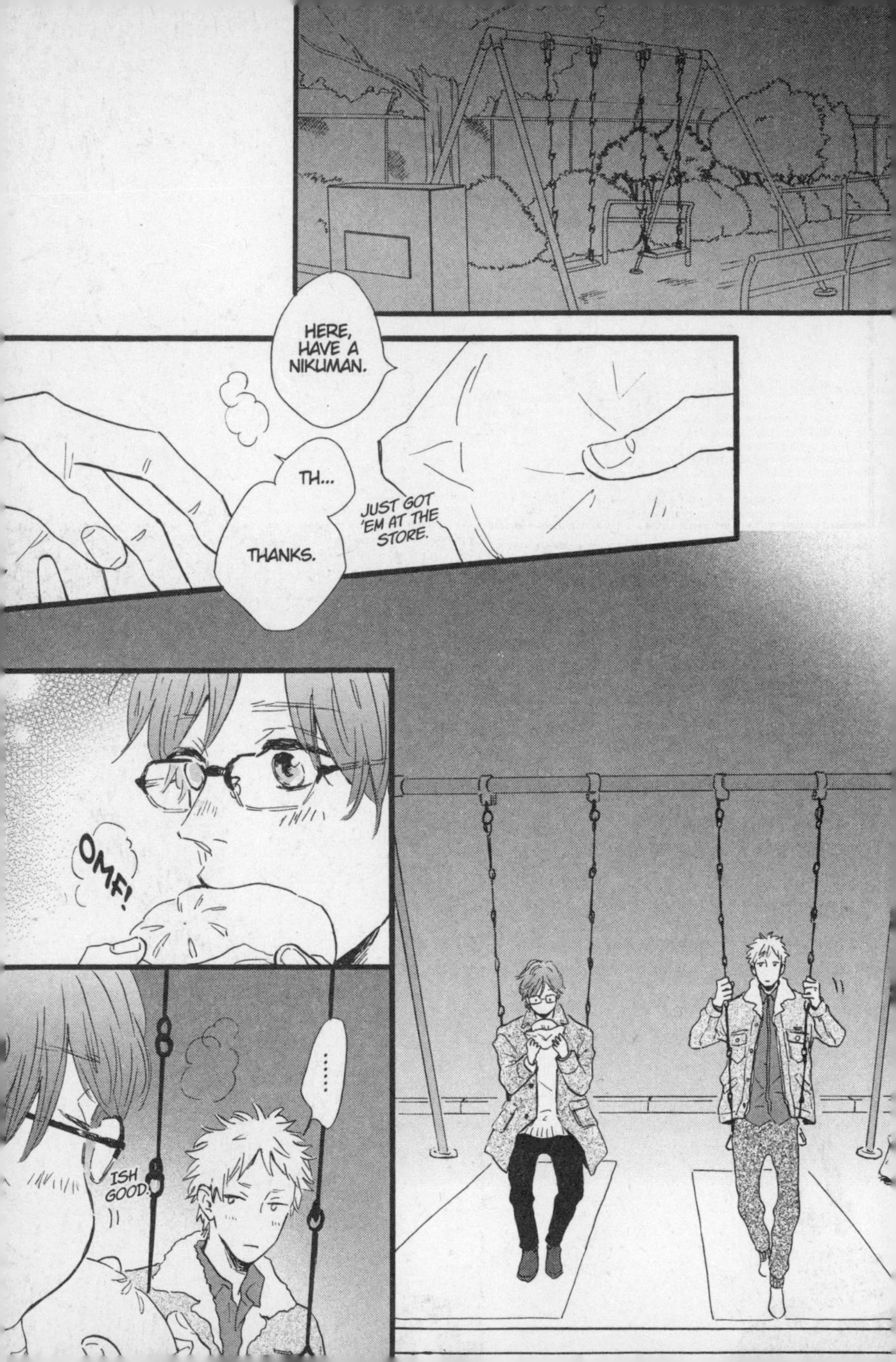
HERE, HAVE A NIKUMAN.
JUST GOT 'EM AT THE STORE.
TH...
THANKS.
OMF!
......
ISH GOOD.

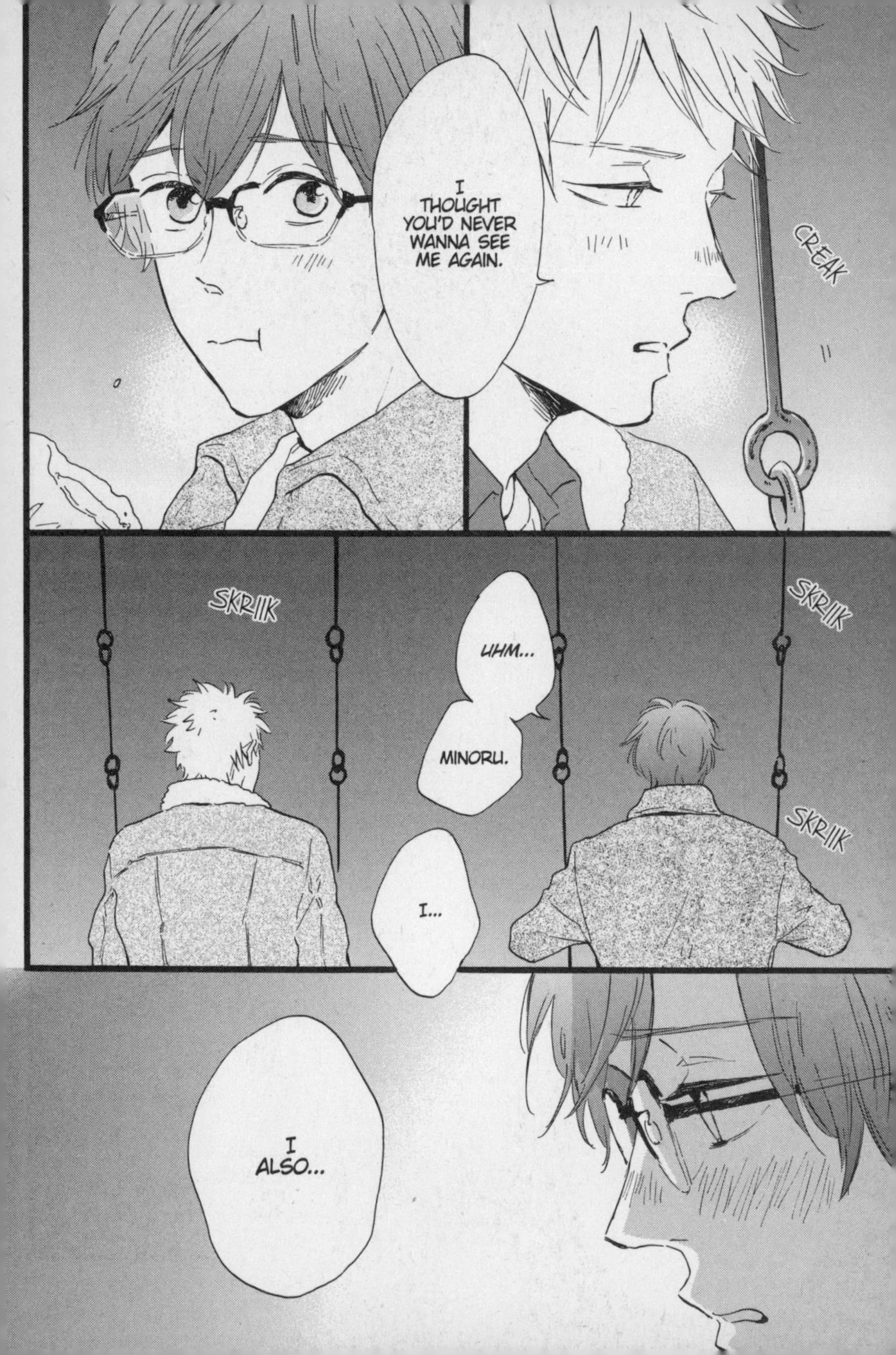
CREAK
I THOUGHT YOU'D NEVER WANNA SEE ME AGAIN.
SKRIIK
UHM...
MINORU.
SKRIIK
I...
SKRIIK
I ALSO...

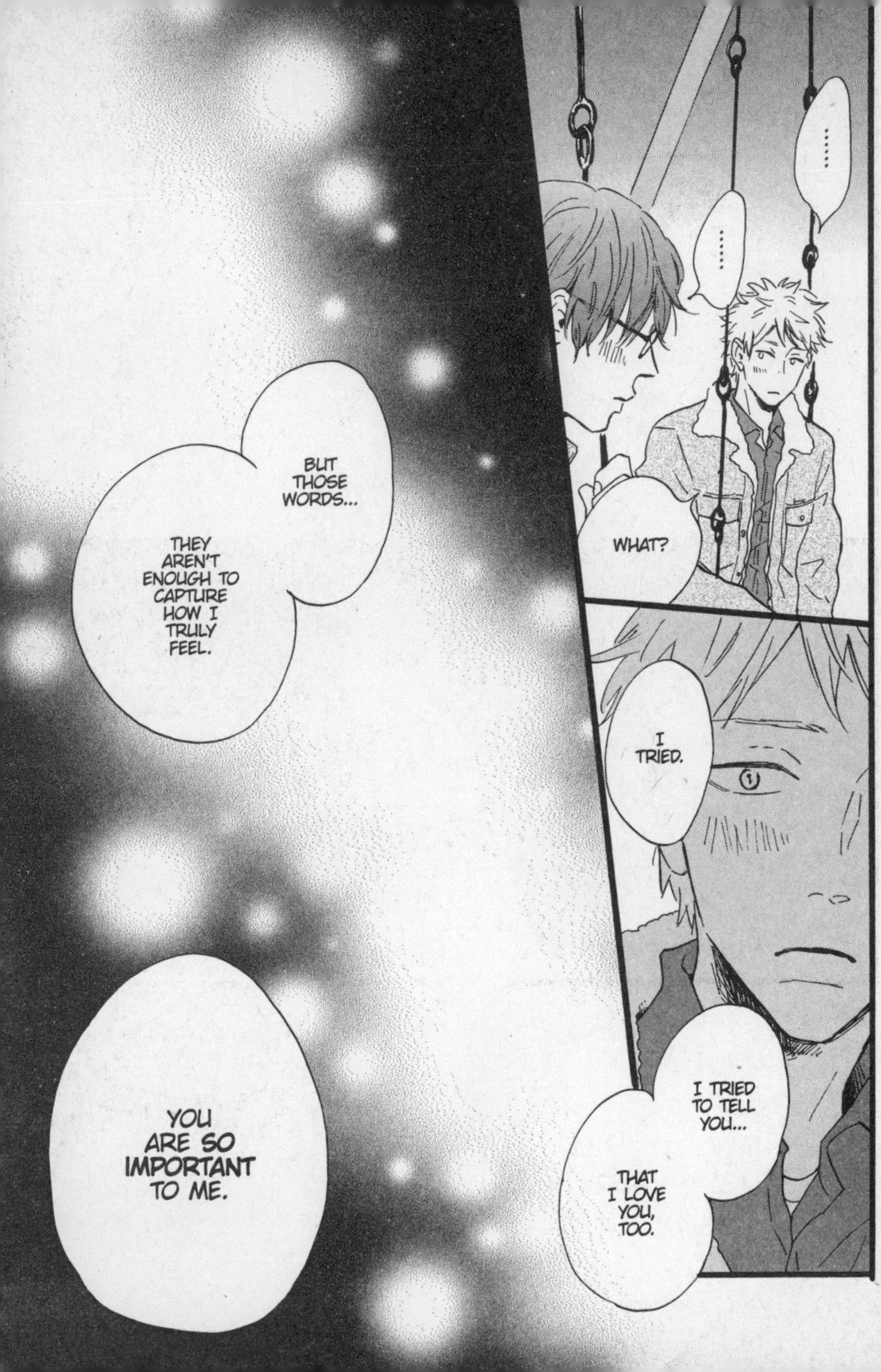
……
……
WHAT?
I TRIED.
I TRIED TO TELL YOU...
THAT I LOVE YOU, TOO.
BUT THOSE WORDS...
THEY AREN'T ENOUGH TO CAPTURE HOW I TRULY FEEL.
YOU ARE SO IMPORTANT TO ME.

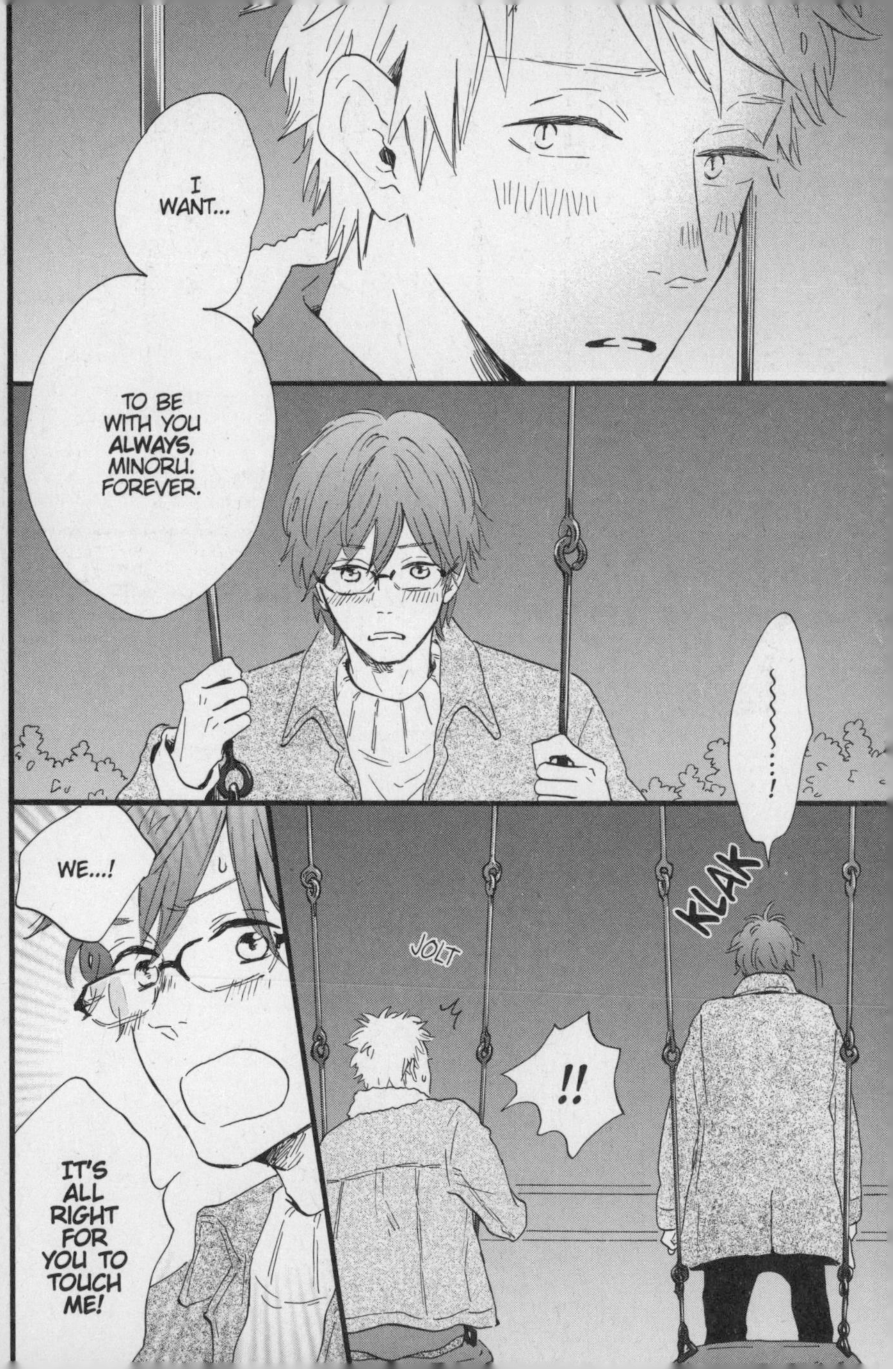
I WANT...
TO BE WITH YOU ALWAYS, MINORU. FOREVER.
......!
KLAK
JOLT
!!
WE...!
IT'S ALL RIGHT FOR YOU TO TOUCH ME!

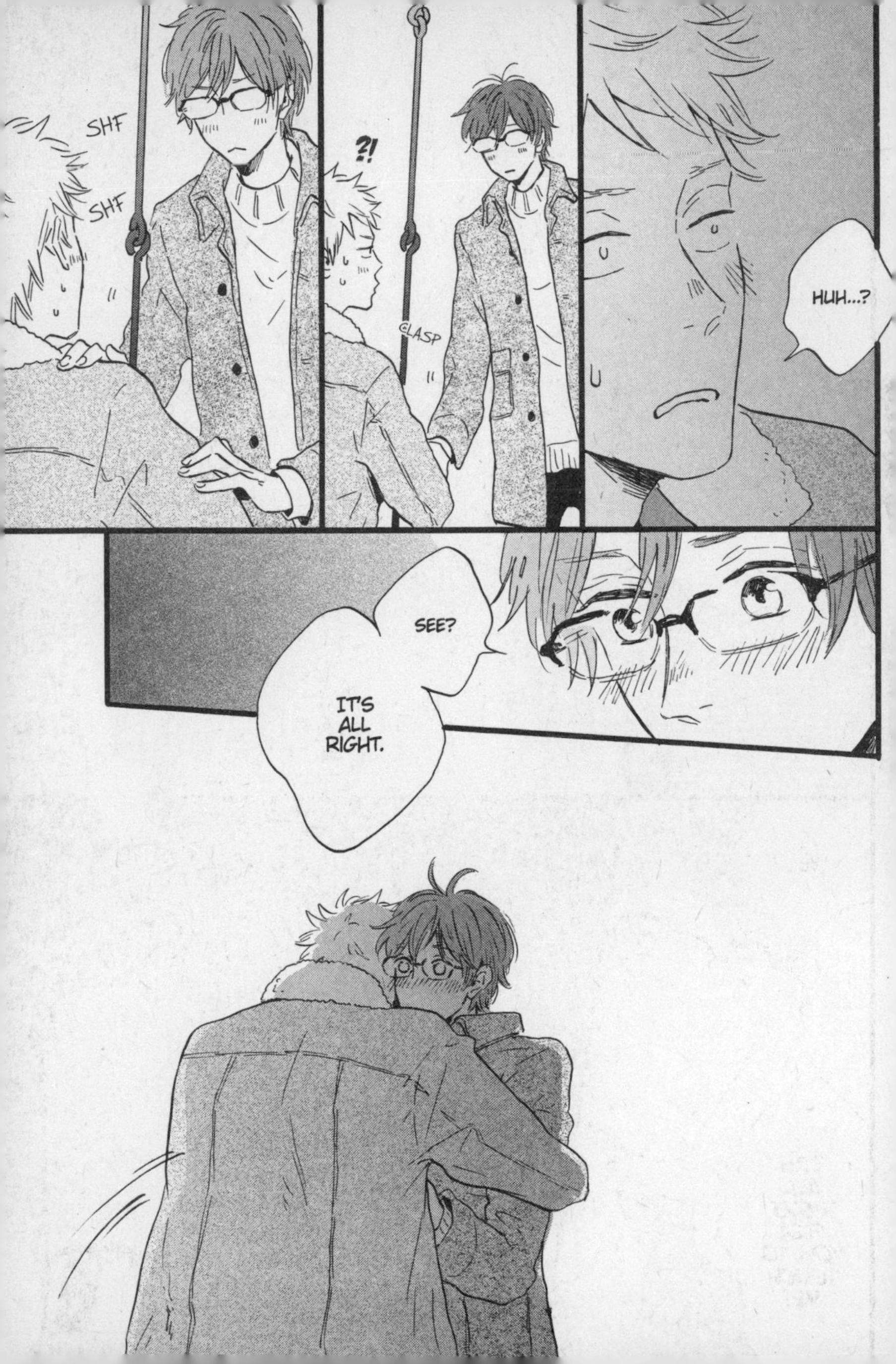
HUH...?
?!
CLASP
SHF
SHF
SEE?
IT'S ALL RIGHT.

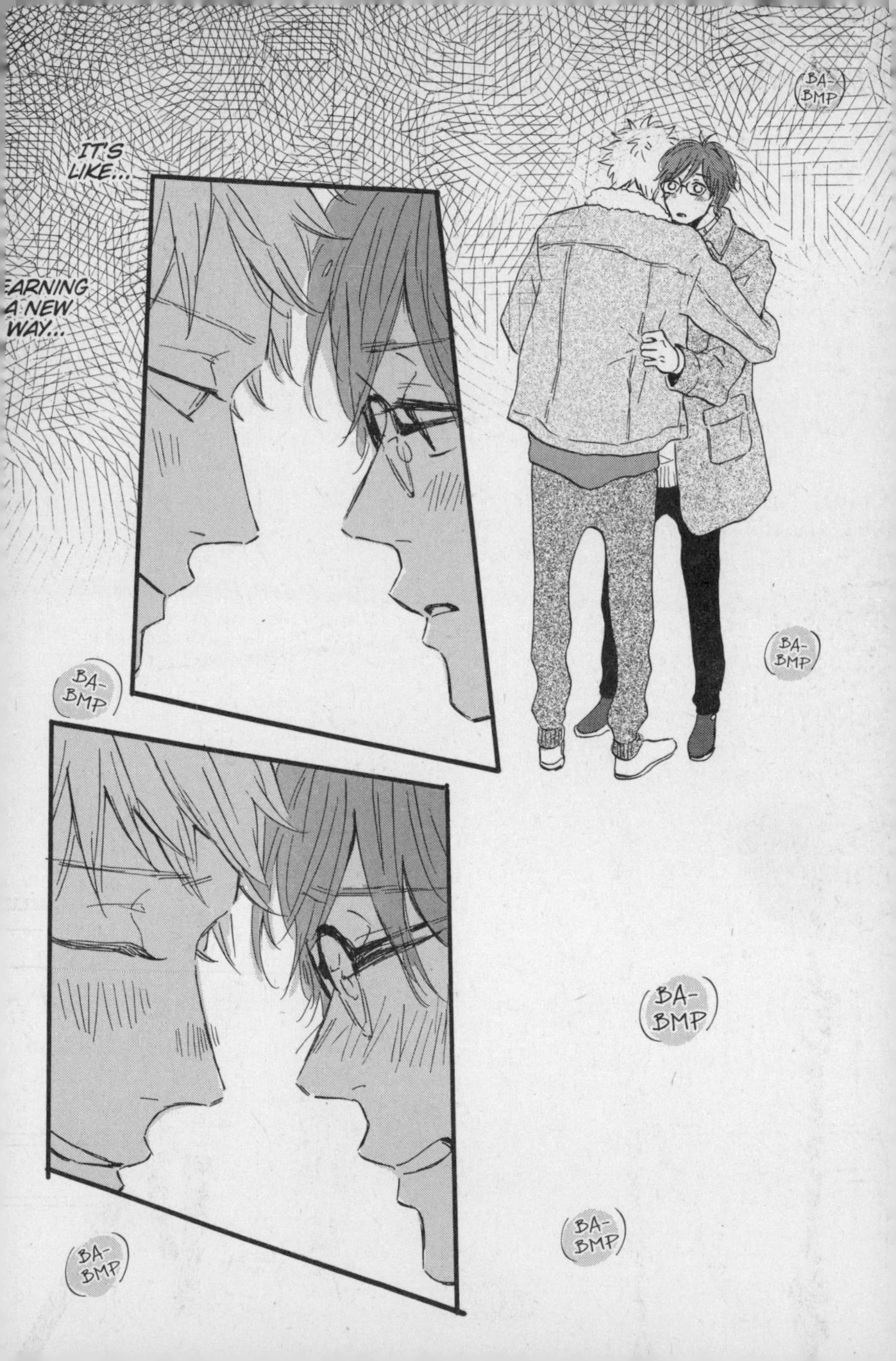
BA-BMP
BA-BMP
IT'S LIKE...
EARNING A NEW WAY...
BA-BMP
BA-BMP
BA-BMP
BA-BMP

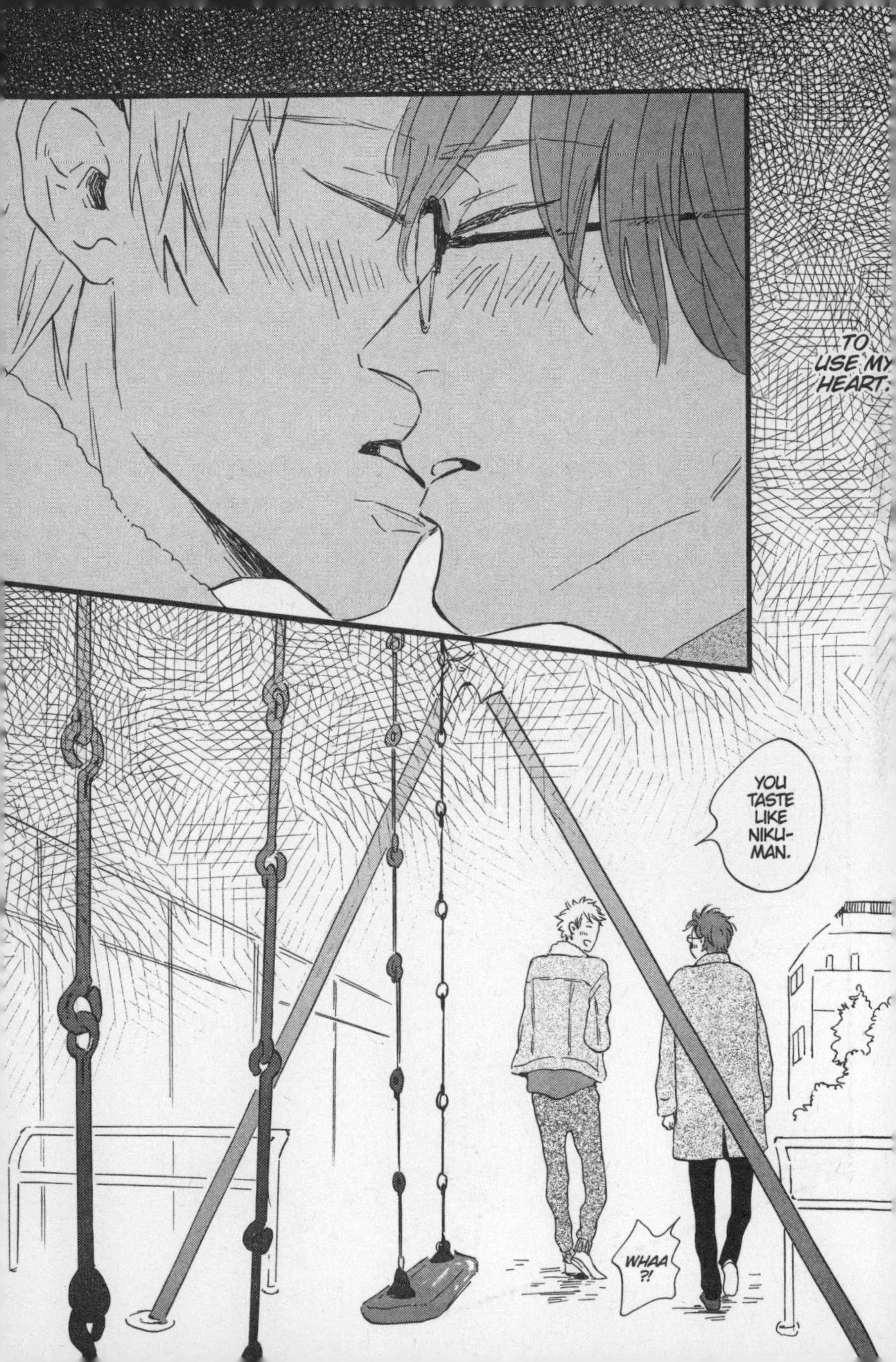
TO USE MY HEART...
YOU TASTE LIKE NIKU-MAN.
WHAA ?!

OUR DINING TABLE

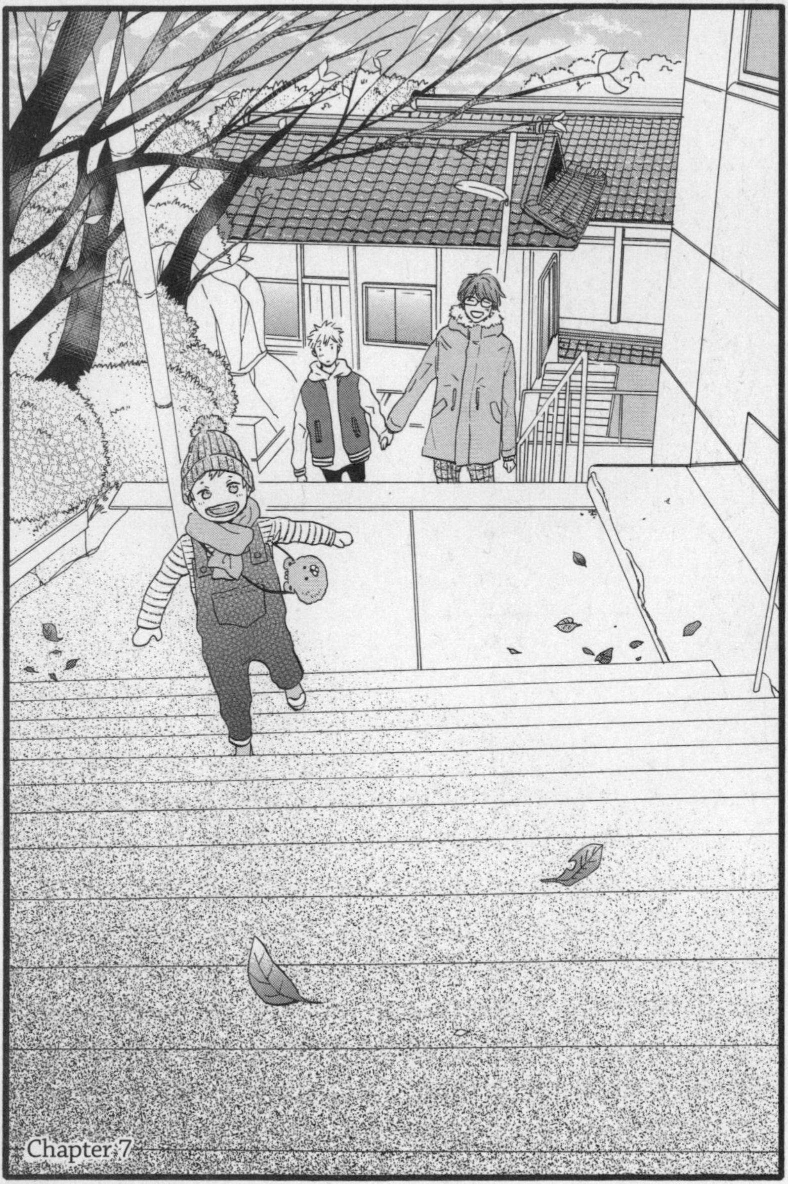
Chapter 7

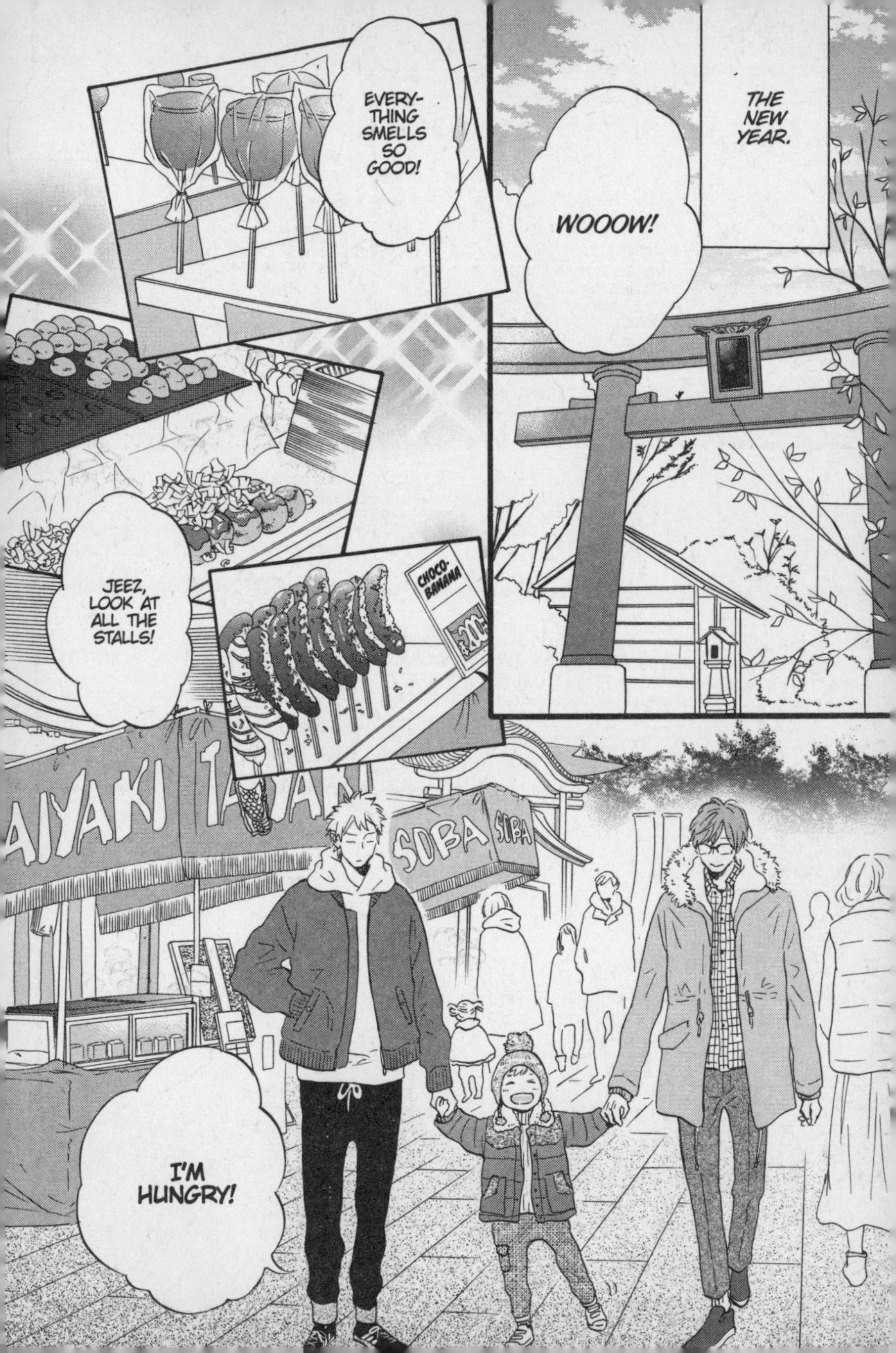
THE NEW YEAR.
WOOOW!
EVERY-THING SMELLS SO GOOD!
JEEZ, LOOK AT ALL THE STALLS!
CHOCO-BANANA
SOBA
SOBA
I'M HUNGRY!

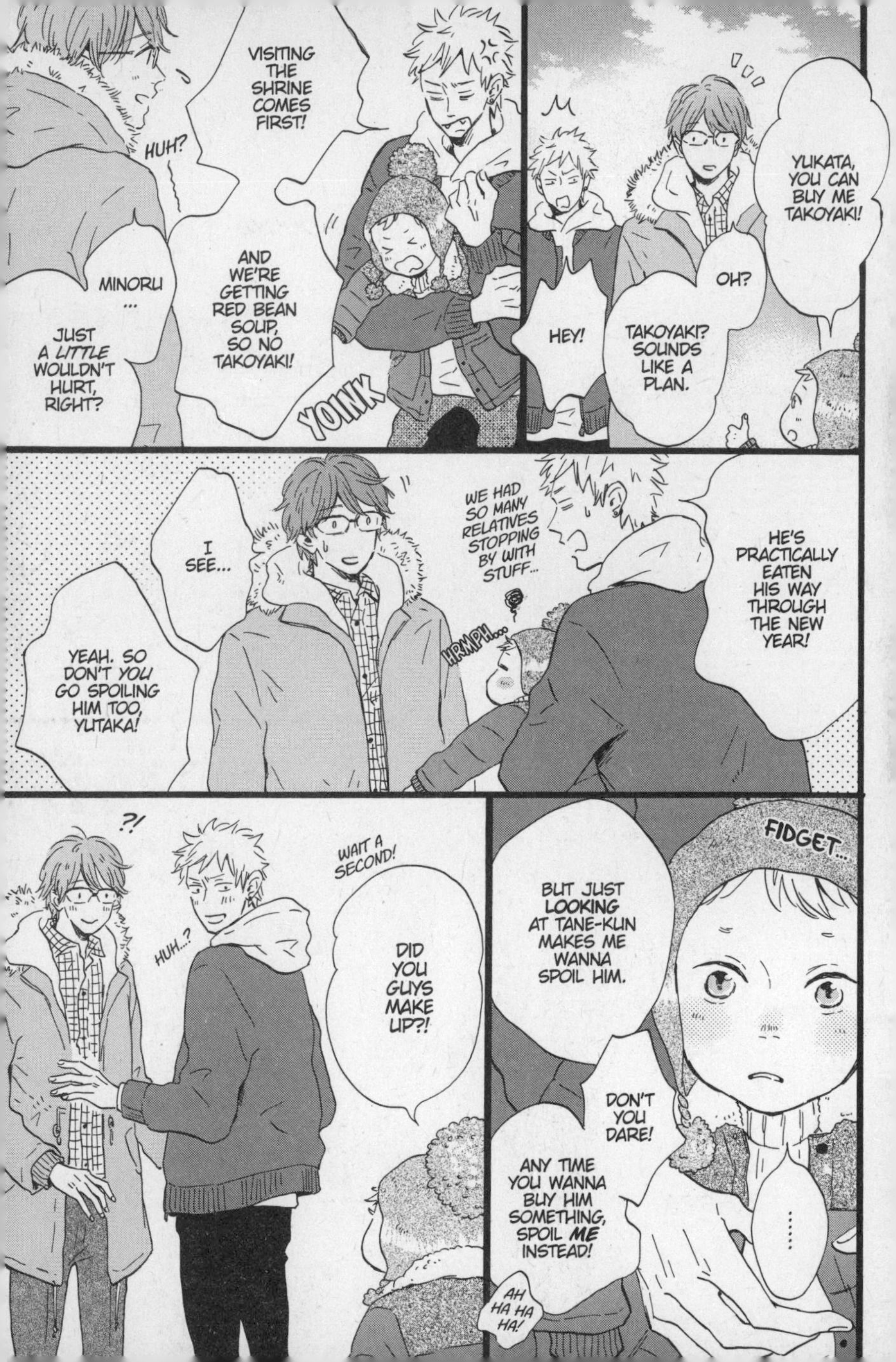

YUKATA, YOU CAN BUY ME TAKOYAKI!
OH?
TAKOYAKI? SOUNDS LIKE A PLAN.
HEY!
VISITING THE SHRINE COMES FIRST!
AND WE'RE GETTING RED BEAN SOUP, SO NO TAKOYAKI!
YOINK
HUH?
MINORU ...
JUST A *LITTLE* WOULDN'T HURT, RIGHT?
HE'S PRACTICALLY EATEN HIS WAY THROUGH THE NEW YEAR!
WE HAD SO MANY RELATIVES STOPPING BY WITH STUFF...
HRMPH...
I SEE...
YEAH. SO DON'T *YOU* GO SPOILING HIM TOO, YUTAKA!
FIDGET...
BUT JUST **LOOKING** AT TANE-KUN MAKES ME WANNA SPOIL HIM.
DON'T YOU DARE!
......
ANY TIME YOU WANNA BUY HIM SOMETHING, SPOIL ***ME*** INSTEAD!
AH HA HA HA!
WAIT A SECOND!
DID YOU GUYS MAKE UP?!
HUH...?
?!

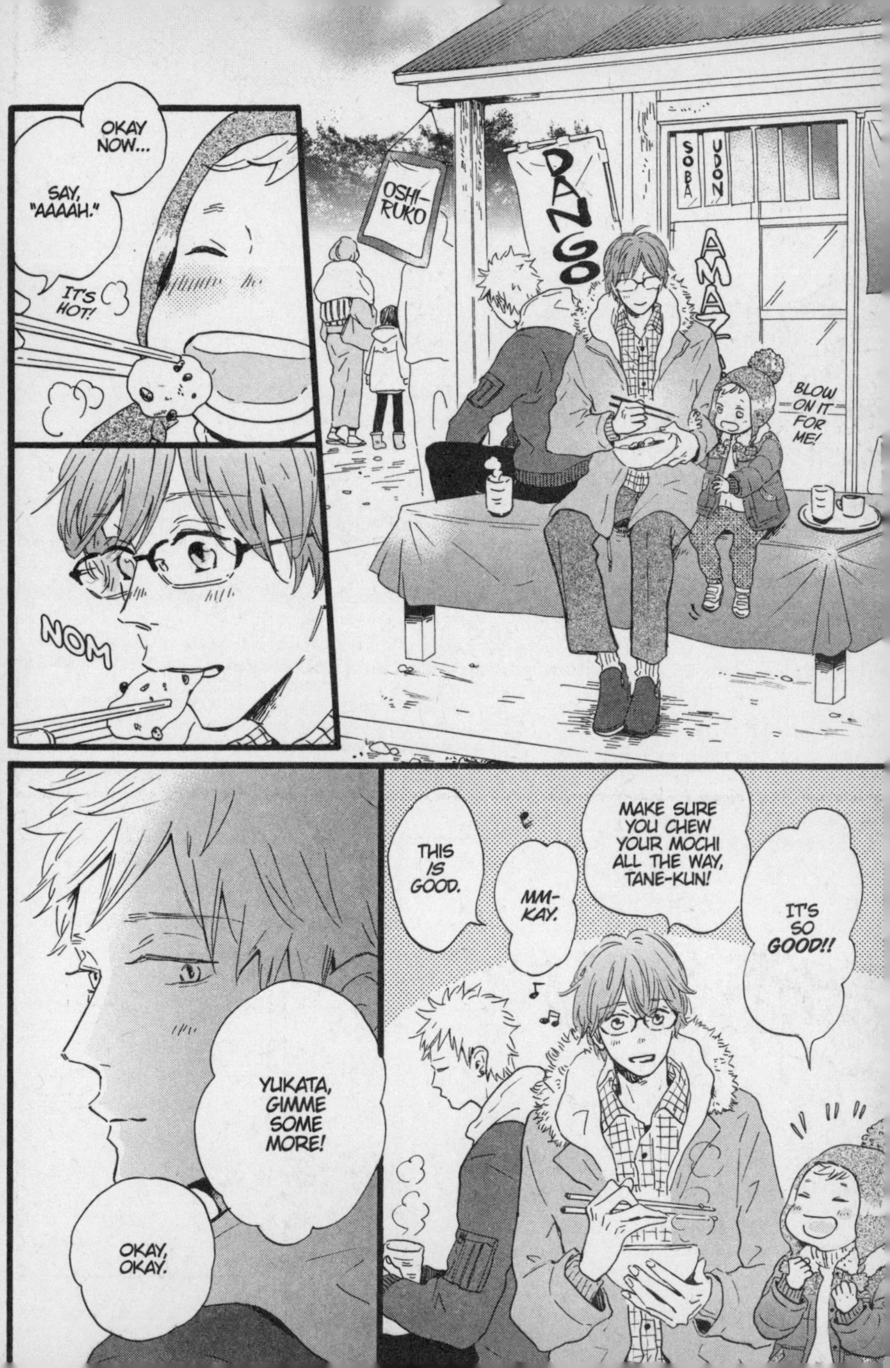
SOBA
UDON
DANGO
OSHI-RUKO
BLOW ON IT FOR ME!
OKAY NOW...
SAY, "AAAAH."
IT'S HOT!
NOM
IT'S SO GOOD!!
MAKE SURE YOU CHEW YOUR MOCHI ALL THE WAY, TANE-KUN!
MM-KAY.
THIS IS GOOD.
YUKATA, GIMME SOME MORE!
OKAY, OKAY.

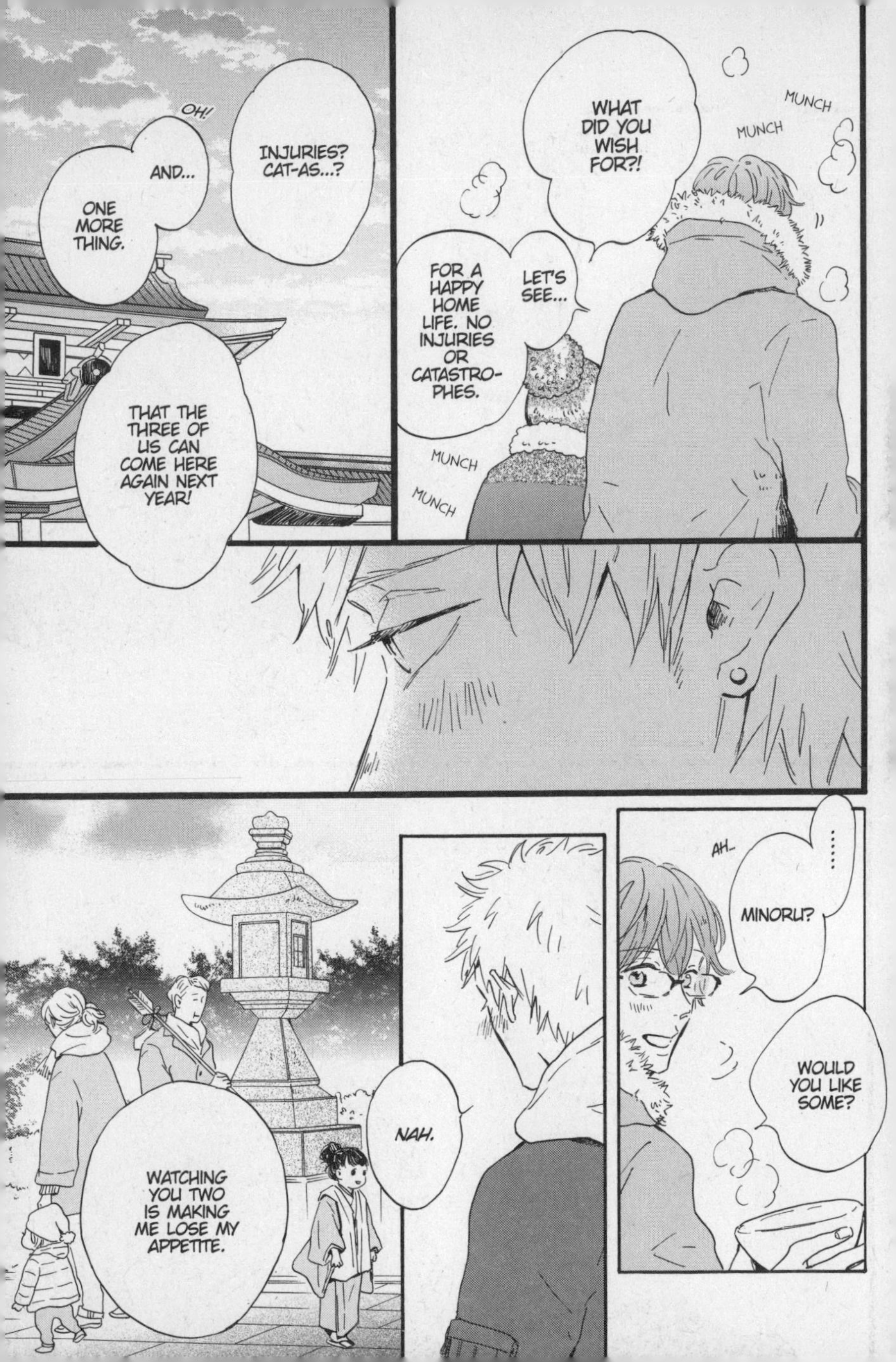

WHAT DID YOU WISH FOR?!
MUNCH
MUNCH
LET'S SEE...
FOR A HAPPY HOME LIFE. NO INJURIES OR CATASTROPHES.
MUNCH
MUNCH
INJURIES? CAT-AS...?
OH!
AND...
ONE MORE THING.
THAT THE THREE OF US CAN COME HERE AGAIN NEXT YEAR!
......
AH...
MINORU?
WOULD YOU LIKE SOME?
NAH.
WATCHING YOU TWO IS MAKING ME LOSE MY APPETITE.

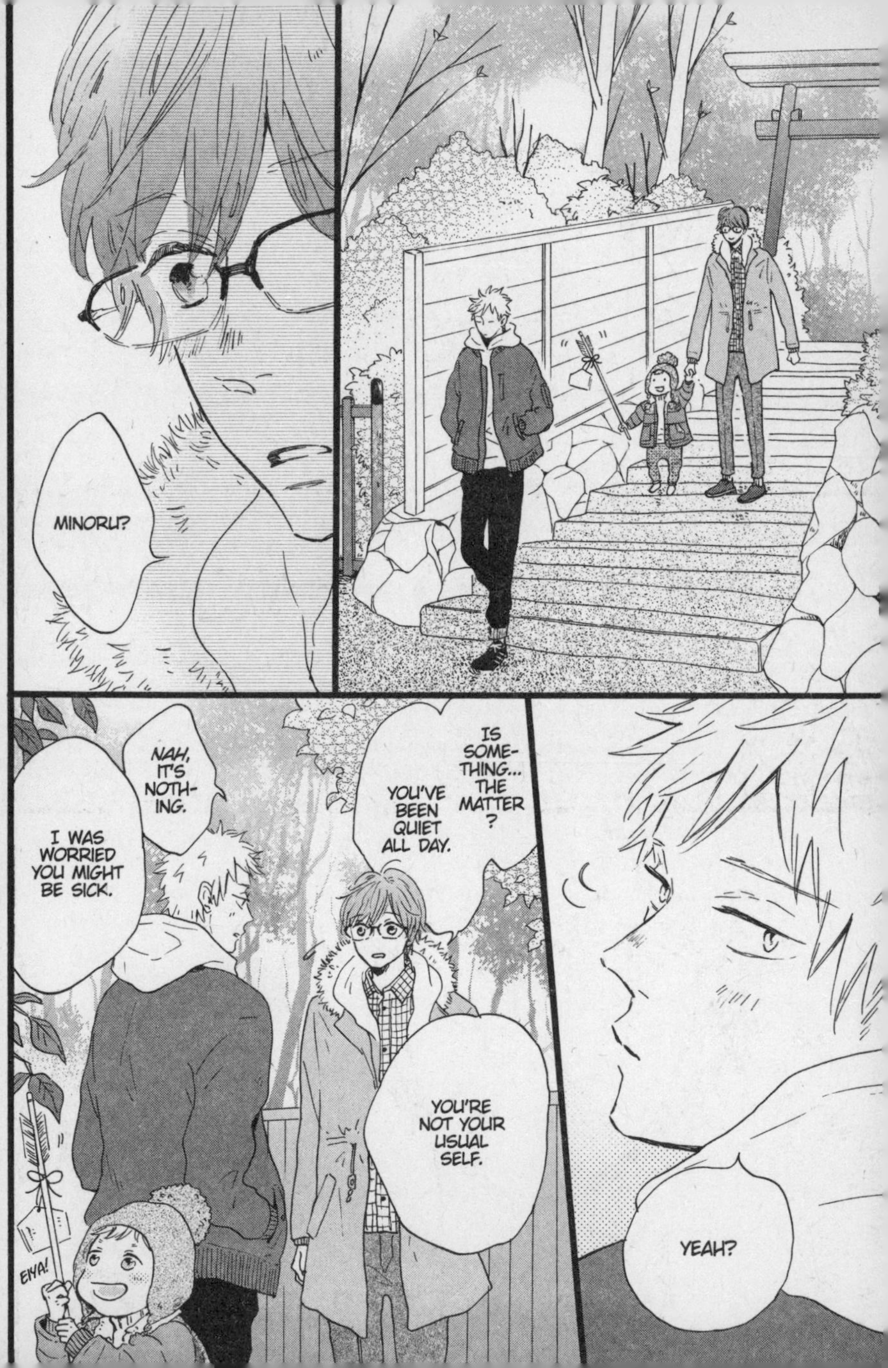
MINORU?
YEAH?
IS SOMETHING... THE MATTER?
YOU'VE BEEN QUIET ALL DAY.
YOU'RE NOT YOUR USUAL SELF.
NAH, IT'S NOTHING.
I WAS WORRIED YOU MIGHT BE SICK.
EIYA!

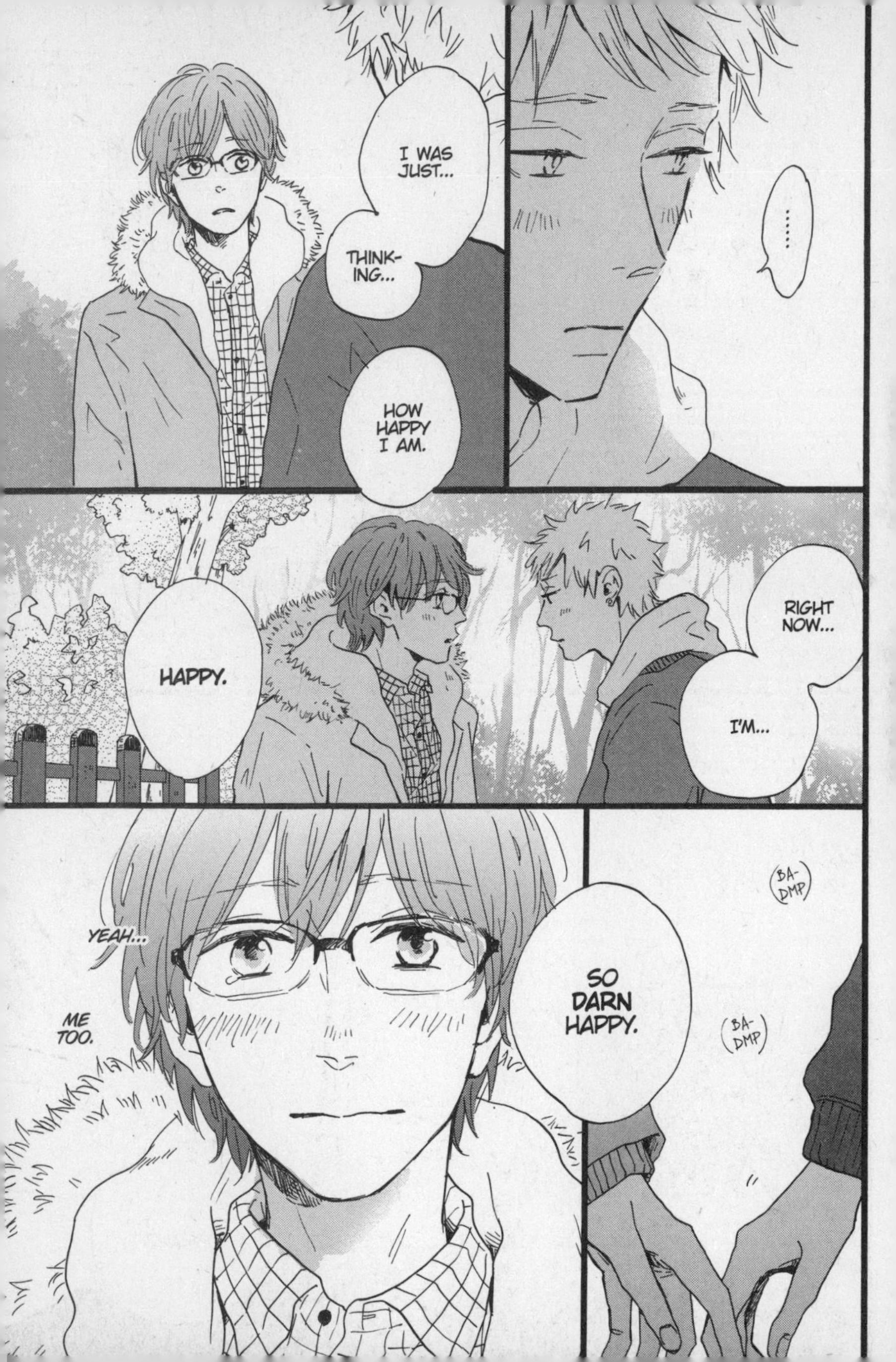
......
I WAS JUST...
THINKING...
HOW HAPPY I AM.
RIGHT NOW...
I'M...
HAPPY.
(BA-DMP)
(BA-DMP)
SO DARN HAPPY.
YEAH...
ME TOO.

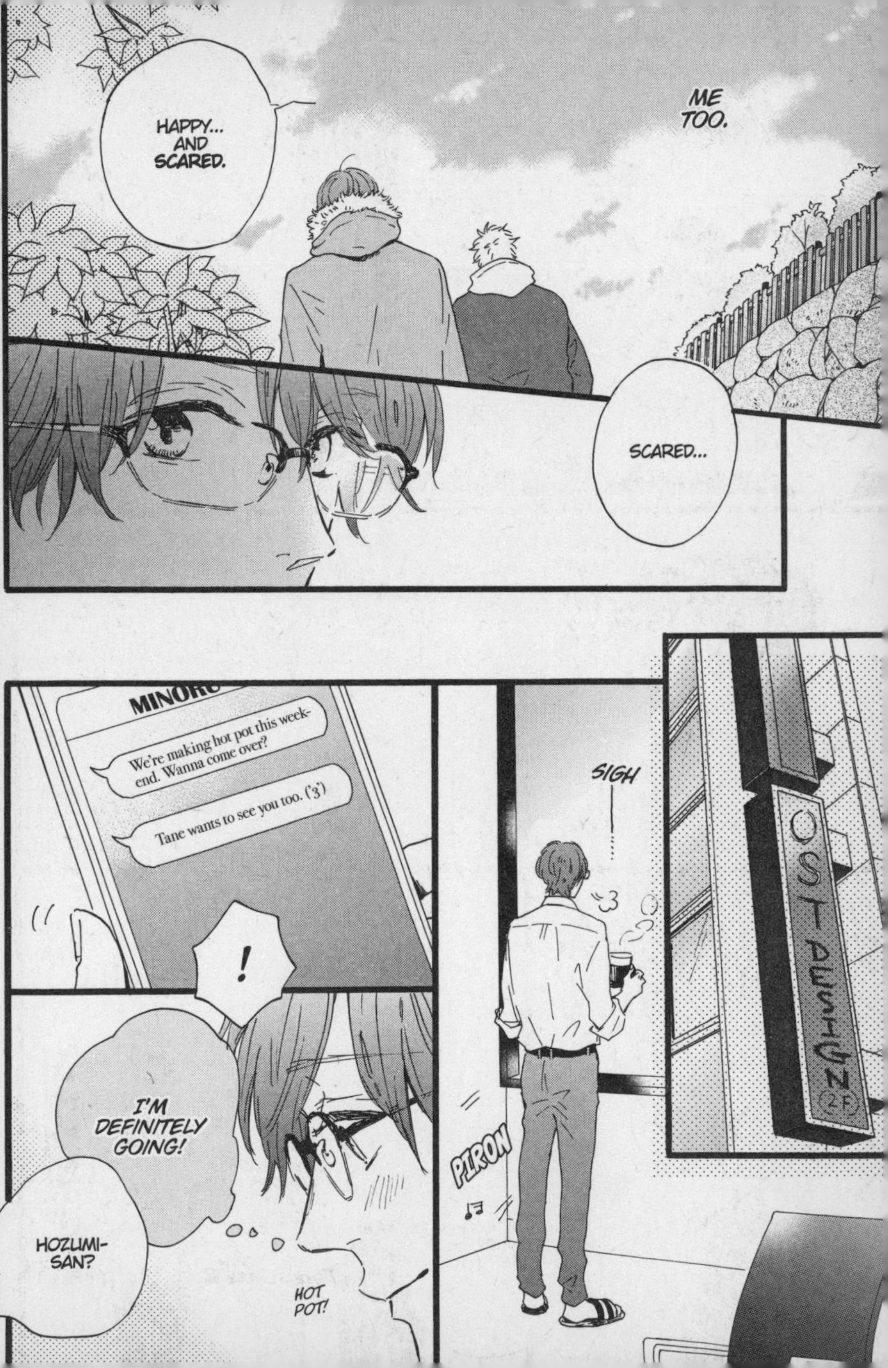
ME TOO.
HAPPY... AND SCARED.
SCARED...
SIGH
OST DESIGN
2F
PIRON
MINORU
We're making hot pot this weekend. Wanna come over?
Tane wants to see you too. ('3')
!
I'M DEFINITELY GOING!
HOT POT!
HOZUMI-SAN?

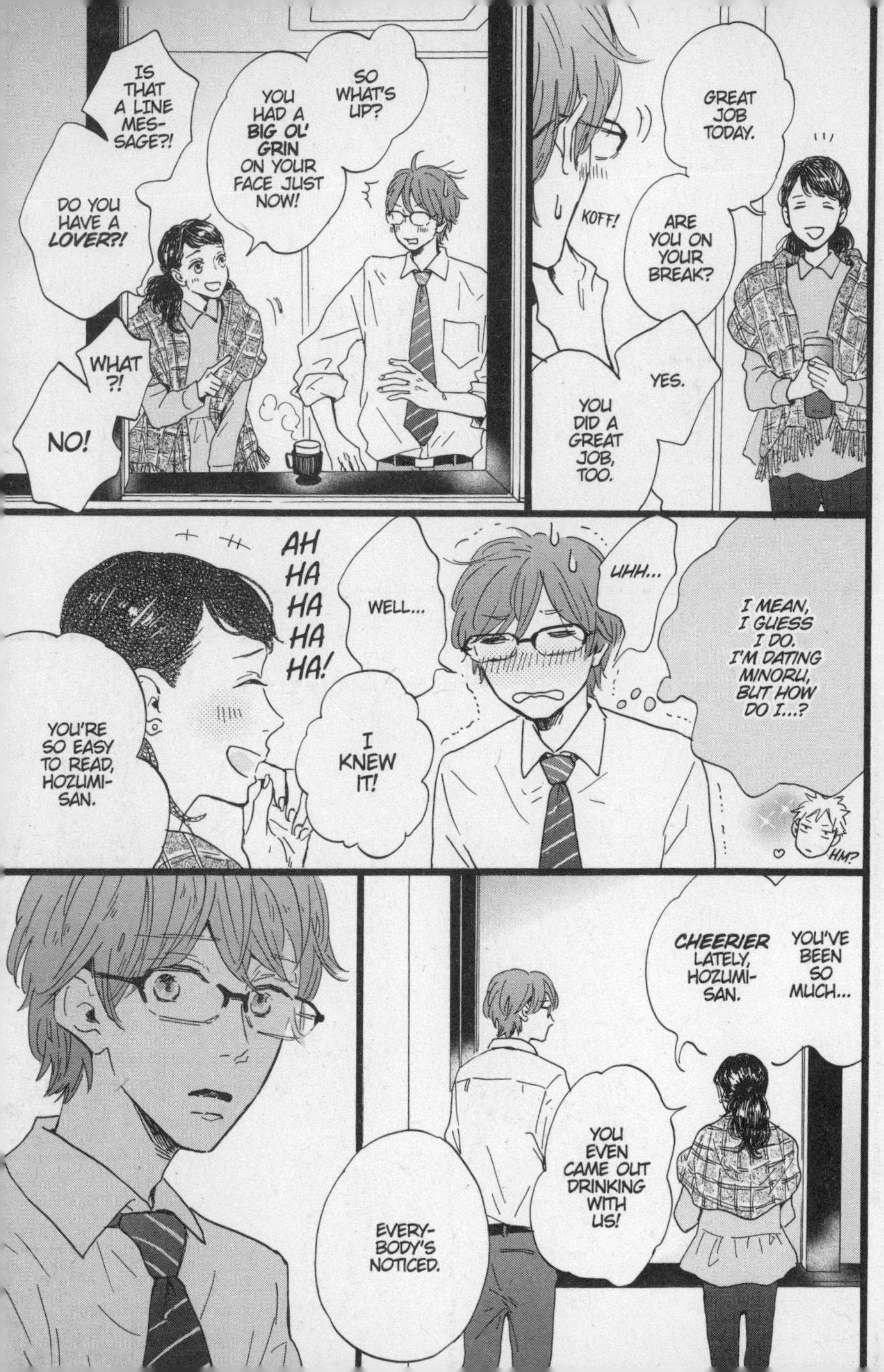
GREAT JOB TODAY.
ARE YOU ON YOUR BREAK?
KOFF!
YES.
YOU DID A GREAT JOB, TOO.
SO WHAT'S UP?
YOU HAD A BIG OL' GRIN ON YOUR FACE JUST NOW!
IS THAT A LINE MES-SAGE?!
DO YOU HAVE A LOVER?!
WHAT?!
NO!
I MEAN, I GUESS I DO. I'M DATING MINORU, BUT HOW DO I...?
HM?
UHH...
WELL...
AH HA HA HA HA HA!
I KNEW IT!
YOU'RE SO EASY TO READ, HOZUMI-SAN.
YOU'VE BEEN SO MUCH...
CHEERIER LATELY, HOZUMI-SAN.
YOU EVEN CAME OUT DRINKING WITH US!
EVERY-BODY'S NOTICED.

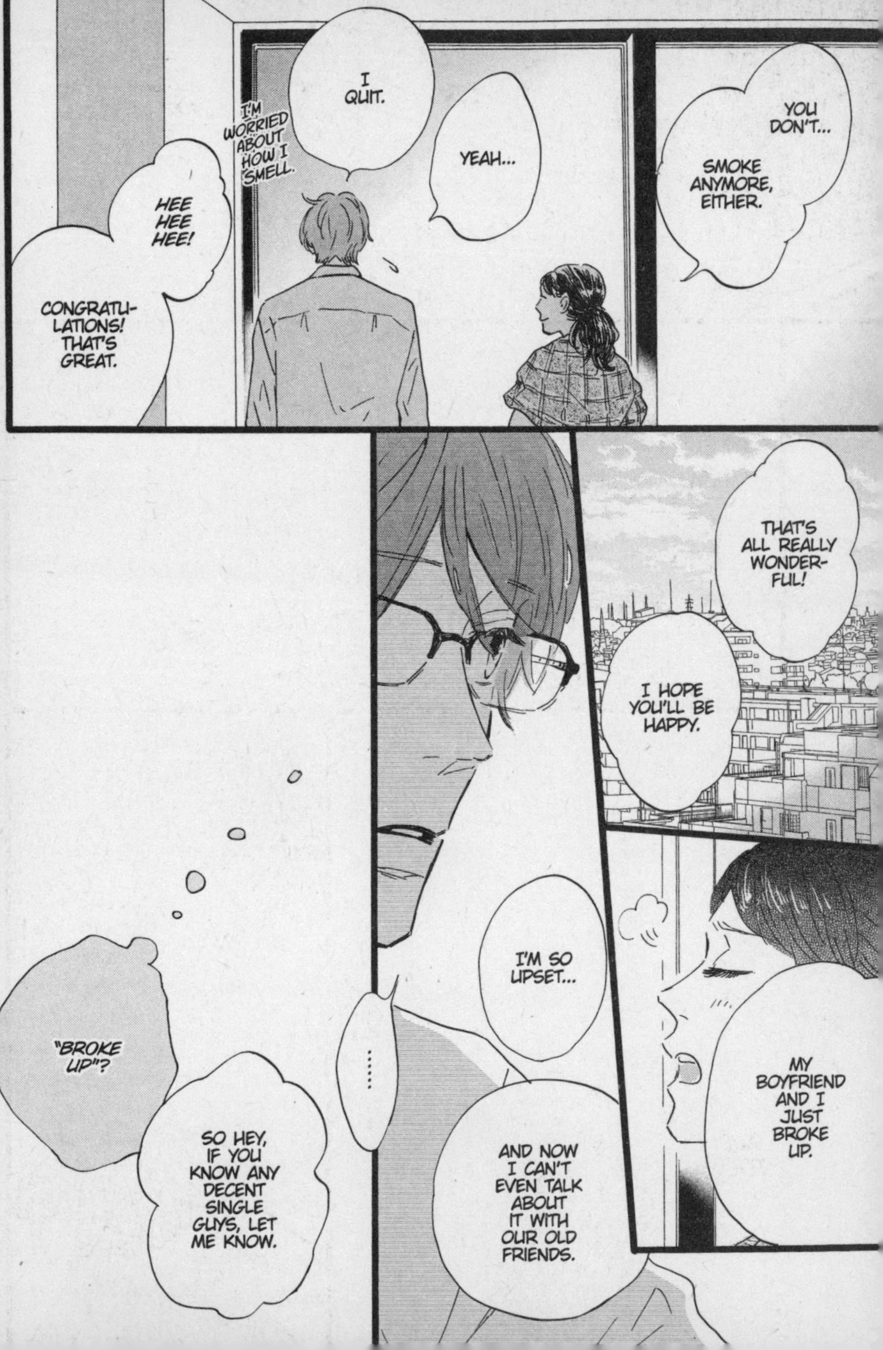
YOU DON'T... SMOKE ANYMORE, EITHER.
YEAH...
I QUIT.
I'M WORRIED ABOUT HOW I SMELL.
HEE HEE HEE!
CONGRATULATIONS! THAT'S GREAT.
THAT'S ALL REALLY WONDERFUL!
I HOPE YOU'LL BE HAPPY.
MY BOYFRIEND AND I JUST BROKE UP.
I'M SO UPSET...
AND NOW I CAN'T EVEN TALK ABOUT IT WITH OUR OLD FRIENDS.
......
SO HEY, IF YOU KNOW ANY DECENT SINGLE GUYS, LET ME KNOW.
"BROKE UP"?

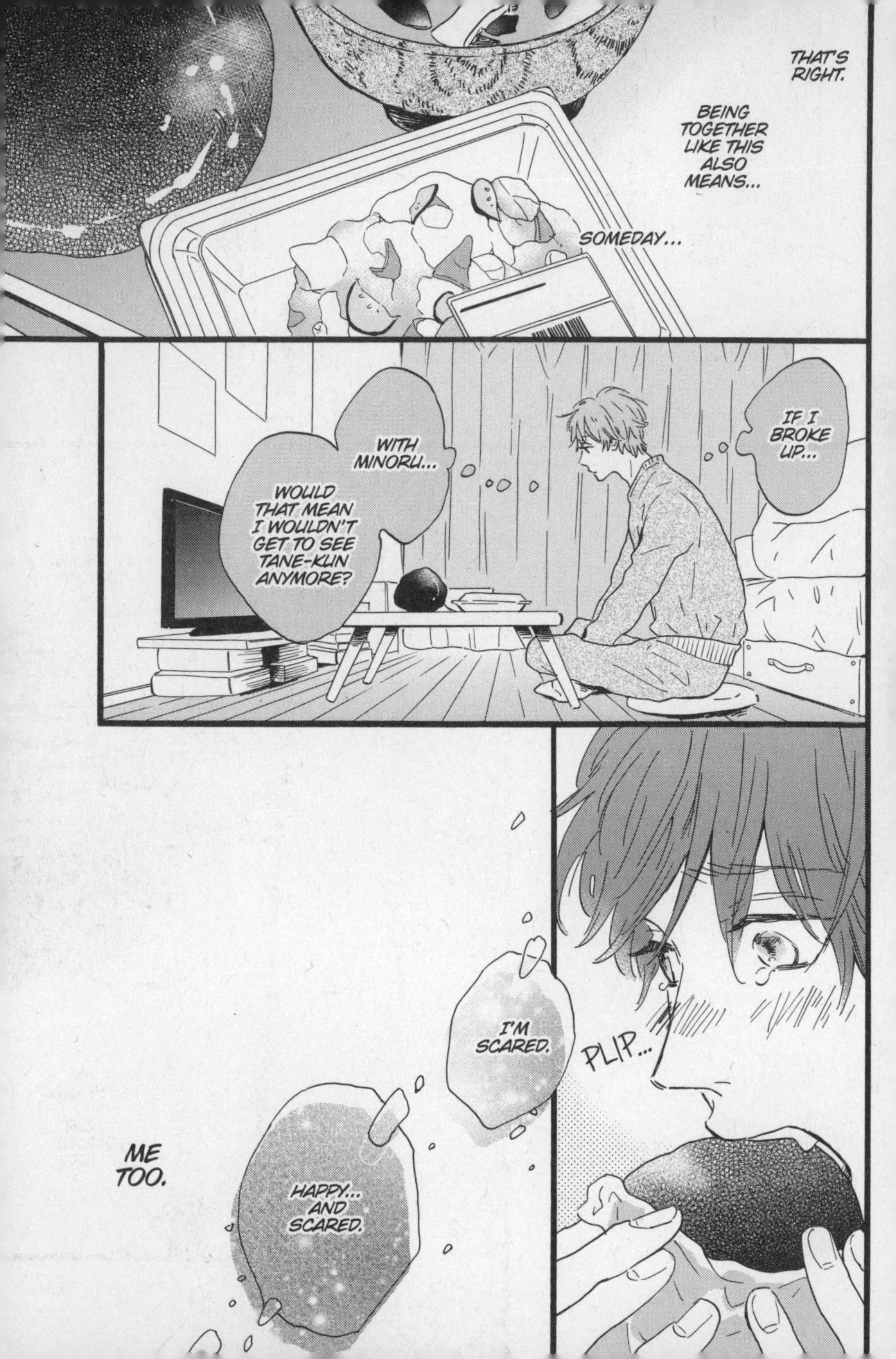

THAT'S RIGHT.
BEING TOGETHER LIKE THIS ALSO MEANS...
SOMEDAY...
IF I BROKE UP...
WITH MINORU...
WOULD THAT MEAN I WOULDN'T GET TO SEE TANE-KUN ANYMORE?
PLIP...
I'M SCARED.
HAPPY... AND SCARED.
ME TOO.

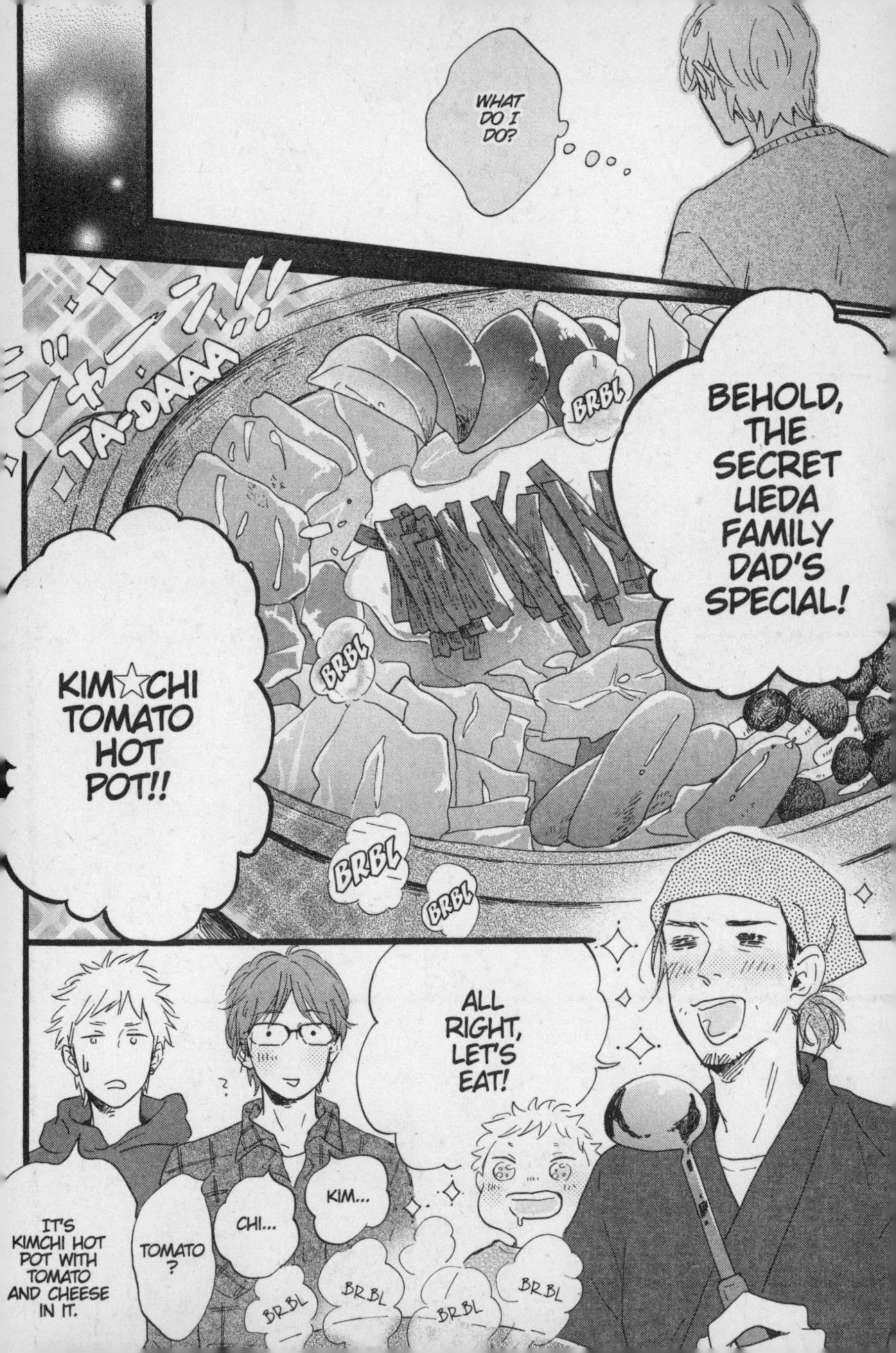
WHAT DO I DO?
BEHOLD, THE SECRET UEDA FAMILY DAD'S SPECIAL!
BRBL
TA-DAAA
BRBL
KIM☆CHI TOMATO HOT POT!!
BRBL
BRBL
ALL RIGHT, LET'S EAT!
KIM...
CHI...
TOMATO?
IT'S KIMCHI HOT POT WITH TOMATO AND CHEESE IN IT.
BR.BL
BR.BL
BR.BL
BR.BL

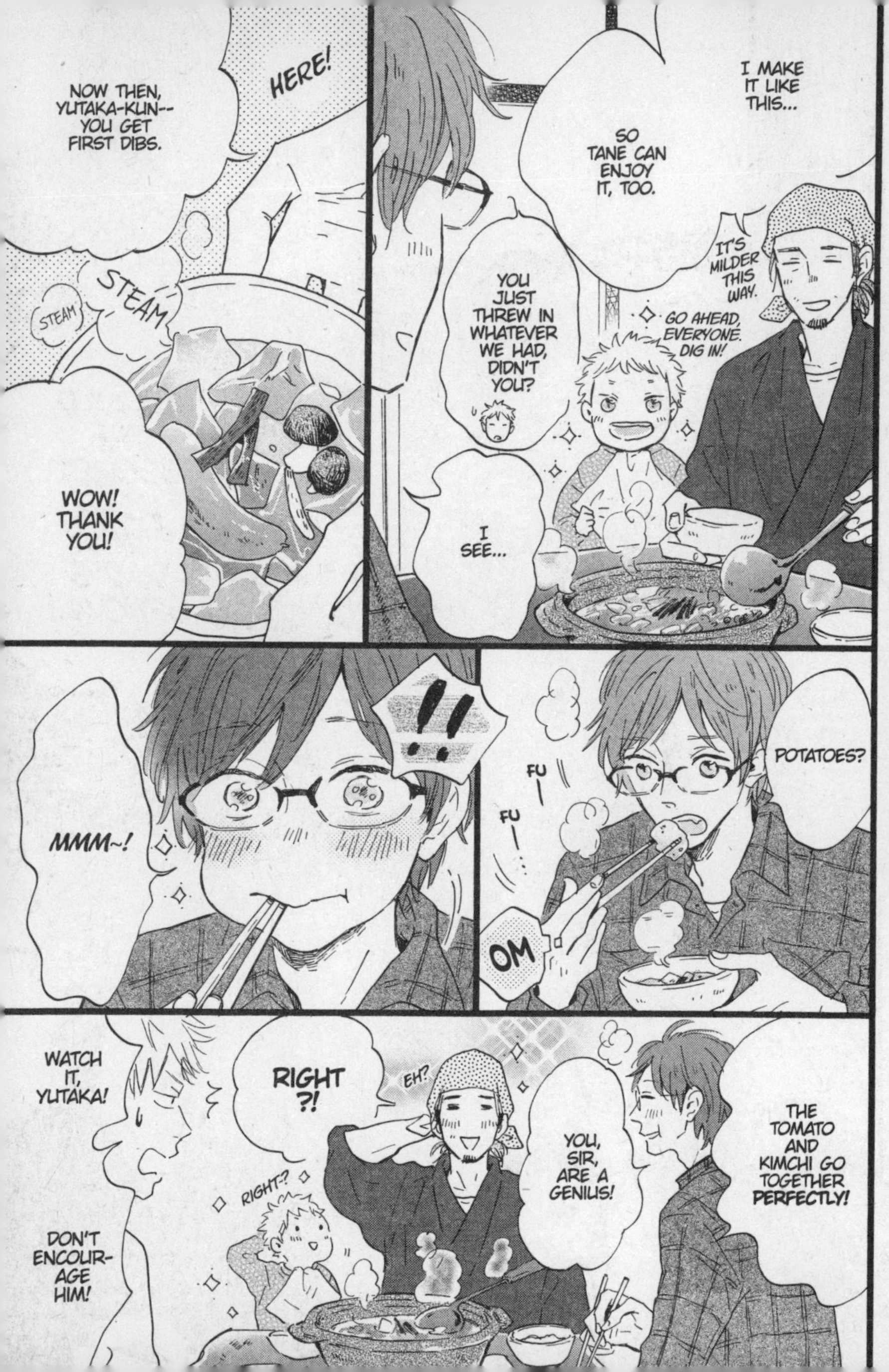
I MAKE IT LIKE THIS...
SO TANE CAN ENJOY IT, TOO.
IT'S MILDER THIS WAY.
GO AHEAD, EVERYONE. DIG IN!
YOU JUST THREW IN WHATEVER WE HAD, DIDN'T YOU?
I SEE...
HERE!
NOW THEN, YUTAKA-KUN-- YOU GET FIRST DIBS.
STEAM
STEAM
WOW! THANK YOU!
POTATOES?
FU
FU
OM
!!
MMM~!
THE TOMATO AND KIMCHI GO TOGETHER PERFECTLY!
YOU, SIR, ARE A GENIUS!
EH?
RIGHT ?!
RIGHT?
WATCH IT, YUTAKA!
DON'T ENCOURAGE HIM!

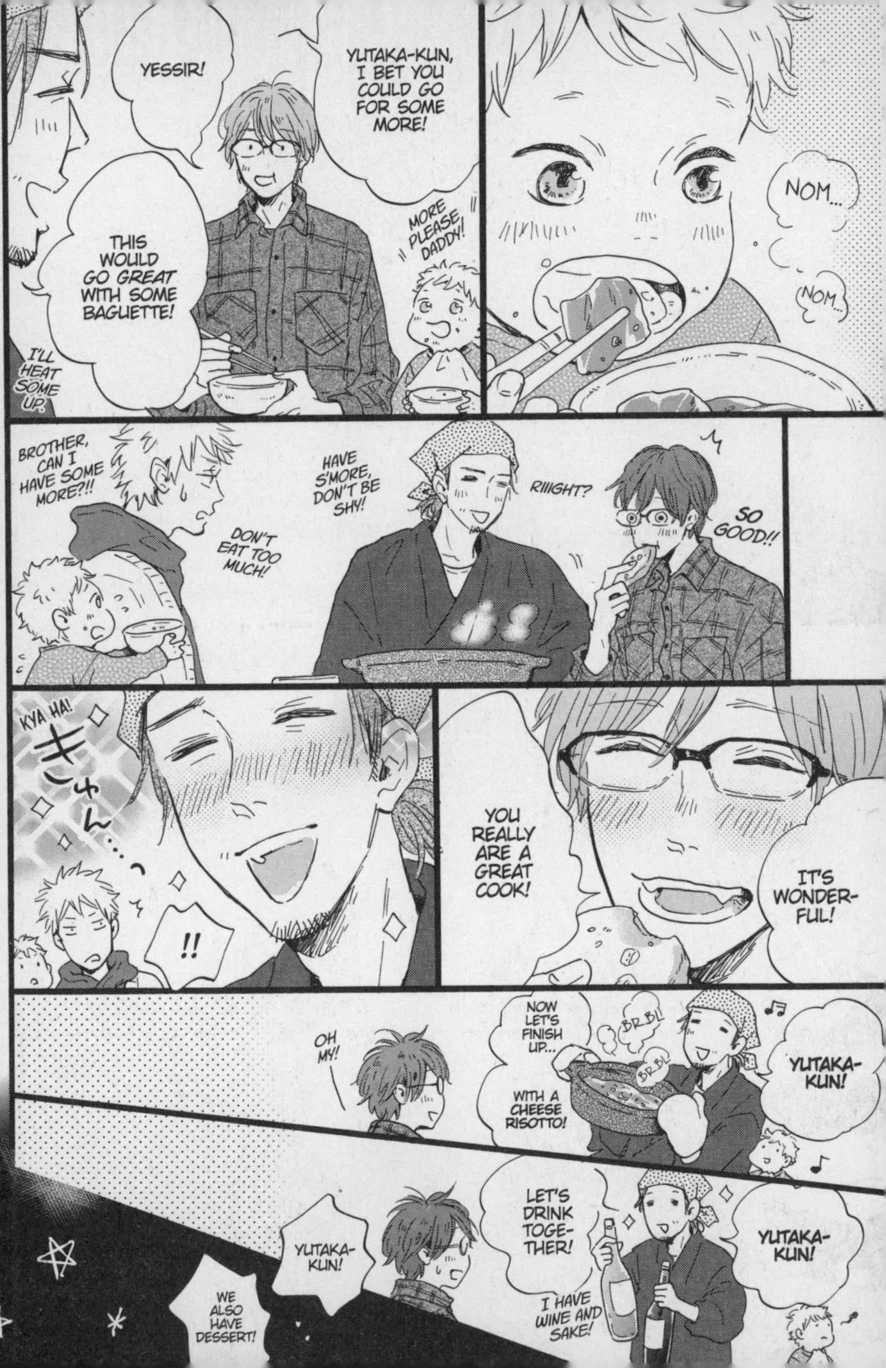
NOM...
NOM...
YUTAKA-KUN, I BET YOU COULD GO FOR SOME MORE!
YESSIR!
MORE PLEASE, DADDY!
THIS WOULD GO GREAT WITH SOME BAGUETTE!
I'LL HEAT SOME UP.
SO GOOD!!
RIIIGHT?
HAVE S'MORE, DON'T BE SHY!
BROTHER, CAN I HAVE SOME MORE?!!
DON'T EAT TOO MUCH!
IT'S WONDER-FUL!
YOU REALLY ARE A GREAT COOK!
KYA HA!
きゅん…
!!
YUTAKA-KUN!
NOW LET'S FINISH UP...
BR BL
BR BL
WITH A CHEESE RISOTTO!
OH MY!
YUTAKA-KUN!
LET'S DRINK TOGE-THER!
I HAVE WINE AND SAKE!
YUTAKA-KUN!
WE ALSO HAVE DESSERT!

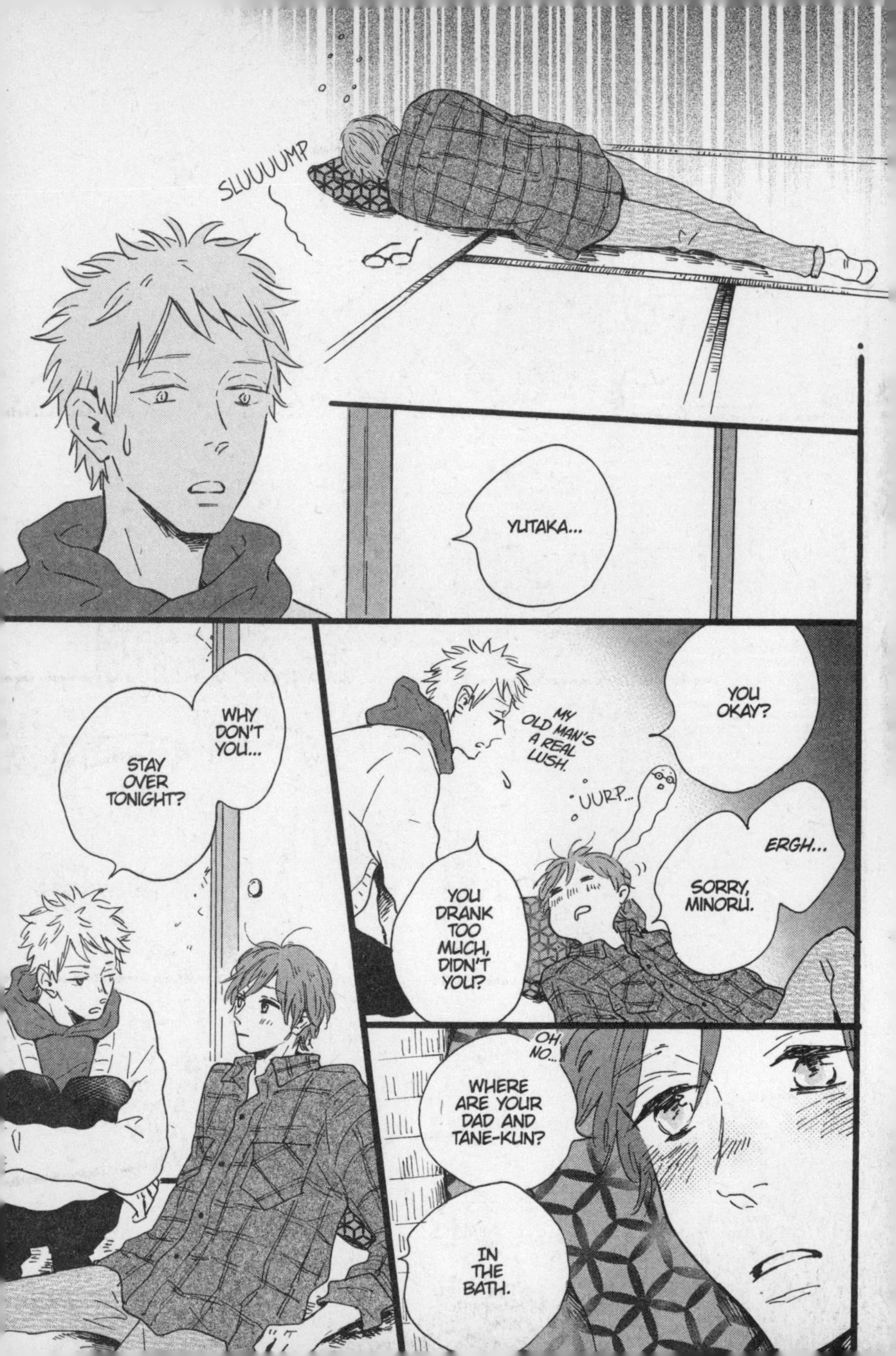
SLUUUUMP
YUTAKA...
YOU OKAY?
ERGH...
SORRY, MINORU.
MY OLD MAN'S A REAL LUSH.
UURP...
YOU DRANK TOO MUCH, DIDN'T YOU?
OH NO...
WHERE ARE YOUR DAD AND TANE-KUN?
IN THE BATH.
WHY DON'T YOU...
STAY OVER TONIGHT?

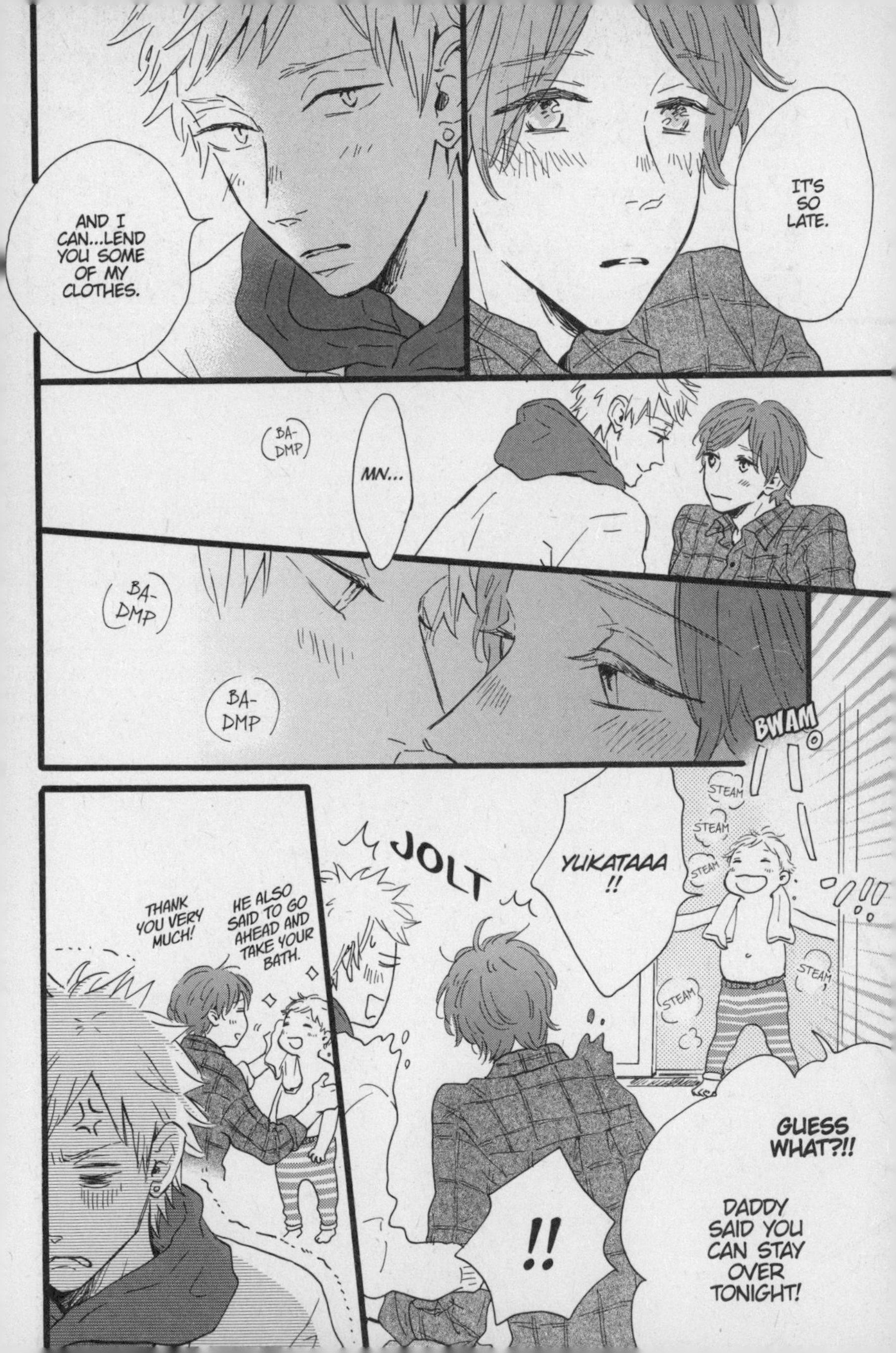
IT'S SO LATE.
AND I CAN...LEND YOU SOME OF MY CLOTHES.
MN...
BA-DMP
BA-DMP
BA-DMP
BWAM
STEAM
STEAM
STEAM
STEAM
STEAM
YUKATAAA!!
GUESS WHAT?!!
DADDY SAID YOU CAN STAY OVER TONIGHT!
JOLT
!!
HE ALSO SAID TO GO AHEAD AND TAKE YOUR BATH.
THANK YOU VERY MUCH!
...

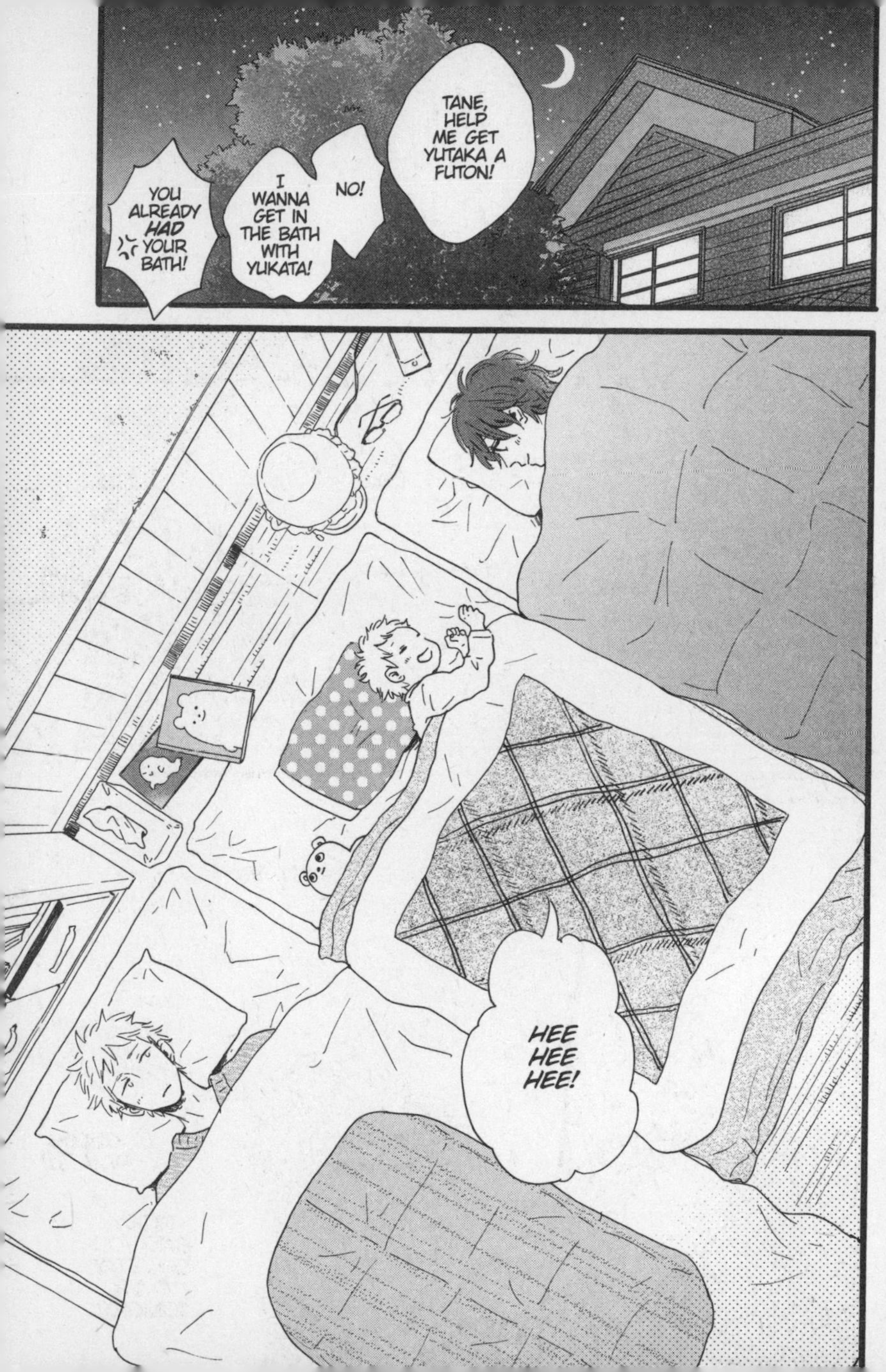
TANE, HELP ME GET YUTAKA A FUTON!
NO!
I WANNA GET IN THE BATH WITH YUKATA!
YOU ALREADY *HAD* YOUR BATH!
HEE HEE HEE!

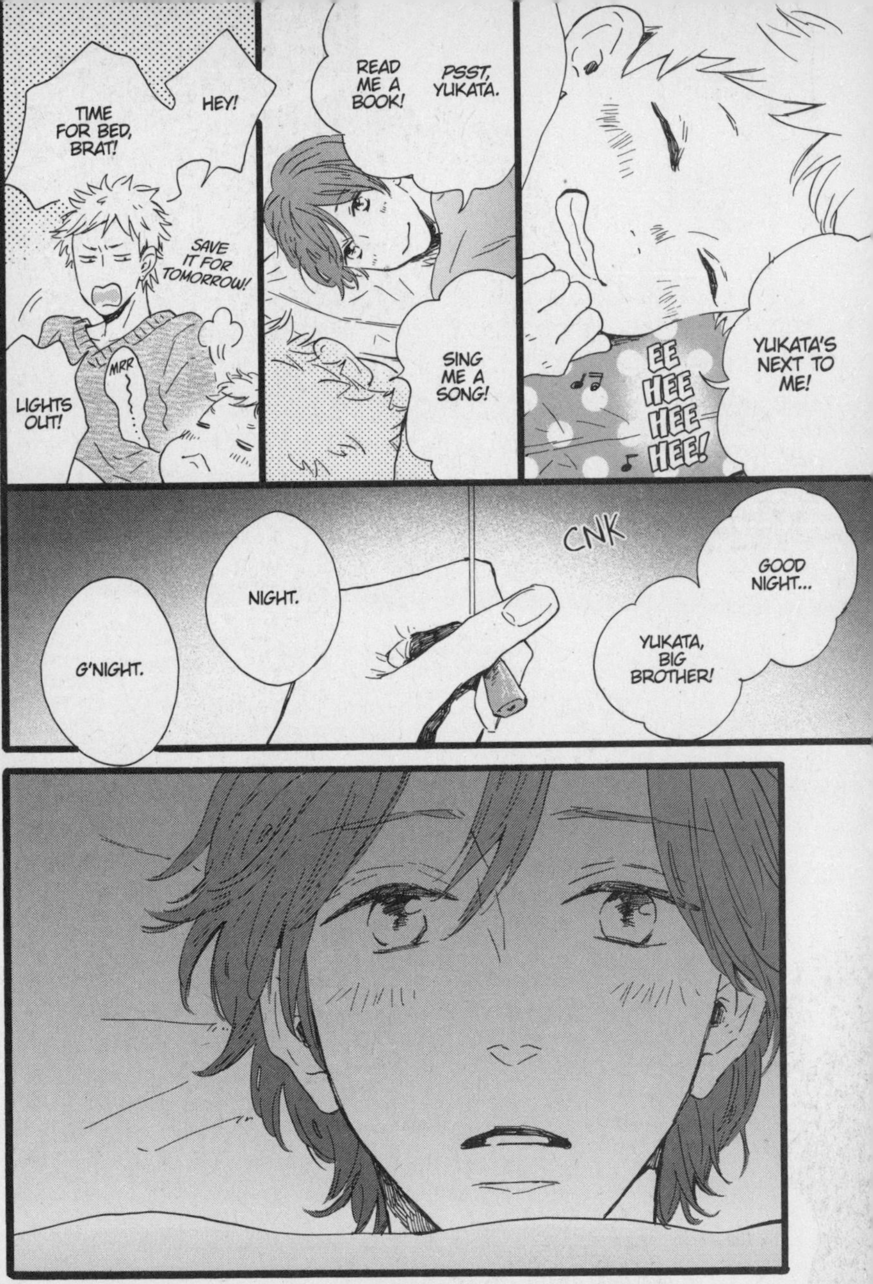
YUKATA'S NEXT TO ME!
EE HEE HEE HEE!
PSST, YUKATA.
READ ME A BOOK!
SING ME A SONG!
HEY!
TIME FOR BED, BRAT!
SAVE IT FOR TOMORROW!
MRR
LIGHTS OUT!
GOOD NIGHT...
YUKATA, BIG BROTHER!
CNK
NIGHT.
G'NIGHT.

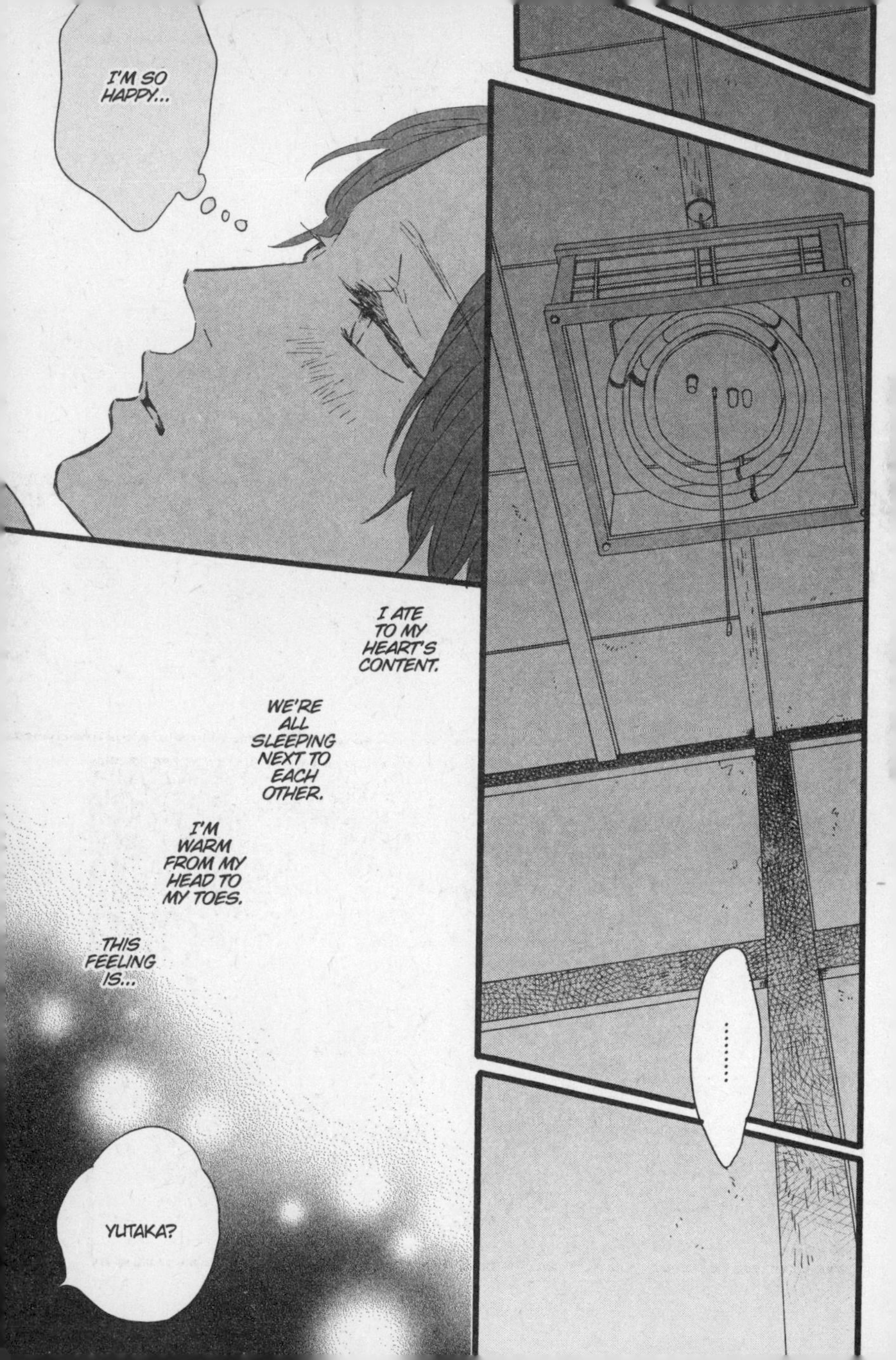
......
I'M SO HAPPY...
I ATE TO MY HEART'S CONTENT.
WE'RE ALL SLEEPING NEXT TO EACH OTHER.
I'M WARM FROM MY HEAD TO MY TOES.
THIS FEELING IS...
YUTAKA?

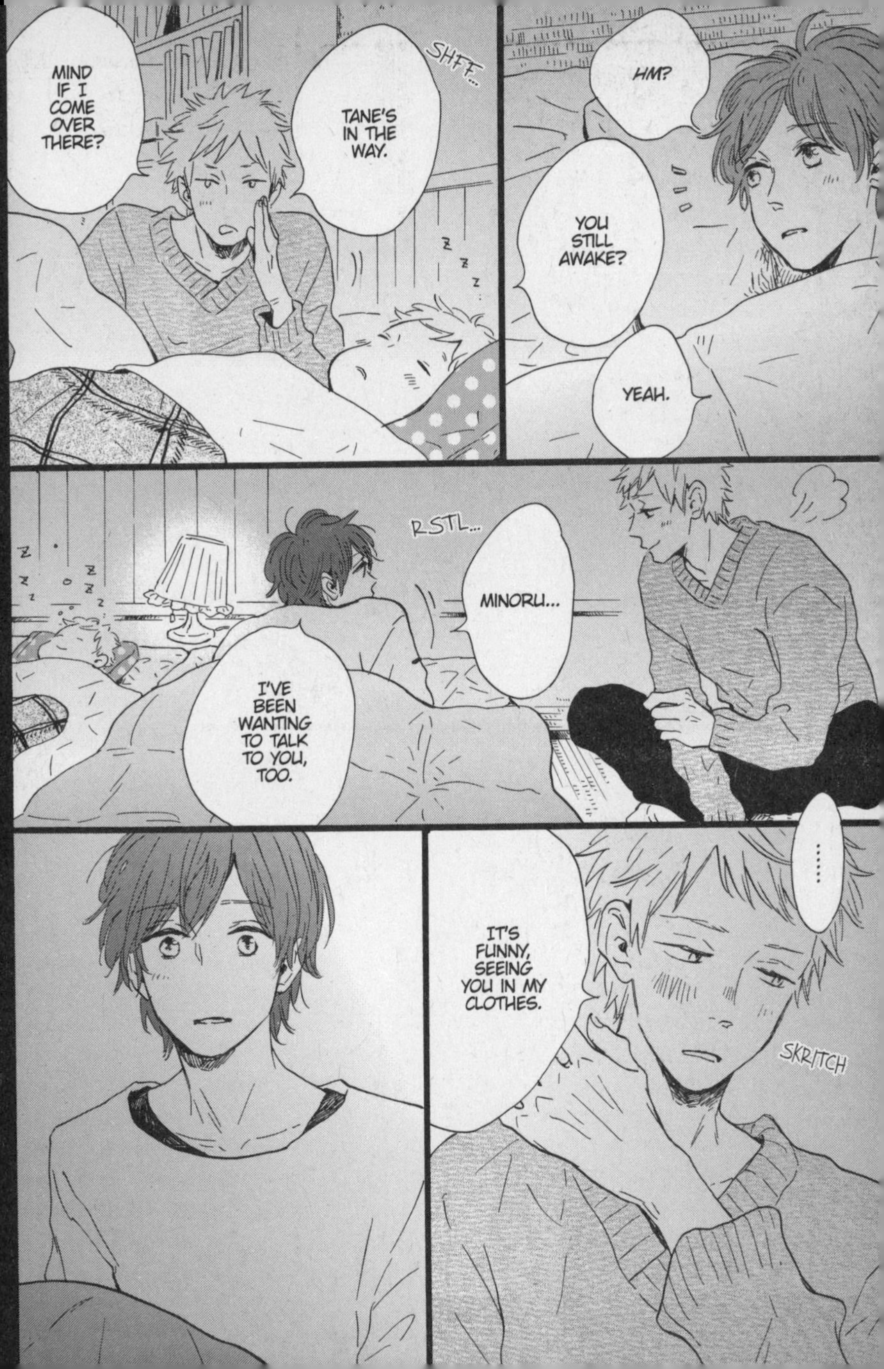
HM?
YOU STILL AWAKE?
YEAH.
SHFF...
TANE'S IN THE WAY.
MIND IF I COME OVER THERE?
RSTL...
MINORU...
I'VE BEEN WANTING TO TALK TO YOU, TOO.
......
IT'S FUNNY, SEEING YOU IN MY CLOTHES.
SKRITCH

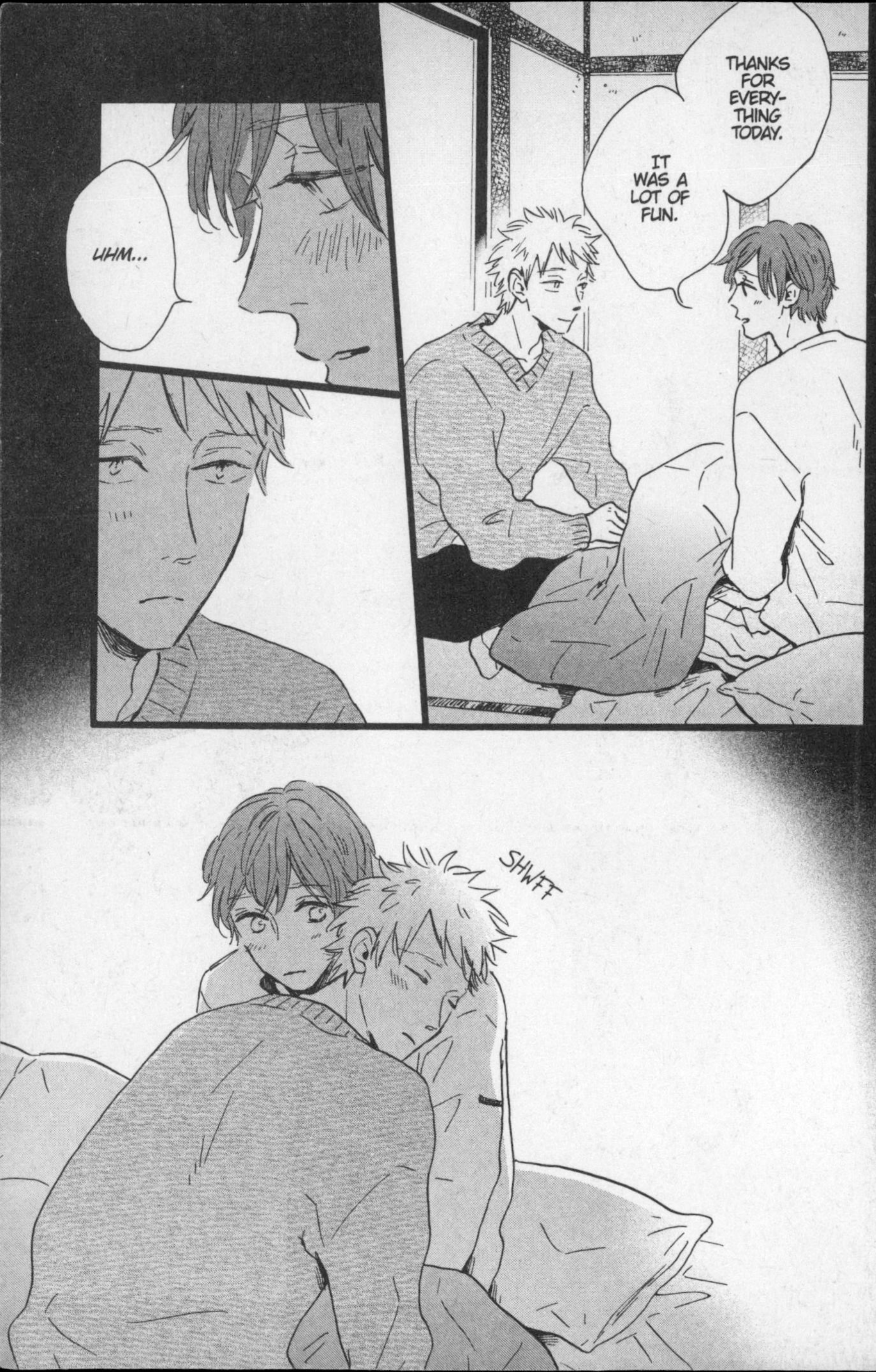
THANKS FOR EVERYTHING TODAY.
IT WAS A LOT OF FUN.
UHM...
SHWFF

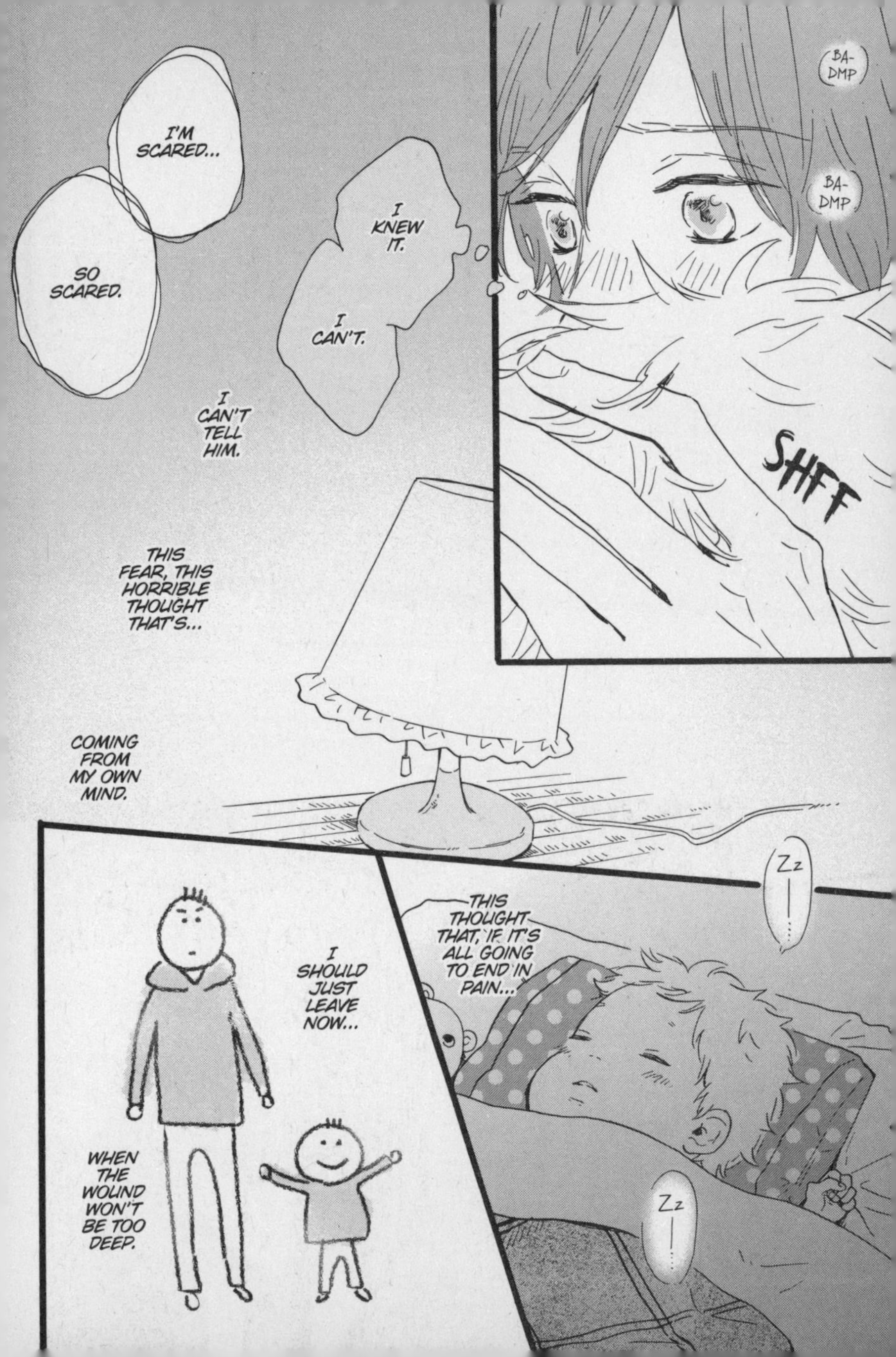
BA-DMP
BA-DMP
SHFF
I KNEW IT.
I CAN'T.
I'M SCARED...
SO SCARED.
I CAN'T TELL HIM.
THIS FEAR, THIS HORRIBLE THOUGHT THAT'S...
COMING FROM MY OWN MIND.
Zz
THIS THOUGHT THAT, IF IT'S ALL GOING TO END IN PAIN...
Zz
I SHOULD JUST LEAVE NOW...
WHEN THE WOUND WON'T BE TOO DEEP.

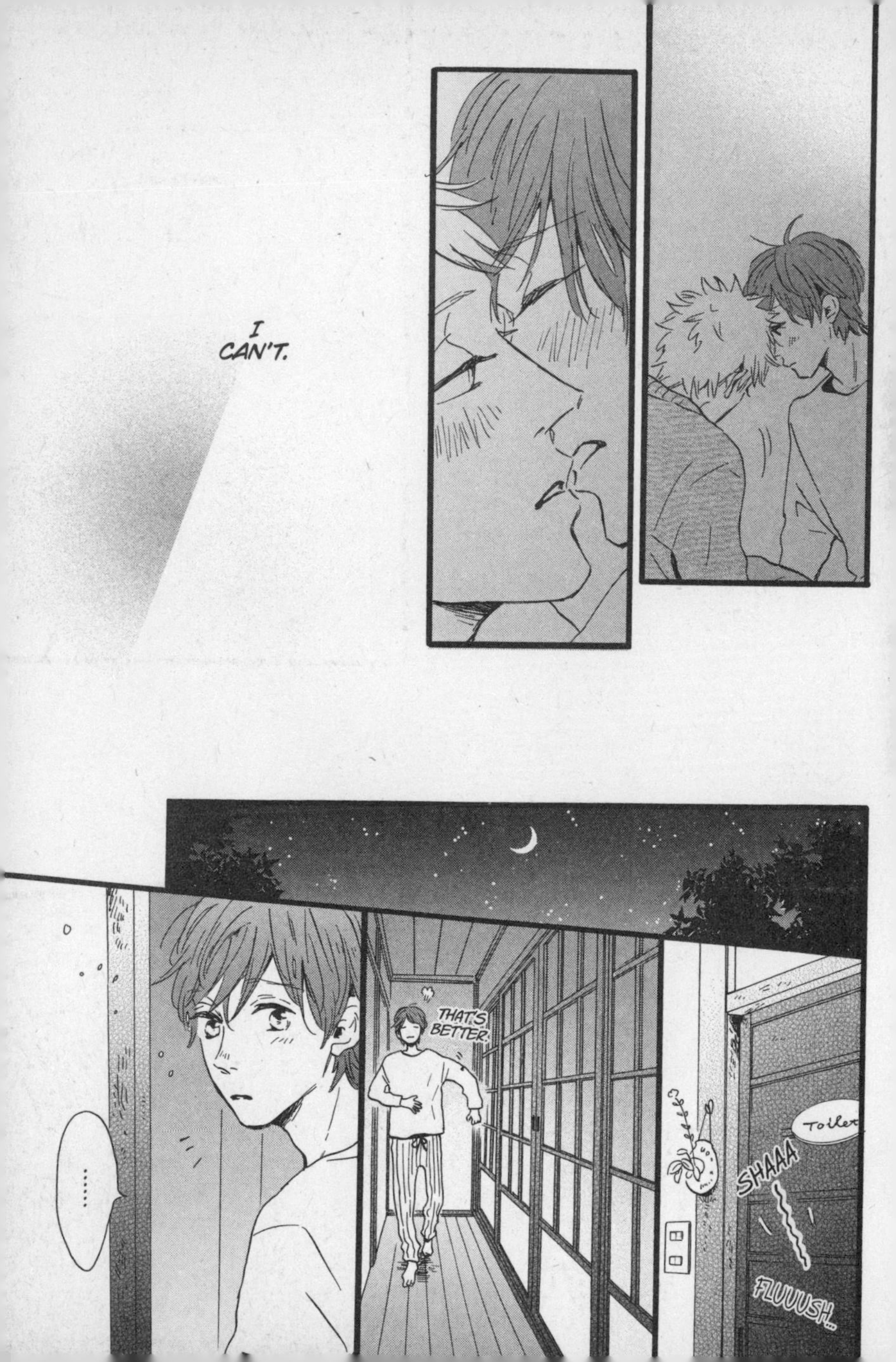
I CAN'T.
Toilet
SHAAA
FLUUUSH...
THAT'S BETTER.
......

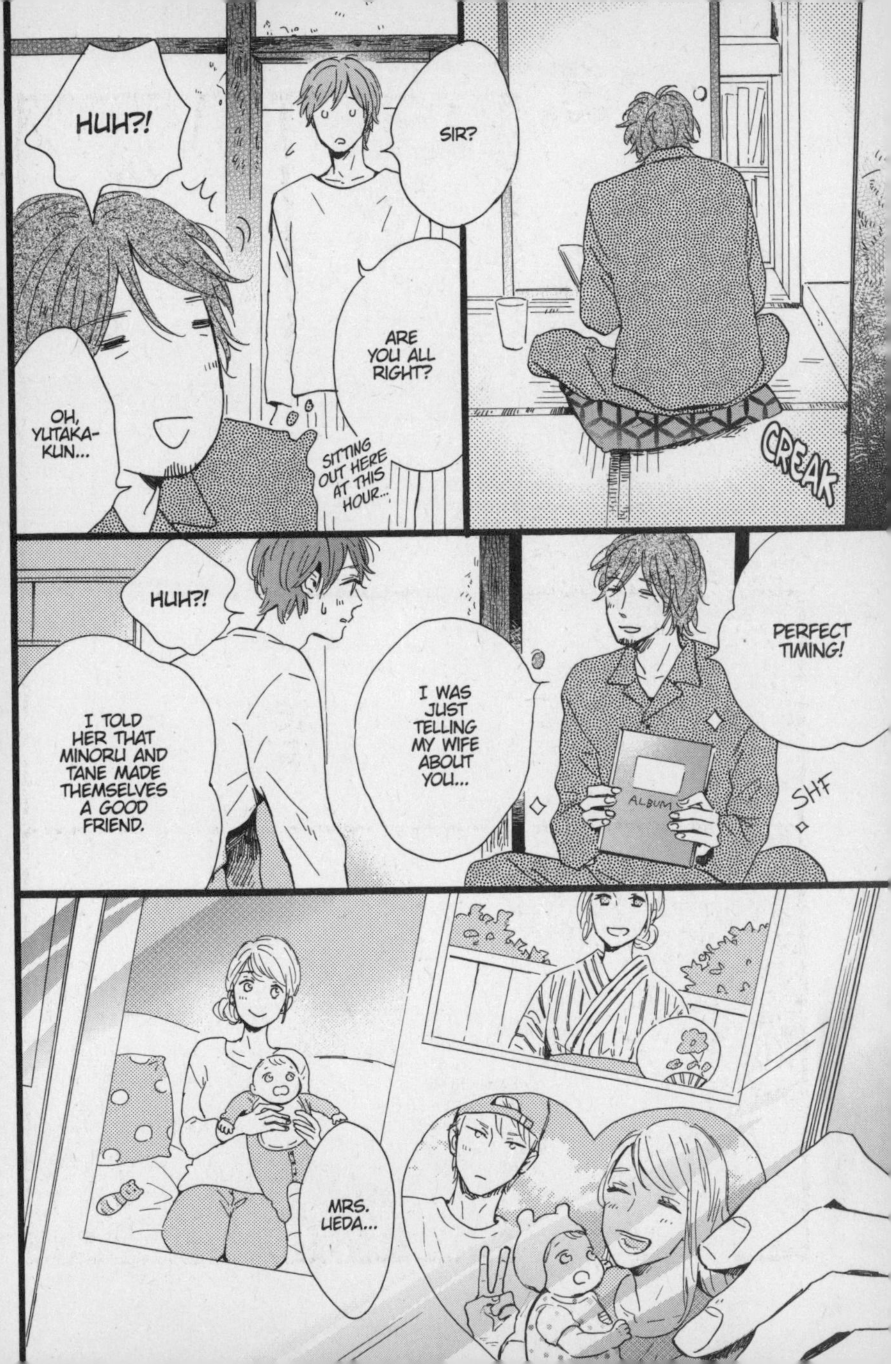
CREAK
SIR?
HUH?!
ARE YOU ALL RIGHT?
SITTING OUT HERE AT THIS HOUR...
OH, YUTAKA-KUN...
PERFECT TIMING!
SHF
I WAS JUST TELLING MY WIFE ABOUT YOU...
HUH?!
I TOLD HER THAT MINORU AND TANE MADE THEMSELVES A GOOD FRIEND.
ALBUM
MRS. UEDA...

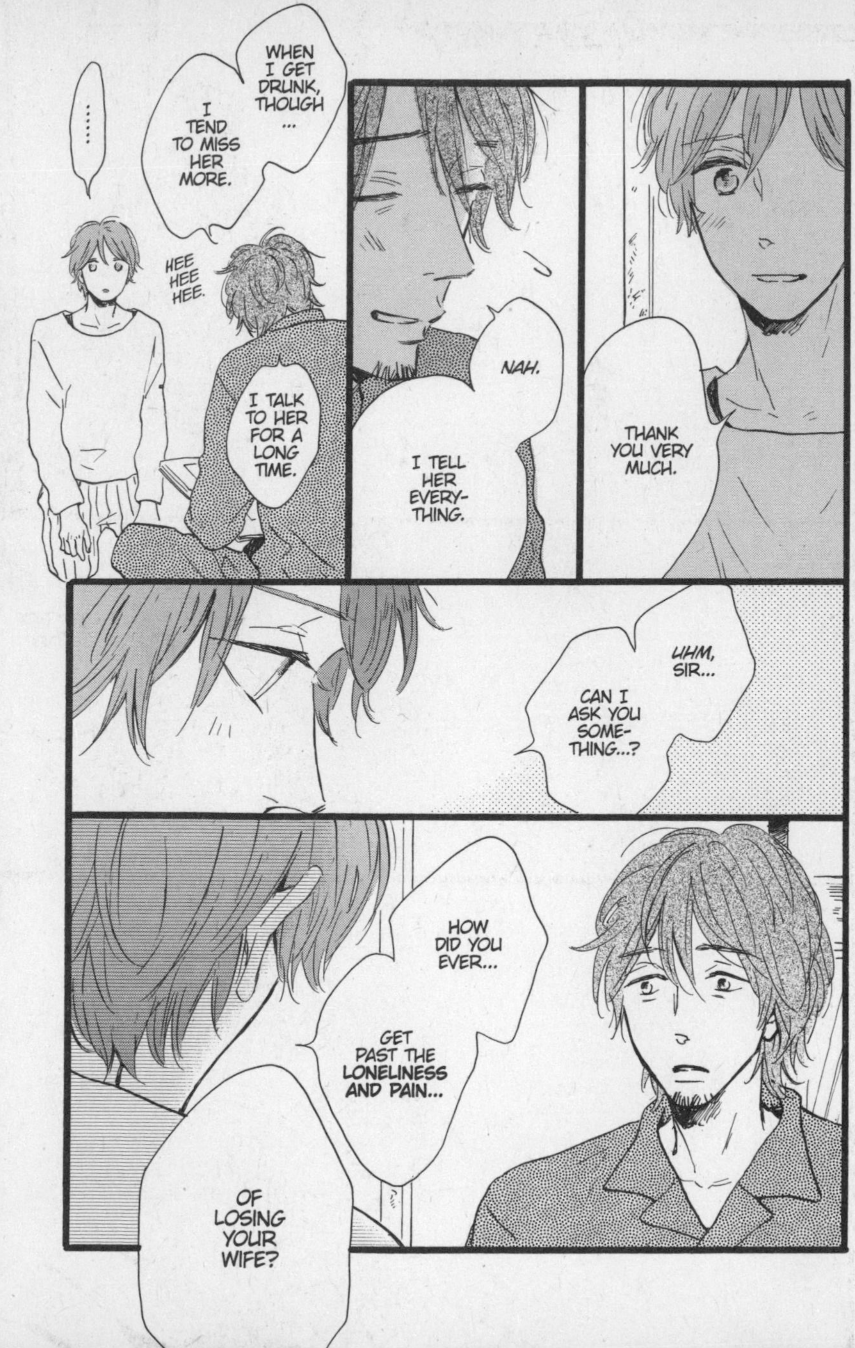
THANK YOU VERY MUCH.
NAH.
I TELL HER EVERYTHING.
WHEN I GET DRUNK, THOUGH ...
I TEND TO MISS HER MORE.
......
HEE HEE HEE.
I TALK TO HER FOR A LONG TIME.
UHM, SIR...
CAN I ASK YOU SOMETHING...?
HOW DID YOU EVER...
GET PAST THE LONELINESS AND PAIN...
OF LOSING YOUR WIFE?

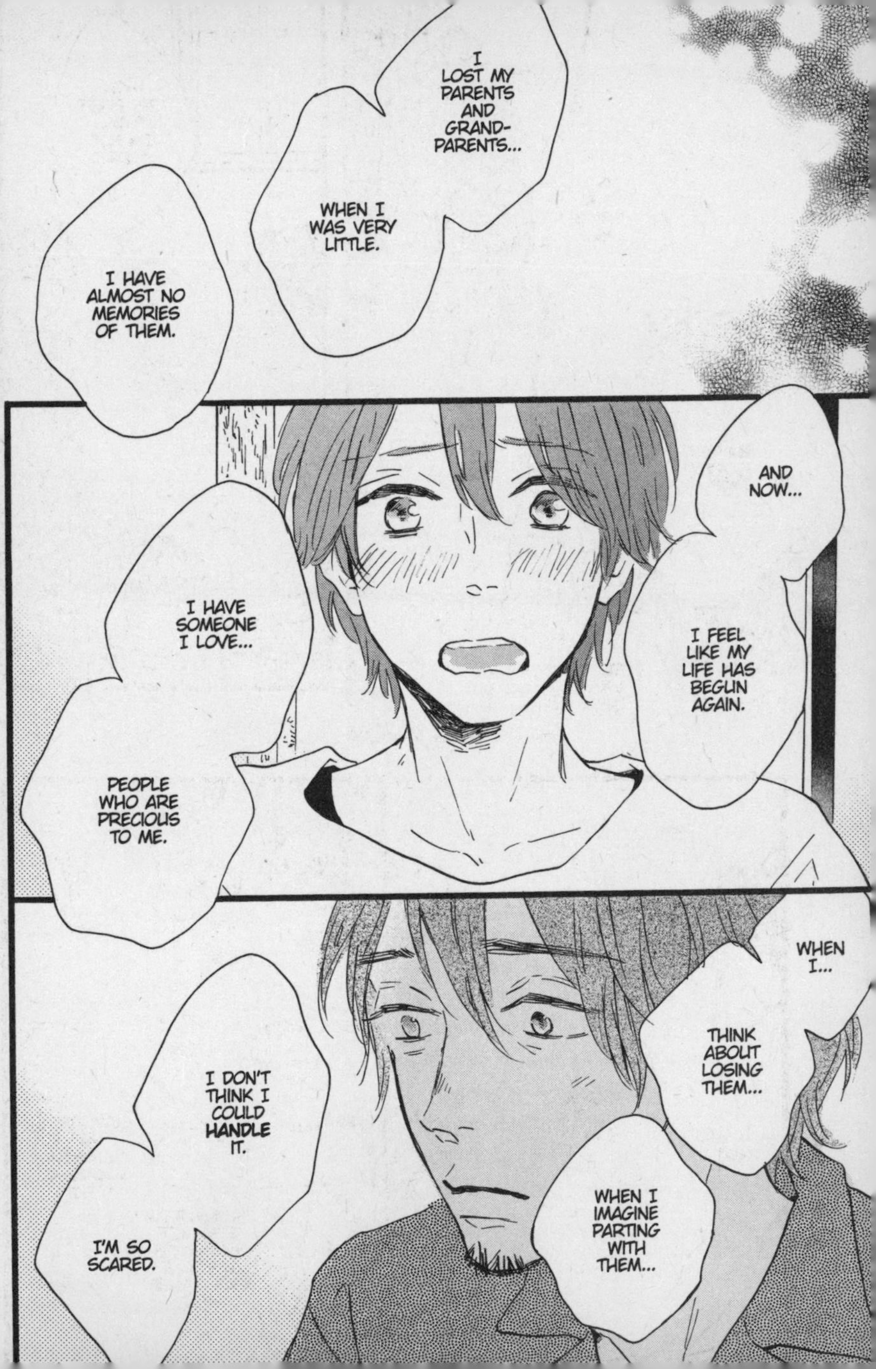
I LOST MY PARENTS AND GRAND-PARENTS...
WHEN I WAS VERY LITTLE.
I HAVE ALMOST NO MEMORIES OF THEM.
AND NOW...
I FEEL LIKE MY LIFE HAS BEGUN AGAIN.
I HAVE SOMEONE I LOVE...
PEOPLE WHO ARE PRECIOUS TO ME.
WHEN I...
THINK ABOUT LOSING THEM...
WHEN I IMAGINE PARTING WITH THEM...
I DON'T THINK I COULD HANDLE IT.
I'M SO SCARED.

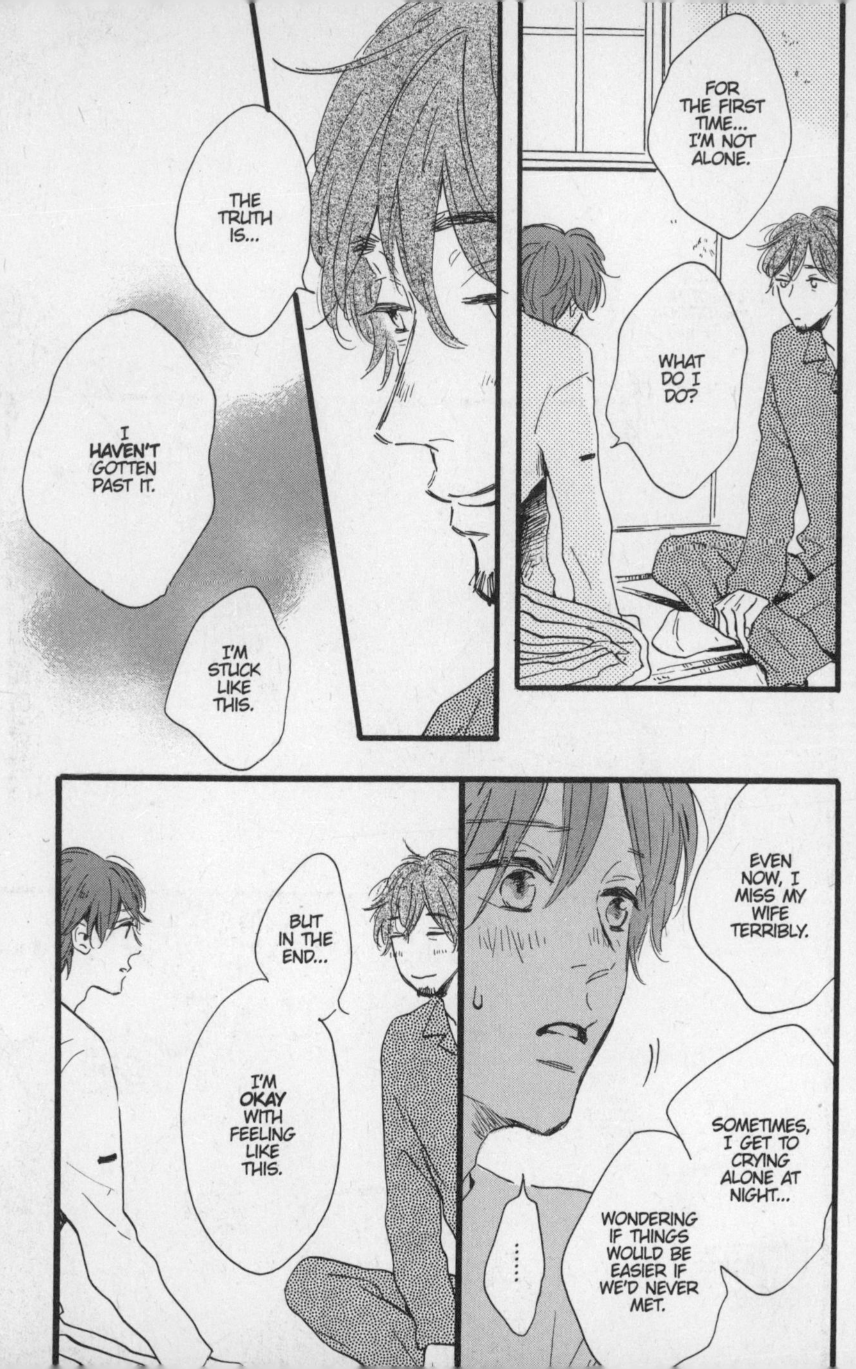
FOR THE FIRST TIME... I'M NOT ALONE.
WHAT DO I DO?
THE TRUTH IS...
I HAVEN'T GOTTEN PAST IT.
I'M STUCK LIKE THIS.
EVEN NOW, I MISS MY WIFE TERRIBLY.
SOMETIMES, I GET TO CRYING ALONE AT NIGHT...
WONDERING IF THINGS WOULD BE EASIER IF WE'D NEVER MET.
......
BUT IN THE END...
I'M OKAY WITH FEELING LIKE THIS.

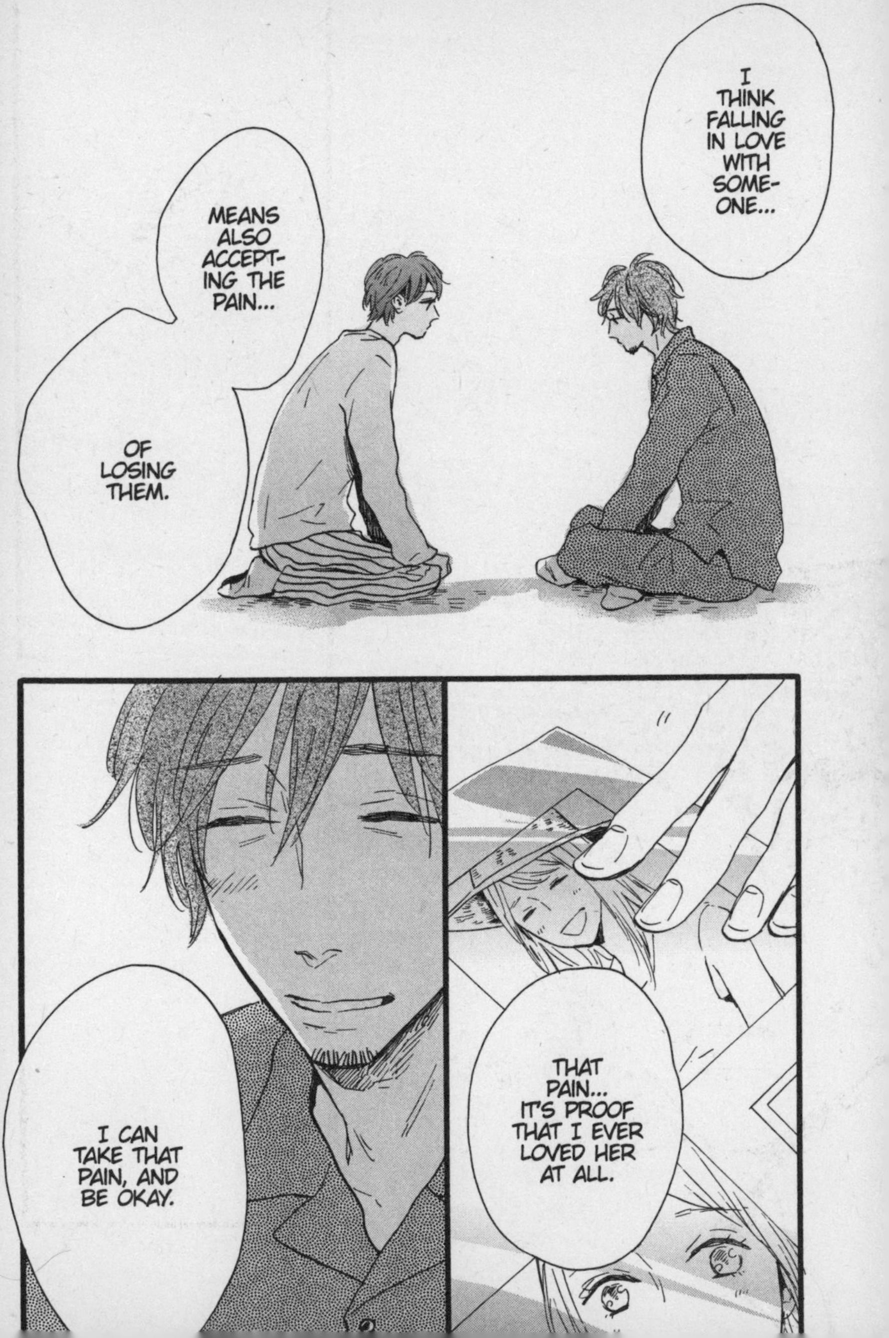
I THINK FALLING IN LOVE WITH SOME-ONE...
MEANS ALSO ACCEPT-ING THE PAIN...
OF LOSING THEM.
THAT PAIN... IT'S PROOF THAT I EVER LOVED HER AT ALL.
I CAN TAKE THAT PAIN, AND BE OKAY.

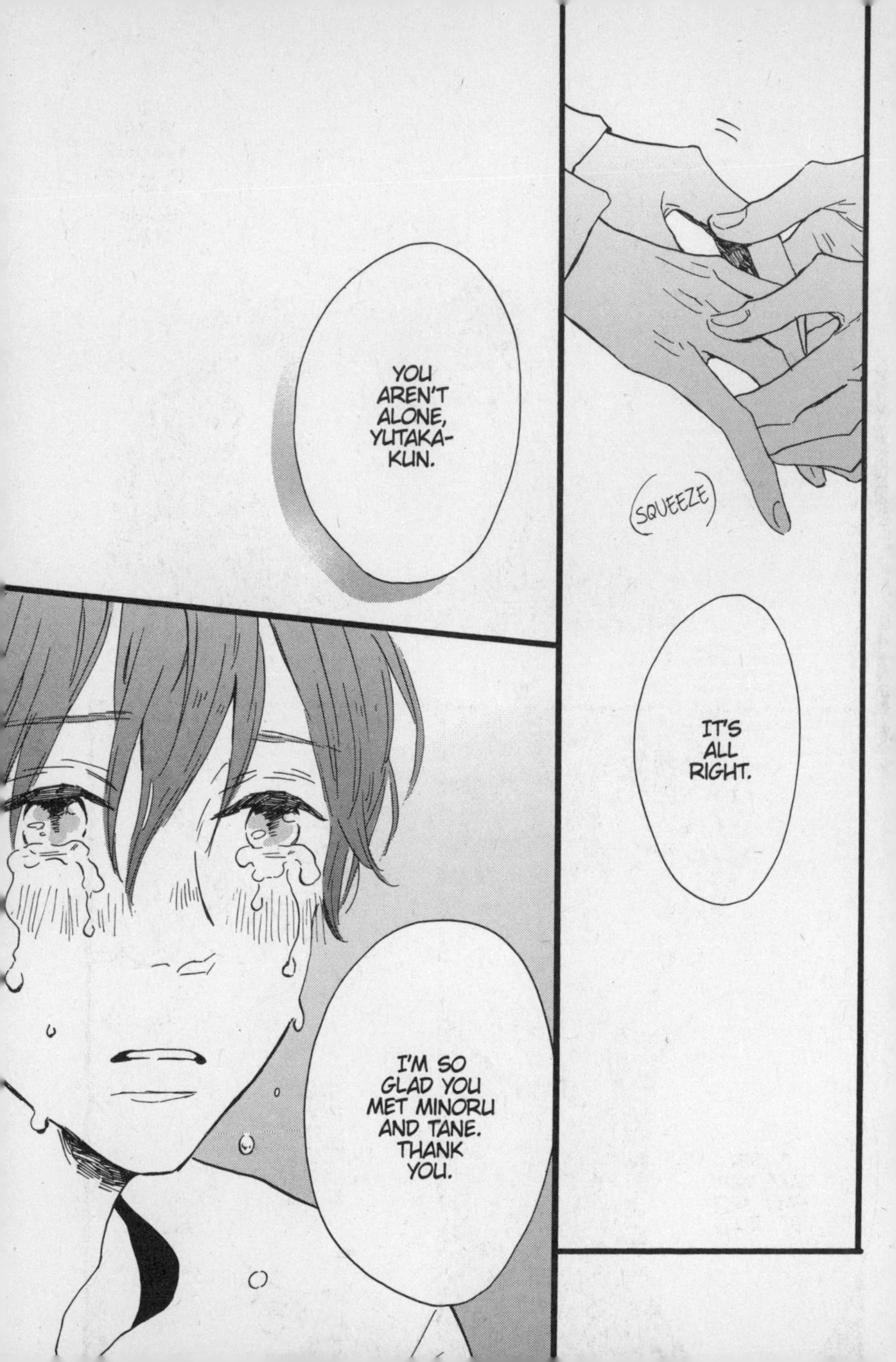
SQUEEZE
IT'S ALL RIGHT.
YOU AREN'T ALONE, YUTAKA-KUN.
I'M SO GLAD YOU MET MINORU AND TANE. THANK YOU.

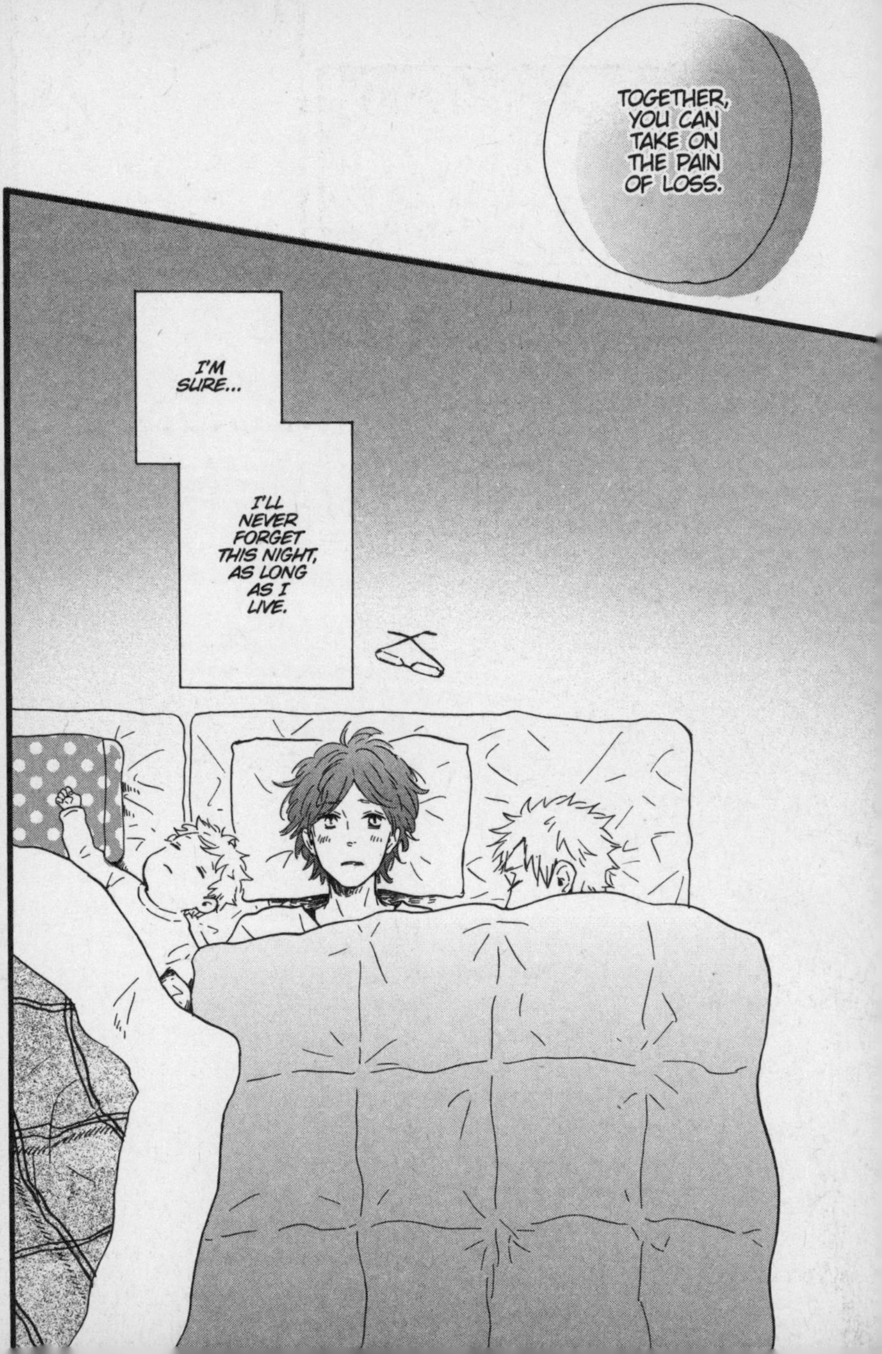
TOGETHER, YOU CAN TAKE ON THE PAIN OF LOSS.
I'M SURE...
I'LL NEVER FORGET THIS NIGHT, AS LONG AS I LIVE.

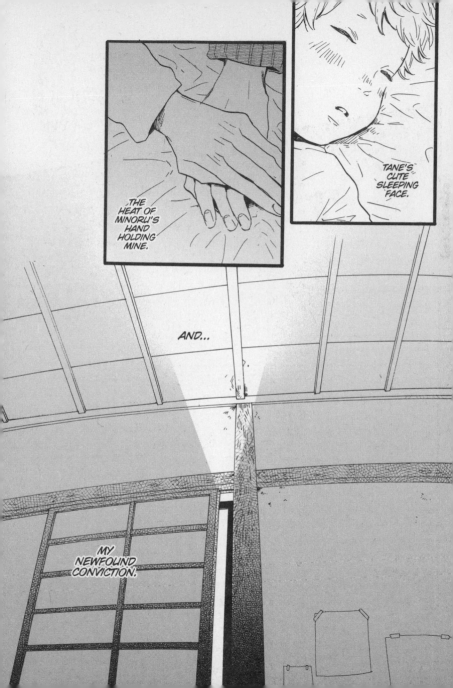

TANE'S CUTE SLEEPING FACE.

THE HEAT OF MINORU'S HAND HOLDING MINE.

AND...

MY NEWFOUND CONVICTION.

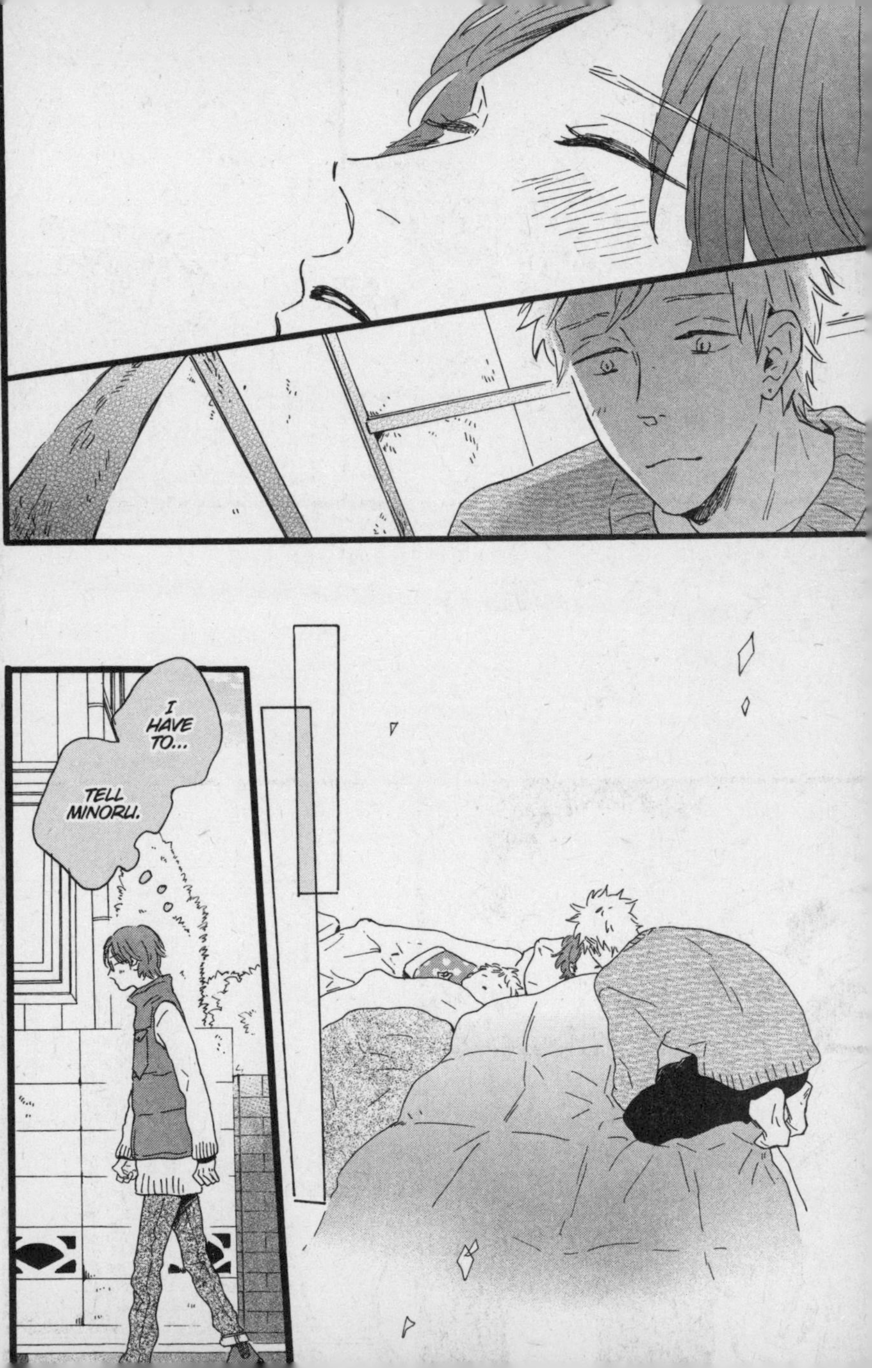
I HAVE TO...
TELL MINORU.

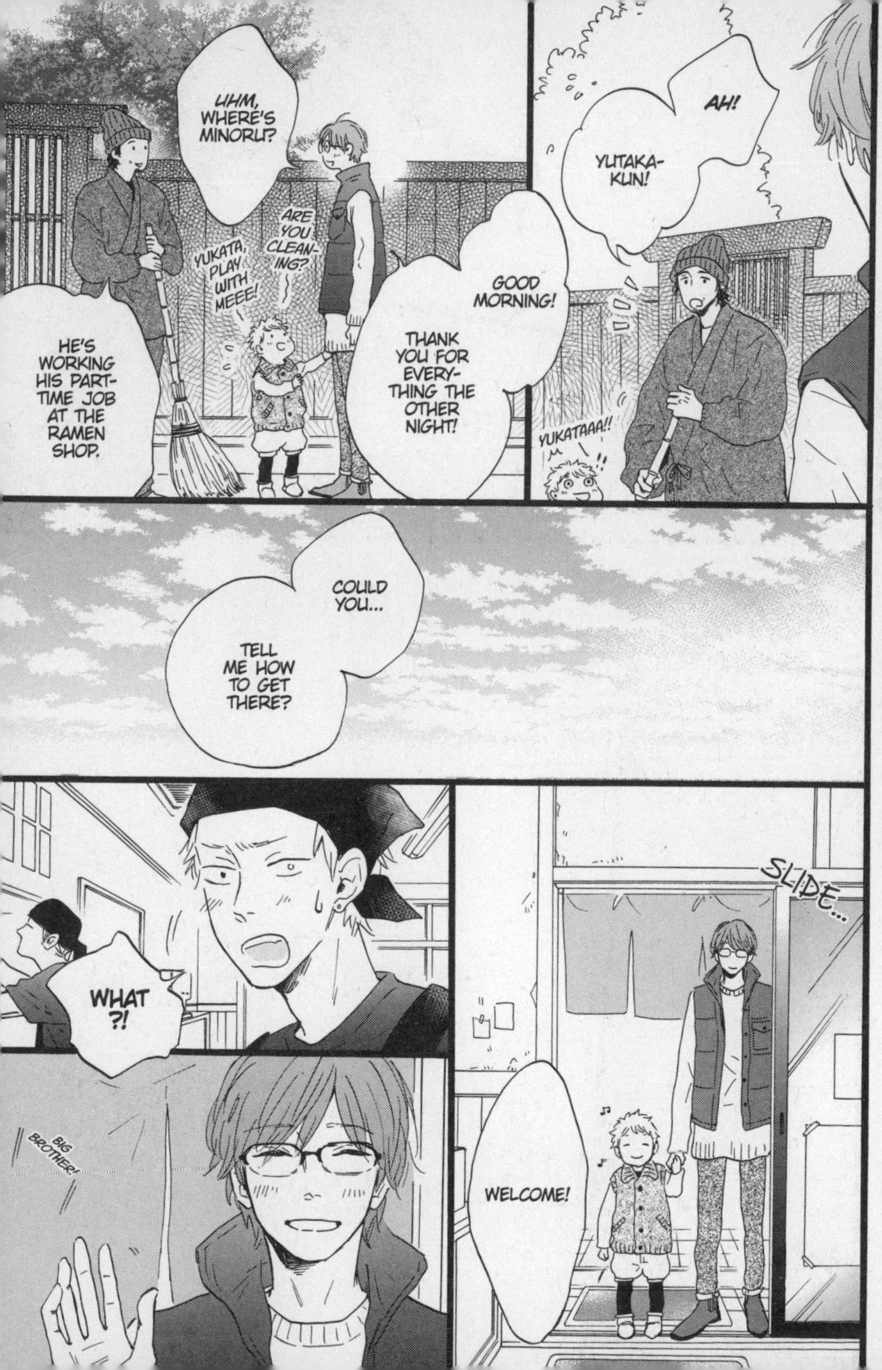
AH!
YUTAKA-KUN!
GOOD MORNING!
THANK YOU FOR EVERY-THING THE OTHER NIGHT!
YUKATAAA!!
UHM, WHERE'S MINORU?
ARE YOU CLEAN-ING?
YUKATA, PLAY WITH MEEE!
HE'S WORKING HIS PART-TIME JOB AT THE RAMEN SHOP.
COULD YOU...
TELL ME HOW TO GET THERE?
SLIDE...
WELCOME!
WHAT?!
BIG BROTHER!

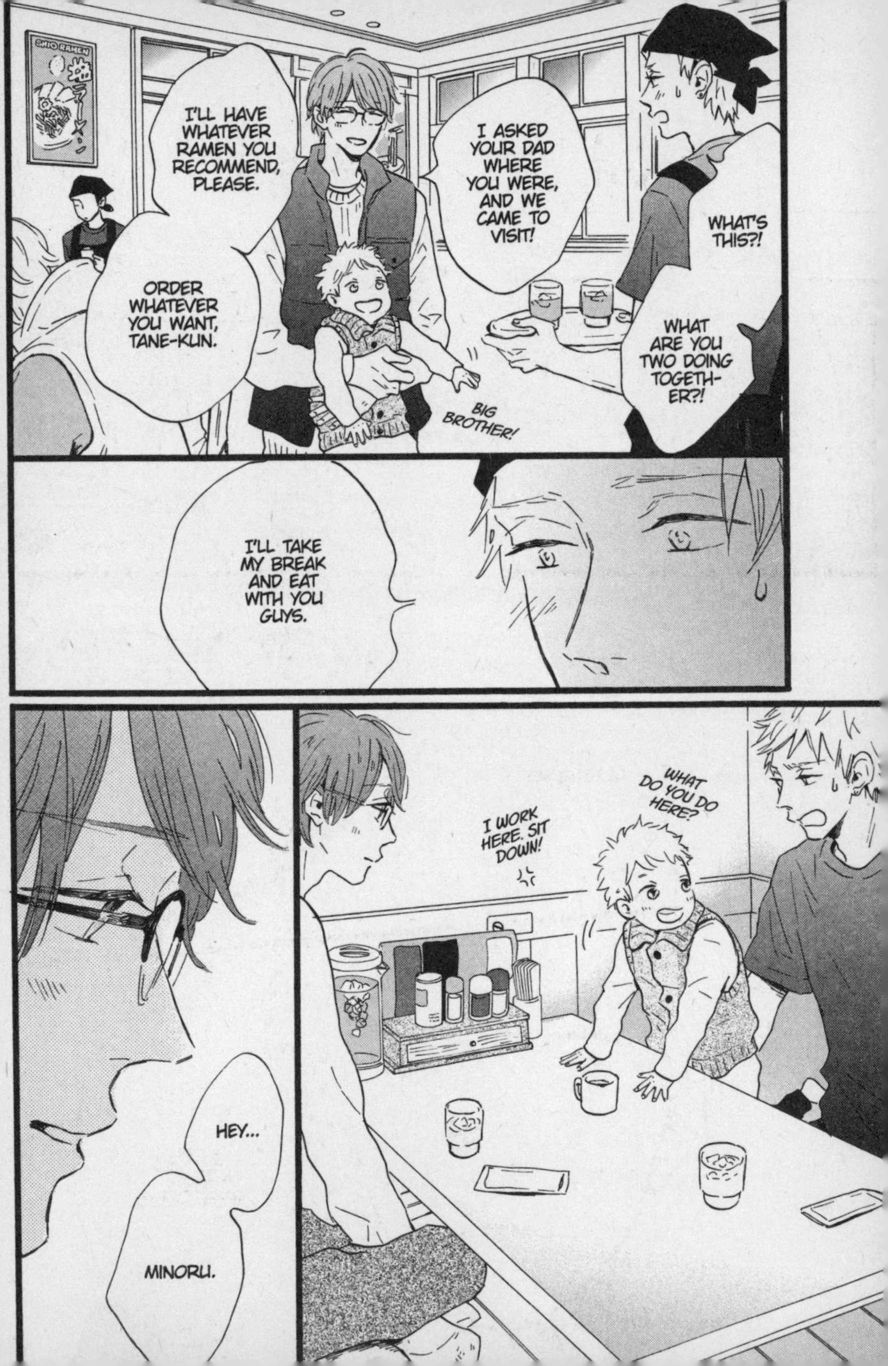
WHAT'S THIS?!
WHAT ARE YOU TWO DOING TOGETH-ER?!
I ASKED YOUR DAD WHERE YOU WERE, AND WE CAME TO VISIT!
BIG BROTHER!
SHIO RAMEN
I'LL HAVE WHATEVER RAMEN YOU RECOMMEND, PLEASE.
ORDER WHATEVER YOU WANT, TANE-KUN.
I'LL TAKE MY BREAK AND EAT WITH YOU GUYS.
WHAT DO YOU DO HERE?
I WORK HERE. SIT DOWN!
HEY...
MINORU.

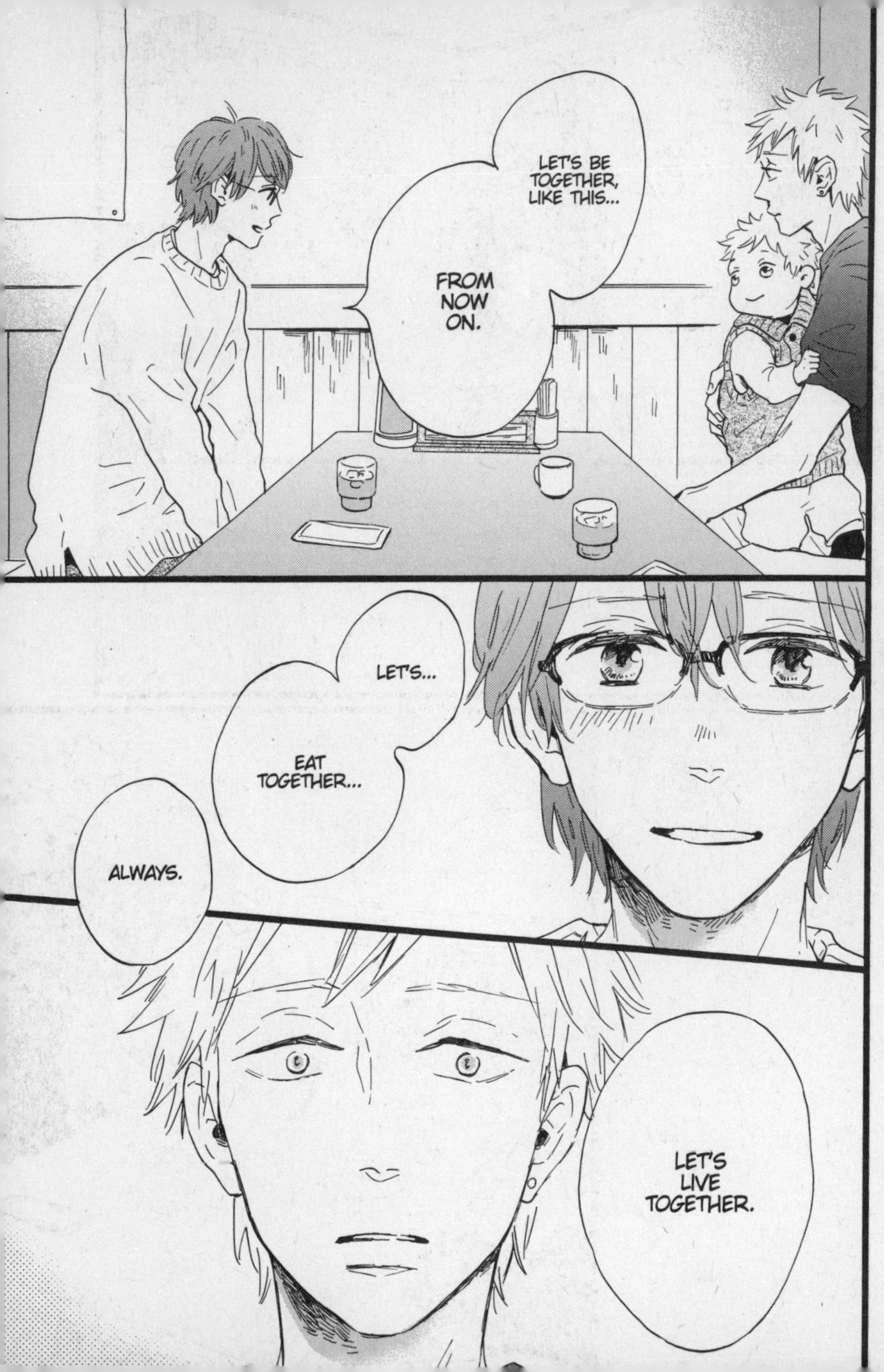
LET'S BE TOGETHER, LIKE THIS...
FROM NOW ON.
LET'S...
EAT TOGETHER...
ALWAYS.
LET'S LIVE TOGETHER.

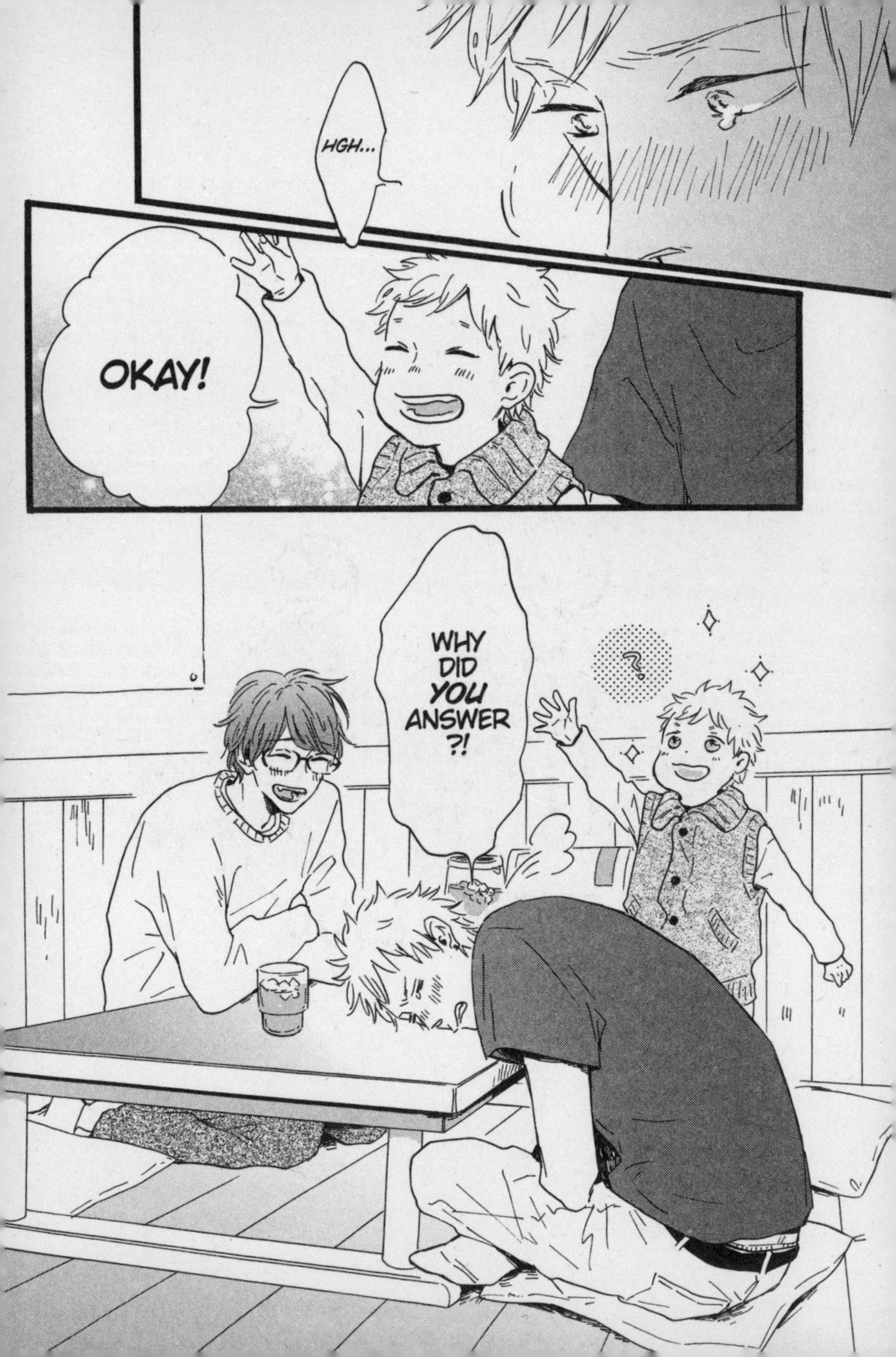
HGH...
OKAY!
WHY DID *YOU* ANSWER ?!

THE END

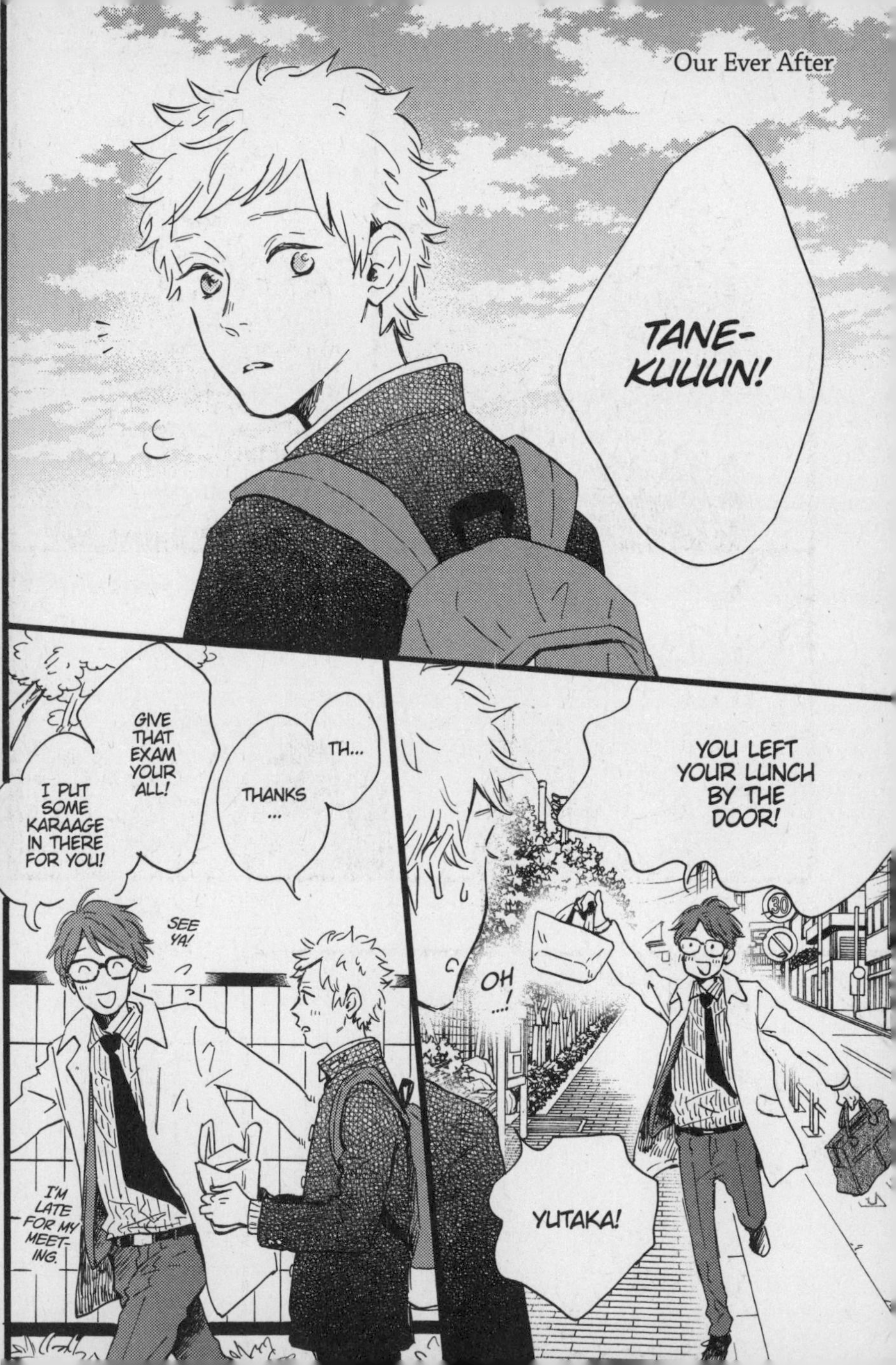
TANE-KUUUN!
YOU LEFT YOUR LUNCH BY THE DOOR!
OH ...!
YUTAKA!
TH...
THANKS ...
GIVE THAT EXAM YOUR ALL!
I PUT SOME KARAAGE IN THERE FOR YOU!
SEE YA!
I'M LATE FOR MY MEET-ING.

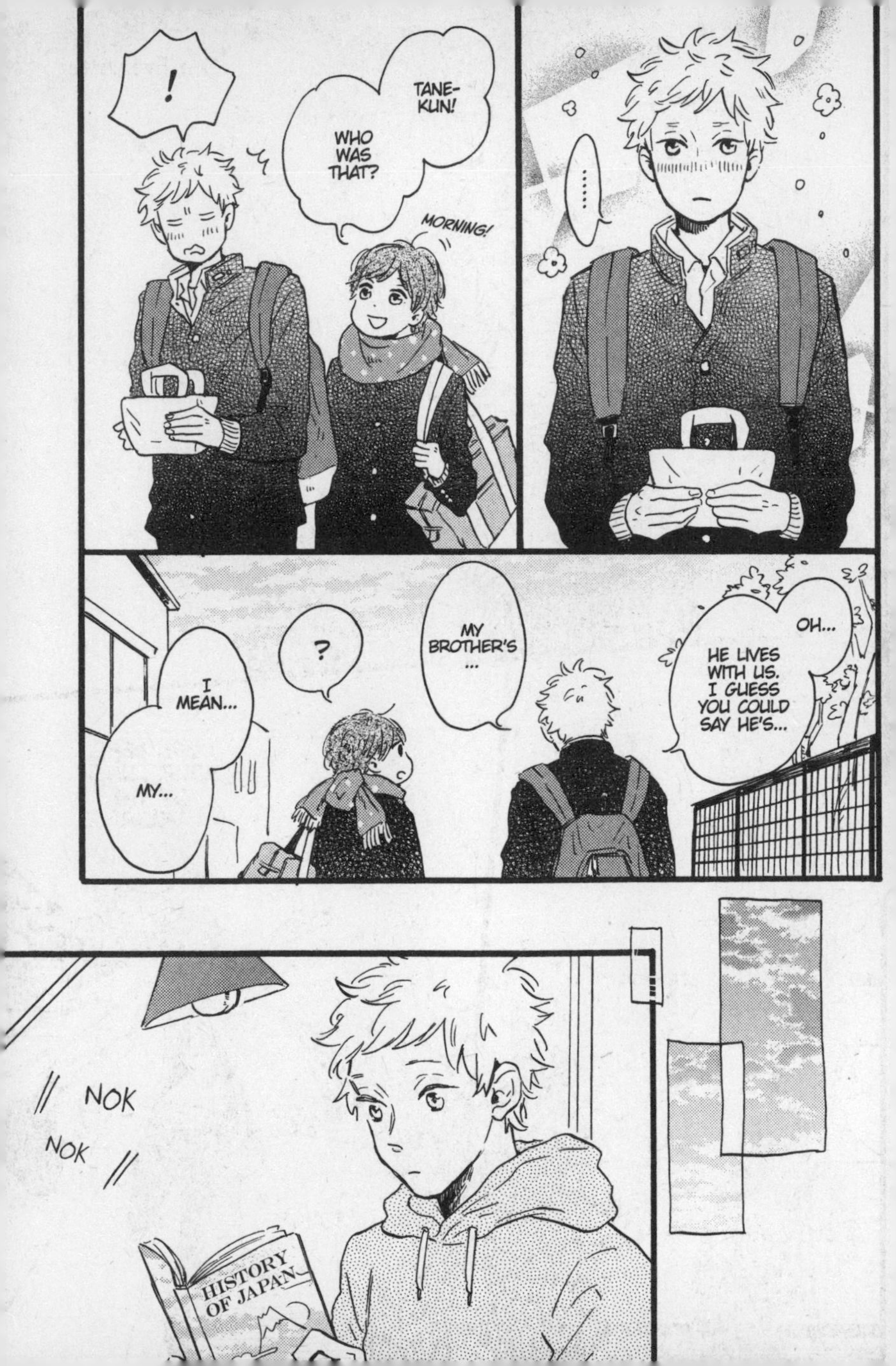
......
TANE-KUN! WHO WAS THAT?
MORNING!
!
OH... HE LIVES WITH US. I GUESS YOU COULD SAY HE'S...
MY BROTHER'S ...
?
I MEAN... MY...
NOK
NOK
HISTORY OF JAPAN

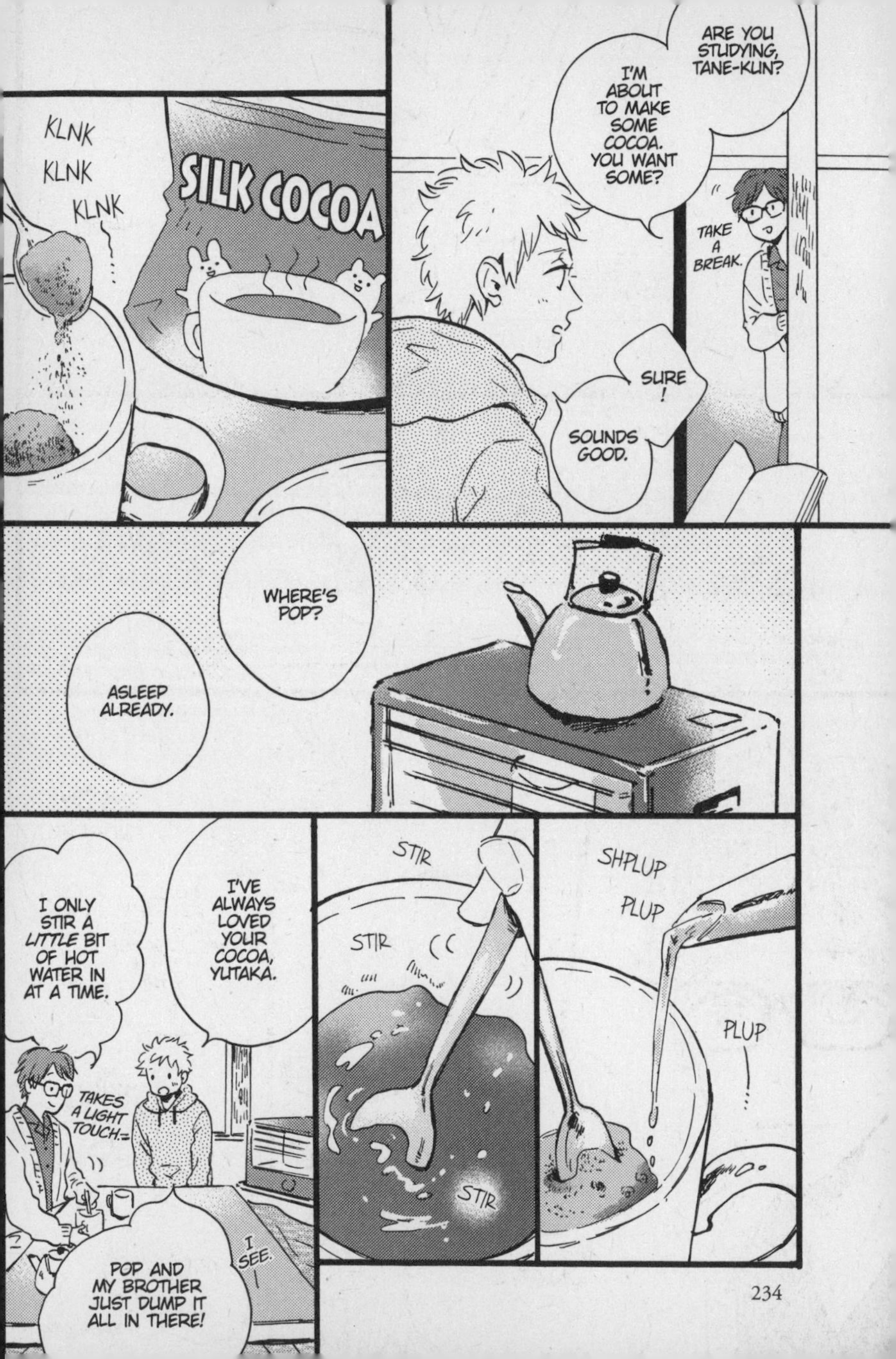
ARE YOU STUDYING, TANE-KUN?
I'M ABOUT TO MAKE SOME COCOA. YOU WANT SOME?
TAKE A BREAK.
SURE!
SOUNDS GOOD.
KLNK
KLNK
KLNK
SILK COCOA
WHERE'S POP?
ASLEEP ALREADY.
SHPLUP
PLUP
PLUP
STIR
STIR
STIR
I'VE ALWAYS LOVED YOUR COCOA, YUTAKA.
I ONLY STIR A *LITTLE* BIT OF HOT WATER IN AT A TIME.
TAKES A LIGHT TOUCH.
I SEE.
POP AND MY BROTHER JUST DUMP IT ALL IN THERE!

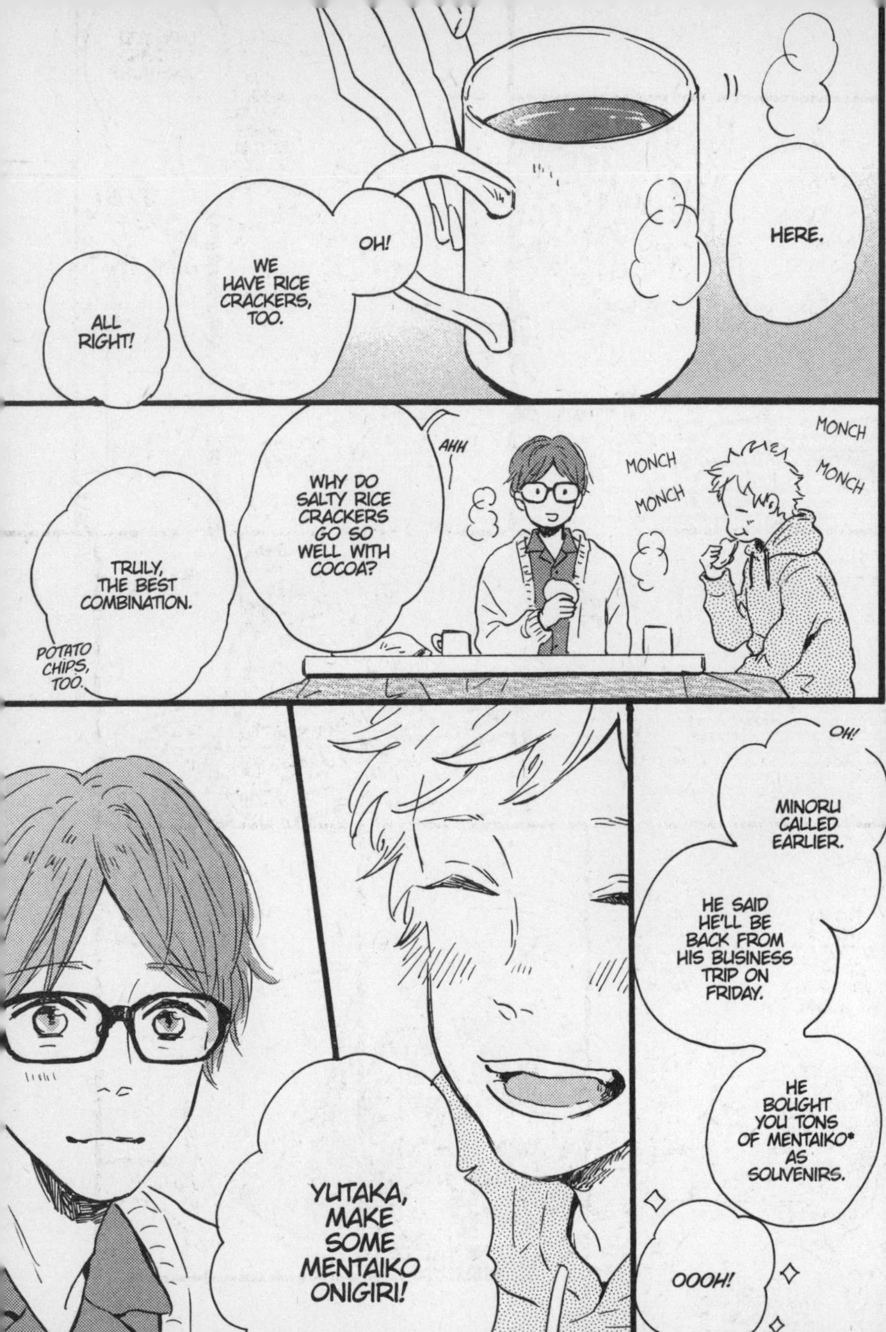
HERE.
OH!
WE HAVE RICE CRACKERS, TOO.
ALL RIGHT!
MONCH
MONCH
MONCH
MONCH
AHH
WHY DO SALTY RICE CRACKERS GO SO WELL WITH COCOA?
TRULY, THE BEST COMBINATION.
POTATO CHIPS, TOO.
OH!
MINORU CALLED EARLIER.
HE SAID HE'LL BE BACK FROM HIS BUSINESS TRIP ON FRIDAY.
HE BOUGHT YOU TONS OF MENTAIKO* AS SOUVENIRS.
OOOH!
YUTAKA, MAKE SOME MENTAIKO ONIGIRI!

*Salted pollock roe.

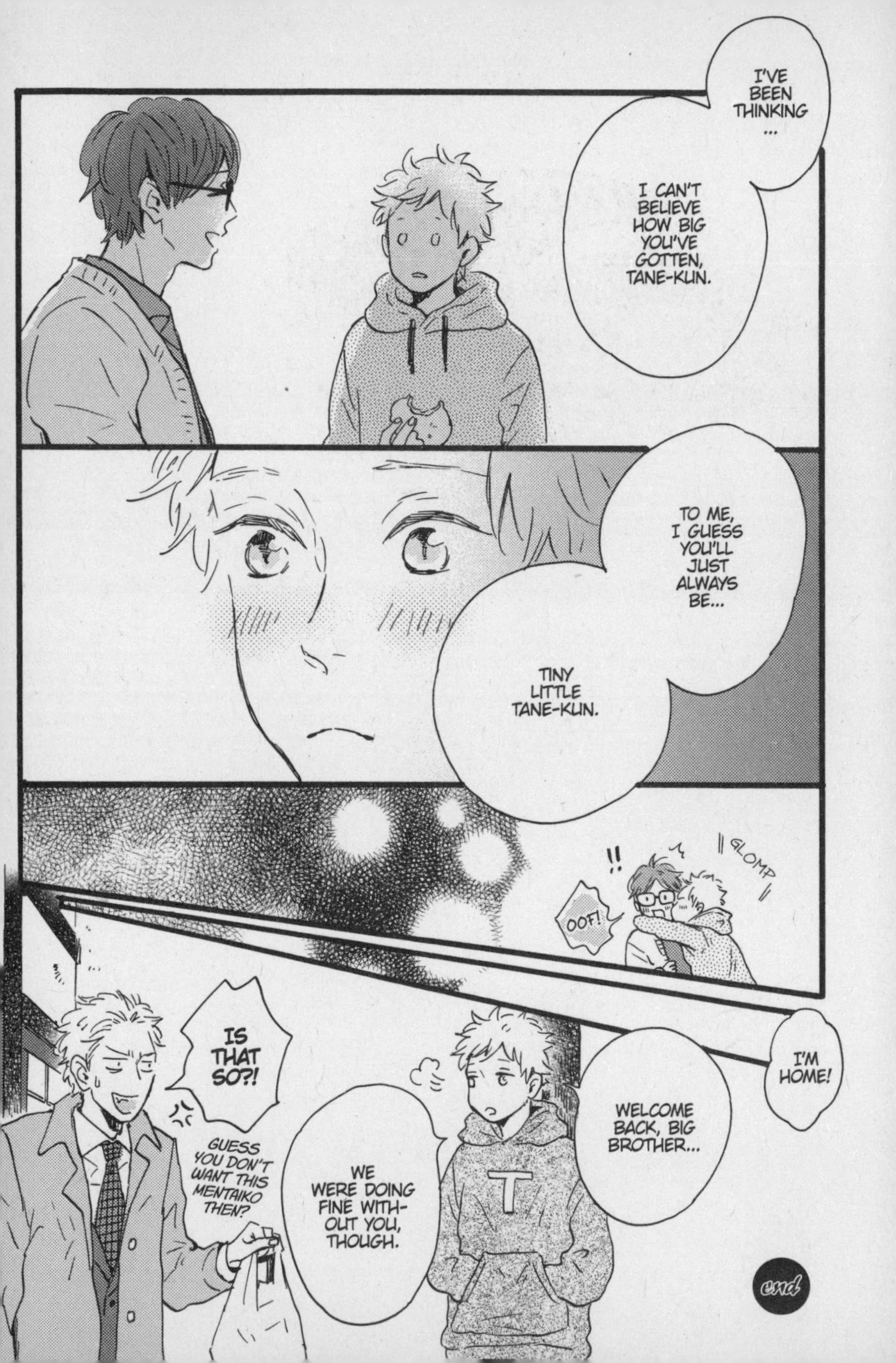

I'VE BEEN THINKING...
I CAN'T BELIEVE HOW BIG YOU'VE GOTTEN, TANE-KUN.
TO ME, I GUESS YOU'LL JUST ALWAYS BE...
TINY LITTLE TANE-KUN.
GLOMP
!!
OOF!
I'M HOME!
WELCOME BACK, BIG BROTHER...
WE WERE DOING FINE WITH-OUT YOU, THOUGH.
IS THAT SO?!
GUESS YOU DON'T WANT THIS MENTAIKO THEN?
end

TANE-TARAKO*

*Tarako is salted roe.

Afterword

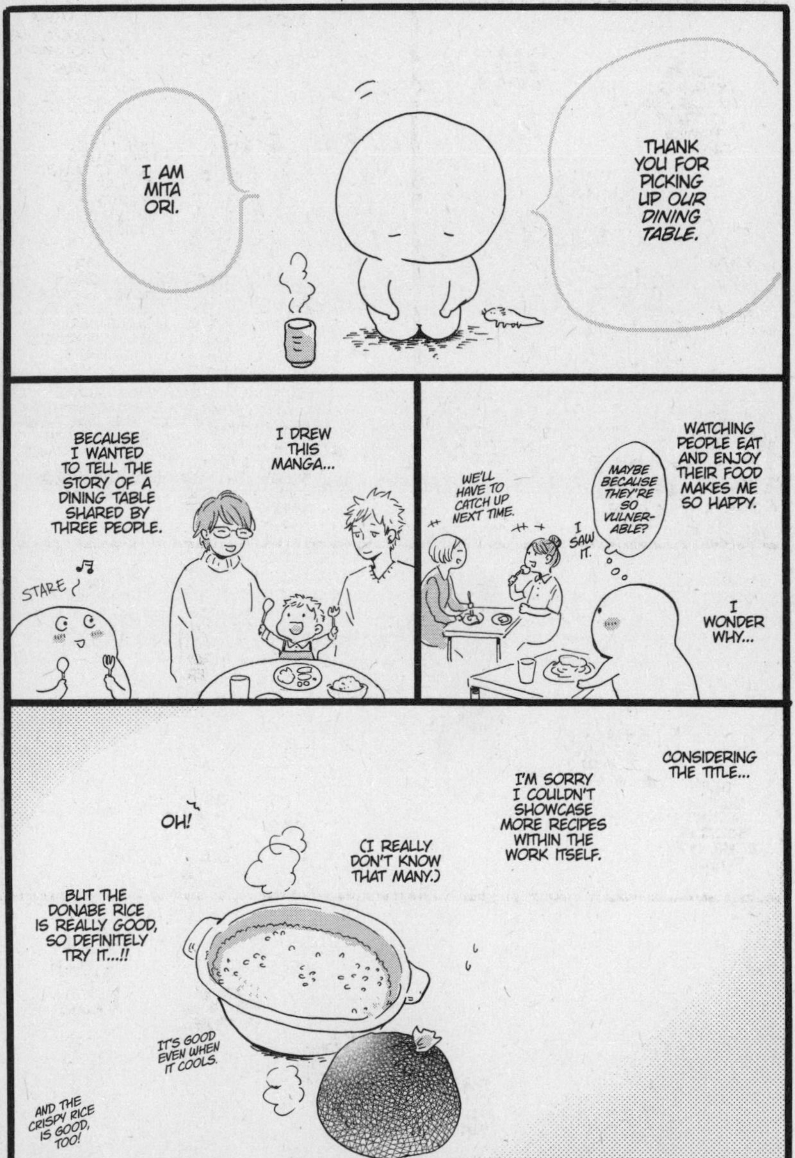

THANK YOU FOR PICKING UP OUR DINING TABLE.
I AM MITA ORI.
WATCHING PEOPLE EAT AND ENJOY THEIR FOOD MAKES ME SO HAPPY.
I WONDER WHY...
MAYBE BECAUSE THEY'RE SO VULNER-ABLE?
I SAW IT.
WE'LL HAVE TO CATCH UP NEXT TIME.
I DREW THIS MANGA...
BECAUSE I WANTED TO TELL THE STORY OF A DINING TABLE SHARED BY THREE PEOPLE.
STARE
CONSIDERING THE TITLE...
I'M SORRY I COULDN'T SHOWCASE MORE RECIPES WITHIN THE WORK ITSELF.
(I REALLY DON'T KNOW THAT MANY.)
OH!
BUT THE DONABE RICE IS REALLY GOOD, SO DEFINITELY TRY IT...!!
IT'S GOOD EVEN WHEN IT COOLS.
AND THE CRISPY RICE IS GOOD, TOO!

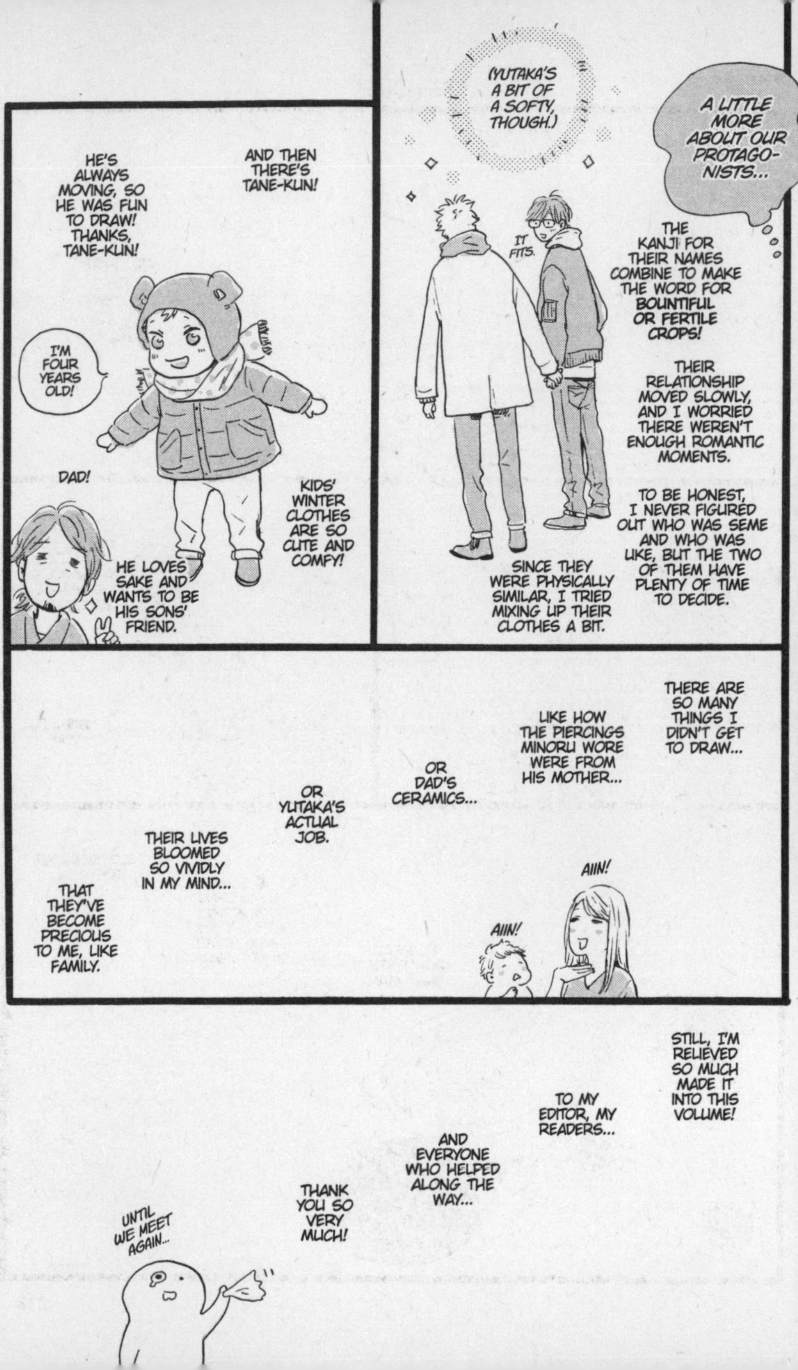
A LITTLE MORE ABOUT OUR PROTAGO-NISTS...
THE KANJI FOR THEIR NAMES COMBINE TO MAKE THE WORD FOR BOUNTIFUL OR FERTILE CROPS!
THEIR RELATIONSHIP MOVED SLOWLY, AND I WORRIED THERE WEREN'T ENOUGH ROMANTIC MOMENTS.
TO BE HONEST, I NEVER FIGURED OUT WHO WAS SEME AND WHO WAS UKE, BUT THE TWO OF THEM HAVE PLENTY OF TIME TO DECIDE.
SINCE THEY WERE PHYSICALLY SIMILAR, I TRIED MIXING UP THEIR CLOTHES A BIT.
IT FITS.
(YUTAKA'S A BIT OF A SOFTY, THOUGH.)
AND THEN THERE'S TANE-KUN!
HE'S ALWAYS MOVING, SO HE WAS FUN TO DRAW! THANKS, TANE-KUN!
I'M FOUR YEARS OLD!
KIDS' WINTER CLOTHES ARE SO CUTE AND COMFY!
DAD!
HE LOVES SAKE AND WANTS TO BE HIS SONS' FRIEND.
THERE ARE SO MANY THINGS I DIDN'T GET TO DRAW...
LIKE HOW THE PIERCINGS MINORU WORE WERE FROM HIS MOTHER...
OR DAD'S CERAMICS...
OR YUTAKA'S ACTUAL JOB.
AIIN!
AIIN!
THEIR LIVES BLOOMED SO VIVIDLY IN MY MIND...
THAT THEY'VE BECOME PRECIOUS TO ME, LIKE FAMILY.
STILL, I'M RELIEVED SO MUCH MADE IT INTO THIS VOLUME!
TO MY EDITOR, MY READERS...
AND EVERYONE WHO HELPED ALONG THE WAY...
THANK YOU SO VERY MUCH!
UNTIL WE MEET AGAIN...

TANE-NIGIRI

SEVEN SEAS ENTERTAINMENT PRESENTS

OUR DINING TABLE

story and art by **MITA ORI**

TRANSLATION
Amber Tamosaitis

ADAPTATION
Marykate Jasper

LETTERING
Laura Heo

COVER DESIGN
KC Fabellon

PROOFREADER
Kurestin Armada
Autumn Kassel

EDITOR
Jenn Grunigen

PRODUCTION MANAGER
Lissa Pattillo

MANAGING EDITOR
Julie Davis

EDITOR-IN-CHIEF
Adam Arnold

PUBLISHER
Jason DeAngelis

Bokura no Shokutaku by MITA ORI

Original Japanese edition published in 2017 by GENTOSHA COMICS Inc.
English translation rights arranged worldwide with GENTOSHA COMICS Inc. through Digital Catapult Inc., Tokyo.

Seven Seas press and purchase enquiries can be sent to Marketing Manager Lianne Sentar at press@gomanga.com. Information regarding the distribution and purchase of digital editions is available from Digital Manager CK Russell at digital@gomanga.com.

ISBN: 978-1-64275-756-9

Printed in Canada

First Printing: December 2019

10 9 8 7 6 5 4 3 2 1

FOLLOW US ONLINE: ***www.sevenseasentertainment.com***

READING DIRECTIONS

This book reads from ***right to left***, Japanese style. If this is your first time reading manga, you start reading from the top right panel on each page and take it from there. If you get lost, just follow the numbered diagram here. It may seem backwards at first, but you'll get the hang of it! Have fun!!

1
2
3
4
5
6
7
8
9

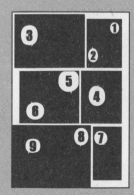